סידור קורן לימות החול • נוסח אשכנז

The Koren Weekday Siddur • Nusaḥ Ashkenaz

קורן ירושלים

THE LOBEL EDITION

סידור קורן לימות החול
THE KOREN WEEKDAY SIDDUR

WITH INTRODUCTION, TRANSLATION
AND COMMENTARY BY

Rabbi Lord Jonathan Sacks שליט״א

•

KOREN PUBLISHERS JERUSALEM

The Lobel Edition
of
The Koren Siddur
is dedicated to the hundreds of thousands
who use this Siddur for their daily prayers.

*May your prayers be speedily answered
and be a source of blessing
for each of you, your families,
and Klal Yisrael.*

The Lobel Family
New York, USA

The Koren Weekday Siddur
The Lobel Edition
Nusaḥ Ashkenaz
First Hebrew/English Edition, 2014

Koren Publishers Jerusalem Ltd.
POB 4044, Jerusalem 91040, ISRAEL
POB 8531, New Milford, CT 06776, USA

www.korenpub.com

The English translation and commentary in this edition are based on the English translation and commentary first published in Great Britain in 2006 in the Authorised Daily Prayer Book of the United Hebrew Congregations of the Commonwealth: New Translation and Commentary by Rabbi Jonathan Sacks, (Fourth Edition, Compilation © United Synagogue) by Collins, a division of HarperCollins Publishers, London.

The creation of this Siddur was made possible with the generous support of Torah Education in Israel.

Compact Size, Hardcover, ISBN 978 965 301 713 9
Compact Size, Softcover, ISBN 978 965 301 714 6
Compact Size, Hardcover, artwork by Emanuel, ISBN 978 965 301 715 3
Compact Size, Hardcover, Leather, ISBN 978 965 301 716 0

SWA1

CONTENTS

PREFACE TO THE FIRST HEBREW EDITION

"My help comes from the Lord…"

"And their fear toward Me is as a commandment of men learned by rote" (Is. 29:13) laments the prophet, referring to those who turn prayer into routine habit. Even when they pray before the Lord, "With their mouth and with their lips do [they] honor Me, but have removed their heart far from Me." This is precisely as our sages cautioned, saying: "When you pray, do not do so as a fixed routine, but as a plea for mercy and grace before God" (*Avot* 2:18). Bartenura elaborates, "[Do not say] as a person who has a duty to fulfill says: I shall relieve myself from this burden." Thus is the nature of ritual duties: when they become routine habit, their original meaning is diminished.

The prayers in this Siddur – the same words, those same sentences we repeat daily and even several times each day – become routine verbiage, "a chirping of a starling" which lacks the deep concentration and the vital sense of "knowing before whom one stands."

This unfortunate situation – which is natural – became our inspiration to present worshipers with the means to connect to prayer, both to the words of the prayers and to the content and meaning our sages infused into the phrases. We resolved to bring the prayers before the worshiper not in a secular form, as a regular book, but in a more sacred manner, so as to enable the worldly structure to become a source of inspiration, reverence, sanctity and awe.

To achieve this, we created an original design of the printed font and the layout of the words in accordance with the meaning of the prayers, line-by-line, page-by-page. From a visual standpoint, the contents of the prayers are presented in a style that does not spur habit and hurry, but rather encourages the worshiper to engross his mind and heart in prayer.

One possible hazard that undermines the beauty and the purity of the prayers is carelessness of diction when pronouncing the words. Disregard for grammar and punctuation, disrespect, or lack of knowledge of the laws of the *dagesh*, the quiescent *sh'va* and the mobile *sh'va*, and so forth, that our sages – the authors of the *Mesora*, the scholars of the linguistic form of the language, the adjudicators of the laws and students of the Torah and Kabbala – were so meticulous about perfecting. In parts of prayers (such as the Shema and the Blessing of the Kohanim), they viewed this meticulous pronunciation as obligatory.

In order to relieve the worshiper of these details – for the sake of his praying – we have presented him (excluding Biblical quotations) with a different notation between the two *sh'va*s (the mobile *sh'va* is more predominant, which is a sign for the worshiper to express the vowel as a brief *segol*, while the quiescent *sh'va* is smaller, as it is not pronounced), and a special form of the *kamatz* (the "small *kamatz*" has a longer foot).

"A window thou shalt make to the ark," says God to Noaḥ, and our sages took this also to mean that the correct pronunciation of the words is an embellishment to the prayers. It is fitting that our conversations with God be clear, pure and unblemished, open and lit as this window.

The Nusaḥ Ashkenaz edition of this Siddur is based upon that of the "first Ashkenazic scholars," incorporating the revisions that were accepted in the land of Israel by the pupils of the Vilna Ga'on, and are customary in synagogues in Israel and the Diaspora (with different customs indicated).

I am very grateful to the excellent proofreaders Shmuel Vexler and Abraham Frankel, for their diligent work, and to Esther Be'er, who skillfully prepared the difficult typesetting of this Siddur.

All this would not have been possible without the help and guidance of my friend Meir Medan, who helped us reach this goal. Using his vast knowledge and careful comparison between different versions, we strived together to make this Siddur as perfect as humanly possible.

And let the beauty of the Lord our God be upon us: and establish the work of our hands upon us; O prosper it, the work of our hands.

Eliyahu Koren

PREFACE TO THE HEBREW/ENGLISH EDITION

"One generation will praise Your works to the next…"

It is with gratitude and pride that we introduce this first Hebrew/English Edition of the Koren Weekday Siddur. Since its publication in 1981, The Koren Siddur has been recognized for its textual accuracy and innovative graphic design. We have remained committed to these qualities, as we have had the privilege of enriching the Siddur with the eloquent English translation and insightful commentary of one of the most articulate and original Jewish thinkers of our time, Rabbi Lord Jonathan Sacks.

Since the very successful introduction of the full Koren Siddur five years ago, we have had many requests for a compact edition for weekday prayer, that provides these same qualities in a convenient and portable format. By not including prayers for Shabbat, Ḥagim and Ḥol HaMo'ed, but still retaining the textual integrity and aesthetics that Koren is renowned for, we hope this new edition fulfills the need for a dedicated Weekday Siddur.

It is also our hope that through this project we have realized the aim of master typographer Eliyahu Koren, founder of Koren Publishers Jerusalem, "to present to worshipers a means to draw and connect them not only to the words of the prayers, but also to the contents and meaning that were before our sages when engraving the phrases of the prayers, and our rabbis throughout the ages when compiling versions of the prayers."

It is always a privilege to collaborate on a project with those who share our commitment and enthusiasm for bringing out the beauty of *Tefilla*. We are grateful to Judith and David Lobel for their support and proud to have their name grace this edition. On behalf of the scholars, editors and designers of this volume, we thank you; on behalf of the users of this Siddur, we are forever in your debt.

Those new to The Koren Siddur will note several unique features:

- Two, distinct fonts, designed by Eliyahu Koren and recently digitized, are used throughout the Siddur. Koren Tanakh Font is used for Tanakh texts (except when embedded in prayers,) and Koren Siddur Font is used for prayers, in keeping with Mr. Koren's belief that the presentation of Tanakh text should be distinctive.

◂ Reading

- Reading aids, fully explained in the Guide to the Reader, facilitate correct reading.
- The graphic layout distinguishes poetry from prose, and provides space to allow pages to "breathe." We have developed a parallel style for the English text that balances the weight of the Hebrew letters to further Mr. Koren's intention of presenting the texts "in a style that does not spur habit and hurry, but rather encourages the worshiper to engross his mind and heart in prayer."

This Hebrew/English Edition also includes new features. We have added Rabbi Sacks' commentary to illuminate and clarify practice and tradition. We have introduced concise instructions and practical *halakha* guides. Finally, we have incorporated prayers for visitors to Israel, for Yom HaZikaron and Yom HaAtzma'ut to reflect the essential and integral connection between the Jewish people in Israel and around the world, and the centrality of Jerusalem to us all.

We wish to thank Rabbi Sacks שליט״א for his exceptional translation and commentary, and his dedicated involvement throughout the preparation of this Siddur; and Rabbi Eli Clark for his extraordinarily helpful section on *Halakha*.

Raphaël Freeman designed the full edition of the Siddur, from which this is derived; an outstanding team at Koren, including Rabbi David Fuchs, Rachel Hanstater Meghnagi and Esther Be'er, brought it to life.

We can only hope that we have extended the vision of Eliyahu Koren to a new generation and a larger audience, furthering *Avodat HaShem* for Jews everywhere.

Matthew Miller, Publisher
Jerusalem 5775 (2014)

סידור קורן
THE KOREN SIDDUR

ימות החול

WEEKDAYS

Shaḥarit

The following order of prayers and blessings, which departs from that of most prayer books, is based on the consensus of recent halakhic authorities. See laws 2–9.

ON WAKING

On waking, our first thought should be that we are in the presence of God. Since we are forbidden to speak God's name until we have washed our hands, the following prayer is said, which, without mentioning God's name, acknowledges His presence and gives thanks for a new day and for the gift of life.

מוֹדֶה I thank You, living and eternal King,
for giving me back my soul in mercy.
Great is Your faithfulness.

Wash hands and say the following blessings.
Some have the custom to say "Wisdom begins" on page 10 at this point.

בָּרוּךְ Blessed are You, LORD our God, King of the Universe,
who has made us holy through His commandments,
and has commanded us about washing hands.

בָּרוּךְ Blessed are You, LORD our God, King of the Universe,
who formed man in wisdom
and created in him many orifices and cavities.
It is revealed and known before the throne of Your glory
that were one of them to be ruptured or blocked,
it would be impossible to survive
and stand before You.
Blessed are You, LORD,
Healer of all flesh who does wondrous deeds.

אֲשֶׁר יָצַר *Who formed man in wisdom:* A blessing of thanks for the intricate wonders of the human body. *Were one of them to be ruptured or blocked* – even the smallest variation in the human genome can cause potentially fatal illness. The more we understand of the complexity of life, the more we appreciate "How numerous are Your works, LORD; You made them all in wisdom; the earth is full of Your creations" (Psalm 104:24). This blessing is a rejection of the idea that the spirit alone is holy, and physical life bereft of God.

שחרית

The following order of prayers and blessings, which departs from that of most prayer books, is based on the consensus of recent halakhic authorities. See laws 2–9.

השכמת הבוקר

On waking, our first thought should be that we are in the presence of God. Since we are forbidden to speak God's name until we have washed our hands, the following prayer is said, which, without mentioning God's name, acknowledges His presence and gives thanks for a new day and for the gift of life.

מוֹדֶה/women מוֹדָה/ אֲנִי לְפָנֶיךָ מֶלֶךְ חַי וְקַיָּם
שֶׁהֶחֱזַרְתָּ בִּי נִשְׁמָתִי בְּחֶמְלָה
רַבָּה אֱמוּנָתֶךָ.

Wash hands and say the following blessings.
Some have the custom to say רֵאשִׁית חָכְמָה *on page 11 at this point.*

בָּרוּךְ אַתָּה יהוה אֱלֹהֵינוּ מֶלֶךְ הָעוֹלָם
אֲשֶׁר קִדְּשָׁנוּ בְּמִצְוֹתָיו וְצִוָּנוּ עַל נְטִילַת יָדָיִם.

בָּרוּךְ אַתָּה יהוה אֱלֹהֵינוּ מֶלֶךְ הָעוֹלָם
אֲשֶׁר יָצַר אֶת הָאָדָם בְּחָכְמָה
וּבָרָא בוֹ נְקָבִים נְקָבִים, חֲלוּלִים חֲלוּלִים.
גָּלוּי וְיָדוּעַ לִפְנֵי כִסֵּא כְבוֹדֶךָ
שֶׁאִם יִפָּתֵחַ אֶחָד מֵהֶם אוֹ יִסָּתֵם אֶחָד מֵהֶם
אִי אֶפְשַׁר לְהִתְקַיֵּם וְלַעֲמֹד לְפָנֶיךָ.
בָּרוּךְ אַתָּה יהוה, רוֹפֵא כָל בָּשָׂר וּמַפְלִיא לַעֲשׂוֹת.

מוֹדֶה אֲנִי *I thank You:* These words are to be said immediately on waking from sleep. In them we thank God for life itself, renewed each day. Sleep, said the sages, is "one-sixtieth of death" (*Berakhot* 57b). Waking, therefore, is a miniature rebirth. Despite its brevity, this sentence articulates a transformative act of faith: the recognition that life is a gift from God. Expressing gratitude at the fact of being alive, we prepare ourselves to celebrate and sanctify the new day.

אֱלֹהַי My God,
the soul You placed within me is pure.
You created it, You formed it, You breathed it into me,
and You guard it while it is within me.
One day You will take it from me,
and restore it to me in the time to come.
As long as the soul is within me,
I will thank You,
LORD my God and God of my ancestors,
Master of all works, LORD of all souls.
Blessed are You, LORD,
who restores souls to lifeless bodies.

TZITZIT

The following blessing is said before putting on tzitzit. Neither it nor the subsequent prayer is said by those who wear a tallit. The blessing over the latter exempts the former. See laws 10–16.

בָּרוּךְ Blessed are You, LORD our God, King of the Universe,
who has made us holy through His commandments,
and has commanded us about the command of tasseled garments.

After putting on tzitzit, say:

יְהִי רָצוֹן May it be Your will, LORD my God and God of my ancestors,
that the commandment of the tasseled garment be considered before You
as if I had fulfilled it in all its specifics,
details and intentions,
as well as the 613 commandments
dependent on it, Amen, Selah.

---

them. The blessing ends with a reference to the resurrection of the dead, returning to the theme of the first words said in the morning.

אֱלֹהַי

נְשָׁמָה שֶׁנָּתַתָּ בִּי טְהוֹרָה הִיא.
אַתָּה בְרָאתָהּ, אַתָּה יְצַרְתָּהּ, אַתָּה נְפַחְתָּהּ בִּי
וְאַתָּה מְשַׁמְּרָהּ בְּקִרְבִּי, וְאַתָּה עָתִיד לִטְּלָהּ מִמֶּנִּי
וּלְהַחֲזִירָהּ בִּי לֶעָתִיד לָבוֹא.
כָּל זְמַן שֶׁהַנְּשָׁמָה בְקִרְבִּי, מוֹדֶה/*women* מוֹדָה/ אֲנִי לְפָנֶיךָ
יהוה אֱלֹהַי וֵאלֹהֵי אֲבוֹתַי
רִבּוֹן כָּל הַמַּעֲשִׂים, אֲדוֹן כָּל הַנְּשָׁמוֹת.
בָּרוּךְ אַתָּה יהוה, הַמַּחֲזִיר נְשָׁמוֹת לִפְגָרִים מֵתִים.

לבישת ציצית

The following blessing is said before putting on a טלית קטן*. Neither it nor* יְהִי רָצוֹן *is said by those who wear a* טלית*. The blessing over the latter exempts the former. See laws 10–16.*

בָּרוּךְ אַתָּה יהוה אֱלֹהֵינוּ מֶלֶךְ הָעוֹלָם
אֲשֶׁר קִדְּשָׁנוּ בְּמִצְוֹתָיו וְצִוָּנוּ עַל מִצְוַת צִיצִית.

After putting on the טלית קטן*, say:*

יְהִי רָצוֹן מִלְּפָנֶיךָ, יהוה אֱלֹהַי וֵאלֹהֵי אֲבוֹתַי
שֶׁתְּהֵא חֲשׁוּבָה מִצְוַת צִיצִית לְפָנֶיךָ
כְּאִלּוּ קִיַּמְתִּיהָ בְּכָל פְּרָטֶיהָ וְדִקְדּוּקֶיהָ וְכַוָּנוֹתֶיהָ
וְתַרְיַ״ג מִצְוֹת הַתְּלוּיוֹת בָּהּ, אָמֵן סֶלָה.

אֱלֹהַי *My God, the soul You placed within me is pure:* An affirmation of Jewish belief in the freedom and responsibility of each human being. The soul as such is pure. We have good instincts and bad, and we must choose between

BLESSINGS OVER THE TORAH

In Judaism, study is greater even than prayer. So, before beginning to pray, we engage in a miniature act of study, preceded by the appropriate blessings. The blessings are followed by brief selections from Scripture, Mishna and Gemara, the three foundational texts of Judaism.

בָּרוּךְ Blessed are You, LORD our God, King of the Universe,
who has made us holy through His commandments,
and has commanded us to engage in study
of the words of Torah.
Please, LORD our God, make the words of Your Torah
sweet in our mouths and in the mouths of Your people,
the house of Israel,
so that we, our descendants (and their descendants)
and the descendants of Your people,
the house of Israel,
may all know Your name
and study Your Torah for its own sake.
Blessed are You, LORD,
who teaches Torah to His people Israel.

בָּרוּךְ Blessed are You, LORD our God, King of the Universe,
who has chosen us from all the peoples
and given us His Torah.
Blessed are You, LORD, Giver of the Torah.

---

chosenness means responsibility, and is inseparably linked to the study and practice of Torah.

So as to follow the blessings immediately with an act that fulfills the commandment, we read three texts whose recitation forms an act of study. The Talmud (*Kiddushin* 30a) rules that Torah study must be divided into three: study of (1) Torah, (2) Mishna, and (3) Gemara. Hence we read: (1) a biblical text – the priestly blessings, (2) a passage from the Mishna about commandments that have no fixed measure, and (3) a passage from the Gemara about the reward of good deeds in this world and the next.

ברכות התורה

In Judaism, study is greater even than prayer. So, before beginning to pray, we engage in a miniature act of study, preceded by the appropriate blessings. The blessings are followed by brief selections from תנ״ך, משנה *and* גמרא*, the three foundational texts of Judaism.*

בָּרוּךְ אַתָּה יהוה אֱלֹהֵינוּ מֶלֶךְ הָעוֹלָם
אֲשֶׁר קִדְּשָׁנוּ בְּמִצְוֹתָיו
וְצִוָּנוּ לַעֲסֹק בְּדִבְרֵי תוֹרָה.
וְהַעֲרֶב נָא יהוה אֱלֹהֵינוּ אֶת דִּבְרֵי תוֹרָתְךָ
בְּפִינוּ וּבְפִי עַמְּךָ בֵּית יִשְׂרָאֵל
וְנִהְיֶה אֲנַחְנוּ וְצֶאֱצָאֵינוּ (וְצֶאֱצָאֵי צֶאֱצָאֵינוּ)
וְצֶאֱצָאֵי עַמְּךָ בֵּית יִשְׂרָאֵל
כֻּלָּנוּ יוֹדְעֵי שְׁמֶךָ וְלוֹמְדֵי תוֹרָתְךָ לִשְׁמָהּ.
בָּרוּךְ אַתָּה יהוה, הַמְלַמֵּד תּוֹרָה לְעַמּוֹ יִשְׂרָאֵל.

בָּרוּךְ אַתָּה יהוה אֱלֹהֵינוּ מֶלֶךְ הָעוֹלָם
אֲשֶׁר בָּחַר בָּנוּ מִכָּל הָעַמִּים
וְנָתַן לָנוּ אֶת תּוֹרָתוֹ.
בָּרוּךְ אַתָּה יהוה, נוֹתֵן הַתּוֹרָה.

BLESSINGS OVER THE TORAH

The history of Judaism is a story of the love of a people for the Book of Books, the Torah. As a preliminary to study, we pronounce two blessings and a prayer. The first, "who has made us holy through His commandments," is a blessing over the commandment to engage in study of the Torah, a declaration that we do not simply study as an intellectual or cultural exercise but as the fulfillment of a divine commandment. This is followed by a prayer that God make Torah study sweet, and help us to hand it on to our children. The final blessing, "who has chosen us," is a blessing of acknowledgment that

יְבָרֶכְךָ May the LORD bless you and protect you. *Num. 6*
May the LORD make His face shine on you
and be gracious to you.
May the LORD turn His face toward you
and grant you peace.

אֵלּוּ These are the things *Mishna Pe'ah 1:1*
for which there is no fixed measure:
the corner of the field, first-fruits,
appearances before the LORD
[on festivals, with offerings],
acts of kindness and the study of Torah.

אֵלּוּ These are the things *Shabbat 127a*
whose fruits we eat in this world
but whose full reward awaits us
in the World to Come:
honoring parents; acts of kindness;
arriving early at the house of study
morning and evening;
hospitality to strangers; visiting the sick;
helping the needy bride; attending to the dead;
devotion in prayer;
and bringing peace between people –
but the study of Torah is equal to them all.

Some say:

רֵאשִׁית חָכְמָה Wisdom begins in awe of the LORD; *Ps. 111*
all who fulfill [His commandments] gain good understanding;
His praise is ever-lasting.
The Torah Moses commanded us *Deut. 33*
is the heritage of the congregation of Jacob.
Listen, my son, to your father's instruction, *Prov. 1*
and do not forsake your mother's teaching.
May the Torah be my faith and Almighty God my help.
Blessed be the name of His glorious kingdom for ever and all time.

יְבָרֶכְךָ יהוה וְיִשְׁמְרֶךָ: במדבר ו
יָאֵר יהוה פָּנָיו אֵלֶיךָ וִיחֻנֶּךָּ:
יִשָּׂא יהוה פָּנָיו אֵלֶיךָ וְיָשֵׂם לְךָ שָׁלוֹם:

אֵלּוּ דְבָרִים שֶׁאֵין לָהֶם שִׁעוּר משנה, פאה א: א
הַפֵּאָה וְהַבִּכּוּרִים וְהָרֵאָיוֹן
וּגְמִילוּת חֲסָדִים וְתַלְמוּד תּוֹרָה.

אֵלּוּ דְבָרִים שֶׁאָדָם אוֹכֵל פֵּרוֹתֵיהֶם בָּעוֹלָם הַזֶּה שבת קכז.
וְהַקֶּרֶן קַיֶּמֶת לוֹ לָעוֹלָם הַבָּא
וְאֵלּוּ הֵן
כִּבּוּד אָב וָאֵם, וּגְמִילוּת חֲסָדִים
וְהַשְׁכָּמַת בֵּית הַמִּדְרָשׁ שַׁחֲרִית וְעַרְבִית
וְהַכְנָסַת אוֹרְחִים, וּבִקּוּר חוֹלִים
וְהַכְנָסַת כַּלָּה, וּלְוָיַת הַמֵּת
וְעִיּוּן תְּפִלָּה
וַהֲבָאַת שָׁלוֹם בֵּין אָדָם לַחֲבֵרוֹ
וְתַלְמוּד תּוֹרָה כְּנֶגֶד כֻּלָּם.

Some say:

רֵאשִׁית חָכְמָה יִרְאַת יהוה תהלים קיא
שֵׂכֶל טוֹב לְכָל־עֹשֵׂיהֶם
תְּהִלָּתוֹ עֹמֶדֶת לָעַד:
תּוֹרָה צִוָּה־לָנוּ מֹשֶׁה, מוֹרָשָׁה קְהִלַּת יַעֲקֹב: דברים לג
שְׁמַע בְּנִי מוּסַר אָבִיךָ וְאַל־תִּטֹּשׁ תּוֹרַת אִמֶּךָ: משלי א
תּוֹרָה תְּהֵא אֱמוּנָתִי, וְאֵל שַׁדַּי בְּעֶזְרָתִי.
בָּרוּךְ שֵׁם כְּבוֹד מַלְכוּתוֹ לְעוֹלָם וָעֶד.

TALLIT

Say the following meditation before putting on the tallit. Meditations before the fulfillment of mitzvot are to ensure that we do so with the requisite intention (kavana). This particularly applies to mitzvot whose purpose is to induce in us certain states of mind, as is the case with tallit and tefillin, both of which are external symbols of inward commitment to the life of observance of the mitzvot.

בָּרְכִי נַפְשִׁי Bless the LORD, my soul. LORD, my God, You are very great, clothed in majesty and splendor, wrapped in a robe of light, spreading out the heavens like a tent. *Ps. 104*

Some say:

For the sake of the unification of the Holy One, blessed be He, and His Divine Presence, in reverence and love, to unify the name *Yod-Heh* with *Vav-Heh* in perfect unity in the name of all Israel.

I am about to wrap myself in this tasseled garment (tallit). So may my soul, my 248 limbs and 365 sinews be wrapped in the light of the tassel (*hatzitzit*) which amounts to 613 [commandments]. And just as I cover myself with a tasseled garment in this world, so may I be worthy of rabbinical dress and a fine garment in the World to Come in the Garden of Eden. Through the commandment of tassels may my life's-breath, spirit, soul and prayer be delivered from external impediments, and may the tallit spread its wings over them like an eagle stirring up its nest, hovering over its young. *Deut. 32* May the commandment of the tasseled garment be considered before the Holy One, blessed be He, as if I had fulfilled it in all its specifics, details and intentions, as well as the 613 commandments dependent on it, Amen, Selah.

Before wrapping oneself in the tallit, say:

בָּרוּךְ Blessed are You, LORD our God, King of the Universe,
who has made us holy through His commandments,
and has commanded us to wrap ourselves
in the tasseled garment.

According to the Shela (R. Isaiah Horowitz), one should say these verses after wrapping oneself in the tallit:

מַה־יָּקָר How precious is Your loving-kindness, O God, and the children of men find refuge under the shadow of Your wings. They are filled with the rich plenty of Your House. You give them drink from Your river of delights. For with You is the fountain of life; in Your light, we see light. Continue Your loving-kindness to those who know You, and Your righteousness to the upright in heart. *Ps. 36*

---

an undergarment *beneath* our outer clothes. Though they fulfill a single commandment, they were deemed so different as to warrant two different blessings.

עטיפת טלית

Say the following meditation before putting on the טלית*. Meditations before the fulfillment of* מצוות *are to ensure that we do so with the requisite intention (*כוונה*). This particularly applies to* מצוות *whose purpose is to induce in us certain states of mind, as is the case with* טלית *and* תפילין*, both of which are external symbols of inward commitment to the life of observance of the* מצוות*.*

בָּרְכִי נַפְשִׁי אֶת־יהוה, יהוה אֱלֹהַי גָּדַלְתָּ מְּאֹד, הוֹד וְהָדָר לָבָשְׁתָּ: תהלים קד
עֹטֶה־אוֹר כַּשַּׂלְמָה, נוֹטֶה שָׁמַיִם כַּיְרִיעָה:

Some say:

לְשֵׁם יִחוּד קֻדְשָׁא בְּרִיךְ הוּא וּשְׁכִינְתֵּהּ בִּדְחִילוּ וּרְחִימוּ, לְיַחֵד שֵׁם י״ה בו״ה בְּיִחוּדָא שְׁלִים בְּשֵׁם כָּל יִשְׂרָאֵל.

הֲרֵינִי מִתְעַטֵּף בְּצִיצִת. כֵּן תִּתְעַטֵּף נִשְׁמָתִי וּרְמַ״ח אֵבָרַי וּשְׁסָ״ה גִידַי בְּאוֹר הַצִּיצִת
הָעוֹלָה תַּרְיַ״ג. וּכְשֵׁם שֶׁאֲנִי מִתְכַּסֶּה בְּטַלִּית בָּעוֹלָם הַזֶּה, כָּךְ אֶזְכֶּה לַחֲלוּקָא
דְרַבָּנָן וּלְטַלִּית נָאָה לָעוֹלָם הַבָּא בְּגַן עֵדֶן. וְעַל יְדֵי מִצְוַת צִיצִת תִּנָּצֵל נַפְשִׁי רוּחִי
וְנִשְׁמָתִי וּתְפִלָּתִי מִן הַחִיצוֹנִים. וְהַטַּלִּית תִּפְרֹשׂ כְּנָפֶיהָ עֲלֵיהֶם וְתַצִּילֵם, כְּנֶשֶׁר יָעִיר דברים לב
קִנּוֹ, עַל גּוֹזָלָיו יְרַחֵף: וּתְהֵא חֲשׁוּבָה מִצְוַת צִיצִת לִפְנֵי הַקָּדוֹשׁ בָּרוּךְ הוּא, כְּאִלּוּ
קִיַּמְתִּיהָ בְּכָל פְּרָטֶיהָ וְדִקְדּוּקֶיהָ וְכַוָּנוֹתֶיהָ וְתַרְיַ״ג מִצְוֹת הַתְּלוּיוֹת בָּהּ, אָמֵן סֶלָה.

Before wrapping oneself in the טלית*, say:*

בָּרוּךְ אַתָּה יהוה אֱלֹהֵינוּ מֶלֶךְ הָעוֹלָם
אֲשֶׁר קִדְּשָׁנוּ בְּמִצְוֹתָיו וְצִוָּנוּ לְהִתְעַטֵּף בַּצִּיצִת.

According to the Shela (R. Isaiah Horowitz), one should say these verses after wrapping oneself in the טלית*:*

מַה־יָּקָר חַסְדְּךָ אֱלֹהִים, וּבְנֵי אָדָם בְּצֵל כְּנָפֶיךָ יֶחֱסָיוּן: יִרְוְיֻן תהלים לו
מִדֶּשֶׁן בֵּיתֶךָ, וְנַחַל עֲדָנֶיךָ תַשְׁקֵם: כִּי־עִמְּךָ מְקוֹר חַיִּים, בְּאוֹרְךָ
נִרְאֶה־אוֹר: מְשֹׁךְ חַסְדְּךָ לְיֹדְעֶיךָ, וְצִדְקָתְךָ לְיִשְׁרֵי־לֵב:

TALLIT AND TEFILLIN

The mitzva of tzitzit, placing tassels on the corner of our garments, is to recall us constantly to our vocation: "Thus you will be reminded to keep all My commandments, and be holy to your God" (Num. 15:40). Over the course of time, the fulfillment of this commandment took two different forms: the tallit, worn as a robe during prayer, *over* our clothes, and the tallit katan, worn as

TEFILLIN

Some say the following meditation before putting on the tefillin.

For the sake of the unification of the Holy One, blessed be He, and His Divine Presence, in reverence and love, to unify the name *Yod-Heh* with *Vav-Heh* in perfect unity in the name of all Israel.

By putting on the tefillin I hereby intend to fulfill the commandment of my Creator who commanded us to wear tefillin, as it is written in His Torah: "Bind them as a sign on your hand, and they shall be an emblem on the center of your head." They contain these four sections of the Torah: one beginning with *Shema* [Deut. 6:4–9]; another with *Vehaya im shamo'a* [ibid. 11:13–21]; the third with *Kadesh Li* [Ex. 13:1–10]; and the fourth with *Vehaya ki yevi'akha* [ibid. 13:11–16]. These proclaim the uniqueness and unity of God, blessed be His name in the world. They also remind us of the miracles and wonders which He did for us when He brought us out of Egypt, and that He has the power and the dominion over the highest and the lowest to deal with them as He pleases. He commanded us to place one of the tefillin on the arm in memory of His "outstretched arm" (of redemption), setting it opposite the heart, to subject the desires and designs of our heart to His service, blessed be His name. The other is to be on the head, opposite the brain, so that my mind, whose seat is in the brain, together with my other senses and faculties, may be subjected to His service, blessed be His name. May the spiritual influence of the commandment of the tefillin be with me so that I may have a long life, a flow of holiness, and sacred thoughts, free from any suggestion of sin or iniquity. May the evil inclination neither incite nor entice us, but leave us to serve the Lord, as it is in our hearts to do.

Deut. 6

And may it be Your will, Lord our God and God of our ancestors, that the commandment of tefillin be considered before You as if I had fulfilled it in all its specifics, details and intentions, as well as the 613 commandments dependent on it, Amen, Selah.

---

this is the head-tefillin opposite the seat of consciousness, the soul. *All your might:* this is the strap of the hand-tefillin, symbolizing action, power, might. Tefillin thus symbolize the love for God in emotion (heart), thought (head) and deed (hand).

הנחת תפילין

Some say the following meditation before putting on the תפילין.

לְשֵׁם יִחוּד קֻדְשָׁא בְּרִיךְ הוּא וּשְׁכִינְתֵּהּ בִּדְחִילוּ וּרְחִימוּ, לְיַחֵד שֵׁם י״ה בו״ה בְּיִחוּדָא שְׁלִים בְּשֵׁם כָּל יִשְׂרָאֵל.

הִנְנִי מְכַוֵּן בַּהֲנָחַת תְּפִלִּין לְקַיֵּם מִצְוַת בּוֹרְאִי, שֶׁצִּוָּנוּ לְהָנִיחַ תְּפִלִּין,
כַּכָּתוּב בְּתוֹרָתוֹ: וּקְשַׁרְתָּם לְאוֹת עַל־יָדֶךָ, וְהָיוּ לְטֹטָפֹת בֵּין עֵינֶיךָ: דברים ו
וְהֵן אַרְבַּע פָּרָשִׁיּוֹת אֵלּוּ, שְׁמַע, וְהָיָה אִם שָׁמֹעַ, קַדֶּשׁ לִי, וְהָיָה כִּי יְבִאֲךָ, שֶׁיֵּשׁ בָּהֶם יִחוּדוֹ וְאַחְדוּתוֹ יִתְבָּרַךְ שְׁמוֹ בָּעוֹלָם, וְשֶׁנִּזְכֹּר נִסִּים וְנִפְלָאוֹת שֶׁעָשָׂה עִמָּנוּ בְּהוֹצִיאוֹ אוֹתָנוּ מִמִּצְרַיִם, וַאֲשֶׁר לוֹ הַכֹּחַ וְהַמֶּמְשָׁלָה בָּעֶלְיוֹנִים וּבַתַּחְתּוֹנִים לַעֲשׂוֹת בָּהֶם כִּרְצוֹנוֹ. וְצִוָּנוּ לְהָנִיחַ עַל הַיָּד לְזִכְרוֹן זְרוֹעַ הַנְּטוּיָה, וְשֶׁהִיא נֶגֶד הַלֵּב, לְשַׁעְבֵּד בָּזֶה תַּאֲווֹת וּמַחְשְׁבוֹת לִבֵּנוּ לַעֲבוֹדָתוֹ יִתְבָּרַךְ שְׁמוֹ. וְעַל הָרֹאשׁ נֶגֶד הַמֹּחַ, שֶׁהַנְּשָׁמָה שֶׁבְּמֹחִי עִם שְׁאָר חוּשַׁי וְכֹחוֹתַי כֻּלָּם יִהְיוּ מְשֻׁעְבָּדִים לַעֲבוֹדָתוֹ, יִתְבָּרַךְ שְׁמוֹ. וּמִשֶּׁפַע מִצְוַת תְּפִלִּין יִתְמַשֵּׁךְ עָלַי לִהְיוֹת לִי חַיִּים אֲרוּכִים וְשֶׁפַע קֹדֶשׁ וּמַחֲשָׁבוֹת קְדוֹשׁוֹת בְּלִי הִרְהוּר חֵטְא וְעָוֹן כְּלָל, וְשֶׁלֹּא יְפַתֵּנוּ וְלֹא יִתְגָּרֶה בָּנוּ יֵצֶר הָרָע, וְיַנִּיחֵנוּ לַעֲבֹד אֶת יהוה כַּאֲשֶׁר עִם לְבָבֵנוּ.

וִיהִי רָצוֹן מִלְּפָנֶיךָ, יהוה אֱלֹהֵינוּ וֵאלֹהֵי אֲבוֹתֵינוּ, שֶׁתְּהֵא חֲשׁוּבָה מִצְוַת הֲנָחַת תְּפִלִּין לִפְנֵי הַקָּדוֹשׁ בָּרוּךְ הוּא, כְּאִלּוּ קִיַּמְתִּיהָ בְּכָל פְּרָטֶיהָ וְדִקְדּוּקֶיהָ וְכַוָּנוֹתֶיהָ וְתַרְיַ״ג מִצְוֹת הַתְּלוּיוֹת בָּהּ, אָמֵן סֶלָה.

Tefillin: The word tefillin (called *totafot* in the Torah) means "emblem, sign, insignia," the visible symbol of an abstract idea. Tefillin are our reminder of the commandment of the Shema: "Love the LORD your God your with all your heart, with all your soul and with all your might" (Deut. 6:5). *All your heart:* this is the tefillin on the upper arm opposite the heart. *All your soul:*

Stand and place the hand-tefillin on the biceps of the left arm (or right arm if you are left-handed), angled toward the heart, and before tightening the strap, say:

בָּרוּךְ Blessed are You, Lord our God,
King of the Universe,
who has made us holy through His commandments,
and has commanded us to put on tefillin.

Wrap the strap of the hand-tefillin seven times around the arm. Place the head-tefillin above the hairline, centered between the eyes, and say quietly:

בָּרוּךְ Blessed are You, Lord our God,
King of the Universe,
who has made us holy through His commandments,
and has commanded us about the commandment of tefillin.

Adjust the head-tefillin and say:

בָּרוּךְ Blessed be the name of His glorious kingdom for ever and all time.

Some say:

From Your wisdom, God most high, grant me [wisdom], and from Your understanding, give me understanding. May Your loving-kindness be greatly upon me, and in Your might may my enemies and those who rise against me be subdued. Pour Your goodly oil on the seven branches of the menora so that Your good flows down upon Your creatures. You open *Ps. 145* Your hand, and satisfy every living thing with favor.

Wind the strap of the hand-tefillin three times around the middle finger, saying:

וְאֵרַשְׂתִּיךְ I will betroth you to Me for ever; *Hos. 2*
I will betroth you to Me in righteousness and justice,
loving-kindness and compassion;
I will betroth you to Me in faithfulness;
and you shall know the Lord.

---

like a wedding ring, we remind ourselves of God's love for Israel, and Israel's love for God.

Stand and place the תפילין של יד *on the biceps of the left arm (or right arm if you are left-handed), angled toward the heart, and before tightening the strap, say:*

בָּרוּךְ אַתָּה יהוה אֱלֹהֵינוּ מֶלֶךְ הָעוֹלָם
אֲשֶׁר קִדְּשָׁנוּ בְּמִצְוֹתָיו
וְצִוָּנוּ לְהָנִיחַ תְּפִלִּין.

Wrap the strap of the תפילין של יד *seven times around the arm.*
Place the תפילין של ראש *above the hairline, centered between the eyes, and say quietly:*

בָּרוּךְ אַתָּה יהוה אֱלֹהֵינוּ מֶלֶךְ הָעוֹלָם
אֲשֶׁר קִדְּשָׁנוּ בְּמִצְוֹתָיו
וְצִוָּנוּ עַל מִצְוַת תְּפִלִּין.

Adjust the תפילין של ראש *and say:*

בָּרוּךְ שֵׁם כְּבוֹד מַלְכוּתוֹ לְעוֹלָם וָעֶד

Some say:

וּמֵחָכְמָתְךָ אֵל עֶלְיוֹן תַּאֲצִיל עָלַי, וּמִבִּינָתְךָ תְּבִינֵנִי, וּבְחַסְדְּךָ תַּגְדִּיל
עָלַי, וּבִגְבוּרָתְךָ תַּצְמִית אוֹיְבַי וְקָמַי. וְשֶׁמֶן הַטּוֹב תָּרִיק עַל שִׁבְעָה
קְנֵי הַמְּנוֹרָה, לְהַשְׁפִּיעַ טוּבְךָ לִבְרִיּוֹתֶיךָ. פּוֹתֵחַ אֶת־יָדֶךָ וּמַשְׂבִּיעַ תהלים קמה
לְכָל־חַי רָצוֹן:

Wind the strap of the תפילין של יד *three times around the middle finger, saying:*

וְאֵרַשְׂתִּיךְ לִי לְעוֹלָם הושע ב
וְאֵרַשְׂתִּיךְ לִי בְּצֶדֶק וּבְמִשְׁפָּט וּבְחֶסֶד וּבְרַחֲמִים:
וְאֵרַשְׂתִּיךְ לִי בֶּאֱמוּנָה, וְיָדַעַתְּ אֶת־יהוה:

וְאֵרַשְׂתִּיךְ *I will betroth you to Me:* These exquisite lines from the book of Hosea speak of God's covenant with Israel as a marriage – a mutual pledge of faith, born of love. Wrapping the strap of the hand-tefillin around the middle finger

After putting on the tefillin, say the following:

וַיְדַבֵּר The LORD spoke to Moses, saying, "Consecrate to Me every firstborn male. The first offspring of every womb among the Israelites, whether man or beast, belongs to Me." Then Moses said to the people, "Remember this day on which you left Egypt, the slave-house, when the LORD brought you out of it with a mighty hand. No leaven shall be eaten. You are leaving on this day, in the month of Aviv. When the LORD brings you into the land of the Canaanites, Hittites, Amorites, Hivites and Jebusites, the land He swore to your ancestors to give you, a land flowing with milk and honey, you are to observe this service in this same month. For seven days you shall eat unleavened bread, and make the seventh day a festival to the LORD. Unleavened bread shall be eaten throughout the seven days. No leavened bread may be seen in your possession, and no leaven shall be seen anywhere within your borders. On that day you shall tell your son, 'This is because of what the LORD did for me when I left Egypt.' [These words] shall also be a sign on your hand, and a reminder above your forehead, so that the LORD's Torah may always be in your mouth, because with a mighty hand the LORD brought you out of Egypt. You shall therefore keep this statute at its appointed time from year to year." Ex. 13

וְהָיָה After the LORD has brought you into the land of the Canaanites, as He swore to you and your ancestors, and He has given it to you, you shall set apart for the LORD the first offspring of every womb. All the firstborn males of your cattle belong to the LORD. Every firstling donkey you shall redeem with a lamb. If you do not redeem it, you must break its neck. Every firstborn among your sons you must redeem. If, in time to come, your son asks you, "What does this mean?" you shall say to him, "With a mighty hand the LORD brought us out of Egypt, out of the slave-house. When Pharaoh stubbornly refused to let us leave, the LORD killed all the firstborn in the land of Egypt, both man and beast. That is why I sacrifice to the LORD the first male offspring of every womb, and redeem all the firstborn of my sons." [These words] shall be a sign on your hand and as an emblem above your forehead, that with a mighty hand the LORD brought us out of Egypt.

After putting on the תפילין, say the following:

וַיְדַבֵּר יהוה אֶל־מֹשֶׁה לֵּאמֹר: קַדֶּשׁ־לִי כָל־בְּכוֹר, פֶּטֶר כָּל־רֶחֶם שמות יג
בִּבְנֵי יִשְׂרָאֵל, בָּאָדָם וּבַבְּהֵמָה, לִי הוּא: וַיֹּאמֶר מֹשֶׁה אֶל־הָעָם, זָכוֹר
אֶת־הַיּוֹם הַזֶּה, אֲשֶׁר יְצָאתֶם מִמִּצְרַיִם מִבֵּית עֲבָדִים, כִּי בְּחֹזֶק יָד
הוֹצִיא יהוה אֶתְכֶם מִזֶּה, וְלֹא יֵאָכֵל חָמֵץ: הַיּוֹם אַתֶּם יֹצְאִים, בְּחֹדֶשׁ
הָאָבִיב: וְהָיָה כִי־יְבִיאֲךָ יהוה אֶל־אֶרֶץ הַכְּנַעֲנִי וְהַחִתִּי וְהָאֱמֹרִי
וְהַחִוִּי וְהַיְבוּסִי, אֲשֶׁר נִשְׁבַּע לַאֲבֹתֶיךָ לָתֶת לָךְ, אֶרֶץ זָבַת חָלָב
וּדְבָשׁ, וְעָבַדְתָּ אֶת־הָעֲבֹדָה הַזֹּאת בַּחֹדֶשׁ הַזֶּה: שִׁבְעַת יָמִים תֹּאכַל
מַצֹּת, וּבַיּוֹם הַשְּׁבִיעִי חַג לַיהוה: מַצּוֹת יֵאָכֵל אֵת שִׁבְעַת הַיָּמִים,
וְלֹא־יֵרָאֶה לְךָ חָמֵץ וְלֹא־יֵרָאֶה לְךָ שְׂאֹר, בְּכָל־גְּבֻלֶךָ: וְהִגַּדְתָּ לְבִנְךָ
בַּיּוֹם הַהוּא לֵאמֹר, בַּעֲבוּר זֶה עָשָׂה יהוה לִי בְּצֵאתִי מִמִּצְרָיִם: וְהָיָה
לְךָ לְאוֹת עַל־יָדְךָ וּלְזִכָּרוֹן בֵּין עֵינֶיךָ, לְמַעַן תִּהְיֶה תּוֹרַת יהוה בְּפִיךָ,
כִּי בְּיָד חֲזָקָה הוֹצִאֲךָ יהוה מִמִּצְרָיִם: וְשָׁמַרְתָּ אֶת־הַחֻקָּה הַזֹּאת
לְמוֹעֲדָהּ, מִיָּמִים יָמִימָה:

וְהָיָה כִּי־יְבִאֲךָ יהוה אֶל־אֶרֶץ הַכְּנַעֲנִי כַּאֲשֶׁר נִשְׁבַּע לְךָ וְלַאֲבֹתֶיךָ, וּנְתָנָהּ לָךְ: וְהַעֲבַרְתָּ כָל־פֶּטֶר־רֶחֶם לַיהוה, וְכָל־פֶּטֶר שֶׁגֶר בְּהֵמָה אֲשֶׁר יִהְיֶה לְךָ הַזְּכָרִים, לַיהוה: וְכָל־פֶּטֶר חֲמֹר תִּפְדֶּה בְשֶׂה, וְאִם־לֹא תִפְדֶּה וַעֲרַפְתּוֹ, וְכֹל בְּכוֹר אָדָם בְּבָנֶיךָ תִּפְדֶּה: וְהָיָה כִּי־יִשְׁאָלְךָ בִנְךָ מָחָר, לֵאמֹר מַה־זֹּאת, וְאָמַרְתָּ אֵלָיו, בְּחֹזֶק יָד הוֹצִיאָנוּ יהוה מִמִּצְרַיִם מִבֵּית עֲבָדִים: וַיְהִי כִּי־הִקְשָׁה פַרְעֹה לְשַׁלְּחֵנוּ, וַיַּהֲרֹג יהוה כָּל־בְּכוֹר בְּאֶרֶץ מִצְרַיִם, מִבְּכֹר אָדָם וְעַד־בְּכוֹר בְּהֵמָה, עַל־כֵּן אֲנִי זֹבֵחַ לַיהוה כָּל־פֶּטֶר רֶחֶם הַזְּכָרִים, וְכָל־בְּכוֹר בָּנַי אֶפְדֶּה: וְהָיָה לְאוֹת עַל־יָדְכָה וּלְטוֹטָפֹת בֵּין עֵינֶיךָ, כִּי בְּחֹזֶק יָד הוֹצִיאָנוּ יהוה מִמִּצְרָיִם:

PREPARATION FOR PRAYER

On entering the synagogue:

HOW GOODLY *Num. 24*

are your tents, Jacob, your dwelling places, Israel.
As for me, *Ps. 5*
in Your great loving-kindness,
I will come into Your House.
I will bow down to Your holy Temple
in awe of You.
LORD, I love the habitation of Your House, *Ps. 26*
the place where Your glory dwells.

As for me,
I will bow in worship;
I will bend the knee
before the LORD my Maker.

As for me, *Ps. 69*
may my prayer come to You, LORD,
at a time of favor.
God, in Your great loving-kindness,
answer me with Your faithful salvation.

הכנה לתפילה

On entering the בית כנסת:

במדבר כד מַה־טֹּבוּ

אֹהָלֶיךָ יַעֲקֹב, מִשְׁכְּנֹתֶיךָ יִשְׂרָאֵל:

תהלים ה וַאֲנִי בְּרֹב חַסְדְּךָ אָבוֹא בֵיתֶךָ

אֶשְׁתַּחֲוֶה אֶל־הֵיכַל־קָדְשְׁךָ

בְּיִרְאָתֶךָ:

תהלים כו יהוה אָהַבְתִּי מְעוֹן בֵּיתֶךָ

וּמְקוֹם מִשְׁכַּן כְּבוֹדֶךָ:

וַאֲנִי אֶשְׁתַּחֲוֶה

וְאֶכְרָעָה

אֶבְרְכָה לִפְנֵי יהוה עֹשִׂי.

תהלים סט וַאֲנִי תְפִלָּתִי־לְךָ יהוה

עֵת רָצוֹן

אֱלֹהִים בְּרָב־חַסְדֶּךָ

עֲנֵנִי בֶּאֱמֶת יִשְׁעֶךָ:

The following poems, on this page and the next, both from the Middle Ages, are summary statements of Jewish faith, orienting us to the spiritual contours of the world that we actualize in the mind by the act of prayer.

Lord of the universe,

who reigned before the birth of any thing –

When by His will all things were made
then was His name proclaimed King.

And when all things shall cease to be
He alone will reign in awe.

He was, He is, and He shall be
glorious for evermore.

He is One, there is none else,
alone, unique, beyond compare;

Without beginning, without end,
His might, His rule are everywhere.

He is my God; my Redeemer lives.
He is the Rock on whom I rely –

My banner and my safe retreat,
my cup, my portion when I cry.

Into His hand my soul I place,
when I awake and when I sleep.

The Lord is with me, I shall not fear;
body and soul from harm will He keep.

The following poems, on this page and the next, both from the Middle Ages, are summary statements of Jewish faith, orienting us to the spiritual contours of the world that we actualize in the mind by the act of prayer.

אֲדוֹן עוֹלָם

אֲשֶׁר מָלַךְ בְּטֶרֶם כָּל־יְצִיר נִבְרָא.
לְעֵת נַעֲשָׂה בְחֶפְצוֹ כֹּל אֲזַי מֶלֶךְ שְׁמוֹ נִקְרָא.
וְאַחֲרֵי כִּכְלוֹת הַכֹּל לְבַדּוֹ יִמְלֹךְ נוֹרָא.

וְהוּא הָיָה וְהוּא הֹוֶה וְהוּא יִהְיֶה בְּתִפְאָרָה.
וְהוּא אֶחָד וְאֵין שֵׁנִי לְהַמְשִׁיל לוֹ לְהַחְבִּירָה.
בְּלִי רֵאשִׁית בְּלִי תַכְלִית וְלוֹ הָעֹז וְהַמִּשְׂרָה.
וְהוּא אֵלִי וְחַי גּוֹאֲלִי וְצוּר חֶבְלִי בְּעֵת צָרָה.
וְהוּא נִסִּי וּמָנוֹס לִי מְנָת כּוֹסִי בְּיוֹם אֶקְרָא.

בְּיָדוֹ אַפְקִיד רוּחִי בְּעֵת אִישַׁן וְאָעִירָה.
וְעִם רוּחִי גְּוִיָּתִי יהוה לִי וְלֹא אִירָא.

GREAT
is the living God and praised.
He exists, and His existence is beyond time.

He is One, and there is no unity like His.
Unfathomable, His oneness is infinite.

He has neither bodily form nor substance;
His holiness is beyond compare.

He preceded all that was created.
He was first: there was no beginning to His beginning.

Behold He is Master of the Universe; and every creature
shows His greatness and majesty.

The rich flow of His prophecy He gave
to His treasured people in whom He gloried.

Never in Israel has there arisen another like Moses,
a prophet who beheld God's image.

God gave His people a Torah of truth
by the hand of His prophet, most faithful of His House.

God will not alter or change His law
for any other, for eternity.

He sees and knows our secret thoughts;
as soon as something is begun, He foresees its end.

He rewards people with loving-kindness according to their deeds;
He punishes the wicked according to his wickedness.

At the end of days He will send our Messiah
to redeem those who await His final salvation.

God will revive the dead in His great loving-kindness.
Blessed for evermore is His glorious name!

יִגְדַּל

אֱלֹהִים חַי וְיִשְׁתַּבַּח, נִמְצָא וְאֵין עֵת אֶל מְצִיאוּתוֹ.

אֶחָד וְאֵין יָחִיד כְּיִחוּדוֹ, נֶעְלָם וְגַם אֵין סוֹף לְאַחְדוּתוֹ.

אֵין לוֹ דְּמוּת הַגּוּף וְאֵינוֹ גוּף, לֹא נַעֲרֹךְ אֵלָיו קְדֻשָּׁתוֹ.

קַדְמוֹן לְכָל דָּבָר אֲשֶׁר נִבְרָא, רִאשׁוֹן וְאֵין רֵאשִׁית לְרֵאשִׁיתוֹ.

הִנּוֹ אֲדוֹן עוֹלָם, וְכָל נוֹצָר יוֹרֶה גְדֻלָּתוֹ וּמַלְכוּתוֹ.

שֶׁפַע נְבוּאָתוֹ נְתָנוֹ אֶל־אַנְשֵׁי סְגֻלָּתוֹ וְתִפְאַרְתּוֹ.

לֹא קָם בְּיִשְׂרָאֵל כְּמֹשֶׁה עוֹד נָבִיא וּמַבִּיט אֶת תְּמוּנָתוֹ.

תּוֹרַת אֱמֶת נָתַן לְעַמּוֹ אֵל עַל יַד נְבִיאוֹ נֶאֱמַן בֵּיתוֹ.

לֹא יַחֲלִיף הָאֵל וְלֹא יָמִיר דָּתוֹ לְעוֹלָמִים לְזוּלָתוֹ.

צוֹפֶה וְיוֹדֵעַ סְתָרֵינוּ, מַבִּיט לְסוֹף דָּבָר בְּקַדְמָתוֹ.

גּוֹמֵל לְאִישׁ חֶסֶד כְּמִפְעָלוֹ, נוֹתֵן לְרָשָׁע רָע כְּרִשְׁעָתוֹ.

יִשְׁלַח לְקֵץ יָמִין מְשִׁיחֵנוּ לִפְדּוֹת מְחַכֵּי קֵץ יְשׁוּעָתוֹ.

מֵתִים יְחַיֶּה אֵל בְּרֹב חַסְדּוֹ, בָּרוּךְ עֲדֵי עַד שֵׁם תְּהִלָּתוֹ.

MORNING BLESSINGS

The following blessings are said aloud by the Leader, but each individual should say them quietly as well. It is our custom to say them standing.

בָּרוּךְ Blessed are You, LORD our God,
King of the Universe,
who gives the heart understanding
to distinguish day from night.

Blessed are You, LORD our God,
King of the Universe,
who has not made me a heathen.

Blessed are You, LORD our God,
King of the Universe,
who has not made me a slave.

Blessed are You, LORD our God,
King of the Universe,
men: who has not made me a woman.
women: who has made me according to His will.

שֶׁלֹּא עָשַׂנִי *Who has not made me a heathen, a slave, a woman:* These three blessings are mentioned in the Talmud (*Menaḥot* 43b). Before we bless God for the universalities of human life, we bless Him for the particularities of our identity. We belong to the people of the covenant; we are free; and we have differentiated responsibilities as women and men. These blessings have nothing to do with hierarchies of dignity, for we believe that every human being is equally formed in the image of God. Rather, they are expressions of acknowledgment of the special duties of Jewish life. Heathens, slaves and women are exempt from certain commands which apply to Jewish men. By these blessings, we express our faith that the commandments are not a burden but a cherished vocation.

ברכות השחר

The following blessings are said aloud by the שליח ציבור*, but each individual should say them quietly as well. It is our custom to say them standing.*

בָּרוּךְ אַתָּה יהוה אֱלֹהֵינוּ מֶלֶךְ הָעוֹלָם
אֲשֶׁר נָתַן לַשֶּׂכְוִי בִינָה
לְהַבְחִין בֵּין יוֹם וּבֵין לָיְלָה.

בָּרוּךְ אַתָּה יהוה אֱלֹהֵינוּ מֶלֶךְ הָעוֹלָם
שֶׁלֹּא עָשַׂנִי גּוֹי.

בָּרוּךְ אַתָּה יהוה אֱלֹהֵינוּ מֶלֶךְ הָעוֹלָם
שֶׁלֹּא עָשַׂנִי עָבֶד.

בָּרוּךְ אַתָּה יהוה אֱלֹהֵינוּ מֶלֶךְ הָעוֹלָם
men שֶׁלֹּא עָשַׂנִי אִשָּׁה. / *women* שֶׁעָשַׂנִי כִּרְצוֹנוֹ.

בָּרוּךְ אַתָּה *Blessed are You:* These blessings, itemized in the Talmud (*Berakhot* 60b), were originally said at home to accompany the various stages of waking and rising. "Who gives sight to the blind" was said on opening one's eyes, "Who clothes the naked" on putting on clothes, and so on. Several medieval authorities, however, held that they should be said in the synagogue.

Their purpose is to make us conscious of what we might otherwise take for granted. Praise is an act of focused attention, foregrounding what is usually in the background of awareness. "The world is full of the light of God, but to see it we must learn to open our eyes" (Rabbi Naḥman of Bratslav).

אֲשֶׁר נָתַן לַשֶּׂכְוִי *Who gives the heart:* This is the translation according to Rabbeinu Asher (Rosh); Rashi and Abudarham read it, "who gives the cockerel." According to Rosh's reading, the first blessing mirrors the first request of the Amida, for human understanding, as well as the first act of creation in which God created light, separating it from darkness.

Blessed are You, Lord our God,
King of the Universe,
who gives sight to the blind.

Blessed are You, Lord our God,
King of the Universe,
who clothes the naked.

Blessed are You, Lord our God,
King of the Universe,
who sets captives free.

Blessed are You, Lord our God,
King of the Universe,
who raises those bowed down.

Blessed are You, Lord our God,
King of the Universe,
who spreads the earth above the waters.

Blessed are You, Lord our God,
King of the Universe,
who has provided me with all I need.

Blessed are You, Lord our God,
King of the Universe,
who makes firm the steps of man.

Blessed are You, Lord our God,
King of the Universe,
who girds Israel with strength.

Blessed are You, Lord our God,
King of the Universe,
who crowns Israel with glory.

Blessed are You, Lord our God,
King of the Universe,
who gives strength to the weary.

בָּרוּךְ אַתָּה יהוה אֱלֹהֵינוּ מֶלֶךְ הָעוֹלָם
פּוֹקֵחַ עִוְרִים.

בָּרוּךְ אַתָּה יהוה אֱלֹהֵינוּ מֶלֶךְ הָעוֹלָם
מַלְבִּישׁ עֲרֻמִּים.

בָּרוּךְ אַתָּה יהוה אֱלֹהֵינוּ מֶלֶךְ הָעוֹלָם
מַתִּיר אֲסוּרִים.

בָּרוּךְ אַתָּה יהוה אֱלֹהֵינוּ מֶלֶךְ הָעוֹלָם
זוֹקֵף כְּפוּפִים.

בָּרוּךְ אַתָּה יהוה אֱלֹהֵינוּ מֶלֶךְ הָעוֹלָם
רוֹקַע הָאָרֶץ עַל הַמָּיִם.

בָּרוּךְ אַתָּה יהוה אֱלֹהֵינוּ מֶלֶךְ הָעוֹלָם
שֶׁעָשָׂה לִי כָּל צָרְכִּי.

בָּרוּךְ אַתָּה יהוה אֱלֹהֵינוּ מֶלֶךְ הָעוֹלָם
הַמֵּכִין מִצְעֲדֵי גָבֶר.

בָּרוּךְ אַתָּה יהוה אֱלֹהֵינוּ מֶלֶךְ הָעוֹלָם
אוֹזֵר יִשְׂרָאֵל בִּגְבוּרָה.

בָּרוּךְ אַתָּה יהוה אֱלֹהֵינוּ מֶלֶךְ הָעוֹלָם
עוֹטֵר יִשְׂרָאֵל בְּתִפְאָרָה.

בָּרוּךְ אַתָּה יהוה אֱלֹהֵינוּ מֶלֶךְ הָעוֹלָם
הַנּוֹתֵן לַיָּעֵף כֹּחַ.

בָּרוּךְ Blessed are You, LORD our God, King of the Universe,
who removes sleep from my eyes
and slumber from my eyelids.
And may it be Your will, LORD our God
and God of our ancestors,
to accustom us to Your Torah,
and make us attached to Your commandments.
Lead us not into error, transgression,
iniquity, temptation or disgrace.
Do not let the evil instinct dominate us.
Keep us far from a bad man and a bad companion.
Help us attach ourselves to the good instinct and to good deeds
and bend our instincts to be subservient to You.
Grant us, this day and every day,
grace, loving-kindness and compassion in Your eyes
and in the eyes of all who see us,
and bestow loving-kindness upon us.
Blessed are You, LORD,
who bestows loving-kindness on His people Israel.

יְהִי רָצוֹן May it be Your will, LORD my God and God of my ancestors, to save me today and every day, from the arrogant and from arrogance itself, from a bad man, a bad friend, a bad neighbor, a bad mishap, a destructive adversary, a harsh trial and a harsh opponent, whether or not he is a son of the covenant. *Berakhot 16b*

---

us of the verse from Psalms (92:3): "To proclaim Your loving-kindness in the morning and Your faithfulness at night."

יְהִי רָצוֹן *May it be Your will:* A meditation composed by Rabbi Judah the Prince (late second–early third century), redactor of the Mishna and leader of the Jewish community in Israel. We are social beings, influenced by our environment (Maimonides); therefore, we pray to be protected from harmful people, events and temptations. The prayer reflects the "social fabric of faith" (Rabbi Lord Jakobovits).

בָּרוּךְ אַתָּה יהוה אֱלֹהֵינוּ מֶלֶךְ הָעוֹלָם
הַמַּעֲבִיר שֵׁנָה מֵעֵינַי וּתְנוּמָה מֵעַפְעַפָּי.
וִיהִי רָצוֹן מִלְּפָנֶיךָ יהוה אֱלֹהֵינוּ וֵאלֹהֵי אֲבוֹתֵינוּ
שֶׁתַּרְגִּילֵנוּ בְּתוֹרָתֶךָ
וְדַבְּקֵנוּ בְּמִצְוֹתֶיךָ
וְאַל תְּבִיאֵנוּ לֹא לִידֵי חֵטְא
וְלֹא לִידֵי עֲבֵרָה וְעָוֹן
וְלֹא לִידֵי נִסָּיוֹן וְלֹא לִידֵי בִזָּיוֹן
וְאַל תַּשְׁלֶט בָּנוּ יֵצֶר הָרָע
וְהַרְחִיקֵנוּ מֵאָדָם רָע וּמֵחָבֵר רָע
וְדַבְּקֵנוּ בְּיֵצֶר הַטּוֹב וּבְמַעֲשִׂים טוֹבִים
וְכֹף אֶת יִצְרֵנוּ לְהִשְׁתַּעְבֶּד לָךְ
וּתְנֵנוּ הַיּוֹם וּבְכָל יוֹם לְחֵן וּלְחֶסֶד וּלְרַחֲמִים
בְּעֵינֶיךָ, וּבְעֵינֵי כָל רוֹאֵינוּ
וְתִגְמְלֵנוּ חֲסָדִים טוֹבִים.
בָּרוּךְ אַתָּה יהוה, גּוֹמֵל חֲסָדִים טוֹבִים לְעַמּוֹ יִשְׂרָאֵל.

יְהִי רָצוֹן מִלְּפָנֶיךָ יהוה אֱלֹהַי וֵאלֹהֵי אֲבוֹתַי, שֶׁתַּצִּילֵנִי הַיּוֹם וּבְכָל יוֹם מֵעַזֵּי פָנִים וּמֵעַזּוּת פָּנִים, מֵאָדָם רָע, וּמֵחָבֵר רָע, וּמִשָּׁכֵן רָע, וּמִפֶּגַע רָע, וּמִשָּׂטָן הַמַּשְׁחִית, מִדִּין קָשֶׁה, וּמִבַּעַל דִּין קָשֶׁה בֵּין שֶׁהוּא בֶן בְּרִית וּבֵין שֶׁאֵינוֹ בֶן בְּרִית. ברכות טז:

הַמַּעֲבִיר *Who removes sleep from my eyes:* Having thanked God for the blessings with which we are surrounded, we conclude by asking for His help in dedicating our lives to His service, undeterred by obstacles that may stand in our way. The prayer ends with thanksgiving for God's kindness, reminding

THE BINDING OF ISAAC

On the basis of Jewish mystical tradition, some have the custom of saying daily the biblical passage recounting the Binding of Isaac, the supreme trial of faith in which Abraham demonstrated his love of God above all other loves.

Our God and God of our ancestors, remember us with a favorable memory, and recall us with a remembrance of salvation and compassion from the highest of high heavens. Remember, LORD our God, on our behalf, the love of the ancients, Abraham, Isaac and Yisrael Your servants; the covenant, the loving-kindness, and the oath You swore to Abraham our father on Mount Moriah, and the Binding, when he bound Isaac his son on the altar, as is written in Your Torah:

It happened after these things that God tested Abraham. He said to him, "Abraham!" "Here I am," he replied. He said, "Take your son, your only son, Isaac, whom you love, and go to the land of Moriah and offer him there as a burnt-offering on one of the mountains which I shall say to you." Early the next morning Abraham rose and saddled his donkey and took his two lads with him, and Isaac his son, and he cut wood for the burnt-offering, and he set out for the place of which God had told him. On the third day Abraham looked up and saw the place from afar. Abraham said to his lads, "Stay here with the donkey while I and the boy go on ahead. We will worship and we will return to you." Abraham took the wood for the burnt-offering and placed it on Isaac his son, and he took in his hand the fire and the knife, and the two of them went together. Isaac said to Abraham his father, "Father?" and he said "Here I am, my son." And he said, "Here are the fire and the wood, but where is the sheep for the burnt-offering?" Abraham said, "God will see to the sheep for the burnt-offering, my son." And the two of them went together. They came to the place God had told him about, and Abraham built there an altar and arranged the wood and bound Isaac his son and laid him on the altar on top of the wood. He reached out his hand and took the knife to slay his son. Then an angel of the LORD called out to him from heaven, "Abraham! Abraham!" He said, "Here I am." He said, "Do not reach out your hand against the boy; do not do anything to him, for now I know that you fear God, because you have not held back your son, your only son, from Me." Abraham looked up and there he saw a ram caught in a thicket by its horns, and Abraham went and took the ram and offered it as a burnt-offering instead of his son. Abraham called that place "The LORD will see," as is said to this day, "On the mountain of the LORD He will be seen." The *Gen. 22*

פרשת העקדה

On the basis of Jewish mystical tradition, some have the custom of saying daily the biblical passage recounting the Binding of Isaac, the supreme trial of faith in which Abraham demonstrated his love of God above all other loves.

אֱלֹהֵינוּ וֵאלֹהֵי אֲבוֹתֵינוּ, זָכְרֵנוּ בְּזִכָּרוֹן טוֹב לְפָנֶיךָ, וּפָקְדֵנוּ בִּפְקֻדַּת יְשׁוּעָה וְרַחֲמִים מִשְּׁמֵי שְׁמֵי קֶדֶם, וּזְכָר לָנוּ יהוה אֱלֹהֵינוּ, אַהֲבַת הַקַּדְמוֹנִים אַבְרָהָם יִצְחָק וְיִשְׂרָאֵל עֲבָדֶיךָ, אֶת הַבְּרִית וְאֶת הַחֶסֶד וְאֶת הַשְּׁבוּעָה שֶׁנִּשְׁבַּעְתָּ לְאַבְרָהָם אָבִינוּ בְּהַר הַמּוֹרִיָּה, וְאֶת הָעֲקֵדָה שֶׁעָקַד אֶת יִצְחָק בְּנוֹ עַל גַּבֵּי הַמִּזְבֵּחַ, כַּכָּתוּב בְּתוֹרָתֶךָ:

וַיְהִי אַחַר הַדְּבָרִים הָאֵלֶּה, וְהָאֱלֹהִים נִסָּה אֶת־אַבְרָהָם, וַיֹּאמֶר אֵלָיו אַבְרָהָם, בראשית כב
וַיֹּאמֶר הִנֵּנִי: וַיֹּאמֶר קַח־נָא אֶת־בִּנְךָ אֶת־יְחִידְךָ אֲשֶׁר־אָהַבְתָּ, אֶת־יִצְחָק,
וְלֶךְ־לְךָ אֶל־אֶרֶץ הַמֹּרִיָּה, וְהַעֲלֵהוּ שָׁם לְעֹלָה עַל אַחַד הֶהָרִים אֲשֶׁר אֹמַר
אֵלֶיךָ: וַיַּשְׁכֵּם אַבְרָהָם בַּבֹּקֶר, וַיַּחֲבֹשׁ אֶת־חֲמֹרוֹ, וַיִּקַּח אֶת־שְׁנֵי נְעָרָיו אִתּוֹ
וְאֵת יִצְחָק בְּנוֹ, וַיְבַקַּע עֲצֵי עֹלָה, וַיָּקָם וַיֵּלֶךְ אֶל־הַמָּקוֹם אֲשֶׁר־אָמַר־לוֹ
הָאֱלֹהִים: בַּיּוֹם הַשְּׁלִישִׁי וַיִּשָּׂא אַבְרָהָם אֶת־עֵינָיו וַיַּרְא אֶת־הַמָּקוֹם מֵרָחֹק:
וַיֹּאמֶר אַבְרָהָם אֶל־נְעָרָיו, שְׁבוּ־לָכֶם פֹּה עִם־הַחֲמוֹר, וַאֲנִי וְהַנַּעַר נֵלְכָה עַד־
כֹּה, וְנִשְׁתַּחֲוֶה וְנָשׁוּבָה אֲלֵיכֶם: וַיִּקַּח אַבְרָהָם אֶת־עֲצֵי הָעֹלָה וַיָּשֶׂם עַל־יִצְחָק
בְּנוֹ, וַיִּקַּח בְּיָדוֹ אֶת־הָאֵשׁ וְאֶת־הַמַּאֲכֶלֶת, וַיֵּלְכוּ שְׁנֵיהֶם יַחְדָּו: וַיֹּאמֶר יִצְחָק
אֶל־אַבְרָהָם אָבִיו, וַיֹּאמֶר אָבִי, וַיֹּאמֶר הִנֶּנִּי בְנִי, וַיֹּאמֶר, הִנֵּה הָאֵשׁ וְהָעֵצִים,
וְאַיֵּה הַשֶּׂה לְעֹלָה: וַיֹּאמֶר אַבְרָהָם, אֱלֹהִים יִרְאֶה־לּוֹ הַשֶּׂה לְעֹלָה, בְּנִי, וַיֵּלְכוּ
שְׁנֵיהֶם יַחְדָּו: וַיָּבֹאוּ אֶל־הַמָּקוֹם אֲשֶׁר אָמַר־לוֹ הָאֱלֹהִים, וַיִּבֶן שָׁם אַבְרָהָם
אֶת־הַמִּזְבֵּחַ וַיַּעֲרֹךְ אֶת־הָעֵצִים, וַיַּעֲקֹד אֶת־יִצְחָק בְּנוֹ, וַיָּשֶׂם אֹתוֹ עַל־הַמִּזְבֵּחַ
מִמַּעַל לָעֵצִים: וַיִּשְׁלַח אַבְרָהָם אֶת־יָדוֹ, וַיִּקַּח אֶת־הַמַּאֲכֶלֶת, לִשְׁחֹט אֶת־
בְּנוֹ: וַיִּקְרָא אֵלָיו מַלְאַךְ יהוה מִן־הַשָּׁמַיִם, וַיֹּאמֶר אַבְרָהָם אַבְרָהָם, וַיֹּאמֶר
הִנֵּנִי: וַיֹּאמֶר אַל־תִּשְׁלַח יָדְךָ אֶל־הַנַּעַר, וְאַל־תַּעַשׂ לוֹ מְאוּמָה, כִּי עַתָּה
יָדַעְתִּי כִּי־יְרֵא אֱלֹהִים אַתָּה, וְלֹא חָשַׂכְתָּ אֶת־בִּנְךָ אֶת־יְחִידְךָ מִמֶּנִּי: וַיִּשָּׂא
אַבְרָהָם אֶת־עֵינָיו, וַיַּרְא וְהִנֵּה־אַיִל, אַחַר נֶאֱחַז בַּסְּבַךְ בְּקַרְנָיו, וַיֵּלֶךְ אַבְרָהָם
וַיִּקַּח אֶת־הָאַיִל, וַיַּעֲלֵהוּ לְעֹלָה תַּחַת בְּנוֹ: וַיִּקְרָא אַבְרָהָם שֵׁם־הַמָּקוֹם
הַהוּא יהוה יִרְאֶה, אֲשֶׁר יֵאָמֵר הַיּוֹם בְּהַר יהוה יֵרָאֶה: וַיִּקְרָא מַלְאַךְ יהוה

angel of the LORD called to Abraham a second time from heaven, and said, "By Myself I swear, declares the LORD, that because you have done this and have not held back your son, your only son, I will greatly bless you and greatly multiply your descendants, as the stars of heaven and the sand of the seashore, and your descendants shall take possession of the gates of their enemies. Through your descendants, all the nations of the earth will be blessed, because you have heeded My voice." Then Abraham returned to his lads, and they rose and went together to Beersheba, and Abraham stayed in Beersheba.

Master of the Universe, just as Abraham our father suppressed his compassion to do Your will wholeheartedly, so may Your compassion suppress Your anger from us and may Your compassion prevail over Your other attributes. Deal with us, LORD our God, with the attributes of loving-kindness and compassion, and in Your great goodness may Your anger be turned away from Your people, Your city, Your land and Your inheritance. Fulfill in us, LORD our God, the promise You made in Your Torah through the hand of Moses Your servant, as it is said: "I will remember My covenant with Jacob, and also My covenant with Isaac, and also My covenant with Abraham I will remember, and the land I will remember." *Lev. 26*

ACCEPTING THE SOVEREIGNTY OF HEAVEN

לְעוֹלָם A person should always be God-fearing, privately and publicly, acknowledging the truth and speaking it in his heart.
He should rise early and say: *Tanna DeVei Eliyahu, ch. 21*

Master of all worlds,
not because of our righteousness *Dan. 9*
do we lay our pleas before You,
but because of Your great compassion.

"privately" and "speaking it [truth] in his heart" (that is, the secret practice of Judaism) and the recitation here of the first lines of the Shema, which could not be said at the normal time. The final blessing, "Who sanctifies His name among the multitudes," refers to the martyrdom of those who went to their deaths rather than renounce their faith. Martyrdom is called *Kiddush HaShem*, "sanctifying [God's] name."

רִבּוֹן *Master of all worlds:* This passage also appears in the *Ne'ila* prayer on Yom

אֶל־אַבְרָהָם שֵׁנִית מִן־הַשָּׁמָיִם: וַיֹּאמֶר, בִּי נִשְׁבַּעְתִּי נְאֻם־יהוה, כִּי יַעַן אֲשֶׁר עָשִׂיתָ אֶת־הַדָּבָר הַזֶּה, וְלֹא חָשַׂכְתָּ אֶת־בִּנְךָ אֶת־יְחִידֶךָ: כִּי־בָרֵךְ אֲבָרֶכְךָ, וְהַרְבָּה אַרְבֶּה אֶת־זַרְעֲךָ כְּכוֹכְבֵי הַשָּׁמַיִם, וְכַחוֹל אֲשֶׁר עַל־שְׂפַת הַיָּם, וְיִרַשׁ זַרְעֲךָ אֵת שַׁעַר אֹיְבָיו: וְהִתְבָּרְכוּ בְזַרְעֲךָ כֹּל גּוֹיֵי הָאָרֶץ, עֵקֶב אֲשֶׁר שָׁמַעְתָּ בְּקֹלִי: וַיָּשָׁב אַבְרָהָם אֶל־נְעָרָיו, וַיָּקֻמוּ וַיֵּלְכוּ יַחְדָּו אֶל־בְּאֵר שָׁבַע, וַיֵּשֶׁב אַבְרָהָם בִּבְאֵר שָׁבַע:

רִבּוֹנוֹ שֶׁל עוֹלָם, כְּמוֹ שֶׁכָּבַשׁ אַבְרָהָם אָבִינוּ אֶת רַחֲמָיו לַעֲשׂוֹת רְצוֹנְךָ בְּלֵבָב שָׁלֵם, כֵּן יִכְבְּשׁוּ רַחֲמֶיךָ אֶת כַּעַסְךָ מֵעָלֵינוּ וְיָגֹלּוּ רַחֲמֶיךָ עַל מִדּוֹתֶיךָ. וְתִתְנַהֵג עִמָּנוּ יהוה אֱלֹהֵינוּ בְּמִדַּת הַחֶסֶד וּבְמִדַּת הָרַחֲמִים, וּבְטוּבְךָ הַגָּדוֹל יָשׁוּב חֲרוֹן אַפְּךָ מֵעַמְּךָ וּמֵעִירְךָ וּמֵאַרְצְךָ וּמִנַּחֲלָתֶךָ. וְקַיֶּם לָנוּ יהוה אֱלֹהֵינוּ אֶת הַדָּבָר שֶׁהִבְטַחְתָּנוּ בְּתוֹרָתֶךָ
עַל יְדֵי מֹשֶׁה עַבְדֶּךָ, כָּאָמוּר: וְזָכַרְתִּי אֶת־בְּרִיתִי יַעֲקוֹב וְאַף אֶת־בְּרִיתִי יִצְחָק, וְאַף (ויקרא כו)
אֶת־בְּרִיתִי אַבְרָהָם אֶזְכֹּר, וְהָאָרֶץ אֶזְכֹּר:

קבלת עול מלכות שמים

לְעוֹלָם יְהֵא אָדָם יְרֵא שָׁמַיִם בְּסֵתֶר וּבְגָלוּי (תנא דבי אליהו, פרק כא)
וּמוֹדֶה עַל הָאֱמֶת, וְדוֹבֵר אֱמֶת בִּלְבָבוֹ
וְיַשְׁכֵּם וְיֹאמַר

רִבּוֹן כָּל הָעוֹלָמִים

לֹא עַל־צִדְקוֹתֵינוּ אֲנַחְנוּ מַפִּילִים תַּחֲנוּנֵינוּ לְפָנֶיךָ (דניאל ט)
כִּי עַל־רַחֲמֶיךָ הָרַבִּים:

לְעוֹלָם *A person should always:* This whole section until "Who sanctifies His name among the multitudes" appears in the tenth-century Midrash, *Tanna DeVei Eliyahu* (chapter 21). Some believe that it dates from a period of persecution under the Persian ruler Yazdegerd II who, in 456 CE, forbade the observance of Shabbat and the reading of the Torah. Jews continued to practice their faith in secret, saying prayers at times and in ways that would not be detected by their persecutors. This explains the reference to fearing God

What are we? What are our lives?
What is our loving-kindness? What is our righteousness?
What is our salvation? What is our strength?
What is our might? What shall we say before You,
Lord our God and God of our ancestors?
Are not all the mighty like nothing before You,
the men of renown as if they had never been,
the wise as if they know nothing,
and the understanding as if they lack intelligence?
For their many works are in vain,
and the days of their lives like a fleeting breath before You.
The pre-eminence of man over the animals is nothing, *Eccl. 3*
for all is but a fleeting breath.

אֲבָל Yet we are Your people, the children of Your covenant,
the children of Abraham, Your beloved,
to whom You made a promise on Mount Moriah;
the offspring of Isaac his only one who was bound on the altar;
the congregation of Jacob Your firstborn son
whom – because of the love with which You loved him
and the joy with which You rejoiced in him –
You called Yisrael and Yeshurun.

לְפִיכָךְ Therefore it is our duty
to thank You, and to praise, glorify, bless, sanctify
and give praise and thanks to Your name.
Happy are we, how good is our portion,
how lovely our fate, how beautiful our heritage.

---

empty, futile." However, it literally means "a short breath." It conveys a sense of the brevity and insubstantiality of life as a physical phenomenon. All that lives soon dies, and is as if it had never been. *Yet:* You created us, made us, chose us. We are infinitesimally small, yet brushed by the wings of Infinity. We are dust; yet *we are Your people, children of Your covenant,* descendants

מָה אָנוּ, מֶה חַיֵּינוּ, מֶה חַסְדֵּנוּ, מַה צִּדְקוֹתֵינוּ
מַה יְּשׁוּעָתֵנוּ, מַה כֹּחֵנוּ, מַה גְּבוּרָתֵנוּ
מַה נֹּאמַר לְפָנֶיךָ, יהוה אֱלֹהֵינוּ וֵאלֹהֵי אֲבוֹתֵינוּ
הֲלֹא כָּל הַגִּבּוֹרִים כְּאַיִן לְפָנֶיךָ
וְאַנְשֵׁי הַשֵּׁם כְּלֹא הָיוּ
וַחֲכָמִים כִּבְלִי מַדָּע, וּנְבוֹנִים כִּבְלִי הַשְׂכֵּל
כִּי רֹב מַעֲשֵׂיהֶם תֹּהוּ, וִימֵי חַיֵּיהֶם הֶבֶל לְפָנֶיךָ
וּמוֹתַר הָאָדָם מִן־הַבְּהֵמָה אָיִן קהלת ג
כִּי הַכֹּל הָבֶל:

אֲבָל אֲנַחְנוּ עַמְּךָ בְּנֵי בְרִיתֶךָ
בְּנֵי אַבְרָהָם אֹהַבְךָ שֶׁנִּשְׁבַּעְתָּ לּוֹ בְּהַר הַמּוֹרִיָּה
זֶרַע יִצְחָק יְחִידוֹ שֶׁנֶּעֱקַד עַל גַּבֵּי הַמִּזְבֵּחַ
עֲדַת יַעֲקֹב בִּנְךָ בְּכוֹרֶךָ
שֶׁמֵּאַהֲבָתְךָ שֶׁאָהַבְתָּ אוֹתוֹ, וּמִשִּׂמְחָתְךָ שֶׁשָּׂמַחְתָּ בּוֹ
קָרָאתָ אֶת שְׁמוֹ יִשְׂרָאֵל וִישֻׁרוּן.

לְפִיכָךְ אֲנַחְנוּ חַיָּבִים
לְהוֹדוֹת לְךָ וּלְשַׁבֵּחֲךָ וּלְפָאֶרְךָ
וּלְבָרֵךְ וּלְקַדֵּשׁ וְלָתֵת שֶׁבַח וְהוֹדָיָה לִשְׁמֶךָ.
אַשְׁרֵינוּ, מַה טּוֹב חֶלְקֵנוּ
וּמַה נָּעִים גּוֹרָלֵנוּ, וּמַה יָּפָה יְרֻשָּׁתֵנוּ.

Kippur. It expresses the paradox of the human condition in the presence of God. We know how small we are and how brief our lives. *Fleeting breath:* the Hebrew word *hevel* – the key word of the opening chapters of Ecclesiastes, from which this line is taken – has been translated as "vain, meaningless,

▸ Happy are we who, early and late,
evening and morning,
say twice each day –

Listen, Israel: the LORD is our God, the LORD is One. *Deut. 6*

Quietly: Blessed be the name of His glorious kingdom for ever and all time.

Some congregations say the entire first paragraph of the Shema (below) at this point. If there is a concern that the Shema will not be recited within the prescribed time, then all three paragraphs should be said. See law 26.

Love the LORD your God with all your heart, with all your soul, and with all your might. These words which I command you today shall be on your heart. Teach them repeatedly to your children, speaking of them when you sit at home and when you travel on the way, when you lie down and when you rise. Bind them as a sign on your hand, and they shall be an emblem between your eyes. Write them on the doorposts of your house and gates.

אַתָּה הוּא It was You who existed
before the world was created,
it is You now that the world has been created.
It is You in this world
and You in the World to Come.
▸ Sanctify Your name
through those who sanctify Your name,
and sanctify Your name
throughout Your world.
By Your salvation may our pride be exalted;
raise high our pride.
Blessed are You, LORD,
who sanctifies His name among the multitudes.

---

the refusal of Jews to abandon their faith. God does not alter or revoke His covenant; therefore, we may not renounce our religion or identity: "I, God, do not change; so you, children of Jacob, are not destroyed" (Mal. 3:6).

◂ אַשְׁרֵינוּ, שֶׁאֲנַחְנוּ מַשְׁכִּימִים וּמַעֲרִיבִים עֶרֶב וָבֹקֶר
וְאוֹמְרִים פַּעֲמַיִם בְּכָל יוֹם

דברים ו
שְׁמַע יִשְׂרָאֵל, יהוה אֱלֹהֵינוּ, יהוה אֶחָד:

Quietly בָּרוּךְ שֵׁם כְּבוֹד מַלְכוּתוֹ לְעוֹלָם וָעֶד.

Some congregations say the entire first paragraph of the שמע *(below) at this point. If there is a concern that the* שמע *will not be recited within the prescribed time, then all three paragraphs should be said. See law 26.*

וְאָהַבְתָּ אֵת יהוה אֱלֹהֶיךָ, בְּכָל־לְבָבְךָ, וּבְכָל־נַפְשְׁךָ, וּבְכָל־מְאֹדֶךָ: וְהָיוּ הַדְּבָרִים הָאֵלֶּה, אֲשֶׁר אָנֹכִי מְצַוְּךָ הַיּוֹם, עַל־לְבָבֶךָ: וְשִׁנַּנְתָּם לְבָנֶיךָ, וְדִבַּרְתָּ בָּם, בְּשִׁבְתְּךָ בְּבֵיתֶךָ, וּבְלֶכְתְּךָ בַדֶּרֶךְ, וּבְשָׁכְבְּךָ וּבְקוּמֶךָ: וּקְשַׁרְתָּם לְאוֹת עַל־יָדֶךָ וְהָיוּ לְטֹטָפֹת בֵּין עֵינֶיךָ: וּכְתַבְתָּם עַל־מְזֻזוֹת בֵּיתֶךָ וּבִשְׁעָרֶיךָ:

אַתָּה הוּא עַד שֶׁלֹּא נִבְרָא הָעוֹלָם
אַתָּה הוּא מִשֶּׁנִּבְרָא הָעוֹלָם.
אַתָּה הוּא בָּעוֹלָם הַזֶּה
וְאַתָּה הוּא לָעוֹלָם הַבָּא.
◂ קַדֵּשׁ אֶת שִׁמְךָ עַל מַקְדִּישֵׁי שְׁמֶךָ
וְקַדֵּשׁ אֶת שִׁמְךָ בְּעוֹלָמֶךָ
וּבִישׁוּעָתְךָ תָּרוּם וְתַגְבִּיהַּ קַרְנֵנוּ.
בָּרוּךְ אַתָּה יהוה
הַמְקַדֵּשׁ אֶת שְׁמוֹ בָּרַבִּים.

---

of those You singled out to be witnesses to the world of Your existence and majesty.

אַתָּה הוּא *It was You who existed:* This prayer, with its emphasis on the changelessness of God, may have been incorporated at a time of persecution, expressing

אַתָּה הוּא You are the LORD our God
in heaven and on earth,
and in the highest heaven of heavens.
Truly, You are the first
and You are the last,
and besides You there is no god.
Gather those who hope in You
from the four quarters of the earth.
May all mankind recognize and know
that You alone are God
over all the kingdoms on earth.

You made the heavens and the earth,
the sea and all they contain.
Who among all the works of Your hands,
above and below,
can tell You what to do?

Heavenly Father,
deal kindly with us
for the sake of Your great name
by which we are called,
and fulfill for us,
LORD our God,
that which is written:

"At that time I will bring you home, and at that time I will gather you, for I will give you renown and praise among all the peoples of the earth when I bring back your exiles before your eyes, says the LORD." *Zeph. 3*

---

ingathering of Jews and of a time when "I will give you renown and praise among all the peoples of the earth." This entire sequence of prayers is eloquent testimony to how Jews sustained faith and hope, dignity and pride, during some of the most prolonged periods of persecution in history.

אַתָּה הוּא יהוה אֱלֹהֵינוּ
בַּשָּׁמַיִם וּבָאָרֶץ
וּבִשְׁמֵי הַשָּׁמַיִם הָעֶלְיוֹנִים.
אֱמֶת, אַתָּה הוּא רִאשׁוֹן
וְאַתָּה הוּא אַחֲרוֹן
וּמִבַּלְעָדֶיךָ אֵין אֱלֹהִים.
קַבֵּץ קוֶֹיךָ מֵאַרְבַּע כַּנְפוֹת הָאָרֶץ.
יַכִּירוּ וְיֵדְעוּ כָּל בָּאֵי עוֹלָם
כִּי אַתָּה הוּא הָאֱלֹהִים לְבַדְּךָ לְכֹל מַמְלְכוֹת הָאָרֶץ.

אַתָּה עָשִׂיתָ אֶת הַשָּׁמַיִם וְאֶת הָאָרֶץ
אֶת הַיָּם וְאֶת כָּל אֲשֶׁר בָּם
וּמִי בְּכָל מַעֲשֵׂי יָדֶיךָ בָּעֶלְיוֹנִים אוֹ בַתַּחְתּוֹנִים
שֶׁיֹּאמַר לְךָ מַה תַּעֲשֶׂה.
אָבִינוּ שֶׁבַּשָּׁמַיִם
עֲשֵׂה עִמָּנוּ חֶסֶד
בַּעֲבוּר שִׁמְךָ הַגָּדוֹל שֶׁנִּקְרָא עָלֵינוּ
וְקַיֶּם לָנוּ יהוה אֱלֹהֵינוּ
מַה שֶּׁכָּתוּב:

בָּעֵת הַהִיא אָבִיא אֶתְכֶם, וּבָעֵת קַבְּצִי אֶתְכֶם, צפניה ג
כִּי־אֶתֵּן אֶתְכֶם לְשֵׁם וְלִתְהִלָּה בְּכֹל עַמֵּי הָאָרֶץ,
בְּשׁוּבִי אֶת־שְׁבוּתֵיכֶם לְעֵינֵיכֶם, אָמַר יהוה:

אַתָּה הוּא *You are the* L*ORD our God:* This second prayer, for the end of exile, culminates with the verse from Zephania (3:20) which speaks of the

OFFERINGS

The sages held that, in the absence of the Temple, studying the laws of sacrifices is the equivalent of offering them. Hence the following texts. There are different customs as to how many passages are to be said, and one should follow the custom of one's congregation. The minimum requirement is to say the verses relating to The Daily Sacrifice on the next page.

THE BASIN

The Lord spoke to Moses, saying: Make a bronze basin, with its bronze stand for washing, and place it between the Tent of Meeting and the altar, and put water in it. From it, Aaron and his sons are to wash their hands and feet. When they enter the Tent of Meeting, they shall wash with water so that they will not die; likewise when they approach the altar to minister, presenting a fire-offering to the Lord. They must wash their hands and feet so that they will not die. This shall be an everlasting ordinance for Aaron and his descendants throughout their generations. *Ex. 30*

TAKING OF THE ASHES

The Lord spoke to Moses, saying: Instruct Aaron and his sons, saying, This is the law of the burnt-offering. The burnt-offering shall remain on the altar hearth throughout the night until morning, and the altar fire shall be kept burning on it. The priest shall then put on his linen garments, and linen breeches next to his body, and shall remove the ashes of the burnt-offering that the fire has consumed on the altar and place them beside the altar. Then he shall take off these clothes and put on others, and carry the ashes outside the camp to a clean place. The fire on the altar must be kept burning; it must not go out. Each morning the priest shall burn wood on it, and prepare on it the burnt-offering and burn the fat of the peace-offerings. A perpetual fire must be kept burning on the altar; it must not go out. *Lev. 6*

May it be Your will, Lord our God and God of our ancestors, that You have compassion on us and pardon us all our sins, grant atonement for all our iniquities and forgive all our transgressions. May You rebuild the Temple swiftly in our days so that we may offer You the continual-offering that it may atone for us as You have prescribed for us in Your Torah through Moses Your servant, from the mouthpiece of Your glory, as it is said:

---

about sacrifice was a substitute for sacrifice itself (*Ta'anit* 27b). The passage from the Mishna (*Zevaḥim* 5) is also about sacrifices, and was chosen because it does not contain any disagreement between the sages, and thus accords with the rule that one should pray "after a decided *halakha*," that is, an item of Jewish law about which there is no debate.

סדר הקרבנות

חז״ל held that, in the absence of the Temple, studying the laws of sacrifices is the equivalent of offering them. Hence the following texts. There are different customs as to how many passages are to be said, and one should follow the custom of one's congregation. The minimum requirement is to say the verses relating to the קרבן תמיד on the next page.

פרשת הכיור

וַיְדַבֵּר יהוה אֶל־מֹשֶׁה לֵּאמֹר: וְעָשִׂיתָ כִּיּוֹר נְחֹשֶׁת וְכַנּוֹ נְחֹשֶׁת לְרָחְצָה, שמות ל
וְנָתַתָּ אֹתוֹ בֵּין־אֹהֶל מוֹעֵד וּבֵין הַמִּזְבֵּחַ, וְנָתַתָּ שָׁמָּה מָיִם: וְרָחֲצוּ אַהֲרֹן
וּבָנָיו מִמֶּנּוּ אֶת־יְדֵיהֶם וְאֶת־רַגְלֵיהֶם: בְּבֹאָם אֶל־אֹהֶל מוֹעֵד יִרְחֲצוּ־מַיִם,
וְלֹא יָמֻתוּ, אוֹ בְגִשְׁתָּם אֶל־הַמִּזְבֵּחַ לְשָׁרֵת, לְהַקְטִיר אִשֶּׁה לַיהוה: וְרָחֲצוּ
יְדֵיהֶם וְרַגְלֵיהֶם וְלֹא יָמֻתוּ, וְהָיְתָה לָהֶם חָק־עוֹלָם, לוֹ וּלְזַרְעוֹ לְדֹרֹתָם:

פרשת תרומת הדשן

וַיְדַבֵּר יהוה אֶל־מֹשֶׁה לֵּאמֹר: צַו אֶת־אַהֲרֹן וְאֶת־בָּנָיו לֵאמֹר, זֹאת תּוֹרַת ויקרא ו
הָעֹלָה, הִוא הָעֹלָה עַל מוֹקְדָה עַל־הַמִּזְבֵּחַ כָּל־הַלַּיְלָה עַד־הַבֹּקֶר, וְאֵשׁ
הַמִּזְבֵּחַ תּוּקַד בּוֹ: וְלָבַשׁ הַכֹּהֵן מִדּוֹ בַד, וּמִכְנְסֵי־בַד יִלְבַּשׁ עַל־בְּשָׂרוֹ,
וְהֵרִים אֶת־הַדֶּשֶׁן אֲשֶׁר תֹּאכַל הָאֵשׁ אֶת־הָעֹלָה, עַל־הַמִּזְבֵּחַ, וְשָׂמוֹ אֵצֶל
הַמִּזְבֵּחַ: וּפָשַׁט אֶת־בְּגָדָיו, וְלָבַשׁ בְּגָדִים אֲחֵרִים, וְהוֹצִיא אֶת־הַדֶּשֶׁן אֶל־
מִחוּץ לַמַּחֲנֶה, אֶל־מָקוֹם טָהוֹר: וְהָאֵשׁ עַל־הַמִּזְבֵּחַ תּוּקַד־בּוֹ, לֹא תִכְבֶּה,
וּבִעֵר עָלֶיהָ הַכֹּהֵן עֵצִים בַּבֹּקֶר בַּבֹּקֶר, וְעָרַךְ עָלֶיהָ הָעֹלָה, וְהִקְטִיר עָלֶיהָ
חֶלְבֵי הַשְּׁלָמִים: אֵשׁ, תָּמִיד תּוּקַד עַל־הַמִּזְבֵּחַ, לֹא תִכְבֶּה:

יְהִי רָצוֹן מִלְּפָנֶיךָ יהוה אֱלֹהֵינוּ וֵאלֹהֵי אֲבוֹתֵינוּ, שֶׁתְּרַחֵם עָלֵינוּ, וְתִמְחֹל לָנוּ עַל כָּל חַטֹּאתֵינוּ וּתְכַפֵּר לָנוּ עַל כָּל עֲוֹנוֹתֵינוּ וְתִסְלַח לָנוּ עַל כָּל פְּשָׁעֵינוּ, וְתִבְנֶה בֵּית הַמִּקְדָּשׁ בִּמְהֵרָה בְיָמֵינוּ, וְנַקְרִיב לְפָנֶיךָ קָרְבַּן הַתָּמִיד שֶׁיְּכַפֵּר בַּעֲדֵנוּ, כְּמוֹ שֶׁכָּתַבְתָּ עָלֵינוּ בְּתוֹרָתֶךָ עַל יְדֵי מֹשֶׁה עַבְדֶּךָ מִפִּי כְבוֹדֶךָ, כָּאָמוּר

OFFERINGS

There now follows a second cycle of study, with the same structure as the first, with passages from (1) the Torah, (2) the Mishna, and (3) the Gemara. The passages from the Torah relate to the daily, weekly and monthly sacrifices because, in the absence of the Temple, the sages held that study of the laws

THE DAILY SACRIFICE

וַיְדַבֵּר The Lord said to Moses, "Command the Israelites and tell them: 'Be careful to offer to Me at the appointed time My food-offering consumed by fire, as an aroma pleasing to Me.' Tell them: 'This is the fire-offering you shall offer to the Lord – two lambs a year old without blemish, as a regular burnt-offering each day. Prepare one lamb in the morning and the other toward evening, together with a meal-offering of a tenth of an ephah of fine flour mixed with a quarter of a hin of oil from pressed olives. This is the regular burnt-offering instituted at Mount Sinai as a pleasing aroma, a fire-offering made to the Lord. Its libation is to be a quarter of a hin [of wine] with each lamb, poured in the Sanctuary as a libation of strong drink to the Lord. Prepare the second lamb in the afternoon, along with the same meal-offering and libation as in the morning. This is a fire-offering, an aroma pleasing to the Lord.'" *Num. 28*

וְשָׁחַט He shall slaughter it at the north side of the altar before the Lord, and Aaron's sons the priests shall sprinkle its blood against the altar on all sides. *Lev. 1*

May it be Your will, Lord our God and God of our ancestors,
that this recitation be considered accepted and favored before You
as if we had offered the daily sacrifice at its appointed time and place, according to its laws.

It is You, Lord our God, to whom our ancestors offered fragrant incense when the Temple stood, as You commanded them through Moses Your prophet, as is written in Your Torah:

THE INCENSE

The Lord said to Moses: Take fragrant spices – balsam, onycha, galbanum and pure frankincense, all in equal amounts – and make a fragrant blend of incense, the work of a perfumer, well mixed, pure and holy. Grind it very finely and place it in front of the [Ark of] Testimony in the Tent of Meeting, where I will meet with you. It shall be most holy to you. *Ex. 30*

And it is said:

Aaron shall burn fragrant incense on the altar every morning when he cleans the lamps. He shall burn incense again when he lights the lamps toward evening so that there will be incense before the Lord at all times, throughout your generations.

פרשת קרבן התמיד

וַיְדַבֵּר יהוה אֶל־מֹשֶׁה לֵּאמֹר: צַו אֶת־בְּנֵי יִשְׂרָאֵל וְאָמַרְתָּ במדבר כח
אֲלֵהֶם, אֶת־קָרְבָּנִי לַחְמִי לְאִשַּׁי, רֵיחַ נִיחֹחִי, תִּשְׁמְרוּ לְהַקְרִיב
לִי בְּמוֹעֲדוֹ: וְאָמַרְתָּ לָהֶם, זֶה הָאִשֶּׁה אֲשֶׁר תַּקְרִיבוּ לַיהוה,
כְּבָשִׂים בְּנֵי־שָׁנָה תְמִימִם שְׁנַיִם לַיּוֹם, עֹלָה תָמִיד: אֶת־הַכֶּבֶשׂ
אֶחָד תַּעֲשֶׂה בַבֹּקֶר, וְאֵת הַכֶּבֶשׂ הַשֵּׁנִי תַּעֲשֶׂה בֵּין הָעַרְבָּיִם:
וַעֲשִׂירִית הָאֵיפָה סֹלֶת לְמִנְחָה, בְּלוּלָה בְּשֶׁמֶן כָּתִית רְבִיעִת
הַהִין: עֹלַת תָּמִיד, הָעֲשֻׂיָה בְּהַר סִינַי, לְרֵיחַ נִיחֹחַ אִשֶּׁה לַיהוה:
וְנִסְכּוֹ רְבִיעִת הַהִין לַכֶּבֶשׂ הָאֶחָד, בַּקֹּדֶשׁ הַסֵּךְ נֶסֶךְ שֵׁכָר
לַיהוה: וְאֵת הַכֶּבֶשׂ הַשֵּׁנִי תַּעֲשֶׂה בֵּין הָעַרְבָּיִם, כְּמִנְחַת הַבֹּקֶר
וּכְנִסְכּוֹ תַּעֲשֶׂה, אִשֵּׁה רֵיחַ נִיחֹחַ לַיהוה:

וְשָׁחַט אֹתוֹ עַל יֶרֶךְ הַמִּזְבֵּחַ צָפֹנָה לִפְנֵי יהוה, וְזָרְקוּ בְּנֵי אַהֲרֹן ויקרא א
הַכֹּהֲנִים אֶת־דָּמוֹ עַל־הַמִּזְבֵּחַ, סָבִיב:

יְהִי רָצוֹן מִלְּפָנֶיךָ, יהוה אֱלֹהֵינוּ וֵאלֹהֵי אֲבוֹתֵינוּ
שֶׁתְּהֵא אֲמִירָה זוֹ חֲשׁוּבָה וּמְקֻבֶּלֶת וּמְרֻצָּה לְפָנֶיךָ
כְּאִלּוּ הִקְרַבְנוּ קָרְבַּן הַתָּמִיד בְּמוֹעֲדוֹ וּבִמְקוֹמוֹ וּכְהִלְכָתוֹ.

אַתָּה הוּא יהוה אֱלֹהֵינוּ שֶׁהִקְטִירוּ אֲבוֹתֵינוּ לְפָנֶיךָ אֶת קְטֹרֶת הַסַּמִּים בִּזְמַן שֶׁבֵּית
הַמִּקְדָּשׁ הָיָה קַיָּם, כַּאֲשֶׁר צִוִּיתָ אוֹתָם עַל יְדֵי מֹשֶׁה נְבִיאֶךָ, כַּכָּתוּב בְּתוֹרָתֶךָ:

פרשת הקטורת

וַיֹּאמֶר יהוה אֶל־מֹשֶׁה, קַח־לְךָ סַמִּים נָטָף וּשְׁחֵלֶת וְחֶלְבְּנָה, סַמִּים וּלְבֹנָה שמות ל
זַכָּה, בַּד בְּבַד יִהְיֶה: וְעָשִׂיתָ אֹתָהּ קְטֹרֶת, רֹקַח מַעֲשֵׂה רוֹקֵחַ, מְמֻלָּח, טָהוֹר
קֹדֶשׁ: וְשָׁחַקְתָּ מִמֶּנָּה הָדֵק, וְנָתַתָּה מִמֶּנָּה לִפְנֵי הָעֵדֻת בְּאֹהֶל מוֹעֵד אֲשֶׁר
אִוָּעֵד לְךָ שָׁמָּה, קֹדֶשׁ קָדָשִׁים תִּהְיֶה לָכֶם:

וְנֶאֱמַר

וְהִקְטִיר עָלָיו אַהֲרֹן קְטֹרֶת סַמִּים, בַּבֹּקֶר בַּבֹּקֶר בְּהֵיטִיבוֹ אֶת־הַנֵּרֹת
יַקְטִירֶנָּה: וּבְהַעֲלֹת אַהֲרֹן אֶת־הַנֵּרֹת בֵּין הָעַרְבַּיִם יַקְטִירֶנָּה, קְטֹרֶת תָּמִיד
לִפְנֵי יהוה לְדֹרֹתֵיכֶם:

The rabbis taught: How was the incense prepared? It weighed 368 manehs, 365 corresponding to the number of days in a solar year, a maneh for each day, half to be offered in the morning and half in the afternoon, and three additional manehs from which the High Priest took two handfuls on Yom Kippur. These were put back into the mortar on the day before Yom Kippur and ground again very thoroughly so as to be extremely fine. The incense contained eleven kinds of spices: balsam, onycha, galbanum and frankincense, each weighing seventy manehs; myrrh, cassia, spikenard and saffron, each weighing sixteen manehs; twelve manehs of costus, three of aromatic bark; nine of cinnamon; nine kabs of Carsina lye; three seahs and three kabs of Cyprus wine. If Cyprus wine was not available, old white wine might be used. A quarter of a kab of Sodom salt, and a minute amount of a smoke-raising herb. Rabbi Nathan the Babylonian says: also a minute amount of Jordan amber. If one added honey to the mixture, he rendered it unfit for sacred use. If he omitted any one of its ingredients, he is guilty of a capital offence. *Keritot 6a*

Rabban Simeon ben Gamliel says: "Balsam" refers to the sap that drips from the balsam tree. The Carsina lye was used for bleaching the onycha to improve it. The Cyprus wine was used to soak the onycha in it to make it pungent. Though urine is suitable for this purpose, it is not brought into the Temple out of respect.

It was taught, Rabbi Nathan says: While it was being ground, another would say, "Grind well, well grind," because the [rhythmic] sound is good for spices. If it was mixed in half-quantities, it is fit for use, but we have not heard whether this applies to a third or a quarter. Rabbi Judah said: The general rule is that if it was made in the correct proportions, it is fit for use even if made in half-quantity, but if he omitted any one of its ingredients, he is guilty of a capital offence.

It was taught, Bar Kappara says: Once every sixty or seventy years, the accumulated surpluses amounted to half the yearly quantity. Bar Kappara also taught: If a minute quantity of honey had been mixed into the incense, no one could have resisted the scent. Why did they not put honey into it? Because the Torah says, "For you are not to burn any leaven or honey in a fire-offering made to the LORD." *JT Yoma 4:5* *Lev. 2*

The following three verses are each said three times:

The LORD of hosts is with us; the God of Jacob is our stronghold, Selah. *Ps. 46*
LORD of hosts, happy is the one who trusts in You. *Ps. 84*
LORD, save! May the King answer us on the day we call. *Ps. 20*

תָּנוּ רַבָּנָן: פִּטּוּם הַקְּטֹרֶת כֵּיצַד, שְׁלֹשׁ מֵאוֹת וְשִׁשִּׁים וּשְׁמוֹנָה מָנִים הָיוּ בָהּ. שְׁלֹשׁ מֵאוֹת וְשִׁשִּׁים וַחֲמִשָּׁה כְּמִנְיַן יְמוֹת הַחַמָּה, מָנֶה לְכָל יוֹם, פְּרַס בְּשַׁחֲרִית וּפְרַס בֵּין הָעַרְבַּיִם, וּשְׁלֹשָׁה מָנִים יְתֵרִים שֶׁמֵּהֶם מַכְנִיס כֹּהֵן גָּדוֹל מְלֹא חָפְנָיו בְּיוֹם הַכִּפּוּרִים, וּמַחֲזִירָן לְמַכְתֶּשֶׁת בְּעֶרֶב יוֹם הַכִּפּוּרִים וְשׁוֹחֲקָן יָפֶה יָפֶה, כְּדֵי שֶׁתְּהֵא דַקָּה מִן הַדַּקָּה. וְאַחַד עָשָׂר סַמָּנִים הָיוּ בָהּ, וְאֵלּוּ הֵן: הַצֳּרִי, וְהַצִּפֹּרֶן, וְהַחֶלְבְּנָה, וְהַלְּבוֹנָה מִשְׁקַל שִׁבְעִים שִׁבְעִים מָנֶה, מֹר, וּקְצִיעָה, שִׁבֹּלֶת נֵרְדְּ, וְכַרְכֹּם מִשְׁקַל שִׁשָּׁה עָשָׂר שִׁשָּׁה עָשָׂר מָנֶה, הַקֹּשְׁטְ שְׁנֵים עָשָׂר, קִלּוּפָה שְׁלֹשָׁה, קִנָּמוֹן תִּשְׁעָה, בֹּרִית כַּרְשִׁינָה תִּשְׁעָה קַבִּין, יֵין קַפְרִיסִין סְאִין תְּלָת וְקַבִּין תְּלָתָא, וְאִם לֹא מָצָא יֵין קַפְרִיסִין, מֵבִיא חֲמַר חִוַּרְיָן עַתִּיק. מֶלַח סְדוֹמִית רֹבַע, מַעֲלֶה עָשָׁן כָּל שֶׁהוּא. רַבִּי נָתָן הַבַּבְלִי אוֹמֵר: אַף כִּפַּת הַיַּרְדֵּן כָּל שֶׁהוּא, וְאִם נָתַן בָּהּ דְּבַשׁ פְּסָלָהּ, וְאִם חִסַּר אַחַת מִכָּל סַמָּנֶיהָ, חַיָּב מִיתָה. כריתות ו.

רַבָּן שִׁמְעוֹן בֶּן גַּמְלִיאֵל אוֹמֵר: הַצֳּרִי אֵינוֹ אֶלָּא שְׂרָף הַנּוֹטֵף מֵעֲצֵי הַקְּטָף. בֹּרִית כַּרְשִׁינָה שֶׁשָּׁפִין בָּהּ אֶת הַצִּפֹּרֶן כְּדֵי שֶׁתְּהֵא נָאָה, יֵין קַפְרִיסִין שֶׁשּׁוֹרִין בּוֹ אֶת הַצִּפֹּרֶן כְּדֵי שֶׁתְּהֵא עַזָּה, וַהֲלֹא מֵי רַגְלַיִם יָפִין לָהּ, אֶלָּא שֶׁאֵין מַכְנִיסִין מֵי רַגְלַיִם בַּמִּקְדָּשׁ מִפְּנֵי הַכָּבוֹד.

תַּנְיָא, רַבִּי נָתָן אוֹמֵר: כְּשֶׁהוּא שׁוֹחֵק אוֹמֵר, הָדֵק הֵיטֵב הֵיטֵב הָדֵק, מִפְּנֵי שֶׁהַקּוֹל יָפֶה לַבְּשָׂמִים. פִּטְּמָהּ לַחֲצָאִין כְּשֵׁרָה, לִשְׁלִישׁ וְלִרְבִיעַ לֹא שָׁמַעְנוּ. אָמַר רַבִּי יְהוּדָה: זֶה הַכְּלָל, אִם כְּמִדָּתָהּ כְּשֵׁרָה לַחֲצָאִין, וְאִם חִסַּר אַחַת מִכָּל סַמָּנֶיהָ חַיָּב מִיתָה.

תַּנְיָא, בַּר קַפָּרָא אוֹמֵר: אַחַת לְשִׁשִּׁים אוֹ לְשִׁבְעִים שָׁנָה הָיְתָה בָאָה שֶׁל שִׁירַיִם לַחֲצָאִין. וְעוֹד תָּנֵי בַּר קַפָּרָא: אִלּוּ הָיָה נוֹתֵן בָּהּ קָרְטוֹב שֶׁל דְּבַשׁ אֵין אָדָם יָכוֹל לַעֲמֹד מִפְּנֵי רֵיחָהּ, וְלָמָּה אֵין מְעָרְבִין בָּהּ דְּבַשׁ, מִפְּנֵי שֶׁהַתּוֹרָה אָמְרָה: כִּי כָל־שְׂאֹר וְכָל־דְּבַשׁ לֹא־תַקְטִירוּ מִמֶּנּוּ אִשֶּׁה לַיהוה: ירושלמי יומא ד, הלכה ה · ויקרא ב

The following three verses are each said three times:

תהלים מו · יהוה צְבָאוֹת עִמָּנוּ, מִשְׂגָּב לָנוּ אֱלֹהֵי יַעֲקֹב סֶלָה:

תהלים פד · יהוה צְבָאוֹת, אַשְׁרֵי אָדָם בֹּטֵחַ בָּךְ:

תהלים כ · יהוה הוֹשִׁיעָה, הַמֶּלֶךְ יַעֲנֵנוּ בְיוֹם־קָרְאֵנוּ:

You are my hiding place; You will protect me from distress and surround me with songs of salvation, Selah. *Ps. 32*

Then the offering of Judah and Jerusalem will be pleasing to the LORD as in the days of old and as in former years. *Mal. 3*

THE ORDER OF THE PRIESTLY FUNCTIONS

Abaye related the order of the daily priestly functions in the name of tradition and in accordance with Abba Shaul: The large pile [of wood] comes before the second pile for the incense; the second pile for the incense precedes the laying in order of the two logs of wood; the laying in order of the two logs of wood comes before the removing of ashes from the inner altar; the removing of ashes from the inner altar precedes the cleaning of the five lamps; the cleaning of the five lamps comes before the blood of the daily offering; the blood of the daily offering precedes the cleaning of the [other] two lamps; the cleaning of the two lamps comes before the incense-offering; the incense-offering precedes the burning of the limbs; the burning of the limbs comes before the meal-offering; the meal-offering precedes the pancakes; the pancakes come before the wine-libations; the wine-libations precede the additional offerings; the additional offerings come before the [frankincense] censers; the censers precede the daily afternoon offering; as it is said, "On it he shall arrange burnt-offerings, and on it he shall burn the fat of the peace-offerings" – "on it" [the daily offering] all the offerings were completed. *Yoma 33a* *Lev. 6*

Please, by the power of Your great right hand, set the captive nation free.
Accept Your people's prayer. Strengthen us, purify us, You who are revered.
Please, mighty One, guard like the pupil of the eye those who seek Your unity.
Bless them, cleanse them, have compassion on them,
grant them Your righteousness always.
Mighty One, Holy One, in Your great goodness guide Your congregation.
Only One, exalted One, turn to Your people, who proclaim Your holiness.
Accept our plea and heed our cry, You who know all secret thoughts.
Blessed be the name of His glorious kingdom for ever and all time.

Master of the Universe, You have commanded us to offer the daily sacrifice at its appointed time with the priests at their service, the Levites on their platform, and the Israelites at their post. Now, because of our sins, the Temple is destroyed and the daily sacrifice discontinued, and we have no priest at his service, no Levite on his platform, no Israelite at his post. But You said: "We will offer in place of bullocks [the prayer of] our lips." Therefore may it be Your will, LORD our God and God of our ancestors, that the prayer of our lips be considered, accepted and favored before You as if we had offered the daily sacrifice at its appointed time and place, according to its laws. *Hos. 14*

תהלים לב אַתָּה סֵתֶר לִי, מִצַּר תִּצְּרֵנִי, רָנֵּי פַלֵּט תְּסוֹבְבֵנִי סֶלָה:
מלאכי ג וְעָרְבָה לַיהוה מִנְחַת יְהוּדָה וִירוּשָׁלָםִ
כִּימֵי עוֹלָם וּכְשָׁנִים קַדְמֹנִיּוֹת:

סדר המערכה

יומא לג. אַבַּיֵּי הֲוָה מְסַדֵּר סֵדֶר הַמַּעֲרָכָה מִשְּׁמָא דִּגְמָרָא, וְאַלִּבָּא דְאַבָּא שָׁאוּל: מַעֲרָכָה גְדוֹלָה קוֹדֶמֶת לְמַעֲרָכָה שְׁנִיָּה שֶׁל קְטֹרֶת, וּמַעֲרָכָה שְׁנִיָּה שֶׁל קְטֹרֶת קוֹדֶמֶת לְסִדּוּר שְׁנֵי גִזְרֵי עֵצִים, וְסִדּוּר שְׁנֵי גִזְרֵי עֵצִים קוֹדֵם לְדִשּׁוּן מִזְבֵּחַ הַפְּנִימִי, וְדִשּׁוּן מִזְבֵּחַ הַפְּנִימִי קוֹדֵם לַהֲטָבַת חָמֵשׁ נֵרוֹת, וַהֲטָבַת חָמֵשׁ נֵרוֹת קוֹדֶמֶת לְדַם הַתָּמִיד, וְדַם הַתָּמִיד קוֹדֵם לַהֲטָבַת שְׁתֵּי נֵרוֹת, וַהֲטָבַת שְׁתֵּי נֵרוֹת קוֹדֶמֶת לִקְטֹרֶת, וּקְטֹרֶת קוֹדֶמֶת לְאֵבָרִים, וְאֵבָרִים לְמִנְחָה, וּמִנְחָה לַחֲבִתִּין, וַחֲבִתִּין לִנְסָכִין, וּנְסָכִין לְמוּסָפִין, וּמוּסָפִין לְבָזִיכִין, וּבָזִיכִין קוֹדְמִין לְתָמִיד שֶׁל בֵּין הָעַרְבָּיִם. שֶׁנֶּאֱמַר:
ויקרא ו וְעָרַךְ עָלֶיהָ הָעֹלָה, וְהִקְטִיר עָלֶיהָ חֶלְבֵי הַשְּׁלָמִים: עָלֶיהָ הַשְׁלֵם כָּל הַקָּרְבָּנוֹת כֻּלָּם.

אָנָּא, בְּכֹחַ גְּדֻלַּת יְמִינְךָ, תַּתִּיר צְרוּרָה.
קַבֵּל רִנַּת עַמְּךָ, שַׂגְּבֵנוּ, טַהֲרֵנוּ, נוֹרָא.
נָא גִבּוֹר, דּוֹרְשֵׁי יִחוּדְךָ כְּבָבַת שָׁמְרֵם.
בָּרְכֵם, טַהֲרֵם, רַחֲמֵם, צִדְקָתְךָ תָּמִיד גָּמְלֵם.
חֲסִין קָדוֹשׁ, בְּרֹב טוּבְךָ נַהֵל עֲדָתֶךָ.
יָחִיד גֵּאֶה, לְעַמְּךָ פְּנֵה, זוֹכְרֵי קְדֻשָּׁתֶךָ.
שַׁוְעָתֵנוּ קַבֵּל וּשְׁמַע צַעֲקָתֵנוּ, יוֹדֵעַ תַּעֲלוּמוֹת.
בָּרוּךְ שֵׁם כְּבוֹד מַלְכוּתוֹ לְעוֹלָם וָעֶד.

רִבּוֹן הָעוֹלָמִים, אַתָּה צִוִּיתָנוּ לְהַקְרִיב קָרְבַּן הַתָּמִיד בְּמוֹעֲדוֹ וְלִהְיוֹת כֹּהֲנִים בַּעֲבוֹדָתָם וּלְוִיִּם בְּדוּכָנָם וְיִשְׂרָאֵל בְּמַעֲמָדָם, וְעַתָּה בַּעֲוֹנוֹתֵינוּ חָרַב בֵּית הַמִּקְדָּשׁ וּבָטַל הַתָּמִיד וְאֵין לָנוּ לֹא כֹהֵן בַּעֲבוֹדָתוֹ וְלֹא לֵוִי בְּדוּכָנוֹ וְלֹא
הושע יד יִשְׂרָאֵל בְּמַעֲמָדוֹ, וְאַתָּה אָמַרְתָּ: וּנְשַׁלְּמָה פָרִים שְׂפָתֵינוּ: לָכֵן יְהִי רָצוֹן מִלְּפָנֶיךָ יהוה אֱלֹהֵינוּ וֵאלֹהֵי אֲבוֹתֵינוּ, שֶׁיְּהֵא שִׂיחַ שִׂפְתוֹתֵינוּ חָשׁוּב וּמְקֻבָּל וּמְרֻצֶּה לְפָנֶיךָ, כְּאִלּוּ הִקְרַבְנוּ קָרְבַּן הַתָּמִיד בְּמוֹעֲדוֹ וּבִמְקוֹמוֹ וּכְהִלְכָתוֹ.

On Rosh Hodesh:

וּבְרָאשֵׁי חָדְשֵׁיכֶם On your new moons, present as a burnt-offering to the LORD, two young bulls, one ram, and seven yearling lambs without blemish. There shall be a meal-offering of three-tenths of an ephah of fine flour mixed with oil for each bull, two-tenths of an ephah of fine flour mixed with oil for the ram, and one-tenth of an ephah of fine flour mixed with oil for each lamb. This is the burnt-offering – a fire-offering of pleasing aroma to the LORD. Their libations shall be: half a hin of wine for each bull, a third of a hin for the ram, and a quarter of a hin for each lamb. This is the monthly burnt-offering to be made at each new moon throughout the year. One male goat should be offered as a sin-offering to God, in addition to the regular daily burnt-offering and its libation. *Num. 28*

LAWS OF OFFERINGS, MISHNA ZEVAHIM

אֵיזֶהוּ מְקוֹמָן What is the location for sacrifices? The holiest offerings were slaughtered on the north side. The bull and he-goat of Yom Kippur were slaughtered on the north side. Their blood was received in a sacred vessel on the north side, and had to be sprinkled between the poles [of the Ark], toward the veil [screening the Holy of Holies], and on the golden altar. [The omission of] one of these sprinklings invalidated [the atonement ceremony]. The leftover blood was to be poured onto the western base of the outer altar. If this was not done, however, the omission did not invalidate [the ceremony]. *Zevahim Ch. 5*

The bulls and he-goats that were completely burnt were slaughtered on the north side, their blood was received in a sacred vessel on the north side, and had to be sprinkled toward the veil and on the golden altar. [The omission of] one of these sprinklings invalidated [the ceremony]. The leftover blood was to be poured onto the western base of the outer altar. If this was not done, however, the omission did not invalidate [the ceremony]. All these offerings were burnt where the altar ashes were deposited.

The communal and individual sin-offerings – these are the communal sin-offerings: the he-goats offered on Rosh Hodesh and Festivals were slaughtered on the north side, their blood was received in a sacred vessel on the north side, and required four sprinklings, one on each of the four corners of the altar. How was this done? The priest ascended the ramp and turned [right] onto the surrounding ledge. He came to the southeast corner, then went to the northeast, then to the northwest, then to the southwest. The leftover blood he poured onto the southern base. [The meat of these offerings], prepared in any manner, was

בראש חודש:

וּבְרָאשֵׁי חָדְשֵׁיכֶם תַּקְרִיבוּ עֹלָה לַיהוה, פָּרִים בְּנֵי־בָקָר שְׁנַיִם, במדבר כח
וְאַיִל אֶחָד, כְּבָשִׂים בְּנֵי־שָׁנָה שִׁבְעָה, תְּמִימִם: וּשְׁלֹשָׁה עֶשְׂרֹנִים
סֹלֶת מִנְחָה בְּלוּלָה בַשֶּׁמֶן לַפָּר הָאֶחָד, וּשְׁנֵי עֶשְׂרֹנִים סֹלֶת
מִנְחָה בְּלוּלָה בַשֶּׁמֶן לָאַיִל הָאֶחָד: וְעִשָּׂרֹן עִשָּׂרוֹן סֹלֶת
מִנְחָה בְּלוּלָה בַשֶּׁמֶן לַכֶּבֶשׂ הָאֶחָד, עֹלָה רֵיחַ נִיחֹחַ, אִשֶּׁה
לַיהוה: וְנִסְכֵּיהֶם, חֲצִי הַהִין יִהְיֶה לַפָּר, וּשְׁלִישִׁת הַהִין לָאַיִל,
וּרְבִיעִת הַהִין לַכֶּבֶשׂ, יָיִן, זֹאת עֹלַת חֹדֶשׁ בְּחָדְשׁוֹ לְחָדְשֵׁי
הַשָּׁנָה: וּשְׂעִיר עִזִּים אֶחָד לְחַטָּאת לַיהוה, עַל־עֹלַת הַתָּמִיד
יֵעָשֶׂה, וְנִסְכּוֹ:

דיני זבחים

אֵיזֶהוּ מְקוֹמָן שֶׁל זְבָחִים. קָדְשֵׁי קָדָשִׁים שְׁחִיטָתָן בַּצָּפוֹן. פַּר וְשָׂעִיר זבחים פרק ה
שֶׁל יוֹם הַכִּפּוּרִים, שְׁחִיטָתָן בַּצָּפוֹן, וְקִבּוּל דָּמָן בִּכְלֵי שָׁרֵת בַּצָּפוֹן,
וְדָמָן טָעוּן הַזָּיָה עַל בֵּין הַבַּדִּים, וְעַל הַפָּרֹכֶת, וְעַל מִזְבַּח הַזָּהָב. מַתָּנָה
אַחַת מֵהֶן מְעַכָּבֶת. שְׁיָרֵי הַדָּם הָיָה שׁוֹפֵךְ עַל יְסוֹד מַעֲרָבִי שֶׁל מִזְבַּח
הַחִיצוֹן, אִם לֹא נָתַן לֹא עִכֵּב.

פָּרִים הַנִּשְׂרָפִים וּשְׂעִירִים הַנִּשְׂרָפִים, שְׁחִיטָתָן בַּצָּפוֹן, וְקִבּוּל דָּמָן בִּכְלֵי שָׁרֵת בַּצָּפוֹן, וְדָמָן טָעוּן הַזָּיָה עַל הַפָּרֹכֶת וְעַל מִזְבַּח הַזָּהָב. מַתָּנָה אַחַת מֵהֶן מְעַכָּבֶת. שְׁיָרֵי הַדָּם הָיָה שׁוֹפֵךְ עַל יְסוֹד מַעֲרָבִי שֶׁל מִזְבַּח הַחִיצוֹן, אִם לֹא נָתַן לֹא עִכֵּב. אֵלּוּ וָאֵלּוּ נִשְׂרָפִין בְּבֵית הַדָּשֶׁן.

חַטֹּאת הַצִּבּוּר וְהַיָּחִיד. אֵלּוּ הֵן חַטֹּאת הַצִּבּוּר: שְׂעִירֵי רָאשֵׁי חֳדָשִׁים וְשֶׁל מוֹעֲדוֹת. שְׁחִיטָתָן בַּצָּפוֹן, וְקִבּוּל דָּמָן בִּכְלֵי שָׁרֵת בַּצָּפוֹן, וְדָמָן טָעוּן אַרְבַּע מַתָּנוֹת עַל אַרְבַּע קְרָנוֹת. כֵּיצַד, עָלָה בַכֶּבֶשׁ, וּפָנָה לַסּוֹבֵב, וּבָא לוֹ לְקֶרֶן דְּרוֹמִית מִזְרָחִית, מִזְרָחִית צְפוֹנִית, צְפוֹנִית מַעֲרָבִית, מַעֲרָבִית דְּרוֹמִית. שְׁיָרֵי הַדָּם הָיָה שׁוֹפֵךְ עַל יְסוֹד דְּרוֹמִי.

eaten within the [courtyard] curtains, by males of the priest-hood, on that day and the following night, until midnight.

The burnt-offering was among the holiest of sacrifices. It was slaughtered on the north side, its blood was received in a sacred vessel on the north side, and required two sprinklings [at opposite corners of the altar], making four in all. The offering had to be flayed, dismembered and wholly consumed by fire.

The communal peace-offerings and the guilt-offerings – these are the guilt-offerings: the guilt-offering for robbery; the guilt-offering for profane use of a sacred object; the guilt-offering [for violating] a betrothed maidservant; the guilt-offering of a Nazirite [who had become defiled by a corpse]; the guilt-offering of a leper [at his cleansing]; and the guilt-offering in case of doubt. All these were slaughtered on the north side, their blood was received in a sacred vessel on the north side, and required two sprinklings [at opposite corners of the altar], making four in all. [The meat of these offerings], prepared in any manner, was eaten within the [courtyard] curtains, by males of the priesthood, on that day and the following night, until midnight.

The thanksgiving-offering and the ram of a Nazirite were offerings of lesser holiness. They could be slaughtered anywhere in the Temple court, and their blood required two sprinklings [at opposite corners of the altar], making four in all. The meat of these offerings, prepared in any manner, was eaten anywhere within the city [Jerusalem], by anyone during that day and the following night until midnight. This also applied to the portion of these sacrifices [given to the priests], except that the priests' portion was only to be eaten by the priests, their wives, children and servants.

Peace-offerings were [also] of lesser holiness. They could be slaughtered anywhere in the Temple court, and their blood required two sprinklings [at opposite corners of the altar], making four in all. The meat of these offerings, prepared in any manner, was eaten anywhere within the city [Jerusalem], by anyone, for two days and one night. This also applied to the portion of these sacrifices [given to the priests], except that the priests' portion was only to be eaten by the priests, their wives, children and servants.

The firstborn and tithe of cattle and the Pesaḥ lamb were sacrifices of lesser holiness. They could be slaughtered anywhere in the Temple court, and their blood required only one sprinkling, which had to be done at the base of the altar. They differed in their consumption: the firstborn was eaten only by priests, while the tithe could be eaten by anyone. Both could be eaten anywhere within the city, prepared in any manner, during two days and one night. The Pesaḥ lamb had to be eaten that night until midnight. It could only be eaten by those who had been numbered for it, and eaten only roasted.

וְנֶאֱכָלִין לִפְנִים מִן הַקְּלָעִים, לְזִכְרֵי כְהֻנָּה, בְּכָל מַאֲכָל, לְיוֹם וָלַיְלָה עַד חֲצוֹת.

הָעוֹלָה קֹדֶשׁ קָדָשִׁים. שְׁחִיטָתָהּ בַּצָּפוֹן, וְקִבּוּל דָּמָהּ בִּכְלִי שָׁרֵת בַּצָּפוֹן, וְדָמָהּ טָעוּן שְׁתֵּי מַתָּנוֹת שֶׁהֵן אַרְבַּע, וּטְעוּנָה הֶפְשֵׁט וְנִתּוּחַ, וְכָלִיל לָאִשִּׁים.

זִבְחֵי שַׁלְמֵי צִבּוּר וַאֲשָׁמוֹת. אֵלּוּ הֵן אֲשָׁמוֹת: אֲשַׁם גְּזֵלוֹת, אֲשַׁם מְעִילוֹת, אֲשַׁם שִׁפְחָה חֲרוּפָה, אֲשַׁם נָזִיר, אֲשַׁם מְצֹרָע, אָשָׁם תָּלוּי. שְׁחִיטָתָן בַּצָּפוֹן, וְקִבּוּל דָּמָן בִּכְלִי שָׁרֵת בַּצָּפוֹן, וְדָמָן טָעוּן שְׁתֵּי מַתָּנוֹת שֶׁהֵן אַרְבַּע. וְנֶאֱכָלִין לִפְנִים מִן הַקְּלָעִים, לְזִכְרֵי כְהֻנָּה, בְּכָל מַאֲכָל, לְיוֹם וָלַיְלָה עַד חֲצוֹת.

הַתּוֹדָה וְאֵיל נָזִיר קָדָשִׁים קַלִּים. שְׁחִיטָתָן בְּכָל מָקוֹם בָּעֲזָרָה, וְדָמָן טָעוּן שְׁתֵּי מַתָּנוֹת שֶׁהֵן אַרְבַּע, וְנֶאֱכָלִין בְּכָל הָעִיר, לְכָל אָדָם, בְּכָל מַאֲכָל, לְיוֹם וָלַיְלָה עַד חֲצוֹת. הַמּוּרָם מֵהֶם כַּיּוֹצֵא בָהֶם, אֶלָּא שֶׁהַמּוּרָם נֶאֱכָל לַכֹּהֲנִים, לִנְשֵׁיהֶם, וְלִבְנֵיהֶם וּלְעַבְדֵיהֶם.

שְׁלָמִים קָדָשִׁים קַלִּים. שְׁחִיטָתָן בְּכָל מָקוֹם בָּעֲזָרָה, וְדָמָן טָעוּן שְׁתֵּי מַתָּנוֹת שֶׁהֵן אַרְבַּע, וְנֶאֱכָלִין בְּכָל הָעִיר, לְכָל אָדָם, בְּכָל מַאֲכָל, לִשְׁנֵי יָמִים וְלַיְלָה אֶחָד. הַמּוּרָם מֵהֶם כַּיּוֹצֵא בָהֶם, אֶלָּא שֶׁהַמּוּרָם נֶאֱכָל לַכֹּהֲנִים, לִנְשֵׁיהֶם, וְלִבְנֵיהֶם וּלְעַבְדֵיהֶם.

הַבְּכוֹר וְהַמַּעֲשֵׂר וְהַפֶּסַח קָדָשִׁים קַלִּים. שְׁחִיטָתָן בְּכָל מָקוֹם בָּעֲזָרָה, וְדָמָן טָעוּן מַתָּנָה אַחַת, וּבִלְבַד שֶׁיִּתֵּן כְּנֶגֶד הַיְסוֹד. שִׁנָּה בַאֲכִילָתָן, הַבְּכוֹר נֶאֱכָל לַכֹּהֲנִים וְהַמַּעֲשֵׂר לְכָל אָדָם, וְנֶאֱכָלִין בְּכָל הָעִיר, בְּכָל מַאֲכָל, לִשְׁנֵי יָמִים וְלַיְלָה אֶחָד. הַפֶּסַח אֵינוֹ נֶאֱכָל אֶלָּא בַלַּיְלָה, וְאֵינוֹ נֶאֱכָל אֶלָּא עַד חֲצוֹת, וְאֵינוֹ נֶאֱכָל אֶלָּא לִמְנוּיָיו, וְאֵינוֹ נֶאֱכָל אֶלָּא צָלִי.

THE INTERPRETIVE PRINCIPLES OF RABBI YISHMAEL

רַבִּי יִשְׁמָעֵאל Rabbi Yishmael says:

The Torah is expounded by thirteen principles:

1. An inference from a lenient law to a strict one, and vice versa.
2. An inference drawn from identical words in two passages.
3. A general principle derived from one text or two related texts.
4. A general law followed by specific examples [where the law applies exclusively to those examples].
5. A specific example followed by a general law [where the law applies to everything implied in the general statement].
6. A general law followed by specific examples and concluding with a general law: here you may infer only cases similar to the examples.
7. When a general statement requires clarification by a specific example, or a specific example requires clarification by a general statement [then rules 4 and 5 do not apply].
8. When a particular case, already included in the general statement, is expressly mentioned to teach something new, that special provision applies to all other cases included in the general statement.
9. When a particular case, though included in the general statement, is expressly mentioned with a provision similar to the general law, such a case is singled out to lessen the severity of the law, not to increase it.
10. When a particular case, though included in the general statement, is explicitly mentioned with a provision differing from the general law, it is singled out to lessen in some respects, and in others to increase, the severity of the law.
11. When a particular case, though included in the general statement, is explicitly mentioned with a new provision, the terms of the general statement no longer apply to it, unless Scripture indicates explicitly that they do apply.
12. A matter elucidated from its context, or from the following passage.
13. Also, when two passages [seem to] contradict each other, [they are to be elucidated by] a third passage that reconciles them.

May it be Your will, Lord our God and God of our ancestors, that the Temple be speedily rebuilt in our days, and grant us our share in Your Torah. And may we serve You there in reverence, as in the days of old and as in former years.

Torah is interpreted" (Maimonides, Laws of Torah Study 1:11). It was chosen because it appears at the beginning of the *Sifra*, the halakhic commentary to Leviticus, which is the source of most of the laws of offerings. It also reminds us of the indissoluble connection between the Written Law (the Mosaic books) and the Oral Law (Mishna, Midrash and Talmud). Rabbi Yishmael's principles show how the latter can be derived from the former.

ברייתא דרבי ישמעאל

רַבִּי יִשְׁמָעֵאל אוֹמֵר: בִּשְׁלֹשׁ עֶשְׂרֵה מִדּוֹת הַתּוֹרָה נִדְרֶשֶׁת

א מִקַּל וָחֹמֶר

ב וּמִגְּזֵרָה שָׁוָה

ג מִבִּנְיַן אָב מִכָּתוּב אֶחָד, וּמִבִּנְיַן אָב מִשְּׁנֵי כְתוּבִים

ד מִכְּלָל וּפְרָט

ה מִפְּרָט וּכְלָל

ו כְּלָל וּפְרָט וּכְלָל, אִי אַתָּה דָן אֶלָּא כְּעֵין הַפְּרָט

ז מִכְּלָל שֶׁהוּא צָרִיךְ לִפְרָט, וּמִפְּרָט שֶׁהוּא צָרִיךְ לִכְלָל

ח כָּל דָּבָר שֶׁהָיָה בִּכְלָל, וְיָצָא מִן הַכְּלָל לְלַמֵּד
לֹא לְלַמֵּד עַל עַצְמוֹ יָצָא, אֶלָּא לְלַמֵּד עַל הַכְּלָל כֻּלּוֹ יָצָא

ט כָּל דָּבָר שֶׁהָיָה בִּכְלָל, וְיָצָא לִטְעֹן טֹעַן אֶחָד שֶׁהוּא כְעִנְיָנוֹ
יָצָא לְהָקֵל וְלֹא לְהַחֲמִיר

י כָּל דָּבָר שֶׁהָיָה בִּכְלָל, וְיָצָא לִטְעֹן טֹעַן אַחֵר שֶׁלֹּא כְעִנְיָנוֹ
יָצָא לְהָקֵל וּלְהַחֲמִיר

יא כָּל דָּבָר שֶׁהָיָה בִּכְלָל, וְיָצָא לִדּוֹן בַּדָּבָר הֶחָדָשׁ
אִי אַתָּה יָכוֹל לְהַחֲזִירוֹ לִכְלָלוֹ
עַד שֶׁיַּחֲזִירֶנּוּ הַכָּתוּב לִכְלָלוֹ בְּפֵרוּשׁ

יב דָּבָר הַלָּמֵד מֵעִנְיָנוֹ, וְדָבָר הַלָּמֵד מִסּוֹפוֹ

יג וְכֵן שְׁנֵי כְתוּבִים הַמַּכְחִישִׁים זֶה אֶת זֶה
עַד שֶׁיָּבוֹא הַכָּתוּב הַשְּׁלִישִׁי וְיַכְרִיעַ בֵּינֵיהֶם.

יְהִי רָצוֹן מִלְּפָנֶיךָ, יהוה אֱלֹהֵינוּ וֵאלֹהֵי אֲבוֹתֵינוּ, שֶׁיִּבָּנֶה בֵּית הַמִּקְדָּשׁ בִּמְהֵרָה בְיָמֵינוּ, וְתֵן חֶלְקֵנוּ בְּתוֹרָתֶךָ, וְשָׁם נַעֲבָדְךָ בְּיִרְאָה כִּימֵי עוֹלָם וּכְשָׁנִים קַדְמוֹנִיּוֹת.

THE INTERPRETIVE PRINCIPLES OF RABBI YISHMAEL

This passage is included as an item of Talmud, defined in its broadest sense as "deducing conclusions from premises, developing implications of statements, comparing dicta, and studying the hermeneutical principles by which the

THE RABBIS' KADDISH

The following prayer, said by mourners, requires the presence of a minyan.
A transliteration can be found on page 698.

Mourner: יִתְגַּדַּל Magnified and sanctified
may His great name be,
in the world He created by His will.
May He establish His kingdom in your lifetime
and in your days,
and in the lifetime of all the house of Israel,
swiftly and soon –
and say: Amen.

All: May His great name be blessed for ever and all time.

Mourner: Blessed and praised,
glorified and exalted,
raised and honored,
uplifted and lauded
be the name of the Holy One,
blessed be He,
beyond any blessing,
song, praise and consolation uttered in the world –
and say: Amen.

---

mark the end of the Amida and its associated meditations; (3) the Mourner's Kaddish; (4) The Rabbis' Kaddish, said after a passage from the Oral Law; (5) the Kaddish of Renewal, said only at the conclusion of a tractate of the Talmud, or by a child at the funeral of a parent.

The Rabbis' Kaddish is a prayer not only for the establishment of God's kingdom but also for the teachers of Torah and their disciples. It is characteristic of Judaism's value system that this is the first Kaddish we say each morning. Judaism is a faith whose passion is education, whose heroes are teachers, and whose citadels are schools and houses of study. To learn, to teach, to internalize God's will, to join our minds with the great sages and scholars of the past – this is a supreme expression of Judaism, and the one from which all else flows.

קדיש דרבנן

The following prayer, said by mourners, requires the presence of a מנין.
A transliteration can be found on page 698.

אבל: יִתְגַּדַּל וְיִתְקַדַּשׁ שְׁמֵהּ רַבָּא (קהל: אָמֵן)
בְּעָלְמָא דִּי בְרָא כִרְעוּתֵהּ
וְיַמְלִיךְ מַלְכוּתֵהּ
בְּחַיֵּיכוֹן וּבְיוֹמֵיכוֹן וּבְחַיֵּי דְכָל בֵּית יִשְׂרָאֵל
בַּעֲגָלָא וּבִזְמַן קָרִיב
וְאִמְרוּ אָמֵן. (קהל: אָמֵן)

קהל ואבל: יְהֵא שְׁמֵהּ רַבָּא מְבָרַךְ לְעָלַם וּלְעָלְמֵי עָלְמַיָּא.

אבל: יִתְבָּרַךְ וְיִשְׁתַּבַּח וְיִתְפָּאַר וְיִתְרוֹמַם וְיִתְנַשֵּׂא
וְיִתְהַדָּר וְיִתְעַלֶּה וְיִתְהַלָּל
שְׁמֵהּ דְּקֻדְשָׁא בְּרִיךְ הוּא (קהל: בְּרִיךְ הוּא)
לְעֵלָּא מִן כָּל בִּרְכָתָא
/בעשרת ימי תשובה: לְעֵלָּא לְעֵלָּא מִכָּל בִּרְכָתָא/
וְשִׁירָתָא, תֻּשְׁבְּחָתָא וְנֶחֱמָתָא, דַּאֲמִירָן בְּעָלְמָא
וְאִמְרוּ אָמֵן. (קהל: אָמֵן)

THE RABBIS' KADDISH

The Kaddish, one of the most important of all prayers, had its origins not in the synagogue but in the house of study. It grew out of a custom, still widely practiced, of ending every discourse or sermon with the hope that we may speedily see the coming of the messianic age, when the sovereignty of God will be recognized by all the dwellers on earth. It is written mainly in Aramaic, the language most widely spoken by Jews in the first centuries of the Common Era.

It has come to have five forms: (1) Half Kaddish, recited to mark the beginning or end of a section of the prayers; (2) Full Kaddish (*Titkabal*), to

To Israel, to the teachers,
their disciples and their disciples' disciples,
and to all who engage in the study of Torah,
in this (*in Israel add:* holy) place or elsewhere,
may there come to them and you great peace,
grace, kindness and compassion,
long life, ample sustenance and deliverance,
from their Father in Heaven –
and say: Amen.

May there be great peace from heaven,
and (good) life for us and all Israel –
and say: Amen.

Bow, take three steps back, as if taking leave of the Divine Presence, then bow, first left, then right, then center, while saying:
May He who makes peace in His high places,
in His compassion make peace for us and all Israel –
and say: Amen.

On Yom HaAtzma'ut and Yom Yerushalayim, continue Shaḥarit on page 428.

A PSALM BEFORE VERSES OF PRAISE

מִזְמוֹר שִׁיר A psalm of David. A song for the dedication of the House. *Ps. 30*
I will exalt You, Lord, for You have lifted me up, and not let my enemies rejoice over me. Lord, my God, I cried to You for help and You healed me. Lord, You lifted my soul from the grave; You spared me from going down to the pit. Sing to the Lord, you His devoted ones, and give thanks to His holy name. For His anger is for a moment, but His favor for a lifetime. At night there may be weeping, but in the morning there is joy. When I felt secure, I said, "I shall never be shaken." Lord, when You favored me, You made me stand firm as a mountain, but when You hid Your face, I was terrified. To You, Lord, I called; I pleaded with my Lord: "What

עַל יִשְׂרָאֵל וְעַל רַבָּנָן
וְעַל תַּלְמִידֵיהוֹן וְעַל כָּל תַּלְמִידֵי תַלְמִידֵיהוֹן
וְעַל כָּל מָאן דְּעָסְקִין בְּאוֹרַיְתָא
דִּי בְּאַתְרָא (בארץ ישראל: קַדִּישָׁא) הָדֵין, וְדִי בְּכָל אֲתַר וַאֲתַר
יְהֵא לְהוֹן וּלְכוֹן שְׁלָמָא רַבָּא
חִנָּא וְחִסְדָּא, וְרַחֲמֵי, וְחַיֵּי אֲרִיכֵי, וּמְזוֹנֵי רְוִיחֵי
וּפֻרְקָנָא מִן קֳדָם אֲבוּהוֹן דִּי בִשְׁמַיָּא
וְאִמְרוּ אָמֵן. (קהל: אָמֵן)

יְהֵא שְׁלָמָא רַבָּא מִן שְׁמַיָּא
וְחַיִּים (טוֹבִים) עָלֵינוּ וְעַל כָּל יִשְׂרָאֵל, וְאִמְרוּ אָמֵן. (קהל: אָמֵן)

Bow, take three steps back, as if taking leave of the Divine Presence, then bow, first left, then right, then center, while saying:

עֹשֶׂה שָׁלוֹם/ בעשרת ימי תשובה: הַשָּׁלוֹם/ בִּמְרוֹמָיו
הוּא יַעֲשֶׂה בְרַחֲמָיו שָׁלוֹם, עָלֵינוּ וְעַל כָּל יִשְׂרָאֵל
וְאִמְרוּ אָמֵן. (קהל: אָמֵן)

On יום העצמאות *and* יום ירושלים, *continue* שחרית *on page 429.*

מזמור לפני פסוקי דזמרה

מִזְמוֹר שִׁיר־חֲנֻכַּת הַבַּיִת לְדָוִד: אֲרוֹמִמְךָ יהוה כִּי דִלִּיתָנִי, וְלֹא־ תהלים ל
שִׂמַּחְתָּ אֹיְבַי לִי: יהוה אֱלֹהָי, שִׁוַּעְתִּי אֵלֶיךָ וַתִּרְפָּאֵנִי: יהוה,
הֶעֱלִיתָ מִן־שְׁאוֹל נַפְשִׁי, חִיִּיתַנִי מִיָּרְדִי־בוֹר: זַמְּרוּ לַיהוה חֲסִידָיו,
וְהוֹדוּ לְזֵכֶר קָדְשׁוֹ: כִּי רֶגַע בְּאַפּוֹ, חַיִּים בִּרְצוֹנוֹ, בָּעֶרֶב יָלִין בֶּכִי
וְלַבֹּקֶר רִנָּה: וַאֲנִי אָמַרְתִּי בְשַׁלְוִי, בַּל־אֶמּוֹט לְעוֹלָם: יהוה, בִּרְצוֹנְךָ
הֶעֱמַדְתָּה לְהַרְרִי עֹז, הִסְתַּרְתָּ פָנֶיךָ הָיִיתִי נִבְהָל: אֵלֶיךָ יהוה
אֶקְרָא, וְאֶל־אֲדֹנָי אֶתְחַנָּן: מַה־בֶּצַע בְּדָמִי, בְּרִדְתִּי אֶל שָׁחַת,

gain would there be if I died and went down to the grave? Can dust thank You? Can it declare Your truth? Hear, Lord, and be gracious to me; Lord, be my help." ▸ You have turned my sorrow into dancing. You have removed my sackcloth and clothed me with joy, so that my soul may sing to You and not be silent. Lord my God, for ever will I thank You.

MOURNER'S KADDISH

The following prayer, said by mourners, requires the presence of a minyan. A transliteration can be found on page 699.

Mourner: יִתְגַּדַּל Magnified and sanctified
may His great name be,
in the world He created by His will.
May He establish His kingdom
in your lifetime and in your days,
and in the lifetime of all the house of Israel,
swiftly and soon – and say: Amen.

All: May His great name be blessed for ever and all time.

Mourner: Blessed and praised, glorified and exalted,
raised and honored, uplifted and lauded
be the name of the Holy One,
blessed be He,
beyond any blessing,
song, praise and consolation
uttered in the world – and say: Amen.

May there be great peace from heaven,
and life for us and all Israel – and say: Amen.

Bow, take three steps back, as if taking leave of the Divine Presence, then bow, first left, then right, then center, while saying:

May He who makes peace in His high places,
make peace for us and all Israel –
and say: Amen.

הַיּוֹדְךָ עָפָר, הֲיַגִּיד אֲמִתֶּךָ: שְׁמַע־יהוה וְחָנֵּנִי, יהוה הֱיֵה־עֹזֵר לִי:
· הָפַכְתָּ מִסְפְּדִי לְמָחוֹל לִי, פִּתַּחְתָּ שַׂקִּי, וַתְּאַזְּרֵנִי שִׂמְחָה: לְמַעַן
יְזַמֶּרְךָ כָבוֹד וְלֹא יִדֹּם, יהוה אֱלֹהַי, לְעוֹלָם אוֹדֶךָּ:

קדיש יתום

The following prayer, said by mourners, requires the presence of a מנין.
A transliteration can be found on page 699.

אבל: יִתְגַּדַּל וְיִתְקַדַּשׁ שְׁמֵהּ רַבָּא (קהל: אָמֵן)
בְּעָלְמָא דִּי בְרָא כִרְעוּתֵהּ
וְיַמְלִיךְ מַלְכוּתֵהּ
בְּחַיֵּיכוֹן וּבְיוֹמֵיכוֹן וּבְחַיֵּי דְכָל בֵּית יִשְׂרָאֵל
בַּעֲגָלָא וּבִזְמַן קָרִיב, וְאִמְרוּ אָמֵן. (קהל: אָמֵן)

קהל ואבל: יְהֵא שְׁמֵהּ רַבָּא מְבָרַךְ לְעָלַם וּלְעָלְמֵי עָלְמַיָּא.

אבל: יִתְבָּרַךְ וְיִשְׁתַּבַּח וְיִתְפָּאַר
וְיִתְרוֹמַם וְיִתְנַשֵּׂא וְיִתְהַדָּר וְיִתְעַלֶּה וְיִתְהַלָּל
שְׁמֵהּ דְּקֻדְשָׁא בְּרִיךְ הוּא (קהל: בְּרִיךְ הוּא)
לְעֵלָּא מִן כָּל בִּרְכָתָא / בעשרת ימי תשובה: לְעֵלָּא לְעֵלָּא מִכָּל בִּרְכָתָא/
וְשִׁירָתָא, תֻּשְׁבְּחָתָא וְנֶחֱמָתָא
דַּאֲמִירָן בְּעָלְמָא, וְאִמְרוּ אָמֵן. (קהל: אָמֵן)

יְהֵא שְׁלָמָא רַבָּא מִן שְׁמַיָּא
וְחַיִּים, עָלֵינוּ וְעַל כָּל יִשְׂרָאֵל, וְאִמְרוּ אָמֵן. (קהל: אָמֵן)

Bow, take three steps back, as if taking leave of the Divine Presence, then bow, first left, then right, then center, while saying:

עֹשֶׂה שָׁלוֹם/ בעשרת ימי תשובה: הַשָּׁלוֹם/ בִּמְרוֹמָיו
הוּא יַעֲשֶׂה שָׁלוֹם עָלֵינוּ וְעַל כָּל יִשְׂרָאֵל
וְאִמְרוּ אָמֵן. (קהל: אָמֵן)

PESUKEI DEZIMRA

The introductory blessing to the Pesukei DeZimra (Verses of Praise) is said standing, while holding the two front tzitziot of the tallit. They are kissed and released at the end of the blessing at "songs of praise" (on next page). From the beginning of this prayer to the end of the Amida, conversation is forbidden. See table on pages 695–697 for which congregational responses are permitted.

Some say:
I hereby prepare my mouth to thank, praise and laud my Creator, for the sake of the unification of the Holy One, blessed be He, and His Divine Presence, through that which is hidden and concealed, in the name of all Israel.

BLESSED IS HE WHO SPOKE

and the world came into being, blessed is He.
Blessed is He who creates the universe.
Blessed is He who speaks and acts.
Blessed is He who decrees and fulfills.
Blessed is He who shows compassion to the earth.
Blessed is He who shows compassion to all creatures.
Blessed is He who gives a good reward
to those who fear Him.
Blessed is He who lives for ever and exists to eternity.
Blessed is He who redeems and saves.
Blessed is His name.

---

structed in three movements, whose themes are: (1) *Creation:* God as He is in nature; (2) *Revelation:* God as He is in Torah and prayer; and (3) *Redemption:* God as He is in history and our lives. The theme of the Verses of Praise is Creation – God as Architect and Maker of a universe of splendor and diversity, whose orderliness testifies to the single creative will that underlies all that exists. The psalms tell this story not in scientific prose but majestic poetry, not *proving* but *proclaiming* the One at the heart of all.

The core elements of *Pesukei DeZimra* are: (1) Psalm 145 (*Ashrei*), a prayer to which the sages attached particular significance, specifying that it should be said three times daily; and (2) Psalms 146–150, which form the culmination and crescendo of the book of Psalms as a whole. These six psalms

פסוקי דזמרה

The introductory blessing to the פסוקי דזמרה *is said standing, while holding the two front* ציציות *of the* טלית*. They are kissed and released at the end of the blessing at* בַּתִּשְׁבָּחוֹת *(on next page). From the beginning of this prayer to the end of the* עמידה*, conversation is forbidden. See table on pages 695–697 for which congregational responses are permitted.*

Some say:

הֲרֵינִי מְזַמֵּן אֶת פִּי לְהוֹדוֹת וּלְהַלֵּל וּלְשַׁבֵּחַ אֶת בּוֹרְאִי, לְשֵׁם יִחוּד קֻדְשָׁא בְּרִיךְ הוּא וּשְׁכִינְתֵּהּ עַל יְדֵי הַהוּא טָמִיר וְנֶעְלָם בְּשֵׁם כָּל יִשְׂרָאֵל.

בָּרוּךְ שֶׁאָמַר
וְהָיָה הָעוֹלָם, בָּרוּךְ הוּא.
בָּרוּךְ עוֹשֶׂה בְרֵאשִׁית
בָּרוּךְ אוֹמֵר וְעוֹשֶׂה
בָּרוּךְ גּוֹזֵר וּמְקַיֵּם
בָּרוּךְ מְרַחֵם עַל הָאָרֶץ
בָּרוּךְ מְרַחֵם עַל הַבְּרִיּוֹת
בָּרוּךְ מְשַׁלֵּם שָׂכָר טוֹב לִירֵאָיו
בָּרוּךְ חַי לָעַד וְקַיָּם לָנֶצַח
בָּרוּךְ פּוֹדֶה וּמַצִּיל
בָּרוּךְ שְׁמוֹ

PESUKEI DEZIMRA / VERSES OF PRAISE

"A person should first recount the praise of the Holy One, blessed be He, and then pray" (*Berakhot* 32b), hence the passages that follow, known as the "Verses of Praise." The morning service from this point until the end is con-

Blessed are You, Lord our God,
King of the Universe,
God, compassionate Father,
extolled by the mouth of His people,
praised and glorified by the tongue of His devoted ones and those who serve Him.
With the songs of Your servant David
we will praise You, O Lord our God.
With praises and psalms
we will magnify and praise You, glorify You,
Speak Your name and proclaim Your kingship,
our King, our God, ▸ the only One, Giver of life to the worlds,
the King whose great name is praised
and glorified to all eternity.
Blessed are You, Lord,
the King extolled with songs of praise.

הוֹדוּ לַיהוה Thank the Lord, call on His name, make His acts known *1 Chr. 16*
among the peoples. Sing to Him, make music to Him, tell of all His wonders. Glory in His holy name; let the hearts of those who seek the Lord rejoice. Search out the Lord and His strength; seek His presence at all times. Remember the wonders He has done,

---

Blessed are You: The second half of the blessing is a prelude to the biblical verses that follow, mainly from the book of Psalms ("With the songs of Your servant David we will exalt You") but also from the books of Chronicles and Nehemiah ("extolled by the mouth of His people"). To emphasize the significance of this declaration, we recite it standing and, at the end, kiss the two front fringes of the tallit.

הוֹדוּ לַיהוה *Thank the Lord:* A psalm of thanksgiving composed by King David to celebrate the moment when the Ark of the Covenant was brought to Jerusalem. In many communities, the Leader says the verse, "For all the gods," aloud to emphasize the need to make a pause between the word "idols" and the name of God.

בָּרוּךְ אַתָּה יהוה אֱלֹהֵינוּ מֶלֶךְ הָעוֹלָם
הָאֵל הָאָב הָרַחֲמָן הַמְהֻלָּל בְּפִי עַמּוֹ
מְשֻׁבָּח וּמְפֹאָר בִּלְשׁוֹן חֲסִידָיו וַעֲבָדָיו
וּבְשִׁירֵי דָוִד עַבְדֶּךָ
נְהַלֶּלְךָ יהוה אֱלֹהֵינוּ.
בִּשְׁבָחוֹת וּבִזְמִירוֹת
נְגַדֶּלְךָ וּנְשַׁבֵּחֲךָ וּנְפָאֶרְךָ
וְנַזְכִּיר שִׁמְךָ וְנַמְלִיכְךָ
מַלְכֵּנוּ אֱלֹהֵינוּ, ‣ יָחִיד חֵי הָעוֹלָמִים
מֶלֶךְ, מְשֻׁבָּח וּמְפֹאָר עֲדֵי עַד שְׁמוֹ הַגָּדוֹל
בָּרוּךְ אַתָּה יהוה, מֶלֶךְ מְהֻלָּל בַּתִּשְׁבָּחוֹת.

דברי הימים א, טז
הוֹדוּ לַיהוה קִרְאוּ בִשְׁמוֹ, הוֹדִיעוּ בָעַמִּים עֲלִילוֹתָיו: שִׁירוּ לוֹ,
זַמְּרוּ־לוֹ, שִׂיחוּ בְּכָל־נִפְלְאוֹתָיו: הִתְהַלְלוּ בְּשֵׁם קָדְשׁוֹ, יִשְׂמַח

---

correspond to the six days of creation; others are added on Shabbat and festivals. Around this inner core other passages have been woven: some from other biblical books and others from selected verses in the book of Psalms. The section begins and ends with a paragraph of blessings: "Blessed is He who spoke" (*Barukh She'Amar*) at the beginning, and "May Your Name be praised for ever" (*Yishtabaḥ*) at the end.

בָּרוּךְ שֶׁאָמַר *Blessed is He who spoke (previous page):* An introductory blessing to the Verses of Praise, in two parts. The first is a ten-part litany of praise to God as Creator, each phrase introduced with the word "Blessed" (the second phrase, *barukh hu*, "blessed is He," is not a separate verse but was originally a congregational response). The number ten corresponds to the ten times the word *Vayomer*, "And He said," appears in the story of creation in Genesis 1, hence the rabbinic saying that "With ten utterances the world was created."

His miracles, and the judgments He pronounced. Descendants of Yisrael His servant, sons of Jacob His chosen ones: He is the LORD our God. His judgments are throughout the earth. Remember His covenant for ever, the word He commanded for a thousand generations. He made it with Abraham, vowed it to Isaac, and confirmed it to Jacob as a statute and to Israel as an everlasting covenant, saying, "To you I will give the land of Canaan as your allotted heritage." You were then small in number, few, strangers there, wandering from nation to nation, from one kingdom to another, but He let no man oppress them, and for their sake He rebuked kings: "Do not touch My anointed ones, and do My prophets no harm." Sing to the LORD, all the earth; proclaim His salvation daily. Declare His glory among the nations, His marvels among all the peoples. For great is the LORD and greatly to be praised; He is awesome beyond all heavenly powers. ▸ For all the gods of the peoples are mere idols; it was the LORD who made the heavens.

Before Him are majesty and splendor; there is strength and beauty in His holy place. Render to the LORD, families of the peoples, render to the LORD honor and might. Render to the LORD the glory due to His name; bring an offering and come before Him; bow down to the LORD in the splendor of holiness. Tremble before Him, all the earth; the world stands firm, it will not be shaken. Let the heavens rejoice and the earth be glad; let them declare among the nations, "The LORD is King." Let the sea roar, and all that is in it; let the fields be jubilant, and all they contain. Then the trees of the forest will sing for joy before the LORD, for He is coming to judge the earth. Thank the LORD for He is good; His loving-kindness is for ever. Say: "Save us, God of our salvation; gather us and rescue us from the nations, to acknowledge Your holy name and glory in Your praise. Blessed is the LORD, God of Israel, from this world to eternity." And let all the people say "Amen" and "Praise the LORD."

לֵב מְבַקְשֵׁי יהוה: דִּרְשׁוּ יהוה וְעֻזּוֹ, בַּקְּשׁוּ פָנָיו תָּמִיד: זִכְרוּ נִפְלְאֹתָיו אֲשֶׁר עָשָׂה, מֹפְתָיו וּמִשְׁפְּטֵי־פִיהוּ: זֶרַע יִשְׂרָאֵל עַבְדּוֹ, בְּנֵי יַעֲקֹב בְּחִירָיו: הוּא יהוה אֱלֹהֵינוּ בְּכָל־הָאָרֶץ מִשְׁפָּטָיו: זִכְרוּ לְעוֹלָם בְּרִיתוֹ, דָּבָר צִוָּה לְאֶלֶף דּוֹר: אֲשֶׁר כָּרַת אֶת־אַבְרָהָם, וּשְׁבוּעָתוֹ לְיִצְחָק: וַיַּעֲמִידֶהָ לְיַעֲקֹב לְחֹק, לְיִשְׂרָאֵל בְּרִית עוֹלָם: לֵאמֹר, לְךָ אֶתֵּן אֶרֶץ־כְּנָעַן, חֶבֶל נַחֲלַתְכֶם: בִּהְיוֹתְכֶם מְתֵי מִסְפָּר, כִּמְעַט וְגָרִים בָּהּ: וַיִּתְהַלְּכוּ מִגּוֹי אֶל־גּוֹי, וּמִמַּמְלָכָה אֶל־עַם אַחֵר: לֹא־הִנִּיחַ לְאִישׁ לְעָשְׁקָם, וַיּוֹכַח עֲלֵיהֶם מְלָכִים: אַל־תִּגְּעוּ בִּמְשִׁיחָי, וּבִנְבִיאַי אַל־תָּרֵעוּ: שִׁירוּ לַיהוה כָּל־הָאָרֶץ, בַּשְּׂרוּ מִיּוֹם־אֶל־יוֹם יְשׁוּעָתוֹ: סַפְּרוּ בַגּוֹיִם אֶת־כְּבוֹדוֹ, בְּכָל־הָעַמִּים נִפְלְאֹתָיו: כִּי גָדוֹל יהוה וּמְהֻלָּל מְאֹד, וְנוֹרָא הוּא עַל־כָּל־אֱלֹהִים: ◂ כִּי כָּל־אֱלֹהֵי הָעַמִּים אֱלִילִים, וַיהוה שָׁמַיִם עָשָׂה:

הוֹד וְהָדָר לְפָנָיו, עֹז וְחֶדְוָה בִּמְקֹמוֹ: הָבוּ לַיהוה מִשְׁפְּחוֹת עַמִּים, הָבוּ לַיהוה כָּבוֹד וָעֹז: הָבוּ לַיהוה כְּבוֹד שְׁמוֹ, שְׂאוּ מִנְחָה וּבֹאוּ לְפָנָיו, הִשְׁתַּחֲווּ לַיהוה בְּהַדְרַת־קֹדֶשׁ: חִילוּ מִלְּפָנָיו כָּל־הָאָרֶץ, אַף־תִּכּוֹן תֵּבֵל בַּל־תִּמּוֹט: יִשְׂמְחוּ הַשָּׁמַיִם וְתָגֵל הָאָרֶץ, וְיֹאמְרוּ בַגּוֹיִם יהוה מָלָךְ: יִרְעַם הַיָּם וּמְלוֹאוֹ, יַעֲלֹץ הַשָּׂדֶה וְכָל־אֲשֶׁר־בּוֹ: אָז יְרַנְּנוּ עֲצֵי הַיָּעַר, מִלִּפְנֵי יהוה, כִּי־בָא לִשְׁפּוֹט אֶת־הָאָרֶץ: הוֹדוּ לַיהוה כִּי טוֹב, כִּי לְעוֹלָם חַסְדּוֹ: וְאִמְרוּ, הוֹשִׁיעֵנוּ אֱלֹהֵי יִשְׁעֵנוּ, וְקַבְּצֵנוּ וְהַצִּילֵנוּ מִן־הַגּוֹיִם, לְהֹדוֹת לְשֵׁם קָדְשֶׁךָ, לְהִשְׁתַּבֵּחַ בִּתְהִלָּתֶךָ: בָּרוּךְ יהוה אֱלֹהֵי יִשְׂרָאֵל מִן־הָעוֹלָם וְעַד־הָעֹלָם, וַיֹּאמְרוּ כָל־הָעָם אָמֵן, וְהַלֵּל לַיהוה:

▸ Exalt the Lord our God and bow before His footstool: He is *Ps. 99*
holy. Exalt the Lord our God and bow at His holy mountain; for
holy is the Lord our God.

He is compassionate. He forgives iniquity and does not destroy. *Ps. 78*
Repeatedly He suppresses His anger, not rousing His full wrath.
You, Lord: do not withhold Your compassion from me. May Your *Ps. 40*
loving-kindness and truth always guard me. Remember, Lord, *Ps. 25*
Your acts of compassion and love, for they have existed for ever.
Ascribe power to God, whose majesty is over Israel and whose *Ps. 68*
might is in the skies. You are awesome, God, in Your holy places.
It is the God of Israel who gives might and strength to the people,
may God be blessed. God of retribution, Lord, God of retribu- *Ps. 94*
tion, appear. Arise, Judge of the earth, to repay the arrogant their
just deserts. Salvation belongs to the Lord; may Your blessing rest *Ps. 3*
upon Your people, Selah! ▸ The Lord of hosts is with us, the God *Ps. 46*
of Jacob is our stronghold, Selah! Lord of hosts, happy is the one *Ps. 84*
who trusts in You. Lord, save! May the King answer us on the day *Ps. 20*
we call.

Save Your people and bless Your heritage; tend them and carry *Ps. 28*
them for ever. Our soul longs for the Lord; He is our Help and *Ps. 33*
Shield. For in Him our hearts rejoice, for in His holy name we have
trusted. May Your loving-kindness, Lord, be upon us, as we have
put our hope in You. Show us, Lord, Your loving-kindness and *Ps. 85*
grant us Your salvation. Arise, help us and redeem us for the sake *Ps. 44*
of Your love. I am the Lord your God who brought you up from *Ps. 81*
the land of Egypt: open your mouth wide and I will fill it. Happy *Ps. 144*
is the people for whom this is so; happy is the people whose God
is the Lord. ▸ As for me, I trust in Your loving-kindness; my heart *Ps. 13*
rejoices in Your salvation. I will sing to the Lord for He has been
good to me.

---

of King David to today. We may no longer have the Ark, but we still have the covenant.

› רוֹמְמוּ יהוה אֱלֹהֵינוּ וְהִשְׁתַּחֲווּ לַהֲדֹם רַגְלָיו, קָדוֹשׁ הוּא: תהלים צט
רוֹמְמוּ יהוה אֱלֹהֵינוּ וְהִשְׁתַּחֲווּ לְהַר קָדְשׁוֹ, כִּי־קָדוֹשׁ יהוה
אֱלֹהֵינוּ:

וְהוּא רַחוּם, יְכַפֵּר עָוֹן וְלֹא־יַשְׁחִית, וְהִרְבָּה לְהָשִׁיב אַפּוֹ, תהלים עח
וְלֹא־יָעִיר כָּל־חֲמָתוֹ: אַתָּה יהוה לֹא־תִכְלָא רַחֲמֶיךָ מִמֶּנִּי, חַסְדְּךָ תהלים מ
וַאֲמִתְּךָ תָּמִיד יִצְּרוּנִי: זְכֹר־רַחֲמֶיךָ יהוה וַחֲסָדֶיךָ, כִּי מֵעוֹלָם תהלים כה
הֵמָּה: תְּנוּ עֹז לֵאלֹהִים, עַל־יִשְׂרָאֵל גַּאֲוָתוֹ, וְעֻזּוֹ בַּשְּׁחָקִים: תהלים סח
נוֹרָא אֱלֹהִים מִמִּקְדָּשֶׁיךָ, אֵל יִשְׂרָאֵל הוּא נֹתֵן עֹז וְתַעֲצֻמוֹת
לָעָם, בָּרוּךְ אֱלֹהִים: אֵל־נְקָמוֹת יהוה, אֵל נְקָמוֹת הוֹפִיעַ: תהלים צד
הִנָּשֵׂא שֹׁפֵט הָאָרֶץ, הָשֵׁב גְּמוּל עַל־גֵּאִים: לַיהוה הַיְשׁוּעָה, תהלים ג
עַל־עַמְּךָ בִרְכָתֶךָ סֶּלָה: › יהוה צְבָאוֹת עִמָּנוּ, מִשְׂגָּב לָנוּ אֱלֹהֵי תהלים מו
יַעֲקֹב סֶלָה: יהוה צְבָאוֹת, אַשְׁרֵי אָדָם בֹּטֵחַ בָּךְ: יהוה הוֹשִׁיעָה, תהלים פד תהלים כ
הַמֶּלֶךְ יַעֲנֵנוּ בְיוֹם־קָרְאֵנוּ:

הוֹשִׁיעָה אֶת־עַמֶּךָ, וּבָרֵךְ אֶת־נַחֲלָתֶךָ, וּרְעֵם וְנַשְּׂאֵם עַד־ תהלים כח
הָעוֹלָם: נַפְשֵׁנוּ חִכְּתָה לַיהוה, עֶזְרֵנוּ וּמָגִנֵּנוּ הוּא: כִּי־בוֹ יִשְׂמַח תהלים לג
לִבֵּנוּ, כִּי בְשֵׁם קָדְשׁוֹ בָטָחְנוּ: יְהִי־חַסְדְּךָ יהוה עָלֵינוּ, כַּאֲשֶׁר
יִחַלְנוּ לָךְ: הַרְאֵנוּ יהוה חַסְדֶּךָ, וְיֶשְׁעֲךָ תִּתֶּן־לָנוּ: קוּמָה עֶזְרָתָה תהלים פה תהלים מד
לָּנוּ, וּפְדֵנוּ לְמַעַן חַסְדֶּךָ: אָנֹכִי יהוה אֱלֹהֶיךָ הַמַּעַלְךָ מֵאֶרֶץ תהלים פא
מִצְרָיִם, הַרְחֶב־פִּיךָ וַאֲמַלְאֵהוּ: אַשְׁרֵי הָעָם שֶׁכָּכָה לּוֹ, אַשְׁרֵי תהלים קמד
הָעָם שֶׁיהוה אֱלֹהָיו: › וַאֲנִי בְּחַסְדְּךָ בָטַחְתִּי, יָגֵל לִבִּי בִּישׁוּעָתֶךָ, תהלים יג
אָשִׁירָה לַיהוה, כִּי גָמַל עָלָי:

רוֹמְמוּ *Exalt:* These paragraphs (until כִּי גָמַל עָלָי, "for He has been good to me") are a selection of verses from the book of Psalms on the theme of hope and trust in God. It forms a moving transition from then to now, from the days

The following psalm recalls the thanksgiving-offering in Temple times.
It is not said on Erev Pesah, or Erev Yom Kippur
since no thanksgiving-offerings were brought on these days.
To emphasize its sacrificial nature, the custom is to say it standing.

מִזְמוֹר A psalm of thanksgiving. Shout joyously to the LORD, *Ps. 100*
all the earth. Serve the LORD with joy. Come before Him with jubilation. Know that the LORD is God. He made us and we are His. We are His people and the flock He tends. Enter His gates with thanksgiving, His courts with praise. Thank Him and bless His name. ▸ For the LORD is good, His loving-kindness is everlasting, and His faithfulness is for every generation.

יְהִי כְבוֹד May the LORD's glory be for ever; may the LORD rejoice in His *Ps. 104*
works. May the LORD's name be blessed, now and for ever. From the *Ps. 113*
rising of the sun to its setting, may the LORD's name be praised. The
LORD is high above all nations; His glory is above the heavens. LORD, *Ps. 135*
Your name is for ever. Your renown, LORD, is for all generations. The *Ps. 103*
LORD has established His throne in heaven; His kingdom rules all. Let *1 Chr. 16*
the heavens rejoice and the earth be glad. Let them say among the
nations, "The LORD is King." The LORD is King, the LORD was King,
the LORD will be King for ever and all time. The LORD is King for ever *Ps. 10*
and all time; nations will perish from His land. The LORD foils the plans *Ps. 33*
of nations; He frustrates the intentions of peoples. Many are the inten- *Prov. 19*
tions in a person's mind, but the LORD's plan prevails. The LORD's plan *Ps. 33*
shall stand for ever, His mind's intent for all generations. For He spoke
and it was; He commanded and it stood firm. For the LORD has chosen *Ps. 132*
Zion; He desired it for His dwelling. For the LORD has chosen Jacob as *Ps. 135*
His own, Israel as His special treasure. For the LORD will not abandon *Ps. 94*
His people; nor will He forsake His heritage. ▸ He is compassionate. He *Ps. 78*
forgives iniquity and does not destroy. Repeatedly He suppresses His
anger, not rousing His full wrath. LORD, save! May the King answer us *Ps. 20*
on the day we call.

---

birth or danger) in place of the sacrifice. The psalm first appeared as part of the daily service in Yemenite and French prayer books of the Middle Ages. Its presence here is to emphasize the mood of thankfulness that dominates this section of the prayers.

The following psalm recalls the קרבן תודה *in Temple times. It is not said on* ערב פסח*, or* ערב יום כיפור*, since no* קורבנות תודה *were brought on these days. To emphasize its sacrificial nature, the custom is to say it standing.*

מִזְמוֹר לְתוֹדָה, הָרִיעוּ לַיהוה כָּל־הָאָרֶץ: עִבְדוּ אֶת־יהוה תהלים ק
בְּשִׂמְחָה, בֹּאוּ לְפָנָיו בִּרְנָנָה: דְּעוּ כִּי־יהוה הוּא אֱלֹהִים,
הוּא עָשָׂנוּ וְלוֹ אֲנַחְנוּ, עַמּוֹ וְצֹאן מַרְעִיתוֹ: בֹּאוּ שְׁעָרָיו
בְּתוֹדָה, חֲצֵרֹתָיו בִּתְהִלָּה, הוֹדוּ לוֹ, בָּרְכוּ שְׁמוֹ: ◂ כִּי־טוֹב
יהוה, לְעוֹלָם חַסְדּוֹ, וְעַד־דֹּר וָדֹר אֱמוּנָתוֹ:

יְהִי כְבוֹד יהוה לְעוֹלָם, יִשְׂמַח יהוה בְּמַעֲשָׂיו: יְהִי שֵׁם יהוה מְבֹרָךְ, תהלים קד תהלים קיג
מֵעַתָּה וְעַד־עוֹלָם: מִמִּזְרַח־שֶׁמֶשׁ עַד־מְבוֹאוֹ, מְהֻלָּל שֵׁם יהוה:
רָם עַל־כָּל־גּוֹיִם יהוה, עַל הַשָּׁמַיִם כְּבוֹדוֹ: יהוה שִׁמְךָ לְעוֹלָם, תהלים קלה
יהוה זִכְרְךָ לְדֹר־וָדֹר: יהוה בַּשָּׁמַיִם הֵכִין כִּסְאוֹ, וּמַלְכוּתוֹ בַּכֹּל תהלים קג
מָשָׁלָה: יִשְׂמְחוּ הַשָּׁמַיִם וְתָגֵל הָאָרֶץ, וְיֹאמְרוּ בַגּוֹיִם יהוה מָלָךְ: דברי הימים א׳ טז
יהוה מֶלֶךְ, יהוה מָלָךְ, יהוה יִמְלֹךְ לְעוֹלָם וָעֶד. יהוה מֶלֶךְ עוֹלָם תהלים י
וָעֶד, אָבְדוּ גוֹיִם מֵאַרְצוֹ: יהוה הֵפִיר עֲצַת־גּוֹיִם, הֵנִיא מַחְשְׁבוֹת תהלים לג
עַמִּים: רַבּוֹת מַחֲשָׁבוֹת בְּלֶב־אִישׁ, וַעֲצַת יהוה הִיא תָקוּם: עֲצַת משלי יט תהלים לג
יהוה לְעוֹלָם תַּעֲמֹד, מַחְשְׁבוֹת לִבּוֹ לְדֹר וָדֹר: כִּי הוּא אָמַר וַיֶּהִי,
הוּא־צִוָּה וַיַּעֲמֹד: כִּי־בָחַר יהוה בְּצִיּוֹן, אִוָּהּ לְמוֹשָׁב לוֹ: כִּי־יַעֲקֹב תהלים קלב תהלים קלה
בָּחַר לוֹ יָהּ, יִשְׂרָאֵל לִסְגֻלָּתוֹ: כִּי לֹא־יִטֹּשׁ יהוה עַמּוֹ, וְנַחֲלָתוֹ לֹא תהלים צד
יַעֲזֹב: ◂ וְהוּא רַחוּם, יְכַפֵּר עָוֹן וְלֹא־יַשְׁחִית, וְהִרְבָּה לְהָשִׁיב אַפּוֹ, תהלים עח
וְלֹא־יָעִיר כָּל־חֲמָתוֹ: יהוה הוֹשִׁיעָה, הַמֶּלֶךְ יַעֲנֵנוּ בְיוֹם־קָרְאֵנוּ: תהלים כ

מִזְמוֹר לְתוֹדָה *A psalm of thanksgiving:* This psalm accompanied the *korban toda*, a thanksgiving-offering (Lev. 7:12), brought to express gratitude for coming safely through a hazardous situation (recovering from illness, completing a potentially dangerous journey or being released from captivity). Nowadays, we make the *HaGomel* blessing (which is said after surviving illness, child-

The line beginning with "You open Your hand" should be said with special concentration, representing as it does the key idea of this Psalm, and of Pesukei DeZimra as a whole, that God is the creator and sustainer of all. Some have the custom to touch the hand-tefillin at °, and the head-tefillin at °°.

אַשְׁרֵי Happy are those who dwell in Your House; *Ps. 84*
they shall continue to praise You, Selah!
Happy are the people for whom this is so; *Ps. 144*
happy are the people whose God is the LORD.
A song of praise by David. *Ps. 145*

I will exalt You, my God, the King, and bless Your name for ever and all time. Every day I will bless You, and praise Your name for ever and all time. Great is the LORD and greatly to be praised; His greatness is unfathomable. One generation will praise Your works to the next, and tell of Your mighty deeds. On the glorious splendor of Your majesty I will meditate, and on the acts of Your wonders. They shall talk of the power of Your awesome deeds, and I will tell of Your greatness. They shall recite the record of Your great goodness, and sing with joy of Your righteousness. The LORD is gracious and compassionate, slow to anger and great in loving-kindness. The LORD is good to all, and His compassion extends to all His works. All Your works shall thank You, LORD, and Your devoted ones shall bless You. They shall talk of the glory of Your kingship, and speak of Your might. To make known to mankind His mighty deeds and the glorious majesty of His kingship. Your kingdom is an everlasting kingdom, and Your reign is for all generations. The LORD supports all who fall, and raises all who are bowed down. All raise their eyes to You in hope, and You give them their food in due season. °You open Your hand, °°and satisfy every living thing with favor. The LORD is righteous in all His ways, and kind in all He does. The LORD is close to all who call on Him, to all who call on Him in truth. He fulfills the will of those who revere Him; He hears their cry and saves them. The LORD guards all who love Him, but all the wicked He will destroy.
▸ My mouth shall speak the praise of the LORD, and all creatures shall bless His holy name for ever and all time.

We will bless the LORD now and for ever. Halleluya! *Ps. 115*

The line beginning with פּוֹתֵחַ אֶת יָדֶךָ *should be said with special concentration, representing as it does the key idea of this psalm, and of* פסוקי דזמרה *as a whole, that God is the creator and sustainer of all. Some have the custom to touch the* תפילין של יד *at °, and the* תפילין של ראש *at °°.*

תהלים פד אַשְׁרֵי יוֹשְׁבֵי בֵיתֶךָ, עוֹד יְהַלְלוּךָ סֶּלָה:

תהלים קמד אַשְׁרֵי הָעָם שֶׁכָּכָה לּוֹ, אַשְׁרֵי הָעָם שֶׁיהוה אֱלֹהָיו:

תהלים קמה תְּהִלָּה לְדָוִד

אֲרוֹמִמְךָ אֱלוֹהַי הַמֶּלֶךְ, וַאֲבָרְכָה שִׁמְךָ לְעוֹלָם וָעֶד:
בְּכָל־יוֹם אֲבָרְכֶךָּ, וַאֲהַלְלָה שִׁמְךָ לְעוֹלָם וָעֶד:
גָּדוֹל יהוה וּמְהֻלָּל מְאֹד, וְלִגְדֻלָּתוֹ אֵין חֵקֶר:
דּוֹר לְדוֹר יְשַׁבַּח מַעֲשֶׂיךָ, וּגְבוּרֹתֶיךָ יַגִּידוּ:
הֲדַר כְּבוֹד הוֹדֶךָ, וְדִבְרֵי נִפְלְאֹתֶיךָ אָשִׂיחָה:
וֶעֱזוּז נוֹרְאֹתֶיךָ יֹאמֵרוּ, וּגְדוּלָּתְךָ אֲסַפְּרֶנָּה:
זֵכֶר רַב־טוּבְךָ יַבִּיעוּ, וְצִדְקָתְךָ יְרַנֵּנוּ:
חַנּוּן וְרַחוּם יהוה, אֶרֶךְ אַפַּיִם וּגְדָל־חָסֶד:
טוֹב־יהוה לַכֹּל, וְרַחֲמָיו עַל־כָּל־מַעֲשָׂיו:
יוֹדוּךָ יהוה כָּל־מַעֲשֶׂיךָ, וַחֲסִידֶיךָ יְבָרְכוּכָה:
כְּבוֹד מַלְכוּתְךָ יֹאמֵרוּ, וּגְבוּרָתְךָ יְדַבֵּרוּ:
לְהוֹדִיעַ לִבְנֵי הָאָדָם גְּבוּרֹתָיו, וּכְבוֹד הֲדַר מַלְכוּתוֹ:
מַלְכוּתְךָ מַלְכוּת כָּל־עֹלָמִים, וּמֶמְשַׁלְתְּךָ בְּכָל־דּוֹר וָדֹר:
סוֹמֵךְ יהוה לְכָל־הַנֹּפְלִים, וְזוֹקֵף לְכָל־הַכְּפוּפִים:
עֵינֵי־כֹל אֵלֶיךָ יְשַׂבֵּרוּ, וְאַתָּה נוֹתֵן־לָהֶם אֶת־אָכְלָם בְּעִתּוֹ:
°פּוֹתֵחַ אֶת־יָדֶךָ, °°וּמַשְׂבִּיעַ לְכָל־חַי רָצוֹן:
צַדִּיק יהוה בְּכָל־דְּרָכָיו, וְחָסִיד בְּכָל־מַעֲשָׂיו:
קָרוֹב יהוה לְכָל־קֹרְאָיו, לְכֹל אֲשֶׁר יִקְרָאֻהוּ בֶאֱמֶת:
רְצוֹן־יְרֵאָיו יַעֲשֶׂה, וְאֶת־שַׁוְעָתָם יִשְׁמַע, וְיוֹשִׁיעֵם:
שׁוֹמֵר יהוה אֶת־כָּל־אֹהֲבָיו, וְאֵת כָּל־הָרְשָׁעִים יַשְׁמִיד:
‹ תְּהִלַּת יהוה יְדַבֶּר פִּי, וִיבָרֵךְ כָּל־בָּשָׂר שֵׁם קָדְשׁוֹ לְעוֹלָם וָעֶד:

תהלים קטו וַאֲנַחְנוּ נְבָרֵךְ יָהּ מֵעַתָּה וְעַד־עוֹלָם, הַלְלוּיָהּ:

הַלְלוּיָהּ Halleluya! Praise the LORD, my soul. I will praise the LORD all my life; I will sing to my God as long as I live. Put not your trust in princes, or in mortal man who cannot save. His breath expires, he returns to the earth; on that day his plans come to an end. Happy is he whose help is the God of Jacob, whose hope is in the LORD his God who made heaven and earth, the sea and all they contain; He who keeps faith for ever. He secures justice for the oppressed. He gives food to the hungry. The LORD sets captives free. The LORD gives sight to the blind. The LORD raises those bowed down. The LORD loves the righteous. The LORD protects the stranger. He gives courage to the orphan and widow. He thwarts the way of the wicked. ▸ The LORD shall reign for ever. He is your God, Zion, for all generations. Halleluya! *Ps. 146*

הַלְלוּיָהּ Halleluya! How good it is to sing songs to our God; how pleasant and fitting to praise Him. The LORD rebuilds Jerusalem. He gathers the scattered exiles of Israel. He heals the brokenhearted and binds up their wounds. He counts the number of the stars, calling each by name. Great is our LORD and mighty in power; His understanding has no limit. The LORD gives courage to the humble, but casts the wicked to the ground. Sing to the LORD in thanks; make music to our God on the harp. He covers the sky with clouds. He provides the earth with rain and makes grass grow on the hills. He gives food to the cattle and to the ravens when they cry. He does not take delight in the strength of horses nor pleasure in the fleetness of man. The LORD takes pleasure in those who fear Him, who put their hope in His loving care. Praise the LORD, Jerusalem; sing to your God, Zion, for He has strengthened the bars of your gates and blessed your children in your midst. He has brought peace to your borders, and satisfied you with the finest wheat. He sends His commandment to earth; swiftly runs His word. He spreads snow like fleece, sprinkles frost like ashes, scatters hail like crumbs. Who can stand His cold? He sends His word and melts them; He makes the wind blow and the waters flow. ▸ He has declared His words to Jacob, His statutes and laws to Israel. He has done this for no other nation; such laws they do not know. Halleluya! *Ps. 147*

תהלים קמו הַלְלוּיָהּ, הַלְלִי נַפְשִׁי אֶת־יהוה: אֲהַלְלָה יהוה בְּחַיָּי, אֲזַמְּרָה לֵאלֹהַי בְּעוֹדִי: אַל־תִּבְטְחוּ בִנְדִיבִים, בְּבֶן־אָדָם שֶׁאֵין לוֹ תְשׁוּעָה: תֵּצֵא רוּחוֹ, יָשֻׁב לְאַדְמָתוֹ, בַּיּוֹם הַהוּא אָבְדוּ עֶשְׁתֹּנוֹתָיו: אַשְׁרֵי שֶׁאֵל יַעֲקֹב בְּעֶזְרוֹ, שִׂבְרוֹ עַל־יהוה אֱלֹהָיו: עֹשֶׂה שָׁמַיִם וָאָרֶץ, אֶת־הַיָּם וְאֶת־כָּל־אֲשֶׁר־בָּם, הַשֹּׁמֵר אֱמֶת לְעוֹלָם: עֹשֶׂה מִשְׁפָּט לַעֲשׁוּקִים, נֹתֵן לֶחֶם לָרְעֵבִים, יהוה מַתִּיר אֲסוּרִים: יהוה פֹּקֵחַ עִוְרִים, יהוה זֹקֵף כְּפוּפִים, יהוה אֹהֵב צַדִּיקִים: יהוה שֹׁמֵר אֶת־גֵּרִים, יָתוֹם וְאַלְמָנָה יְעוֹדֵד, וְדֶרֶךְ רְשָׁעִים יְעַוֵּת: ◂ יִמְלֹךְ יהוה לְעוֹלָם, אֱלֹהַיִךְ צִיּוֹן לְדֹר וָדֹר, הַלְלוּיָהּ:

תהלים קמז הַלְלוּיָהּ, כִּי־טוֹב זַמְּרָה אֱלֹהֵינוּ, כִּי־נָעִים נָאוָה תְהִלָּה: בּוֹנֵה יְרוּשָׁלַםִ יהוה, נִדְחֵי יִשְׂרָאֵל יְכַנֵּס: הָרוֹפֵא לִשְׁבוּרֵי לֵב, וּמְחַבֵּשׁ לְעַצְּבוֹתָם: מוֹנֶה מִסְפָּר לַכּוֹכָבִים, לְכֻלָּם שֵׁמוֹת יִקְרָא: גָּדוֹל אֲדוֹנֵינוּ וְרַב־כֹּחַ, לִתְבוּנָתוֹ אֵין מִסְפָּר: מְעוֹדֵד עֲנָוִים יהוה, מַשְׁפִּיל רְשָׁעִים עֲדֵי־אָרֶץ: עֱנוּ לַיהוה בְּתוֹדָה, זַמְּרוּ לֵאלֹהֵינוּ בְכִנּוֹר: הַמְכַסֶּה שָׁמַיִם בְּעָבִים, הַמֵּכִין לָאָרֶץ מָטָר, הַמַּצְמִיחַ הָרִים חָצִיר: נוֹתֵן לִבְהֵמָה לַחְמָהּ, לִבְנֵי עֹרֵב אֲשֶׁר יִקְרָאוּ: לֹא בִגְבוּרַת הַסּוּס יֶחְפָּץ, לֹא־בְשׁוֹקֵי הָאִישׁ יִרְצֶה: רוֹצֶה יהוה אֶת־יְרֵאָיו, אֶת־הַמְיַחֲלִים לְחַסְדּוֹ: שַׁבְּחִי יְרוּשָׁלַםִ אֶת־יהוה, הַלְלִי אֱלֹהַיִךְ צִיּוֹן: כִּי־חִזַּק בְּרִיחֵי שְׁעָרָיִךְ, בֵּרַךְ בָּנַיִךְ בְּקִרְבֵּךְ: הַשָּׂם־גְּבוּלֵךְ שָׁלוֹם, חֵלֶב חִטִּים יַשְׂבִּיעֵךְ: הַשֹּׁלֵחַ אִמְרָתוֹ אָרֶץ, עַד־מְהֵרָה יָרוּץ דְּבָרוֹ: הַנֹּתֵן שֶׁלֶג כַּצָּמֶר, כְּפוֹר כָּאֵפֶר יְפַזֵּר: מַשְׁלִיךְ קַרְחוֹ כְפִתִּים, לִפְנֵי קָרָתוֹ מִי יַעֲמֹד: יִשְׁלַח דְּבָרוֹ וְיַמְסֵם, יַשֵּׁב רוּחוֹ יִזְּלוּ־מָיִם: ◂ מַגִּיד דְּבָרָו לְיַעֲקֹב, חֻקָּיו וּמִשְׁפָּטָיו לְיִשְׂרָאֵל: לֹא עָשָׂה כֵן לְכָל־גּוֹי, וּמִשְׁפָּטִים בַּל־יְדָעוּם, הַלְלוּיָהּ:

הַלְלוּיָהּ Halleluya! Praise the Lord from the heavens, praise Him in the heights. Praise Him, all His angels; praise Him, all His hosts. Praise Him, sun and moon; praise Him, all shining stars. Praise Him, highest heavens and the waters above the heavens. Let them praise the name of the Lord, for He commanded and they were created. He established them for ever and all time, issuing a decree that will never change. Praise the Lord from the earth: sea monsters and all the deep seas; fire and hail, snow and mist, storm winds that obey His word; mountains and all hills, fruit trees and all cedars; wild animals and all cattle, creeping things and winged birds; kings of the earth and all nations, princes and all judges on earth; youths and maidens, old and young. ▸ Let them praise the name of the Lord, for His name alone is sublime; His majesty is above earth and heaven. He has raised the pride of His people, for the glory of all His devoted ones, the children of Israel, the people close to Him. Halleluya! *Ps. 148*

הַלְלוּיָהּ Halleluya! Sing to the Lord a new song, His praise in the assembly of the devoted. Let Israel rejoice in its Maker; let the children of Zion exult in their King. Let them praise His name with dancing; sing praises to Him with timbrel and harp. For the Lord delights in His people; He adorns the humble with salvation. Let the devoted revel in glory; let them sing for joy on their beds. Let high praises of God be in their throats, and a two-edged sword in their hand: to impose retribution on the nations, punishment on the peoples, ▸ binding their kings with chains, their nobles with iron fetters, carrying out the judgment written against them. This is the glory of all His devoted ones. Halleluya! *Ps. 149*

הַלְלוּיָהּ Halleluya! Praise God in His holy place; praise Him in the heavens of His power. Praise Him for His mighty deeds; praise Him for His surpassing greatness. Praise Him with blasts of the shofar; praise Him with the harp and lyre. Praise Him with timbrel and dance; praise Him with strings and flute. Praise Him with clashing cymbals; praise Him with resounding cymbals. ▸ Let all that breathes praise the Lord. Halleluya! Let all that breathes praise the Lord. Halleluya! *Ps. 150*

הַלְלוּיָהּ, הַלְלוּ אֶת־יהוה מִן־הַשָּׁמַיִם, הַלְלְוּהוּ בַּמְּרוֹמִים: הַלְלְוּהוּ תהלים קמח
כָל־מַלְאָכָיו, הַלְלְוּהוּ כָּל־צְבָאָו: הַלְלְוּהוּ שֶׁמֶשׁ וְיָרֵחַ, הַלְלְוּהוּ
כָּל־כּוֹכְבֵי אוֹר: הַלְלְוּהוּ שְׁמֵי הַשָּׁמָיִם, וְהַמַּיִם אֲשֶׁר מֵעַל הַשָּׁמָיִם:
יְהַלְלוּ אֶת־שֵׁם יהוה, כִּי הוּא צִוָּה וְנִבְרָאוּ: וַיַּעֲמִידֵם לָעַד לְעוֹלָם,
חָק־נָתַן וְלֹא יַעֲבוֹר: הַלְלוּ אֶת־יהוה מִן־הָאָרֶץ, תַּנִּינִים וְכָל־
תְּהֹמוֹת: אֵשׁ וּבָרָד שֶׁלֶג וְקִיטוֹר, רְוּחַ סְעָרָה עֹשָׂה דְבָרוֹ:
הֶהָרִים וְכָל־גְּבָעוֹת, עֵץ פְּרִי וְכָל־אֲרָזִים: הַחַיָּה וְכָל־בְּהֵמָה, רֶמֶשׂ
וְצִפּוֹר כָּנָף: מַלְכֵי־אֶרֶץ וְכָל־לְאֻמִּים, שָׂרִים וְכָל־שֹׁפְטֵי אָרֶץ:
בַּחוּרִים וְגַם־בְּתוּלוֹת, זְקֵנִים עִם־נְעָרִים: ‹ יְהַלְלוּ אֶת־שֵׁם יהוה,
כִּי־נִשְׂגָּב שְׁמוֹ לְבַדּוֹ, הוֹדוֹ עַל־אֶרֶץ וְשָׁמָיִם: וַיָּרֶם קֶרֶן לְעַמּוֹ,
תְּהִלָּה לְכָל־חֲסִידָיו, לִבְנֵי יִשְׂרָאֵל עַם קְרֹבוֹ, הַלְלוּיָהּ:

הַלְלוּיָהּ, שִׁירוּ לַיהוה שִׁיר חָדָשׁ, תְּהִלָּתוֹ בִּקְהַל חֲסִידִים: יִשְׂמַח תהלים קמט
יִשְׂרָאֵל בְּעֹשָׂיו, בְּנֵי־צִיּוֹן יָגִילוּ בְמַלְכָּם: יְהַלְלוּ שְׁמוֹ בְמָחוֹל, בְּתֹף
וְכִנּוֹר יְזַמְּרוּ־לוֹ: כִּי־רוֹצֶה יהוה בְּעַמּוֹ, יְפָאֵר עֲנָוִים בִּישׁוּעָה:
יַעְלְזוּ חֲסִידִים בְּכָבוֹד, יְרַנְּנוּ עַל־מִשְׁכְּבוֹתָם: רוֹמְמוֹת אֵל
בִּגְרוֹנָם, וְחֶרֶב פִּיפִיּוֹת בְּיָדָם: לַעֲשׂוֹת נְקָמָה בַּגּוֹיִם, תּוֹכֵחוֹת
בַּלְאֻמִּים: ‹ לֶאְסֹר מַלְכֵיהֶם בְּזִקִּים, וְנִכְבְּדֵיהֶם בְּכַבְלֵי בַרְזֶל:
לַעֲשׂוֹת בָּהֶם מִשְׁפָּט כָּתוּב, הָדָר הוּא לְכָל־חֲסִידָיו, הַלְלוּיָהּ:

הַלְלוּיָהּ, הַלְלוּ־אֵל בְּקָדְשׁוֹ, הַלְלְוּהוּ בִּרְקִיעַ עֻזּוֹ: הַלְלְוּהוּ תהלים קנ
בִגְבוּרֹתָיו, הַלְלְוּהוּ כְּרֹב גֻּדְלוֹ: הַלְלְוּהוּ בְּתֵקַע שׁוֹפָר, הַלְלְוּהוּ
בְּנֵבֶל וְכִנּוֹר: הַלְלְוּהוּ בְּתֹף וּמָחוֹל, הַלְלְוּהוּ בְּמִנִּים וְעוּגָב: הַלְלְוּהוּ
בְצִלְצְלֵי־שָׁמַע, הַלְלְוּהוּ בְּצִלְצְלֵי תְרוּעָה: ‹ כֹּל הַנְּשָׁמָה תְּהַלֵּל
יָהּ, הַלְלוּיָהּ: כֹּל הַנְּשָׁמָה תְּהַלֵּל יָהּ, הַלְלוּיָהּ:

בָּרוּךְ Blessed be the LORD for ever. Amen and Amen. *Ps. 89*
Blessed from Zion be the LORD *Ps. 135*
who dwells in Jerusalem. Halleluya!
Blessed be the LORD, God of Israel, *Ps. 72*
who alone does wonders.
▸ Blessed be His glorious name for ever,
and may all the earth be filled with His glory.
Amen and Amen.

Stand (see commentary) until after "Bless the LORD" on page 88.

וַיְבָרֶךְ David blessed the LORD in front of the entire assembly. David *1 Chr. 29*
said, "Blessed are You, LORD, God of our father Yisrael, for ever
and ever. Yours, LORD, are the greatness and the power, the glory,
majesty and splendor, for everything in heaven and earth is Yours.
Yours, LORD, is the kingdom; You are exalted as Head over all. Both
riches and honor are in Your gift and You reign over all things. In
Your hand are strength and might. It is in Your power to make great
and give strength to all. Therefore, our God, we thank You and
praise Your glorious name." You alone are the LORD. You *Neh. 9*
made the heavens, even the highest heavens, and all their hosts,
the earth and all that is on it, the seas and all they contain. You
give life to them all, and the hosts of heaven worship You. ▸ You are
the LORD God who chose Abram and brought him out of Ur of
the Chaldees, changing his name to Abraham. You found his heart
faithful toward You, ◂ and You made a covenant with him to give
to his descendants the land of the Canaanites, Hittites, Amorites,

---

money to charity at this point in the service. Some give this as the reason we stand at this point of the service, since we stand to fulfill a mitzva, in this case, giving to charity.

Others relate the act of standing to the next passage, "You alone," taken from the gathering in the days of Ezra and Nehemiah after the Babylonian exile and return, when the people renewed their covenant with God.

בָּרוּךְ יהוה לְעוֹלָם, אָמֵן וְאָמֵן: תהלים פט
בָּרוּךְ יהוה מִצִּיּוֹן, שֹׁכֵן יְרוּשָׁלָםִ, הַלְלוּיָהּ: תהלים קלה
בָּרוּךְ יהוה אֱלֹהִים אֱלֹהֵי יִשְׂרָאֵל, עֹשֵׂה נִפְלָאוֹת לְבַדּוֹ: תהלים עב
‹ וּבָרוּךְ שֵׁם כְּבוֹדוֹ לְעוֹלָם
וְיִמָּלֵא כְבוֹדוֹ אֶת־כָּל־הָאָרֶץ
אָמֵן וְאָמֵן:

Stand (see commentary) until after בָּרְכוּ *on page 89.*

וַיְבָרֶךְ דָּוִיד אֶת־יהוה לְעֵינֵי כָּל־הַקָּהָל, וַיֹּאמֶר דָּוִיד, בָּרוּךְ דברי הימים א, כט
אַתָּה יהוה, אֱלֹהֵי יִשְׂרָאֵל אָבִינוּ, מֵעוֹלָם וְעַד־עוֹלָם: לְךָ יהוה
הַגְּדֻלָּה וְהַגְּבוּרָה וְהַתִּפְאֶרֶת וְהַנֵּצַח וְהַהוֹד, כִּי־כֹל בַּשָּׁמַיִם
וּבָאָרֶץ, לְךָ יהוה הַמַּמְלָכָה וְהַמִּתְנַשֵּׂא לְכֹל לְרֹאשׁ: וְהָעֹשֶׁר
וְהַכָּבוֹד מִלְּפָנֶיךָ, וְאַתָּה מוֹשֵׁל בַּכֹּל, וּבְיָדְךָ כֹּחַ וּגְבוּרָה, וּבְיָדְךָ
לְגַדֵּל וּלְחַזֵּק לַכֹּל: וְעַתָּה אֱלֹהֵינוּ מוֹדִים אֲנַחְנוּ לָךְ, וּמְהַלְלִים
לְשֵׁם תִּפְאַרְתֶּךָ: אַתָּה־הוּא יהוה לְבַדֶּךָ, אַתָּ עָשִׂיתָ נחמיה ט
אֶת־הַשָּׁמַיִם, שְׁמֵי הַשָּׁמַיִם וְכָל־צְבָאָם, הָאָרֶץ וְכָל־אֲשֶׁר עָלֶיהָ,
הַיַּמִּים וְכָל־אֲשֶׁר בָּהֶם, וְאַתָּה מְחַיֶּה אֶת־כֻּלָּם, וּצְבָא הַשָּׁמַיִם לְךָ
מִשְׁתַּחֲוִים: ‹ אַתָּה הוּא יהוה הָאֱלֹהִים אֲשֶׁר בָּחַרְתָּ בְּאַבְרָם,
וְהוֹצֵאתוֹ מֵאוּר כַּשְׂדִּים, וְשַׂמְתָּ שְּׁמוֹ אַבְרָהָם: וּמָצָאתָ אֶת־
לְבָבוֹ נֶאֱמָן לְפָנֶיךָ, ‹ וְכָרוֹת עִמּוֹ הַבְּרִית לָתֵת אֶת־אֶרֶץ הַכְּנַעֲנִי

וַיְבָרֶךְ דָּוִיד *David blessed:* This passage is part of the prayer of thanksgiving said by King David at the end of his life after he had gathered the resources to build the Temple in Jerusalem, to be undertaken by Solomon his son. As with the Tabernacle, the Temple was made out of the voluntary contributions of the people as a whole. For that reason, many have the custom to give

Perizzites, Jebusites and Girgashites. You fulfilled Your promise for You are righteous. You saw the suffering of our ancestors in Egypt. You heard their cry at the Sea of Reeds. You sent signs and wonders against Pharaoh, all his servants and all the people of his land, because You knew how arrogantly the Egyptians treated them. You created for Yourself renown that remains to this day. ▸ You divided the sea before them, so that they passed through the sea on dry land, but You cast their pursuers into the depths, like a stone into mighty waters.

וַיּוֹשַׁע That day the LORD saved Israel from the hands of the Egyptians, and Israel saw the Egyptians lying dead on the seashore. ▸ When Israel saw the great power the LORD had displayed against the Egyptians, the people feared the LORD, and believed in the LORD and in His servant, Moses. *Ex. 14*

אָז יָשִׁיר־מֹשֶׁה Then Moses and the Israelites sang this song to the LORD, saying: *Ex. 15*
I will sing to the LORD, for He has triumphed gloriously;
horse and rider He has hurled into the sea.
The LORD is my strength and song; He has become my salvation.
This is my God, and I will beautify Him,
my father's God, and I will exalt Him.
The LORD is a Master of war; LORD is His name.
Pharaoh's chariots and army He cast into the sea;
the best of his officers drowned in the Sea of Reeds.
The deep waters covered them;
they went down to the depths like a stone.
Your right hand, LORD, is majestic in power.
Your right hand, LORD, shatters the enemy.
In the greatness of Your majesty, You overthrew those who rose against You.
You sent out Your fury; it consumed them like stubble.

הַחִתִּי הָאֱמֹרִי וְהַפְּרִזִּי וְהַיְבוּסִי וְהַגִּרְגָּשִׁי, לָתֵת לְזַרְעוֹ, וַתָּקֶם
אֶת־דְּבָרֶיךָ, כִּי צַדִּיק אָתָּה: וַתֵּרֶא אֶת־עֳנִי אֲבֹתֵינוּ בְּמִצְרָיִם,
וְאֶת־זַעֲקָתָם שָׁמַעְתָּ עַל־יַם־סוּף: וַתִּתֵּן אֹתֹת וּמֹפְתִים בְּפַרְעֹה
וּבְכָל־עֲבָדָיו וּבְכָל־עַם אַרְצוֹ, כִּי יָדַעְתָּ כִּי הֵזִידוּ עֲלֵיהֶם, וַתַּעַשׂ־
לְךָ שֵׁם כְּהַיּוֹם הַזֶּה: ◂ וְהַיָּם בָּקַעְתָּ לִפְנֵיהֶם, וַיַּעַבְרוּ בְתוֹךְ־הַיָּם
בַּיַּבָּשָׁה, וְאֶת־רֹדְפֵיהֶם הִשְׁלַכְתָּ בִמְצוֹלֹת כְּמוֹ־אֶבֶן, בְּמַיִם עַזִּים:

וַיּוֹשַׁע יהוה בַּיּוֹם הַהוּא אֶת־יִשְׂרָאֵל מִיַּד מִצְרָיִם, וַיַּרְא יִשְׂרָאֵל שמות יד
אֶת־מִצְרַיִם מֵת עַל־שְׂפַת הַיָּם: ◂ וַיַּרְא יִשְׂרָאֵל אֶת־הַיָּד הַגְּדֹלָה
אֲשֶׁר עָשָׂה יהוה בְּמִצְרַיִם, וַיִּירְאוּ הָעָם אֶת־יהוה, וַיַּאֲמִינוּ
בַּיהוה וּבְמֹשֶׁה עַבְדּוֹ:

אָז יָשִׁיר־מֹשֶׁה וּבְנֵי יִשְׂרָאֵל אֶת־הַשִּׁירָה הַזֹּאת לַיהוה, וַיֹּאמְרוּ שמות טו
לֵאמֹר, אָשִׁירָה לַיהוה כִּי־גָאֹה גָּאָה, סוּס
וְרֹכְבוֹ רָמָה בַיָּם: עָזִּי וְזִמְרָת יָהּ וַיְהִי־לִי
לִישׁוּעָה, זֶה אֵלִי וְאַנְוֵהוּ, אֱלֹהֵי
אָבִי וַאֲרֹמְמֶנְהוּ: יהוה אִישׁ מִלְחָמָה, יהוה
שְׁמוֹ: מַרְכְּבֹת פַּרְעֹה וְחֵילוֹ יָרָה בַיָּם, וּמִבְחַר
שָׁלִשָׁיו טֻבְּעוּ בְיַם־סוּף: תְּהֹמֹת יְכַסְיֻמוּ, יָרְדוּ בִמְצוֹלֹת כְּמוֹ־
אָבֶן: יְמִינְךָ יהוה נֶאְדָּרִי בַּכֹּחַ, יְמִינְךָ
יהוה תִּרְעַץ אוֹיֵב: וּבְרֹב גְּאוֹנְךָ תַּהֲרֹס

Immediately prior to this passage, we read that the Levites called on the people to "Rise, bless the Lord your God" (Neh. 9:5). Hence we too stand in remembrance of that gathering (Rabbi Eli Munk).

By the blast of Your nostrils the waters piled up.
  The surging waters stood straight like a wall;
  the deeps congealed in the heart of the sea.
The enemy said, "I will pursue. I will overtake. I will divide the spoil.
  My desire shall have its fill of them.
  I will draw my sword. My hand will destroy them."
You blew with Your wind; the sea covered them.
  They sank in the mighty waters like lead.
Who is like You, LORD, among the mighty?
  Who is like You – majestic in holiness, awesome in glory,
  working wonders?
You stretched out Your right hand,
  the earth swallowed them.
In Your loving-kindness, You led the people You redeemed.
  In Your strength, You guided them to Your holy abode.
Nations heard and trembled;
  terror gripped Philistia's inhabitants.
The chiefs of Edom were dismayed,
  Moab's leaders were seized with trembling,
  the people of Canaan melted away.
Fear and dread fell upon them.
  By the power of Your arm, they were still as stone –
  until Your people crossed, LORD,
  until the people You acquired crossed over.
You will bring them and plant them
  on the mountain of Your heritage –
  the place, LORD, You made for Your dwelling,
  the Sanctuary, LORD, Your hands established.
  The LORD will reign for ever and all time.

The LORD will reign for ever and all time.
The LORD's kingship is established for ever and to all eternity.

When Pharaoh's horses, chariots and riders went into the sea,
  the LORD brought the waters of the sea back over them, but
  the Israelites walked on dry land through the sea.

קָמֶיךָ, תְּשַׁלַּח חֲרֹנְךָ יֹאכְלֵמוֹ כַּקַּשׁ: וּבְרוּחַ
אַפֶּיךָ נֶעֶרְמוּ מַיִם, נִצְּבוּ כְמוֹ־נֵד
נֹזְלִים, קָפְאוּ תְהֹמֹת בְּלֶב־יָם: אָמַר
אוֹיֵב אֶרְדֹּף, אַשִּׂיג, אֲחַלֵּק שָׁלָל, תִּמְלָאֵמוֹ
נַפְשִׁי, אָרִיק חַרְבִּי תּוֹרִישֵׁמוֹ יָדִי: נָשַׁפְתָּ
בְרוּחֲךָ כִּסָּמוֹ יָם, צָלְלוּ כַּעוֹפֶרֶת בְּמַיִם
אַדִּירִים: מִי־כָמֹכָה בָּאֵלִם יהוה, מִי
כָּמֹכָה נֶאְדָּר בַּקֹּדֶשׁ, נוֹרָא תְהִלֹּת עֹשֵׂה
פֶלֶא: נָטִיתָ יְמִינְךָ תִּבְלָעֵמוֹ אָרֶץ: נָחִיתָ
בְחַסְדְּךָ עַם־זוּ גָּאָלְתָּ, נֵהַלְתָּ בְעָזְּךָ אֶל־נְוֵה
קָדְשֶׁךָ: שָׁמְעוּ עַמִּים יִרְגָּזוּן, חִיל
אָחַז יֹשְׁבֵי פְּלָשֶׁת: אָז נִבְהֲלוּ אַלּוּפֵי
אֱדוֹם, אֵילֵי מוֹאָב יֹאחֲזֵמוֹ רָעַד, נָמֹגוּ
כֹּל יֹשְׁבֵי כְנָעַן: תִּפֹּל עֲלֵיהֶם אֵימָתָה
וָפַחַד, בִּגְדֹל זְרוֹעֲךָ יִדְּמוּ כָּאָבֶן, עַד־
יַעֲבֹר עַמְּךָ יהוה, עַד־יַעֲבֹר עַם־זוּ
קָנִיתָ: תְּבִאֵמוֹ וְתִטָּעֵמוֹ בְּהַר נַחֲלָתְךָ, מָכוֹן
לְשִׁבְתְּךָ פָּעַלְתָּ יהוה, מִקְּדָשׁ אֲדֹנָי כּוֹנְנוּ
יָדֶיךָ: יהוה יִמְלֹךְ לְעֹלָם וָעֶד:

יהוה יִמְלֹךְ לְעֹלָם וָעֶד.

יהוה מַלְכוּתֵהּ קָאֵם לְעָלַם וּלְעָלְמֵי עָלְמַיָּא.

כִּי
בָא סוּס פַּרְעֹה בְּרִכְבּוֹ וּבְפָרָשָׁיו בַּיָּם, וַיָּשֶׁב יהוה עֲלֵהֶם אֶת־מֵי
הַיָּם, וּבְנֵי יִשְׂרָאֵל הָלְכוּ בַיַּבָּשָׁה בְּתוֹךְ הַיָּם:

▸ For kingship is the Lord's Ps. 22
and He rules over the nations.
Saviors shall go up to Mount Zion Ob. 1
to judge Mount Esau,
and the Lord's shall be the kingdom.

Then the Lord shall be King over all the earth; Zech. 14
on that day the Lord shall be One and His name One,

(as it is written in Your Torah, saying:
Listen, Israel: the Lord is our God, the Lord is One.) Deut. 6

יִשְׁתַּבַּח May Your name be praised for ever, our King,
the great and holy God, King in heaven and on earth.
For to You,
Lord our God and God of our ancestors,
it is right to offer song and praise,
hymn and psalm,
strength and dominion,
eternity, greatness and power,
song of praise and glory,
holiness and kingship,
▸ blessings and thanks,
from now and for ever.
Blessed are You, Lord,
God and King,
exalted in praises,
God of thanksgivings,
Master of wonders,
who delights in hymns of song,
King, God, Giver of life to the worlds.

תהלים כב ‹ כִּי לַיהוה הַמְּלוּכָה וּמשֵׁל בַּגּוֹיִם:

עובדיה א וְעָלוּ מוֹשִׁעִים בְּהַר צִיּוֹן לִשְׁפֹּט אֶת־הַר עֵשָׂו
וְהָיְתָה לַיהוה הַמְּלוּכָה:

זכריה יד וְהָיָה יהוה לְמֶלֶךְ עַל־כָּל־הָאָרֶץ
בַּיּוֹם הַהוּא יִהְיֶה יהוה אֶחָד וּשְׁמוֹ אֶחָד:

דברים ו (וּבְתוֹרָתְךָ כָּתוּב לֵאמֹר, שְׁמַע יִשְׂרָאֵל, יהוה אֱלֹהֵינוּ יהוה אֶחָד:)

יִשְׁתַּבַּח

שִׁמְךָ לָעַד, מַלְכֵּנוּ
הָאֵל הַמֶּלֶךְ הַגָּדוֹל וְהַקָּדוֹשׁ בַּשָּׁמַיִם וּבָאָרֶץ
כִּי לְךָ נָאֶה, יהוה אֱלֹהֵינוּ וֵאלֹהֵי אֲבוֹתֵינוּ
שִׁיר וּשְׁבָחָה, הַלֵּל וְזִמְרָה
עֹז וּמֶמְשָׁלָה, נֶצַח, גְּדֻלָּה וּגְבוּרָה
תְּהִלָּה וְתִפְאֶרֶת, קְדֻשָּׁה וּמַלְכוּת
‹ בְּרָכוֹת וְהוֹדָאוֹת, מֵעַתָּה וְעַד עוֹלָם.
בָּרוּךְ אַתָּה יהוה
אֵל מֶלֶךְ גָּדוֹל בַּתִּשְׁבָּחוֹת
אֵל הַהוֹדָאוֹת
אֲדוֹן הַנִּפְלָאוֹת
הַבּוֹחֵר בְּשִׁירֵי זִמְרָה
מֶלֶךְ, אֵל, חֵי הָעוֹלָמִים.

Between Rosh HaShana and Yom Kippur, many congregations open the Ark and say this psalm responsively, verse by verse.

שִׁיר הַמַּעֲלוֹת A song of ascents. From the depths I have called to You, LORD. *Ps. 130*
LORD, hear my voice; let Your ears be attentive to my plea. If You, LORD, should keep account of sins, O LORD, who could stand? But with You there is forgiveness, that You may be held in awe. I wait for the LORD, my soul waits, and in His word I put my hope. My soul waits for the LORD more than watchmen wait for the morning, more than watchmen wait for the morning. Israel, put your hope in the LORD, for with the LORD there is loving-kindness, and great is His power to redeem. It is He who will redeem Israel from all their sins.

HALF KADDISH

Leader: יִתְגַּדַּל Magnified and sanctified
may His great name be,
in the world He created by His will.
May He establish His kingdom
in your lifetime and in your days,
and in the lifetime of all the house of Israel,
swiftly and soon –
and say: Amen.

All: May His great name be blessed
for ever and all time.

Leader: Blessed and praised,
glorified and exalted,
raised and honored,
uplifted and lauded
be the name of the Holy One,
blessed be He,
beyond any blessing,
song, praise and consolation
uttered in the world –
and say: Amen.

During the עשרת ימי תשובה*, many congregations open the* ארון קודש *and say this psalm responsively, verse by verse.*

שִׁיר הַמַּעֲלוֹת, מִמַּעֲמַקִּים קְרָאתִיךָ יהוה: אֲדֹנָי שִׁמְעָה בְקוֹלִי, תִּהְיֶינָה אָזְנֶיךָ קַשֻּׁבוֹת לְקוֹל תַּחֲנוּנָי: אִם־עֲוֹנוֹת תִּשְׁמָר־יָהּ, אֲדֹנָי מִי יַעֲמֹד: כִּי־עִמְּךָ הַסְּלִיחָה, לְמַעַן תִּוָּרֵא: קִוִּיתִי יהוה קִוְּתָה נַפְשִׁי, וְלִדְבָרוֹ הוֹחָלְתִּי: נַפְשִׁי לַאדֹנָי, מִשֹּׁמְרִים לַבֹּקֶר, שֹׁמְרִים לַבֹּקֶר: יַחֵל יִשְׂרָאֵל אֶל יהוה, כִּי־עִם־יהוה הַחֶסֶד, וְהַרְבֵּה עִמּוֹ פְדוּת: וְהוּא יִפְדֶּה אֶת־יִשְׂרָאֵל, מִכֹּל עֲוֹנוֹתָיו: תהלים קל

חצי קדיש

ש״ץ: יִתְגַּדַּל וְיִתְקַדַּשׁ שְׁמֵהּ רַבָּא (קהל: אָמֵן)
בְּעָלְמָא דִּי בְרָא כִרְעוּתֵהּ
וְיַמְלִיךְ מַלְכוּתֵהּ
בְּחַיֵּיכוֹן וּבְיוֹמֵיכוֹן וּבְחַיֵּי דְכָל בֵּית יִשְׂרָאֵל
בַּעֲגָלָא וּבִזְמַן קָרִיב
וְאִמְרוּ אָמֵן. (קהל: אָמֵן)

קהל וש״ץ: יְהֵא שְׁמֵהּ רַבָּא מְבָרַךְ לְעָלַם וּלְעָלְמֵי עָלְמַיָּא.

ש״ץ: יִתְבָּרַךְ וְיִשְׁתַּבַּח וְיִתְפָּאַר וְיִתְרוֹמַם וְיִתְנַשֵּׂא
וְיִתְהַדָּר וְיִתְעַלֶּה וְיִתְהַלָּל
שְׁמֵהּ דְּקֻדְשָׁא בְּרִיךְ הוּא (קהל: בְּרִיךְ הוּא)
לְעֵלָּא מִן כָּל בִּרְכָתָא
/בעשרת ימי תשובה: לְעֵלָּא לְעֵלָּא מִכָּל בִּרְכָתָא/
וְשִׁירָתָא, תֻּשְׁבְּחָתָא וְנֶחֱמָתָא, דַּאֲמִירָן בְּעָלְמָא
וְאִמְרוּ אָמֵן. (קהל: אָמֵן)

BLESSINGS OF THE SHEMA

The following blessing and response are said only in the presence of a minyan. They represent a formal summons to the congregation to engage in an act of collective prayer. The custom of bowing at this point is based on 1 Chronicles 29:20, "David said to the whole assembly, 'Now bless the Lord your God.' All the assembly blessed the Lord God of their fathers and bowed their heads low to the Lord and the King."

The Leader says the following, bowing at "Bless," standing straight at "the Lord." The congregation, followed by the Leader, responds, bowing at "Bless," standing straight at "the Lord."

Leader: BLESS
the Lord, the blessed One.

Congregation: Bless the Lord, the blessed One,
for ever and all time.

Leader: Bless the Lord, the blessed One,
for ever and all time.

The custom is to sit from this point until the Amida, since the predominant emotion of this section of the prayers is love rather than awe. Conversation is forbidden until after the Amida. See table on pages 695–697.

בָּרוּךְ Blessed are You, Lord our God,
King of the Universe,
who forms light and creates darkness, *Is. 45*
makes peace and creates all.

---

prayer). Saying the Shema twice daily (morning and evening, "when you lie down and when you rise up") is a biblical institution, and was part of the order of service in Temple times. The transition to congregational prayer is marked by a call – "Bless the Lord" – to those present to join in prayer as a community.

קריאת שמע וברכותיה

The following blessing and response are said only in the presence of a מנין.
They represent a formal summons to the קהל *to engage in an act of collective prayer.*
The custom of bowing at this point is based on דברי הימים א' כט, כ*, "David said to the whole assembly, 'Now bless the Lord your God.' All the assembly blessed the Lord God of their fathers and bowed their heads low to the Lord and the King."*
The שליח ציבור *says the following, bowing at* בָּרְכוּ*, standing straight at* ה'*. The* קהל*, followed by the* שליח ציבור*, responds, bowing at* בָּרוּךְ*, standing straight at* ה'*.*

ש״ץ: **בָּרְכוּ**

אֶת יהוה הַמְבֹרָךְ.

קהל: בָּרוּךְ יהוה הַמְבֹרָךְ לְעוֹלָם וָעֶד.

ש״ץ: בָּרוּךְ יהוה הַמְבֹרָךְ לְעוֹלָם וָעֶד.

The custom is to sit from this point until the עמידה*, since the predominant emotion of this section of the prayers is love rather than awe.*
Conversation is forbidden until after the עמידה*. See table on pages 695–697.*

בָּרוּךְ אַתָּה יהוה אֱלֹהֵינוּ מֶלֶךְ הָעוֹלָם
יוֹצֵר אוֹר וּבוֹרֵא חֹשֶׁךְ ישעיה מה
עֹשֶׂה שָׁלוֹם וּבוֹרֵא אֶת הַכֹּל.

THE SHEMA AND ITS BLESSINGS

The *Pesukei DeZimra* are a prelude to prayer. We now move to congregational prayer, the heart of which is the Shema and the Amida (the "standing"

הַמֵּאִיר In compassion He gives light to the earth
and its inhabitants,
and in His goodness continually renews the work of creation,
day after day.
How numerous are Your works, LORD; *Ps. 104*
You made them all in wisdom;
the earth is full of Your creations.
He is the King exalted alone since the beginning of time –
praised, glorified and elevated since the world began.
Eternal God,
in Your great compassion, have compassion on us,
LORD of our strength, Rock of our refuge,
Shield of our salvation, You are our stronghold.
The blessed God,
great in knowledge,
prepared and made the rays of the sun.
He who is good formed glory for His name,
surrounding His power with radiant stars.
The leaders of His hosts,
the holy ones,
exalt the Almighty,
constantly proclaiming God's glory and holiness.
Be blessed, LORD our God,
for the magnificence of Your handiwork
and for the radiant lights You have made.
May they glorify You, Selah!

---

the sun, moon and stars, made on the fourth day of creation, and the spiritual light created on the first day ("Let there be light"). The prayer modulates from the first to the second: from the universe as we see it, to the mystical vision of God enthroned in glory, surrounded by angels.

הַמֵּאִיר לָאָרֶץ וְלַדָּרִים עָלֶיהָ בְּרַחֲמִים
וּבְטוּבוֹ מְחַדֵּשׁ בְּכָל יוֹם תָּמִיד מַעֲשֵׂה בְרֵאשִׁית.
מָה־רַבּוּ מַעֲשֶׂיךָ יהוה, כֻּלָּם בְּחָכְמָה עָשִׂיתָ תהלים קד
מָלְאָה הָאָרֶץ קִנְיָנֶךָ:
הַמֶּלֶךְ הַמְרוֹמָם לְבַדּוֹ מֵאָז
הַמְשֻׁבָּח וְהַמְפֹאָר וְהַמִּתְנַשֵּׂא מִימוֹת עוֹלָם.
אֱלֹהֵי עוֹלָם
בְּרַחֲמֶיךָ הָרַבִּים רַחֵם עָלֵינוּ
אֲדוֹן עֻזֵּנוּ, צוּר מִשְׂגַּבֵּנוּ
מָגֵן יִשְׁעֵנוּ, מִשְׂגָּב בַּעֲדֵנוּ.
אֵל בָּרוּךְ גְּדוֹל דֵּעָה
הֵכִין וּפָעַל זָהֳרֵי חַמָּה
טוֹב יָצַר כָּבוֹד לִשְׁמוֹ
מְאוֹרוֹת נָתַן סְבִיבוֹת עֻזּוֹ
פִּנּוֹת צְבָאָיו קְדוֹשִׁים, רוֹמְמֵי שַׁדַּי
תָּמִיד מְסַפְּרִים כְּבוֹד אֵל וּקְדֻשָּׁתוֹ.
תִּתְבָּרַךְ יהוה אֱלֹהֵינוּ
עַל שֶׁבַח מַעֲשֵׂה יָדֶיךָ.
וְעַל מְאוֹרֵי אוֹר שֶׁעָשִׂיתָ
יְפָאֲרוּךָ סֶּלָה.

אֵל בָּרוּךְ *The blessed God:* An alphabetical acrostic of twenty-two words. Although the first blessing is about creation as a whole, the morning prayer emphasizes the element of which we are most conscious at the start of the day: the creation of light. Of this, there are two forms: the physical light of

תִּתְבָּרַךְ May You be blessed,
our Rock, King and Redeemer,
Creator of holy beings.
May Your name be praised for ever,
our King, Creator of the ministering angels,
all of whom stand in the universe's heights,
proclaiming together,
in awe, aloud,
the words of the living God, the eternal King.
They are all beloved, all pure, all mighty,
and all perform in awe and reverence the will of their Maker.
▸ All open their mouths in holiness and purity,
with song and psalm,
and bless, praise, glorify,
revere, sanctify and declare the sovereignty of – ◂
The name of the great, mighty
and awesome God and King,
holy is He.
▸ All accept on themselves,
one from another,
the yoke of the kingdom of heaven,
granting permission to one another
to sanctify the One who formed them,
in serene spirit,
pure speech and sweet melody.
All, as one,
proclaim His holiness,
saying in awe:

The theme of this section of the service is *revelation*: God as He has disclosed Himself in the words of the Torah. So at its heart are three passages from the Torah, known collectively by their first word, *Shema*. Around it

תִּתְבָּרַךְ
צוּרֵנוּ מַלְכֵּנוּ וְגוֹאֲלֵנוּ, בּוֹרֵא קְדוֹשִׁים
יִשְׁתַּבַּח שִׁמְךָ לָעַד
מַלְכֵּנוּ, יוֹצֵר מְשָׁרְתִים
וַאֲשֶׁר מְשָׁרְתָיו כֻּלָּם עוֹמְדִים בְּרוּם עוֹלָם
וּמַשְׁמִיעִים בְּיִרְאָה יַחַד בְּקוֹל
דִּבְרֵי אֱלֹהִים חַיִּים וּמֶלֶךְ עוֹלָם.
כֻּלָּם אֲהוּבִים, כֻּלָּם בְּרוּרִים, כֻּלָּם גִּבּוֹרִים
וְכֻלָּם עוֹשִׂים בְּאֵימָה וּבְיִרְאָה רְצוֹן קוֹנָם
◂ וְכֻלָּם פּוֹתְחִים אֶת פִּיהֶם בִּקְדֻשָּׁה וּבְטָהֳרָה
בְּשִׁירָה וּבְזִמְרָה
וּמְבָרְכִים וּמְשַׁבְּחִים וּמְפָאֲרִים
◂ וּמַעֲרִיצִים וּמַקְדִּישִׁים וּמַמְלִיכִים
אֶת שֵׁם הָאֵל הַמֶּלֶךְ הַגָּדוֹל, הַגִּבּוֹר וְהַנּוֹרָא
קָדוֹשׁ הוּא.
◂ וְכֻלָּם מְקַבְּלִים עֲלֵיהֶם עֹל מַלְכוּת שָׁמַיִם זֶה מִזֶּה
וְנוֹתְנִים רְשׁוּת זֶה לָזֶה
לְהַקְדִּישׁ לְיוֹצְרָם בְּנַחַת רוּחַ
בְּשָׂפָה בְרוּרָה וּבִנְעִימָה
קְדֻשָּׁה כֻּלָּם כְּאֶחָד
עוֹנִים וְאוֹמְרִים בְּיִרְאָה

The three blessings and the three paragraphs of the Shema form six passages, leading up to the seventh, the Amida. In Judaism, seven is the number of the holy.

All say aloud: Holy, holy, holy is the LORD of hosts; *Is. 6*
the whole world is filled with His glory.

▸ Then the Ophanim and the Holy Ḥayyot,
with a roar of noise,
raise themselves toward the Seraphim and,
facing them, give praise, saying:

All say aloud: Blessed is the LORD's glory from His place. *Ezek. 3*

לָאֵל To the blessed God they offer melodies.
To the King, living and eternal God,
they say psalms and proclaim praises.
For it is He alone
who does mighty deeds and creates new things,
who is Master of battles, and sows righteousness,
who makes salvation grow and creates cures,
who is revered in praises,
LORD of wonders,
who in His goodness,
continually renews the work of creation, day after day,
as it is said:
"[Praise] Him who made the great lights, *Ps. 136*
for His love endures for ever."
▸ May You make a new light shine over Zion,
and may we all soon be worthy of its light.
Blessed are You, LORD, who forms the radiant lights.

---

renewed daily. The second אַהֲבָה רַבָּה ("You have loved us") is about revelation: the Torah, given in love. The third אֱמֶת וְיַצִּיב ("True and firm") is about redemption.

All say aloud קָדוֹשׁ, קָדוֹשׁ, קָדוֹשׁ יהוה צְבָאוֹת ישעיה ו
מְלֹא כָל־הָאָרֶץ כְּבוֹדוֹ:

‹ וְהָאוֹפַנִּים וְחַיּוֹת הַקֹּדֶשׁ
בְּרַעַשׁ גָּדוֹל מִתְנַשְּׂאִים לְעֻמַּת שְׂרָפִים
לְעֻמָּתָם מְשַׁבְּחִים וְאוֹמְרִים

All say aloud בָּרוּךְ כְּבוֹד־יהוה מִמְּקוֹמוֹ: יחזקאל ג

לְאֵל בָּרוּךְ נְעִימוֹת יִתֵּנוּ, לְמֶלֶךְ אֵל חַי וְקַיָּם
זְמִירוֹת יֹאמֵרוּ וְתִשְׁבָּחוֹת יַשְׁמִיעוּ
כִּי הוּא לְבַדּוֹ
פּוֹעֵל גְּבוּרוֹת, עוֹשֶׂה חֲדָשׁוֹת
בַּעַל מִלְחָמוֹת, זוֹרֵעַ צְדָקוֹת
מַצְמִיחַ יְשׁוּעוֹת, בּוֹרֵא רְפוּאוֹת
נוֹרָא תְהִלּוֹת, אֲדוֹן הַנִּפְלָאוֹת
הַמְחַדֵּשׁ בְּטוּבוֹ בְּכָל יוֹם תָּמִיד מַעֲשֵׂה בְרֵאשִׁית
כָּאָמוּר
לְעֹשֵׂה אוֹרִים גְּדֹלִים, כִּי לְעוֹלָם חַסְדּוֹ: תהלים קלו
‹ אוֹר חָדָשׁ עַל צִיּוֹן תָּאִיר וְנִזְכֶּה כֻלָּנוּ מְהֵרָה לְאוֹרוֹ.
בָּרוּךְ אַתָּה יהוה, יוֹצֵר הַמְּאוֹרוֹת.

---

are three blessings, two before and one after the Shema. Like the morning service as a whole, their themes are creation, revelation and redemption. The first (continuing the theme of the *Pesukei DeZimra*) is about creation,

אַהֲבָה You have loved us with great love, LORD our God,
and with surpassing compassion
have You had compassion on us.
Our Father, our King,
for the sake of our ancestors who trusted in You,
and to whom You taught the laws of life,
be gracious also to us and teach us.
Our Father, compassionate Father,
ever compassionate,
have compassion on us.
Instill in our hearts
the desire to understand and discern,
to listen, learn and teach,
to observe, perform and fulfill
all the teachings of Your Torah in love.
Enlighten our eyes in Your Torah
and let our hearts cling to Your commandments.
Unite our hearts to love and revere Your name,
so that we may never be ashamed.
And because we have trusted
in Your holy, great and revered name,
may we be glad and rejoice in Your salvation.

At this point, gather the four tzitziot of the tallit, holding them in the left hand.

Bring us back in peace from the four quarters of the earth
and lead us upright to our land.
▸ For You are a God who performs acts of salvation,
and You chose us from all peoples and tongues,
bringing us close to Your great name for ever in truth,
that we may thank You
and proclaim Your oneness in love.
Blessed are You, LORD,
who chooses His people Israel in love.

אַהֲבָה רַבָּה אֲהַבְתָּנוּ, יהוה אֱלֹהֵינוּ
חֶמְלָה גְדוֹלָה וִיתֵרָה חָמַלְתָּ עָלֵינוּ.
אָבִינוּ מַלְכֵּנוּ
בַּעֲבוּר אֲבוֹתֵינוּ שֶׁבָּטְחוּ בְךָ
וַתְּלַמְּדֵם חֻקֵּי חַיִּים
כֵּן תְּחָנֵּנוּ וּתְלַמְּדֵנוּ.
אָבִינוּ, הָאָב הָרַחֲמָן, הַמְרַחֵם
רַחֵם עָלֵינוּ
וְתֵן בְּלִבֵּנוּ לְהָבִין וּלְהַשְׂכִּיל
לִשְׁמֹעַ, לִלְמֹד וּלְלַמֵּד, לִשְׁמֹר וְלַעֲשׂוֹת, וּלְקַיֵּם
אֶת כָּל דִּבְרֵי תַלְמוּד תּוֹרָתֶךָ בְּאַהֲבָה.
וְהָאֵר עֵינֵינוּ בְּתוֹרָתֶךָ, וְדַבֵּק לִבֵּנוּ בְּמִצְוֹתֶיךָ
וְיַחֵד לְבָבֵנוּ לְאַהֲבָה וּלְיִרְאָה אֶת שְׁמֶךָ
וְלֹא נֵבוֹשׁ לְעוֹלָם וָעֶד.
כִּי בְשֵׁם קָדְשְׁךָ הַגָּדוֹל וְהַנּוֹרָא בָּטָחְנוּ
נָגִילָה וְנִשְׂמְחָה בִּישׁוּעָתֶךָ.

At this point, gather the four ציציות *of the* טלית*, holding them in the left hand.*

וַהֲבִיאֵנוּ לְשָׁלוֹם מֵאַרְבַּע כַּנְפוֹת הָאָרֶץ
וְתוֹלִיכֵנוּ קוֹמְמִיּוּת לְאַרְצֵנוּ.
◄ כִּי אֵל פּוֹעֵל יְשׁוּעוֹת אָתָּה
וּבָנוּ בָחַרְתָּ מִכָּל עַם וְלָשׁוֹן
וְקֵרַבְתָּנוּ לְשִׁמְךָ הַגָּדוֹל סֶלָה, בֶּאֱמֶת
לְהוֹדוֹת לְךָ וּלְיַחֶדְךָ בְּאַהֲבָה.
בָּרוּךְ אַתָּה יהוה, הַבּוֹחֵר בְּעַמּוֹ יִשְׂרָאֵל בְּאַהֲבָה.

The Shema must be said with intense concentration. In the first paragraph one should accept, with love, the sovereignty of God; in the second, the mitzvot as the will of God. The end of the third paragraph constitutes fulfillment of the mitzva to remember, morning and evening, the exodus from Egypt. See laws 32–41.

When not praying with a minyan, say:

God, faithful King!

The following verse should be said aloud, while covering the eyes with the right hand:

Listen, Israel: the LORD is our God, the LORD is One. *Deut. 6*

Quietly: Blessed be the name of His glorious kingdom for ever and all time.

Touch the hand-tefillin at ° and the head-tefillin at °°.

וְאָהַבְתָּ Love the LORD your God with all your heart, with all your soul, and with all your might. These words which I command you today shall be on your heart. Teach them repeatedly to your children, speaking of them when you sit at home and when you travel on the way, when you lie down and when you rise. °Bind them as a sign on your hand, and °°they shall be an emblem between your eyes. Write them on the doorposts of your house and gates. *Deut. 6*

Touch the hand-tefillin at ° and the head-tefillin at °°.

וְהָיָה If you indeed heed My commandments with which I charge you today, to love the LORD your God and worship Him with all your heart and with all your soul, I will give rain in your land in its season, the early and late rain; and you shall gather in your grain, wine and oil. I will give grass in your field for your cattle, and you shall eat and be satisfied. Be careful lest your heart be tempted and *Deut. 11*

---

biblical readings. It is less a prayer than a prelude to prayer. In prayer, we speak to God. In the Shema, God, through the Torah, speaks to us. The word Shema itself means "listen," and the recital of the Shema is a supreme act of faith-as-listening: to the voice that brought the universe into being, created us in love and guides us through our lives.

The first paragraph represents *kabbalat ol malkhut shamayim*, "acceptance of the yoke of the kingship of heaven." We pledge allegiance to the One God, Sovereign of the universe, to whose authority all earthly powers are answer-

The שמע *must be said with intense concentration. In the first paragraph one should accept, with love, the sovereignty of God; in the second, the* מצוות *as the will of God. The end of the third paragraph constitutes fulfillment of the* מצוה *to remember, morning and evening, the exodus from Egypt. See laws 32–41.*

When not praying with a מנין*, say:*

אֵל מֶלֶךְ נֶאֱמָן

The following verse should be said aloud, while covering the eyes with the right hand:

דברים ו שְׁמַע יִשְׂרָאֵל, יהוה אֱלֹהֵינוּ, יהוה | אֶחָד:

Quietly בָּרוּךְ שֵׁם כְּבוֹד מַלְכוּתוֹ לְעוֹלָם וָעֶד.

Touch the תפילין של יד *at* ° *and the* תפילין של ראש *at* °°.

דברים ו וְאָהַבְתָּ אֵת יהוה אֱלֹהֶיךָ, בְּכָל־לְבָבְךָ וּבְכָל־נַפְשְׁךָ וּבְכָל־
מְאֹדֶךָ: וְהָיוּ הַדְּבָרִים הָאֵלֶּה, אֲשֶׁר אָנֹכִי מְצַוְּךָ הַיּוֹם, עַל־לְבָבֶךָ:
וְשִׁנַּנְתָּם לְבָנֶיךָ וְדִבַּרְתָּ בָּם, בְּשִׁבְתְּךָ בְּבֵיתֶךָ וּבְלֶכְתְּךָ בַדֶּרֶךְ,
וּבְשָׁכְבְּךָ וּבְקוּמֶךָ: °וּקְשַׁרְתָּם לְאוֹת עַל־יָדֶךָ °°וְהָיוּ לְטֹטָפֹת
בֵּין עֵינֶיךָ: וּכְתַבְתָּם עַל־מְזֻזוֹת בֵּיתֶךָ וּבִשְׁעָרֶיךָ:

Touch the תפילין של יד *at* ° *and the* תפילין של ראש *at* °°.

דברים יא וְהָיָה אִם־שָׁמֹעַ תִּשְׁמְעוּ אֶל־מִצְוֺתַי אֲשֶׁר אָנֹכִי מְצַוֶּה אֶתְכֶם
הַיּוֹם, לְאַהֲבָה אֶת־יהוה אֱלֹהֵיכֶם וּלְעָבְדוֹ, בְּכָל־לְבַבְכֶם וּבְכָל־
נַפְשְׁכֶם: וְנָתַתִּי מְטַר־אַרְצְכֶם בְּעִתּוֹ, יוֹרֶה וּמַלְקוֹשׁ, וְאָסַפְתָּ
דְגָנֶךָ וְתִירֹשְׁךָ וְיִצְהָרֶךָ: וְנָתַתִּי עֵשֶׂב בְּשָׂדְךָ לִבְהֶמְתֶּךָ, וְאָכַלְתָּ
וְשָׂבָעְתָּ: הִשָּׁמְרוּ לָכֶם פֶּן־יִפְתֶּה לְבַבְכֶם, וְסַרְתֶּם וַעֲבַדְתֶּם

THE SHEMA

The Shema is the oldest and greatest of our prayers, part of the liturgy since Temple times, recited evening and morning, "when you lie down and when you rise." Its opening line is among the first words taught to a Jewish child, and among the last words spoken by those who went to their deaths because they were Jews. It is the supreme declaration of faith.

The Shema contains no human requests, no praise, no plea. It is a set of you go astray and worship other gods, bowing down to them. Then the LORD's anger will flare against you and He will close the heavens so that there will be no rain. The land will not yield its crops, and you will perish swiftly from the good land that the LORD is giving you. Therefore, set these, My words, on your heart and soul. °Bind them as a sign on your hand, °°and they shall be an emblem between your eyes. Teach them to your children, speaking of them when you sit at home and when you travel on the way, when you lie down and when you rise. Write them on the doorposts of your house and gates, so that you and your children may live long in the land that the LORD swore to your ancestors to give them, for as long as the heavens are above the earth.

Transfer the tzitziot to the right hand, kissing them at °.

וַיֹּאמֶר The LORD spoke to Moses, saying: Speak to the Israelites and tell them to make °tassels on the corners of their garments for all generations. They shall attach to the °tassel at each corner a thread of blue. This shall be your °tassel, and you shall see it and remember all of the LORD's commandments and keep them, not straying after your heart and after your eyes, following your own sinful desires. Thus you will be reminded to keep all My commandments, and be holy to your God. I am the LORD your God, who brought you out of the land of Egypt to be your God. I am the LORD your God. *Num. 15*

°True –

The Leader repeats:

▸ The LORD your God is true –

---

commandments." Whereas the first paragraph speaks to us as individuals, the second speaks to us as a people, defined by our covenant with God and its 613 commandments. "Our nation is only a nation in virtue of its Torah," said Rabbi Sa'adia Gaon, and our collective fate depends on our collective faith. The third paragraph speaks of tzitzit, a perennial reminder of God's commandments. It then leads into the theme of the exodus from Egypt, which we are commanded to remember "all the days of our lives."

אֱלֹהִים אֲחֵרִים וְהִשְׁתַּחֲוִיתֶם לָהֶם: וְחָרָה אַף־יהוה בָּכֶם, וְעָצַר
אֶת־הַשָּׁמַיִם וְלֹא־יִהְיֶה מָטָר, וְהָאֲדָמָה לֹא תִתֵּן אֶת־יְבוּלָהּ,
וַאֲבַדְתֶּם מְהֵרָה מֵעַל הָאָרֶץ הַטֹּבָה אֲשֶׁר יהוה נֹתֵן לָכֶם:
וְשַׂמְתֶּם אֶת־דְּבָרַי אֵלֶּה עַל־לְבַבְכֶם וְעַל־נַפְשְׁכֶם, °וּקְשַׁרְתֶּם
אֹתָם לְאוֹת עַל־יֶדְכֶם, °°וְהָיוּ לְטוֹטָפֹת בֵּין עֵינֵיכֶם: וְלִמַּדְתֶּם
אֹתָם אֶת־בְּנֵיכֶם לְדַבֵּר בָּם, בְּשִׁבְתְּךָ בְּבֵיתֶךָ וּבְלֶכְתְּךָ בַדֶּרֶךְ,
וּבְשָׁכְבְּךָ וּבְקוּמֶךָ: וּכְתַבְתָּם עַל־מְזוּזוֹת בֵּיתֶךָ וּבִשְׁעָרֶיךָ: לְמַעַן
יִרְבּוּ יְמֵיכֶם וִימֵי בְנֵיכֶם עַל הָאֲדָמָה אֲשֶׁר נִשְׁבַּע יהוה לַאֲבֹתֵיכֶם
לָתֵת לָהֶם, כִּימֵי הַשָּׁמַיִם עַל־הָאָרֶץ:

Transfer the ציצית *to the right hand, kissing them at °.*

במדבר טו
וַיֹּאמֶר יהוה אֶל־מֹשֶׁה לֵּאמֹר: דַּבֵּר אֶל־בְּנֵי יִשְׂרָאֵל וְאָמַרְתָּ
אֲלֵהֶם, וְעָשׂוּ לָהֶם °צִיצִת עַל־כַּנְפֵי בִגְדֵיהֶם לְדֹרֹתָם, וְנָתְנוּ
°עַל־צִיצִת הַכָּנָף פְּתִיל תְּכֵלֶת: וְהָיָה לָכֶם °לְצִיצִת, וּרְאִיתֶם
אֹתוֹ וּזְכַרְתֶּם אֶת־כָּל־מִצְוֹת יהוה וַעֲשִׂיתֶם אֹתָם, וְלֹא תָתוּרוּ
אַחֲרֵי לְבַבְכֶם וְאַחֲרֵי עֵינֵיכֶם, אֲשֶׁר־אַתֶּם זֹנִים אַחֲרֵיהֶם: לְמַעַן
תִּזְכְּרוּ וַעֲשִׂיתֶם אֶת־כָּל־מִצְוֹתָי, וִהְיִיתֶם קְדֹשִׁים לֵאלֹהֵיכֶם: אֲנִי
יהוה אֱלֹהֵיכֶם, אֲשֶׁר הוֹצֵאתִי אֶתְכֶם מֵאֶרֶץ מִצְרַיִם, לִהְיוֹת לָכֶם
לֵאלֹהִים, אֲנִי יהוה אֱלֹהֵיכֶם:

אֱמֶת°

The שליח ציבור *repeats:*

‹ יהוה אֱלֹהֵיכֶם אֱמֶת

---

able. We do so not in fear but in love and with the totality of our being: all our heart, our soul, our might. That love suffuses all we do, from our relationships with our children to the homes we make.

The second paragraph represents *kabbalat ol mitzvot,* "acceptance of the

וְיַצִּיב And firm, established and enduring,
right, faithful,
beloved, cherished, delightful, pleasant,
awesome, mighty, perfect, accepted,
good and beautiful
is this faith for us for ever.

True is the eternal God, our King,
Rock of Jacob,
Shield of our salvation.
He exists and His name exists
through all generations.
His throne is established,
His kingship and faithfulness endure for ever.

At °, kiss the tzitziot and release them.

His words live and persist,
faithful and desirable
°for ever and all time.

▸ So they were for our ancestors,
so they are for us,
and so they will be for our children
and all our generations
and for all future generations
of the seed of Israel, Your servants. ◂
For the early and the later generations
this faith has proved good and enduring for ever –
True and faithful, an irrevocable law.

Israel," and the beginning of the Amida (*Berakhot* 14b, 9b). The connection between the two is *redemption*, the theme of this section. The Shema ends by speaking about redemption in the past. In the Amida we pray for redemption in the future. Connecting past and future is "truth" – our faith in God and in His covenant with us.

וְיַצִּיב, וְנָכוֹן וְקַיָּם, וְיָשָׁר וְנֶאֱמָן
וְאָהוּב וְחָבִיב, וְנֶחְמָד וְנָעִים
וְנוֹרָא וְאַדִּיר, וּמְתֻקָּן וּמְקֻבָּל
וְטוֹב וְיָפֶה
הַדָּבָר הַזֶּה עָלֵינוּ לְעוֹלָם וָעֶד.
אֱמֶת אֱלֹהֵי עוֹלָם מַלְכֵּנוּ
צוּר יַעֲקֹב מָגֵן יִשְׁעֵנוּ
לְדוֹר וָדוֹר הוּא קַיָּם וּשְׁמוֹ קַיָּם
וְכִסְאוֹ נָכוֹן
וּמַלְכוּתוֹ וֶאֱמוּנָתוֹ לָעַד קַיָּמֶת.

At °, kiss the ציציות *and release them.*

וּדְבָרָיו חָיִים וְקַיָּמִים
נֶאֱמָנִים וְנֶחֱמָדִים
°לָעַד וּלְעוֹלְמֵי עוֹלָמִים
◂ עַל אֲבוֹתֵינוּ וְעָלֵינוּ
עַל בָּנֵינוּ וְעַל דּוֹרוֹתֵינוּ
וְעַל כָּל דּוֹרוֹת זֶרַע יִשְׂרָאֵל עֲבָדֶיךָ. ◂
עַל הָרִאשׁוֹנִים וְעַל הָאַחֲרוֹנִים
דָּבָר טוֹב וְקַיָּם לְעוֹלָם וָעֶד
אֱמֶת וֶאֱמוּנָה, חֹק וְלֹא יַעֲבֹר.

וְיַצִּיב *And firm:* This section of prayer, joining the Shema to the Amida, goes back to Temple times. The sages emphasized that there must be no separation between the last words of the Shema, "I am the LORD your God," and the first word of the prayer, "*True* and firm," or between its last words, "who redeemed

True You are the LORD: our God and God of our ancestors,
▸ our King and King of our ancestors,
our Redeemer and Redeemer of our ancestors,
our Maker,
Rock of our salvation,
our Deliverer and Rescuer:
this has ever been Your name.
There is no God but You.

עֶזְרַת You have always been the help of our ancestors,
Shield and Savior of their children after them
in every generation.
Your dwelling is in the heights of the universe,
and Your judgments and righteousness
reach to the ends of the earth.
Happy is the one who obeys Your commandments
and takes to heart Your teaching and Your word.
True You are the Master of Your people
and a mighty King who pleads their cause.
True You are the first and You are the last.
Besides You, we have no king,
redeemer or savior.
From Egypt You redeemed us,
LORD our God,
and from the slave-house You delivered us.
All their firstborn You killed,
but Your firstborn You redeemed.
You split the Sea of Reeds
and drowned the arrogant.
You brought Your beloved ones across.
The water covered their foes; *Ps. 106*
not one of them was left.

אֱמֶת שָׁאַתָּה הוּא יהוה אֱלֹהֵינוּ וֵאלֹהֵי אֲבוֹתֵינוּ
› מַלְכֵּנוּ מֶלֶךְ אֲבוֹתֵינוּ
גּוֹאֲלֵנוּ גּוֹאֵל אֲבוֹתֵינוּ
יוֹצְרֵנוּ צוּר יְשׁוּעָתֵנוּ
פּוֹדֵנוּ וּמַצִּילֵנוּ מֵעוֹלָם שְׁמֶךָ
אֵין אֱלֹהִים זוּלָתֶךָ.

עֶזְרַת אֲבוֹתֵינוּ אַתָּה הוּא מֵעוֹלָם
מָגֵן וּמוֹשִׁיעַ לִבְנֵיהֶם אַחֲרֵיהֶם בְּכָל דּוֹר וָדוֹר.
בְּרוּם עוֹלָם מוֹשָׁבֶךָ
וּמִשְׁפָּטֶיךָ וְצִדְקָתְךָ עַד אַפְסֵי אָרֶץ.
אַשְׁרֵי אִישׁ שֶׁיִּשְׁמַע לְמִצְוֹתֶיךָ
וְתוֹרָתְךָ וּדְבָרְךָ יָשִׂים עַל לִבּוֹ.
אֱמֶת אַתָּה הוּא אָדוֹן לְעַמֶּךָ
וּמֶלֶךְ גִּבּוֹר לָרִיב רִיבָם.
אֱמֶת אַתָּה הוּא רִאשׁוֹן וְאַתָּה הוּא אַחֲרוֹן
וּמִבַּלְעָדֶיךָ אֵין לָנוּ מֶלֶךְ גּוֹאֵל וּמוֹשִׁיעַ.
מִמִּצְרַיִם גְּאַלְתָּנוּ, יהוה אֱלֹהֵינוּ
וּמִבֵּית עֲבָדִים פְּדִיתָנוּ
כָּל בְּכוֹרֵיהֶם הָרַגְתָּ, וּבְכוֹרְךָ גָּאָלְתָּ
וְיַם סוּף בָּקַעְתָּ
וְזֵדִים טִבַּעְתָּ
וִידִידִים הֶעֱבַרְתָּ
וַיְכַסּוּ־מַיִם צָרֵיהֶם, אֶחָד מֵהֶם לֹא נוֹתָר: תהלים קו

For this, the beloved ones praised and exalted God,
the cherished ones sang psalms, songs and praises,
blessings and thanksgivings to the King,
the living and enduring God.
High and exalted, great and awesome,
He humbles the haughty and raises the lowly,
freeing captives and redeeming those in need,
helping the poor
and answering His people when they cry out to Him.

Stand in preparation for the Amida. Take three steps back before beginning the Amida.

▸ Praises to God Most High,
the Blessed One who is blessed.
Moses and the children of Israel
recited to You a song with great joy,
and they all exclaimed:
"Who is like You, LORD, among the mighty? *Ex. 15*
Who is like You, majestic in holiness,
awesome in praises, doing wonders?"

▸ With a new song, the redeemed people praised
Your name at the seashore.
Together they all gave thanks,
proclaimed Your kingship,
and declared:
"The LORD shall reign for ever and ever." *Ex. 15*

Congregants should end the following blessing together with the Leader so as to be able to move directly from the words "redeemed Israel" to the Amida, without the interruption of saying Amen.

▸ צוּר יִשְׂרָאֵל Rock of Israel! Arise to the help of Israel.
Deliver, as You promised, Judah and Israel.
Our Redeemer, the LORD of hosts is His name, *Is. 47*
the Holy One of Israel.
Blessed are You, LORD, who redeemed Israel.

עַל זֹאת שִׁבְּחוּ אֲהוּבִים, וְרוֹמְמוּ אֵל
וְנָתְנוּ יְדִידִים זְמִירוֹת, שִׁירוֹת וְתִשְׁבָּחוֹת
בְּרָכוֹת וְהוֹדָאוֹת לַמֶּלֶךְ אֵל חַי וְקַיָּם
רָם וְנִשָּׂא, גָּדוֹל וְנוֹרָא
מַשְׁפִּיל גֵּאִים וּמַגְבִּיהַּ שְׁפָלִים
מוֹצִיא אֲסִירִים, וּפוֹדֶה עֲנָוִים וְעוֹזֵר דַּלִּים
וְעוֹנֶה לְעַמּוֹ בְּעֵת שַׁוְּעָם אֵלָיו.

Stand in preparation for the עמידה*. Take three steps back before beginning the* עמידה*.*

◂ תְּהִלּוֹת לְאֵל עֶלְיוֹן, בָּרוּךְ הוּא וּמְבֹרָךְ
מֹשֶׁה וּבְנֵי יִשְׂרָאֵל
לְךָ עָנוּ שִׁירָה בְּשִׂמְחָה רַבָּה
וְאָמְרוּ כֻלָּם

שמות טו מִי־כָמֹכָה בָּאֵלִם, יהוה
מִי כָּמֹכָה נֶאְדָּר בַּקֹּדֶשׁ, נוֹרָא תְהִלֹּת, עֹשֵׂה פֶלֶא:

◂ שִׁירָה חֲדָשָׁה שִׁבְּחוּ גְאוּלִים
לְשִׁמְךָ עַל שְׂפַת הַיָּם
יַחַד כֻּלָּם הוֹדוּ וְהִמְלִיכוּ
וְאָמְרוּ

שמות טו יהוה יִמְלֹךְ לְעֹלָם וָעֶד:

The קהל *should end the following blessing together with the* שליח ציבור *so as to be able to move directly from the words* גָּאַל יִשְׂרָאֵל *to the* עמידה*, without the interruption of saying* אמן*.*

◂ צוּר יִשְׂרָאֵל, קוּמָה בְּעֶזְרַת יִשְׂרָאֵל
וּפְדֵה כִנְאֻמֶךָ יְהוּדָה וְיִשְׂרָאֵל.

ישעיה מז גֹּאֲלֵנוּ יהוה צְבָאוֹת שְׁמוֹ, קְדוֹשׁ יִשְׂרָאֵל:
בָּרוּךְ אַתָּה יהוה, גָּאַל יִשְׂרָאֵל.

THE AMIDA

The following prayer, until "in former years" on page 134, is said standing with feet together in imitation of the angels in Ezekiel's vision (Ezek. 1:7). The Amida is said silently, following the precedent of Hannah when she prayed for a child (1 Sam. 1:13). If there is a minyan, it is repeated aloud by the Leader. Take three steps forward, as if formally entering the place of the Divine Presence. At the points indicated by ▾, bend the knees at the first word, bow at the second, and stand straight before saying God's name.

O LORD, open my lips, *Ps. 51*
so that my mouth may declare Your praise.

PATRIARCHS

▾בָּרוּךְ Blessed are You, LORD our God and God of our fathers,
God of Abraham, God of Isaac and God of Jacob;
the great, mighty and awesome God, God Most High,
who bestows acts of loving-kindness and creates all,
who remembers the loving-kindness of the fathers and will bring
a Redeemer to their children's children
for the sake of His name, in love.

Between Rosh HaShana & Yom Kippur: Remember us for life, O King who desires life,
and write us in the book of life –
for Your sake, O God of life.

King, Helper, Savior, Shield:
▾Blessed are You, LORD, Shield of Abraham.

Several centuries later, it was canonized in a fuller form by Shimon HaPakuli in the days of Rabban Gamliel II (*Berakhot* 28b).

It is often called the *Shemoneh Esreh*, "Eighteen," because it originally consisted of eighteen blessings (now, nineteen). It has a three-part structure: (1) *praise* (blessings 1–3), (2) *requests* (blessings 4–16), and (3) *thanks* (17–19). Each of these has a tripartite form. The first and last sections each contain three blessings. The middle section is composed of twelve blessings (4–15), six personal requests and six collective ones. The first three personal requests are for spiritual goods (wisdom, repentance and forgiveness). The second are for physical goods (deliverance, healing and livelihood). The first three national requests are for physical events (ingathering of exiles, justice, and an end to internal conflicts). The second three are for the nation's spiritual needs

עמידה

The following prayer, until קַדְמֹנִיּוֹת *on page 135, is said standing with feet together in imitation of the angels in Ezekiel's vision* (יחזקאל א, ז)*. The* עמידה *is said silently, following the precedent of Hannah when she prayed for a child* (שמואל א׳ א, יג)*. If there is a* מנין*, it is repeated aloud by the* שליח ציבור*. Take three steps forward, as if formally entering the place of the Divine Presence. At the points indicated by* ▾*, bend the knees at the first word, bow at the second, and stand straight before saying God's name.*

אֲדֹנָי, שְׂפָתַי תִּפְתָּח, וּפִי יַגִּיד תְּהִלָּתֶךָ: תהלים נא

אבות

▾בָּרוּךְ אַתָּה יהוה, אֱלֹהֵינוּ וֵאלֹהֵי אֲבוֹתֵינוּ
אֱלֹהֵי אַבְרָהָם, אֱלֹהֵי יִצְחָק, וֵאלֹהֵי יַעֲקֹב
הָאֵל הַגָּדוֹל הַגִּבּוֹר וְהַנּוֹרָא, אֵל עֶלְיוֹן
גּוֹמֵל חֲסָדִים טוֹבִים, וְקוֹנֵה הַכֹּל
וְזוֹכֵר חַסְדֵי אָבוֹת
וּמֵבִיא גוֹאֵל לִבְנֵי בְנֵיהֶם לְמַעַן שְׁמוֹ בְּאַהֲבָה.

בעשרת ימי תשובה: זָכְרֵנוּ לְחַיִּים, מֶלֶךְ חָפֵץ בַּחַיִּים
וְכָתְבֵנוּ בְּסֵפֶר הַחַיִּים, לְמַעַנְךָ אֱלֹהִים חַיִּים.

מֶלֶךְ עוֹזֵר וּמוֹשִׁיעַ וּמָגֵן.
▾בָּרוּךְ אַתָּה יהוה, מָגֵן אַבְרָהָם.

THE AMIDA: THE STANDING PRAYER

The Amida is the summit of prayer: in it, we enter the holy of holies of religious experience. We say it standing because we are conscious of being in the unmediated presence of God. The name Amida is also related to its earliest setting: prayers said by the people of the *Ma'amad*, groups of laymen who, in Second Temple times, accompanied their local "watch" (*mishmar*) of priests who officiated in the Temple on a one-in-24-week schedule. The *Ma'amad* was one of the prototypes of congregational prayer.

According to tradition, the Amida in embryonic form dates back to the Great Assembly in the time of Ezra following the Jews' return from Babylon.

DIVINE MIGHT

אַתָּה גִּבּוֹר You are eternally mighty, LORD.
You give life to the dead and have great power to save.

The phrase "He makes the wind blow and the rain fall" is said from Simḥat Torah until Pesaḥ. In Israel the phrase "He causes the dew to fall" is said from Pesaḥ until Shemini Atzeret. See laws 49–51.

In fall & winter: He makes the wind blow and the rain fall.
In Israel, in spring & summer: He causes the dew to fall.

He sustains the living with loving-kindness,
and with great compassion revives the dead.
He supports the fallen, heals the sick,
sets captives free,
and keeps His faith with those who sleep in the dust.
Who is like You, Master of might,
and to whom can You be compared,
O King who brings death and gives life,
and makes salvation grow?

Between Rosh HaShana & Yom Kippur: Who is like You, compassionate Father,
who remembers His creatures in compassion, for life?

Faithful are You to revive the dead.
Blessed are You, LORD, who revives the dead.

---

who was the first person to heed God's call. לְמַעַנְךָ אֱלֹהִים חַיִּים *For Your sake, O* God *of life:* the phrase literally means "Living God." The translation, however, conveys the poetic structure of this short but powerful prayer: four phrases, each ending with the word *ḥayim*, "life."

גבורות *Blessing 2: Divine might.* The fivefold reference to the resurrection of the dead reflects the controversy between the Sadducees and Pharisees in the late Second Temple era. The Sadducees rejected belief in resurrection; the Pharisees, whose heirs we are, affirmed it. Belief that those who died will one day live again is one of Judaism's great principles of hope, set out in the vision of Ezekiel of the valley of dry bones that came to life once more. Jews kept hope alive; hope kept the Jewish people alive.

גבורות

אַתָּה גִּבּוֹר לְעוֹלָם, אֲדֹנָי
מְחַיֵּה מֵתִים אַתָּה, רַב לְהוֹשִׁיעַ

The phrase מַשִּׁיב הָרְוּחַ *is said from* שמחת תורה *until* פסח.
In ארץ ישראל *the phrase* מוֹרִיד הַטָּל *is said from* פסח *until* שמיני עצרת. *See laws 49–51.*

בחורף: מַשִּׁיב הָרְוּחַ וּמוֹרִיד הַגֶּשֶׁם / בארץ ישראל בקיץ: מוֹרִיד הַטָּל

מְכַלְכֵּל חַיִּים בְּחֶסֶד, מְחַיֵּה מֵתִים בְּרַחֲמִים רַבִּים
סוֹמֵךְ נוֹפְלִים, וְרוֹפֵא חוֹלִים, וּמַתִּיר אֲסוּרִים
וּמְקַיֵּם אֱמוּנָתוֹ לִישֵׁנֵי עָפָר.
מִי כָמְוֹךָ, בַּעַל גְּבוּרוֹת
וּמִי דּוֹמֶה לָּךְ
מֶלֶךְ, מֵמִית וּמְחַיֶּה וּמַצְמִיחַ יְשׁוּעָה.

בעשרת ימי תשובה: מִי כָמְוֹךָ אַב הָרַחֲמִים
זוֹכֵר יְצוּרָיו לְחַיִּים בְּרַחֲמִים.

וְנֶאֱמָן אַתָּה לְהַחֲיוֹת מֵתִים.
בָּרוּךְ אַתָּה יהוה, מְחַיֵּה הַמֵּתִים.

(the righteous and pious, the rebuilding of Jerusalem, and the restoration of the Davidic monarchy). One blessing, "Listen to our voice" (the sixteenth, last of the "request" blessings), stands outside this structure because it is a prayer about prayer itself. It is also the point at which individuals can add their personal requests.

אבות *Blessing 1: Patriarchs.* In these opening chords we refer back to the dawn of our people's history – the days of the patriarchs, Abraham, Isaac and Jacob. In so doing, we echo Moses, who constantly referred to the patriarchs when praying for forgiveness for the people. God's love for, and covenant with, those who first heard His call is the supreme ground on which we stand when we turn to Him in prayer. The paragraph ends with a reference to Abraham,

When saying the Amida silently, continue with "You are holy" on the next page.

KEDUSHA

During the Leader's Repetition, the following is said standing with feet together, rising on the toes at the words indicated by ▴.

Cong. then Leader: נְקַדֵּשׁ We will sanctify Your name on earth,
as they sanctify it in the highest heavens,
as is written by Your prophet,
"And they [the angels] call to one another saying: *Is. 6*

Cong. then Leader: ▴Holy, ▴holy, ▴holy is the LORD of hosts
the whole world is filled with His glory."
Those facing them say "Blessed – "

Cong. then Leader: ▴"Blessed is the LORD's glory from His place." *Ezek. 3*
And in Your holy Writings it is written thus:

Cong. then Leader: ▴"The LORD shall reign for ever. He is your God, Zion, *Ps. 146*
from generation to generation, Halleluya!"

Leader: From generation to generation we will declare Your greatness,
and we will proclaim Your holiness for evermore.
Your praise, our God, shall not leave our mouth forever,
for You, God, are a great and holy King. Blessed are You, LORD,
the holy God. / *Between Rosh HaShana & Yom Kippur:* the holy King./

The Leader continues with "You grace humanity" on the next page.

do not require a *minyan* and are said sitting. The second requires a *minyan* and is said standing. The reason is that the first and third are descriptions of the song of the angels; the second is a reenactment. We stand, feet together, rising on our toes, as if we too were angels.

In the *Kedusha* we move beyond the priestly prayer-as-sacrifice and the prophetic prayer-as-dialogue, to prayer as a mystic experience. So holy is it that in Israel in ancient times it was said only on Shabbat and festivals. The *Zohar* interprets Jacob's vision of a ladder stretching from earth to heaven, with angels ascending and descending (Gen. 28:12), as a metaphor for prayer, and this, too, is part of the meaning of *Kedusha*. We have climbed the ladder from earth to heaven. As the Leader repeats the prayer on behalf of the entire community, we reach the summit of religious experience.

When saying the עמידה *silently, continue with* אַתָּה קָדוֹשׁ *on the next page.*

קדושה

During חזרת הש״ץ, *the following is said standing with feet together, rising on the toes at the words indicated by* ·.

then קהל ש״ץ: נְקַדֵּשׁ אֶת שִׁמְךָ בָּעוֹלָם, כְּשֵׁם שֶׁמַּקְדִּישִׁים אוֹתוֹ בִּשְׁמֵי מָרוֹם
כַּכָּתוּב עַל יַד נְבִיאֶךָ, וְקָרָא זֶה אֶל־זֶה וְאָמַר ישעיה ו

then קהל ש״ץ: ·קָדוֹשׁ, ·קָדוֹשׁ, ·קָדוֹשׁ, יהוה צְבָאוֹת, מְלֹא כָל־הָאָרֶץ כְּבוֹדוֹ:
לְעֻמָּתָם בָּרוּךְ יֹאמֵרוּ

then קהל ש״ץ: ·בָּרוּךְ כְּבוֹד־יהוה מִמְּקוֹמוֹ: יחזקאל ג
וּבְדִבְרֵי קָדְשְׁךָ כָּתוּב לֵאמֹר

then קהל ש״ץ: ·יִמְלֹךְ יהוה לְעוֹלָם, אֱלֹהַיִךְ צִיּוֹן לְדֹר וָדֹר, הַלְלוּיָהּ: תהלים קמו

ש״ץ: לְדוֹר וָדוֹר נַגִּיד גָּדְלֶךָ, וּלְנֵצַח נְצָחִים קְדֻשָּׁתְךָ נַקְדִּישׁ
וְשִׁבְחֲךָ אֱלֹהֵינוּ מִפִּינוּ לֹא יָמוּשׁ לְעוֹלָם וָעֶד
כִּי אֵל מֶלֶךְ גָּדוֹל וְקָדוֹשׁ אָתָּה.
בָּרוּךְ אַתָּה יהוה, הָאֵל הַקָּדוֹשׁ./בעשרת ימי תשובה: הַמֶּלֶךְ הַקָּדוֹשׁ./

The שליח ציבור *continues with* אַתָּה חוֹנֵן *on the next page.*

קדושה *Kedusha.* The *Kedusha* is the supreme moment of holiness in prayer. It takes several different forms. Common to them all is that they are built around the two supreme mystical visions in the Hebrew Bible, of Isaiah (chapter 6) and Ezekiel (chapters 1–3). The prophet sees God enthroned in glory, surrounded by angels singing His praises. Isaiah hears them singing, "Holy, holy, holy is the LORD of hosts; the whole world is filled with His glory." Ezekiel (3:12) hears them singing, "Blessed is the LORD's glory from His place." Together they constitute the most sublime expression of prayer as praise in the presence of God.

In the morning, *Kedusha* is said three times at different points in the service. There is *Kedushat Yotzer,* which appears in the first of the three Shema blessings (page 95), *Kedusha DeAmida,* said here during the Leader's Repetition; and *Kedusha DeSidra,* toward the end of the service. The first and third

HOLINESS

אַתָּה קָדוֹשׁ You are holy and Your name is holy,
and holy ones praise You daily, Selah!
Blessed are You, LORD,
the holy God. / *Between Rosh HaShana & Yom Kippur:* the holy King./
(If forgotten, repeat the Amida.)

KNOWLEDGE

אַתָּה חוֹנֵן You grace humanity with knowledge
and teach mortals understanding.
Grace us with the knowledge, understanding
and discernment that come from You.
Blessed are You, LORD, who graciously grants knowledge.

REPENTANCE

הֲשִׁיבֵנוּ Bring us back, our Father,
to Your Torah.
Draw us near, our King,
to Your service.
Lead us back to You in perfect repentance.
Blessed are You, LORD, who desires repentance.

דעת *Blessing 4: Knowledge.* This is the first of the "request" blessings. King Solomon, when asked by God to name the thing he most desired (1 Kings 3:5–15), asked for wisdom; so do we. Knowledge is prior to emotion, because "the heart is deceitful above all things" (Jer. 17:9). Untutored emotion can be misdirected, even destructive.

This paragraph replicates the structure of the Amida as a whole. It begins with praise ("You grace humanity with knowledge"), proceeds to request ("Grace us with the knowledge"), and ends in acknowledgment ("Who graciously grants knowledge").

תשובה *Blessing 5: Repentance.* Knowledge and understanding allow us to see where we have drifted from the right path of life. So we ask God to help us find the way back to repentance.

קדושת השם

אַתָּה קָדוֹשׁ וְשִׁמְךָ קָדוֹשׁ
וּקְדוֹשִׁים בְּכָל יוֹם יְהַלְלוּךָ סֶּלָה.
בָּרוּךְ אַתָּה יהוה, הָאֵל הַקָּדוֹשׁ./ בעשרת ימי תשובה: הַמֶּלֶךְ הַקָּדוֹשׁ./
(*If forgotten, repeat the* עמידה.)

דעת

אַתָּה חוֹנֵן לְאָדָם דַּעַת
וּמְלַמֵּד לֶאֱנוֹשׁ בִּינָה.
חָנֵּנוּ מֵאִתְּךָ דֵּעָה בִּינָה וְהַשְׂכֵּל.
בָּרוּךְ אַתָּה יהוה, חוֹנֵן הַדָּעַת.

תשובה

הֲשִׁיבֵנוּ אָבִינוּ לְתוֹרָתֶךָ
וְקָרְבֵנוּ מַלְכֵּנוּ לַעֲבוֹדָתֶךָ
וְהַחֲזִירֵנוּ בִּתְשׁוּבָה שְׁלֵמָה לְפָנֶיךָ.
בָּרוּךְ אַתָּה יהוה, הָרוֹצֶה בִּתְשׁוּבָה.

קדושת השם *Blessing 3: Holiness.* The threefold reference to holiness ("You are holy and Your name is holy, and holy ones praise You daily") mirrors the threefold declaration of the angels in Isaiah's vision: "Holy, holy, holy is the LORD of hosts." *Kadosh*, "holy," means "set apart, distinct." When used of God, it refers to His transcendence, the fact that He stands outside nature, creating and sustaining it. When used of Israel, it means that we too are summoned to stand apart from the idols of the age, living instead in close and continuous proximity to God.

The first three paragraphs of the Amida (excluding the *Kedusha*), form a composite unit. The first speaks of the beginning of covenantal time in the days of the patriarchs. The second is about the end of time: resurrection. The third is about holiness, beyond space and time.

FORGIVENESS

Strike the left side of the chest at °.

סְלַח לָנוּ Forgive us, our Father, for we have °sinned.
Pardon us, our King, for we have °transgressed;
for You pardon and forgive.
Blessed are You, LORD, the gracious One who repeatedly forgives.

REDEMPTION

רְאֵה Look on our affliction, plead our cause,
and redeem us soon for Your name's sake,
for You are a powerful Redeemer.
Blessed are You, LORD, the Redeemer of Israel.

On Fast Days the Leader adds:

עֲנֵנוּ Answer us, LORD, answer us on our Fast Day, for we are in great distress. Look not at our wickedness. Do not hide Your face from us and do not ignore our plea. Be near to our cry; please let Your loving-kindness comfort us. Even before we call to You, answer us, as is said, "Before they call, I will *Is. 65*
answer. While they are still speaking, I will hear." For You, LORD, are the One who answers in time of distress, redeems and rescues in all times of trouble and anguish. Blessed are You, LORD, who answers in time of distress.

---

or affliction. Rabbi Samson Raphael Hirsch distinguishes between the first two phrases thus: "Look on our affliction" refers to suffering not caused by others, while "Plead our cause" refers to those who seek our harm. Rational argument is often insufficient to cure hatred; therefore we place our fate in the hands of God, asking Him to heal hostility (Rabbi J.H. Hertz). לְמַעַן שְׁמֶךָ *For Your name's sake:* may we be spared suffering not for our own sake but so that we may be free to worship You without distraction (Rabbi Yaakov Tzvi Mecklenburg). גּוֹאֵל יִשְׂרָאֵל *Redeemer of Israel:* in the present, as opposed to the blessing immediately prior to the Amida, which refers to acts of divine redemption in the past.

עֲנֵנוּ *Answer us:* A special prayer to be said on public fasts (*Ta'anit* 11a). The Leader recites it at this point in the Repetition of the Amida.

סליחה

Strike the left side of the chest at °.

סְלַח לָנוּ אָבִינוּ כִּי °חָטָאנוּ
מְחַל לָנוּ מַלְכֵּנוּ כִּי °פָשָׁעְנוּ
כִּי מוֹחֵל וְסוֹלֵחַ אָתָּה.
בָּרוּךְ אַתָּה יהוה, חַנּוּן הַמַּרְבֶּה לִסְלֹחַ.

גאולה

רְאֵה בְעָנְיֵנוּ, וְרִיבָה רִיבֵנוּ
וּגְאָלֵנוּ מְהֵרָה לְמַעַן שְׁמֶךָ
כִּי גּוֹאֵל חָזָק אָתָּה.
בָּרוּךְ אַתָּה יהוה, גּוֹאֵל יִשְׂרָאֵל.

On Fast Days the שליח ציבור *adds:*

עֲנֵנוּ יהוה עֲנֵנוּ בְּיוֹם צוֹם תַּעֲנִיתֵנוּ, כִּי בְצָרָה גְדוֹלָה אֲנָחְנוּ. אַל תֵּפֶן אֶל
רִשְׁעֵנוּ, וְאַל תַּסְתֵּר פָּנֶיךָ מִמֶּנּוּ, וְאַל תִּתְעַלַּם מִתְּחִנָּתֵנוּ. הֱיֵה נָא קָרוֹב
לְשַׁוְעָתֵנוּ, יְהִי נָא חַסְדְּךָ לְנַחֲמֵנוּ, טֶרֶם נִקְרָא אֵלֶיךָ עֲנֵנוּ, כַּדָּבָר שֶׁנֶּאֱמַר:
וְהָיָה טֶרֶם יִקְרָאוּ וַאֲנִי אֶעֱנֶה, עוֹד הֵם מְדַבְּרִים וַאֲנִי אֶשְׁמָע: כִּי אַתָּה יהוה ישעיה סה
הָעוֹנֶה בְּעֵת צָרָה, פּוֹדֶה וּמַצִּיל בְּכָל עֵת צָרָה וְצוּקָה. בָּרוּךְ אַתָּה יהוה,
הָעוֹנֶה בְּעֵת צָרָה.

סליחה *Blessing 6: Forgiveness.* Repentance involves asking God to forgive us. This applies to sins between us and God. Sins between us and our fellow human beings are only forgiven when we have apologized to, and tried to obtain the forgiveness of, those we have wronged. Knowledge, repentance and forgiveness are the three primary needs of the mind and soul.

גאולה *Blessing 7: Redemption.* The commentators explain that this request is not for national redemption, the subject of later blessings. Here the reference is to release from personal crises: captivity, persecution, misfortune

HEALING

רְפָאֵנוּ Heal us, LORD, and we shall be healed.
Save us and we shall be saved,
for You are our praise.
Bring complete recovery for all our ailments,

The following prayer for a sick person may be said here:
May it be Your will, O LORD my God and God of my ancestors, that You speedily send a complete recovery from heaven, a healing of both soul and body, to the patient (*name*), son/daughter of (*mother's name*) among the other afflicted of Israel.

for You, God, King, are a faithful and compassionate Healer.
Blessed are You, LORD, Healer of the sick of His people Israel.

PROSPERITY

The phrase "Grant dew and rain as a blessing" is said from December 5th (in the year before a civil leap year, December 6th) until Pesaḥ. In Israel, it is said from the 7th of Marḥeshvan. The phrase "Grant blessing" is said from Ḥol HaMo'ed Pesaḥ until December 4th (in the year before a civil leap year, December 5th). In Israel it is said through the 6th of Marḥeshvan. See laws 52–54.

בָּרֵךְ Bless this year for us, LORD our God,
and all its types of produce for good.

In winter: Grant dew and rain as a blessing
In other seasons: Grant blessing

on the face of the earth,
and from its goodness satisfy us,
blessing our year as the best of years.
Blessed are You, LORD, who blesses the years.

teaches its inhabitants the need for prayer. וְתֵן טַל וּמָטָר *Grant dew and rain:* unlike the praise "He makes the wind blow and the rain fall" (page 110), which we begin saying on Shemini Atzeret, the actual prayer for rain is said later to coincide with the rainy season itself. Outside Israel, it is said from the sixtieth day after "*Tekufat Tishrei*," the Jewish equivalent of the fall equinox (in the Northern Hemisphere).

רפואה

רְפָאֵנוּ יהוה וְנֵרָפֵא
הוֹשִׁיעֵנוּ וְנִוָּשֵׁעָה, כִּי תְהִלָּתֵנוּ אָתָּה
וְהַעֲלֵה רְפוּאָה שְׁלֵמָה לְכָל מַכּוֹתֵינוּ

The following prayer for a sick person may be said here:

יְהִי רָצוֹן מִלְּפָנֶיךָ יהוה אֱלֹהַי וֵאלֹהֵי אֲבוֹתַי, שֶׁתִּשְׁלַח מְהֵרָה רְפוּאָה שְׁלֵמָה
מִן הַשָּׁמַיִם רְפוּאַת הַנֶּפֶשׁ וּרְפוּאַת הַגּוּף לַחוֹלֶה/לַחוֹלָה *name of patient*
בֶּן/בַּת *mother's name* בְּתוֹךְ שְׁאָר חוֹלֵי יִשְׂרָאֵל.

כִּי אֵל מֶלֶךְ רוֹפֵא נֶאֱמָן וְרַחֲמָן אָתָּה.
בָּרוּךְ אַתָּה יהוה, רוֹפֵא חוֹלֵי עַמּוֹ יִשְׂרָאֵל.

ברכת השנים

The phrase וְתֵן טַל וּמָטָר לִבְרָכָה *is said from December 5th (in the year before a civil leap year, December 6th) until* פסח. *In* ארץ ישראל, *it is said from* ז׳ מרחשון. *The phrase* וְתֵן בְּרָכָה *is said from* חול המועד פסח *until December 4th (in the year before a civil leap year, December 5th). In* ארץ ישראל *it is said through* ו׳ מרחשון. *See laws 52–54.*

בָּרֵךְ עָלֵינוּ יהוה אֱלֹהֵינוּ אֶת הַשָּׁנָה הַזֹּאת
וְאֶת כָּל מִינֵי תְבוּאָתָהּ, לְטוֹבָה
בחורף: וְתֵן טַל וּמָטָר לִבְרָכָה / בקיץ: וְתֵן בְּרָכָה
עַל פְּנֵי הָאֲדָמָה, וְשַׂבְּעֵנוּ מִטּוּבָהּ
וּבָרֵךְ שְׁנָתֵנוּ כַּשָּׁנִים הַטּוֹבוֹת.
בָּרוּךְ אַתָּה יהוה, מְבָרֵךְ הַשָּׁנִים.

רפואה *Blessing 8: Healing.* We pray that medical treatment be successful, and that God Himself be part of the healing process. We are both body and soul: the health of one affects that of the other.

ברכת השנים *Blessing 9: Prosperity.* We pray for God's blessing on our efforts to earn a livelihood. Israel's agriculture depends on rain, so this blessing includes – during the winter months – a prayer for rain. Israel is a land that

INGATHERING OF EXILES

תְּקַע Sound the great shofar for our freedom,
raise high the banner to gather our exiles,
and gather us together from the four quarters of the earth.
Blessed are You, LORD,
who gathers the dispersed of His people Israel.

JUSTICE

הָשִׁיבָה Restore our judges as at first,
and our counselors as at the beginning,
and remove from us sorrow and sighing.
May You alone, LORD,
reign over us with loving-kindness and compassion,
and vindicate us in justice.
Blessed are You, LORD,
the King who loves righteousness and justice.
/ *Between Rosh HaShana & Yom Kippur, end the blessing:* the King of justice./

AGAINST INFORMERS

וְלַמַּלְשִׁינִים For the slanderers let there be no hope,
and may all wickedness perish in an instant.
May all Your people's enemies swiftly be cut down.
May You swiftly uproot, crush, cast down
and humble the arrogant swiftly in our days.
Blessed are You, LORD,
who destroys enemies and humbles the arrogant.

---

leaders of the people (Rabbi Abraham ben HaRambam). The prayer for the restoration of judges, following the ingathering of exiles, is thus a plea for the return of national sovereignty. וְהָסֵר מִמֶּנּוּ יָגוֹן וַאֲנָחָה *Remove from us sorrow and sighing:* the plaint of a people who have known the full precariousness of being dependent on the goodwill of others.

ברכת המינים *Blessing 12: Against Informers.* The text of this paragraph underwent several changes during the centuries. Its original object was the sectarianism that split the Jewish world during the late Second Temple period.

קבוץ גלויות

תְּקַע בְּשׁוֹפָר גָּדוֹל לְחֵרוּתֵנוּ, וְשָׂא נֵס לְקַבֵּץ גָּלֻיּוֹתֵינוּ
וְקַבְּצֵנוּ יַחַד מֵאַרְבַּע כַּנְפוֹת הָאָרֶץ.
בָּרוּךְ אַתָּה יהוה, מְקַבֵּץ נִדְחֵי עַמּוֹ יִשְׂרָאֵל.

השבת המשפט

הָשִׁיבָה שׁוֹפְטֵינוּ כְּבָרִאשׁוֹנָה וְיוֹעֲצֵינוּ כְּבַתְּחִלָּה
וְהָסֵר מִמֶּנּוּ יָגוֹן וַאֲנָחָה
וּמְלֹךְ עָלֵינוּ אַתָּה יהוה לְבַדְּךָ בְּחֶסֶד וּבְרַחֲמִים
וְצַדְּקֵנוּ בַּמִּשְׁפָּט.
בָּרוּךְ אַתָּה יהוה
מֶלֶךְ אוֹהֵב צְדָקָה וּמִשְׁפָּט. / בעשרת ימי תשובה: הַמֶּלֶךְ הַמִּשְׁפָּט./

ברכת המינים

וְלַמַּלְשִׁינִים אַל תְּהִי תִקְוָה, וְכָל הָרִשְׁעָה כְּרֶגַע תֹּאבֵד
וְכָל אוֹיְבֵי עַמְּךָ מְהֵרָה יִכָּרֵתוּ
וְהַזֵּדִים מְהֵרָה תְעַקֵּר וּתְשַׁבֵּר וּתְמַגֵּר וְתַכְנִיעַ בִּמְהֵרָה בְיָמֵינוּ.
בָּרוּךְ אַתָּה יהוה, שׁוֹבֵר אוֹיְבִים וּמַכְנִיעַ זֵדִים.

קבוץ גלויות *Blessing 10: Ingathering of exiles.* With this paragraph, the requests change from individual to collective hopes. They begin with three prayers for political-historical renewal: the return of exiles, the restoration of independence, and an end to the factionalism that caused great damage to the Israelites from the biblical era to the end of the Second Temple period. תְּקַע בְּשׁוֹפָר גָּדוֹל *Sound the great shofar:* A reference to Isaiah 27:13, "On that day a great shofar will sound." וְשָׂא נֵס *Raise high the banner:* Isaiah 11:12, "He will raise a banner for the nations and gather the exiles of Israel; He will assemble the scattered people of Judah from the four quarters of the earth."

משפט *Blessing 11: Justice.* A prayer for self-government. The "Judges" in the biblical book of that name were not merely judges in a legal sense; they were

THE RIGHTEOUS

עַל הַצַּדִּיקִים To the righteous, the pious,
the elders of Your people the house of Israel,
the remnant of their scholars,
the righteous converts, and to us,
may Your compassion be aroused,
LORD our God.
Grant a good reward to all who sincerely trust in Your name.
Set our lot with them,
so that we may never be ashamed, for in You we trust.
Blessed are You, LORD,
who is the support and trust of the righteous.

REBUILDING JERUSALEM

וְלִירוּשָׁלַיִם To Jerusalem, Your city,
may You return in compassion,
and may You dwell in it as You promised.
May You rebuild it rapidly in our days
as an everlasting structure,
and install within it soon the throne of David.
Blessed are You, LORD, who builds Jerusalem.

פְּלֵיטַת סוֹפְרֵיהֶם *The remnant of their scholars* is a reference to those Jews who endured religious persecution under the Greeks and Romans, and later, those who survived the Crusades and those who lived through the Holocaust. Judaism lost many of its greatest scholars as martyrs.

בנין ירושלים *Blessing 14: Rebuilding Jerusalem.* Jerusalem is the home of the Jewish soul, the place to which we turn in prayer and for whose restoration Jews prayed in every generation. The book of Psalms has left us an indelible description of how Jews felt when the city fell to the Babylonians in the sixth century BCE: "By the rivers of Babylon we sat and wept when we remembered Zion… May my tongue cling to the roof of my mouth if I do not remember you, if I do not consider Jerusalem my highest joy" (Psalm 137). Jerusalem is mentioned more than 600 times in the Hebrew Bible.

על הצדיקים

עַל הַצַּדִּיקִים וְעַל הַחֲסִידִים
וְעַל זִקְנֵי עַמְּךָ בֵּית יִשְׂרָאֵל
וְעַל פְּלֵיטַת סוֹפְרֵיהֶם
וְעַל גֵּרֵי הַצֶּדֶק, וְעָלֵינוּ
יֶהֱמוּ רַחֲמֶיךָ יהוה אֱלֹהֵינוּ
וְתֵן שָׂכָר טוֹב לְכָל הַבּוֹטְחִים בְּשִׁמְךָ בֶּאֱמֶת
וְשִׂים חֶלְקֵנוּ עִמָּהֶם, וּלְעוֹלָם לֹא נֵבוֹשׁ כִּי בְךָ בָּטָחְנוּ.
בָּרוּךְ אַתָּה יהוה, מִשְׁעָן וּמִבְטָח לַצַּדִּיקִים.

בניין ירושלים

וְלִירוּשָׁלַיִם עִירְךָ בְּרַחֲמִים תָּשׁוּב
וְתִשְׁכֹּן בְּתוֹכָהּ כַּאֲשֶׁר דִּבַּרְתָּ
וּבְנֵה אוֹתָהּ בְּקָרוֹב בְּיָמֵינוּ בִּנְיַן עוֹלָם
וְכִסֵּא דָוִד מְהֵרָה לְתוֹכָהּ תָּכִין.
בָּרוּךְ אַתָּה יהוה, בּוֹנֵה יְרוּשָׁלָיִם.

There were Jews in the Hellenistic age who turned against their own people. Faith (*emuna*) in Judaism involves the idea of loyalty – to a people and its heritage. This prayer is a protest against disloyalty.

The Talmud (*Berakhot* 28b) says that, to formulate this prayer, Rabban Gamliel turned to Shmuel HaKatan. Rabbi Kook pointed out that Shmuel HaKatan was known for his attachment to the principle, "Do not rejoice when your enemy falls" (*Avot* 4:24). Only a person who deeply loved his fellow human beings could be entrusted with the task of constructing this prayer, which must be free of animosity and *schadenfreude*.

על הצדיקים *Blessing 13:* הַצַּדִּיקִים *The righteous.* After mentioning those who harm the Jewish people, we go on to describe those who endow it with greatness: the righteous, the pious, the elders, scholars and converts.

KINGDOM OF DAVID

אֶת צֶמַח May the offshoot of Your servant David soon flower,
and may his pride be raised high by Your salvation,
for we wait for Your salvation all day.
Blessed are You, LORD, who makes the glory of salvation flourish.

RESPONSE TO PRAYER

שְׁמַע קוֹלֵנוּ Listen to our voice, LORD our God.
Spare us and have compassion on us,
and in compassion and favor accept our prayer,
for You, God, listen to prayers and pleas.
Do not turn us away, O our King,
empty-handed from Your presence,*
for You listen with compassion
to the prayer of Your people Israel.
Blessed are You, LORD, who listens to prayer.

**In times of drought in Israel, add:*

וַעֲנֵנוּ And answer us through the attribute of compassion, Creator of the universe who chooses His people Israel to make known His greatness and majestic glory. You who listen to prayer, grant dew and rain on the face of the earth, satisfying the whole universe from Your goodness. Fill our hands from Your blessings and Your hand's rich gift. Guard and deliver this year from all evil, all kinds of destruction and punishment, and give it hope and a peaceful end. Spare us and have compassion on us and on all our produce and fruit, blessing us with bounteous rain. May we merit life, plenty and peace as in the good years. Remove from us plague, sword and famine, wild animals, captivity and plunder, the evil instinct and serious and dangerous illnesses and events. Decree for us goodly decrees, and may Your compassion prevail over Your other attributes, that You may act toward Your children through the attribute of compassion, and in compassion and favor accept our prayer.

Continue with "for You listen" above.

שומע תפלה *Blessing 16: Response to Prayer.* An all-inclusive prayer, that our prayers be heard. At this point in the silent Amida, the individual can include any of his or her personal requests.

מלכות בית דוד

אֶת צֶמַח דָּוִד עַבְדְּךָ מְהֵרָה תַצְמִיחַ, וְקַרְנוֹ תָּרוּם בִּישׁוּעָתֶךָ
כִּי לִישׁוּעָתְךָ קִוִּינוּ כָּל הַיּוֹם.
בָּרוּךְ אַתָּה יהוה, מַצְמִיחַ קֶרֶן יְשׁוּעָה.

שומע תפלה

שְׁמַע קוֹלֵנוּ יהוה אֱלֹהֵינוּ
חוּס וְרַחֵם עָלֵינוּ, וְקַבֵּל בְּרַחֲמִים וּבְרָצוֹן אֶת תְּפִלָּתֵנוּ
כִּי אֵל שׁוֹמֵעַ תְּפִלּוֹת וְתַחֲנוּנִים אָתָּה
וּמִלְּפָנֶיךָ מַלְכֵּנוּ רֵיקָם אַל תְּשִׁיבֵנוּ*
כִּי אַתָּה שׁוֹמֵעַ תְּפִלַּת עַמְּךָ יִשְׂרָאֵל בְּרַחֲמִים.
בָּרוּךְ אַתָּה יהוה, שׁוֹמֵעַ תְּפִלָּה.

**In times of drought in* ארץ ישראל*, add:*

וַעֲנֵנוּ בּוֹרֵא עוֹלָם בְּמִדַּת הָרַחֲמִים, בּוֹחֵר בְּעַמּוֹ יִשְׂרָאֵל לְהוֹדִיעַ גָּדְלוֹ וְהַדְרַת כְּבוֹדוֹ. שׁוֹמֵעַ תְּפִלָּה, תֵּן טַל וּמָטָר עַל פְּנֵי הָאֲדָמָה, וְתַשְׂבִּיעַ אֶת הָעוֹלָם כֻּלּוֹ מִטּוּבֶךָ, וּמַלֵּא יָדֵינוּ מִבִּרְכוֹתֶיךָ וּמֵעֹשֶׁר מַתְּנַת יָדֶךָ. שְׁמֹר וְהַצֵּל שָׁנָה זוֹ מִכָּל דָּבָר רָע, וּמִכָּל מִינֵי מַשְׁחִית וּמִכָּל מִינֵי פֻרְעָנִיּוֹת, וַעֲשֵׂה לָהּ תִּקְוָה וְאַחֲרִית שָׁלוֹם. חוּס וְרַחֵם עָלֵינוּ וְעַל כָּל תְּבוּאָתֵנוּ וּפֵרוֹתֵינוּ, וּבָרְכֵנוּ בְּגִשְׁמֵי בְרָכָה, וְנִזְכֶּה לְחַיִּים וְשֹׂבַע וְשָׁלוֹם כַּשָּׁנִים הַטּוֹבוֹת. וְהָסֵר מִמֶּנּוּ דֶּבֶר וָחֶרֶב וְרָעָב, וְחַיָּה רָעָה וּשְׁבִי וּבִזָּה, וְיֵצֶר הָרָע וָחֳלָיִים רָעִים וְקָשִׁים וּמְאֹרָעוֹת רָעִים וְקָשִׁים. וּגְזֹר עָלֵינוּ גְּזֵרוֹת טוֹבוֹת מִלְּפָנֶיךָ, וְיִגֹּלּוּ רַחֲמֶיךָ עַל מִדּוֹתֶיךָ, וְתִתְנַהֵג עִם בָּנֶיךָ בְּמִדַּת הָרַחֲמִים, וְקַבֵּל בְּרַחֲמִים וּבְרָצוֹן אֶת תְּפִלָּתֵנוּ.

Continue with כִּי אַתָּה שׁוֹמֵעַ *above.*

מלכות בית דוד *Blessing 15: Kingdom of David.* David was promised by God that the monarchy would always be the heritage of his children. The Davidic monarchy came to an end with the Babylonian conquest. It will be restored in the messianic age. The word "Messiah" in Hebrew means "anointed"; that is, a duly appointed king of Davidic descent.

TEMPLE SERVICE

רְצֵה Find favor, LORD our God,
in Your people Israel and their prayer.
Restore the service to Your most holy House,
and accept in love and favor
the fire-offerings of Israel and their prayer.
May the service of Your people Israel
always find favor with You.

On Rosh Hodesh, say:

אֱלֹהֵינוּ Our God and God of our ancestors, may there rise, come, reach, appear, be favored, heard, regarded and remembered before You, our recollection and remembrance, as well as the remembrance of our ancestors, and of the Messiah son of David Your servant, and of Jerusalem Your holy city, and of all Your people the house of Israel – for deliverance and well-being, grace, loving-kindness and compassion, life and peace, on this day of Rosh Hodesh. On it remember us, LORD our God, for good; recollect us for blessing, and deliver us for life. In accord with Your promise of salvation and compassion, spare us and be gracious to us; have compassion on us and deliver us, for our eyes are turned to You because You, God, are a gracious and compassionate King.

וְתֶחֱזֶינָה And may our eyes witness
Your return to Zion in compassion.
Blessed are You, LORD,
who restores His Presence to Zion.

Priestly Blessing, but according to Maimonides it means that they said the prayer beginning שִׂים שָׁלוֹם, "Grant peace."

עבודה

רְצֵה יהוה אֱלֹהֵינוּ בְּעַמְּךָ יִשְׂרָאֵל, וּבִתְפִלָּתָם
וְהָשֵׁב אֶת הָעֲבוֹדָה לִדְבִיר בֵּיתֶךָ
וְאִשֵּׁי יִשְׂרָאֵל וּתְפִלָּתָם בְּאַהֲבָה תְקַבֵּל בְּרָצוֹן
וּתְהִי לְרָצוֹן תָּמִיד עֲבוֹדַת יִשְׂרָאֵל עַמֶּךָ.

On ראש חודש, *say:*

אֱלֹהֵינוּ וֵאלֹהֵי אֲבוֹתֵינוּ, יַעֲלֶה וְיָבוֹא וְיַגִּיעַ, וְיֵרָאֶה וְיֵרָצֶה וְיִשָּׁמַע, וְיִפָּקֵד וְיִזָּכֵר זִכְרוֹנֵנוּ וּפִקְדוֹנֵנוּ וְזִכְרוֹן אֲבוֹתֵינוּ, וְזִכְרוֹן מָשִׁיחַ בֶּן דָּוִד עַבְדֶּךָ, וְזִכְרוֹן יְרוּשָׁלַיִם עִיר קָדְשֶׁךָ, וְזִכְרוֹן כָּל עַמְּךָ בֵּית יִשְׂרָאֵל, לְפָנֶיךָ, לִפְלֵיטָה לְטוֹבָה, לְחֵן וּלְחֶסֶד וּלְרַחֲמִים, לְחַיִּים וּלְשָׁלוֹם בְּיוֹם רֹאשׁ הַחֹדֶשׁ הַזֶּה. זָכְרֵנוּ יהוה אֱלֹהֵינוּ בּוֹ לְטוֹבָה, וּפָקְדֵנוּ בוֹ לִבְרָכָה, וְהוֹשִׁיעֵנוּ בוֹ לְחַיִּים. וּבִדְבַר יְשׁוּעָה וְרַחֲמִים, חוּס וְחָנֵּנוּ וְרַחֵם עָלֵינוּ וְהוֹשִׁיעֵנוּ, כִּי אֵלֶיךָ עֵינֵינוּ, כִּי אֵל מֶלֶךְ חַנּוּן וְרַחוּם אָתָּה.

וְתֶחֱזֶינָה עֵינֵינוּ בְּשׁוּבְךָ לְצִיּוֹן בְּרַחֲמִים.
בָּרוּךְ אַתָּה יהוה
הַמַּחֲזִיר שְׁכִינָתוֹ לְצִיּוֹן.

עבודה *Blessing 17: Temple Service.* The last three blessings, called by the sages "Thanksgiving," are linked because they were said by the priests in the Temple (*Tamid* 5:1). This paragraph was originally a prayer that the day's sacrifices be accepted. The priests then said *Modim*, "We give thanks to You" and blessed the people. According to *Tosafot*, this means that they said the threefold

THANKSGIVING

Bow at the first nine words.

מוֹדִים We give thanks to You,
for You are the LORD our God
and God of our ancestors
for ever and all time.
You are the Rock of our lives,
Shield of our salvation
from generation to generation.
We will thank You and
declare Your praise for our lives,
which are entrusted into Your hand;
for our souls,
which are placed in Your charge;
for Your miracles
which are with us every day;
and for Your wonders and favors
at all times, evening,
morning and midday.
You are good –
for Your compassion never fails.
You are compassionate –
for Your loving-
kindnesses never cease.
We have always
placed our hope in You.

During the Leader's Repetition, the congregation says quietly:

מוֹדִים We give thanks to You,
for You are the LORD
our God
and God of our ancestors,
God of all flesh,
who formed us
and formed the universe.
Blessings and thanks are due
to Your great and holy name
for giving us life
and sustaining us.
May You continue
to give us life and sustain us;
and may You gather
our exiles
to Your holy courts,
to keep Your decrees,
do Your will and serve You
with a perfect heart,
for it is for us
to give You thanks.
Blessed be God
to whom
thanksgiving is due.

---

hidden miracles take place within them. God is present not only in signs and wonders, but also in the very laws that govern the universe. To see the miraculous in the everyday is part of the Judaic vision, beautifully expressed in these lines.

הודאה

Bow at the first five words.

מוֹדִים אֲנַחְנוּ לָךְ
שָׁאַתָּה הוּא יהוה אֱלֹהֵינוּ
וֵאלֹהֵי אֲבוֹתֵינוּ לְעוֹלָם וָעֶד.
צוּר חַיֵּינוּ, מָגֵן יִשְׁעֵנוּ
אַתָּה הוּא לְדוֹר וָדוֹר.
נוֹדֶה לְּךָ וּנְסַפֵּר תְּהִלָּתֶךָ
עַל חַיֵּינוּ הַמְּסוּרִים בְּיָדֶךָ
וְעַל נִשְׁמוֹתֵינוּ הַפְּקוּדוֹת לָךְ
וְעַל נִסֶּיךָ שֶׁבְּכָל יוֹם עִמָּנוּ
וְעַל נִפְלְאוֹתֶיךָ וְטוֹבוֹתֶיךָ
שֶׁבְּכָל עֵת
עֶרֶב וָבֹקֶר וְצָהֳרָיִם.
הַטּוֹב, כִּי לֹא כָלוּ רַחֲמֶיךָ
וְהַמְרַחֵם, כִּי לֹא תַמּוּ חֲסָדֶיךָ
מֵעוֹלָם קִוִּינוּ לָךְ.

During חזרת הש״ץ, *the* קהל *says quietly:*

מוֹדִים אֲנַחְנוּ לָךְ
שָׁאַתָּה הוּא יהוה אֱלֹהֵינוּ
וֵאלֹהֵי אֲבוֹתֵינוּ
אֱלֹהֵי כָל בָּשָׂר
יוֹצְרֵנוּ, יוֹצֵר בְּרֵאשִׁית.
בְּרָכוֹת וְהוֹדָאוֹת
לְשִׁמְךָ הַגָּדוֹל וְהַקָּדוֹשׁ
עַל שֶׁהֶחֱיִיתָנוּ וְקִיַּמְתָּנוּ.
כֵּן תְּחַיֵּנוּ וּתְקַיְּמֵנוּ
וְתֶאֱסֹף גָּלֻיּוֹתֵינוּ
לְחַצְרוֹת קָדְשֶׁךָ
לִשְׁמֹר חֻקֶּיךָ
וְלַעֲשׂוֹת רְצוֹנֶךָ וּלְעָבְדְּךָ
בְּלֵבָב שָׁלֵם
עַל שֶׁאֲנַחְנוּ מוֹדִים לָךְ.
בָּרוּךְ אֵל הַהוֹדָאוֹת.

הודאה *Blessing 18: Thanksgiving.* The root *y-d-h* has three meanings: (1) to bow (see *Targum* to II Samuel 16:4), hence we bow at the beginning and end of this blessing; (2) to confess or profess; and (3) to thank. The blessing begins as a confession of faith, and moves to thanks for God's blessings which surround us continually. **וְעַל נִסֶּיךָ שֶׁבְּכָל יוֹם עִמָּנוּ** *For Your miracles which are with us every day:* Nahmanides explained the difference between a "revealed" and a "hidden" miracle. Revealed miracles stand outside the laws of nature;

On Ḥanukka:

עַל הַנִּסִּים [We thank You also] for the miracles, the redemption, the mighty deeds, the salvations, and the victories in battle which You performed for our ancestors in those days, at this time.

בִּימֵי מַתִּתְיָהוּ In the days of Mattityahu, son of Yoḥanan, the High Priest, the Hasmonean, and his sons, the wicked Greek kingdom rose up against Your people Israel to make them forget Your Torah and to force them to transgress the statutes of Your will. It was then that You in Your great compassion stood by them in the time of their distress. You championed their cause, judged their claim, and avenged their wrong. You delivered the strong into the hands of the weak, the many into the hands of the few, the impure into the hands of the pure, the wicked into the hands of the righteous, and the arrogant into the hands of those who were engaged in the study of Your Torah. You made for Yourself great and holy renown in Your world, and for Your people Israel You performed a great salvation and redemption as of this very day. Your children then entered the holiest part of Your House, cleansed Your Temple, purified Your Sanctuary, kindled lights in Your holy courts, and designated these eight days of Ḥanukka for giving thanks and praise to Your great name.

Continue with "For all these things."

On Purim:

עַל הַנִּסִּים [We thank You also] for the miracles, the redemption, the mighty deeds, the salvations, and the victories in battle which You performed for our ancestors in those days, at this time.

בִּימֵי מָרְדְּכַי In the days of Mordekhai and Esther, in Shushan the capital, the
wicked Haman rose up against them and sought to destroy, slay and exterminate *Esther 3*
all the Jews, young and old, children and women, on one day, the thirteenth day of the twelfth month, which is the month of Adar, and to plunder their possessions. Then You in Your great compassion thwarted his counsel, frustrated his plans, and caused his scheme to recoil on his own head, so that they hanged him and his sons on the gallows.

Continue with "For all these things."

וְעַל כֻּלָּם For all these things may Your name be blessed and exalted, our King, continually, for ever and all time.

Between Rosh HaShana & Yom Kippur: And write, for a good life, all the children of Your covenant.

Let all that lives thank You, Selah! and praise Your name in truth, God, our Savior and Help, Selah!

▼Blessed are You, Lord, whose name is "the Good" and to whom thanks are due.

בחנוכה:

עַל הַנִּסִּים וְעַל הַפֻּרְקָן וְעַל הַגְּבוּרוֹת וְעַל הַתְּשׁוּעוֹת וְעַל הַמִּלְחָמוֹת שֶׁעָשִׂיתָ לַאֲבוֹתֵינוּ בַּיָּמִים הָהֵם בַּזְּמַן הַזֶּה.

בִּימֵי מַתִּתְיָהוּ בֶּן יוֹחָנָן כֹּהֵן גָּדוֹל חַשְׁמוֹנַאי וּבָנָיו, כְּשֶׁעָמְדָה מַלְכוּת יָוָן הָרְשָׁעָה עַל עַמְּךָ יִשְׂרָאֵל לְהַשְׁכִּיחָם תּוֹרָתֶךָ וּלְהַעֲבִירָם מֵחֻקֵּי רְצוֹנֶךָ, וְאַתָּה בְּרַחֲמֶיךָ הָרַבִּים עָמַדְתָּ לָהֶם בְּעֵת צָרָתָם, רַבְתָּ אֶת רִיבָם, דַּנְתָּ אֶת דִּינָם, נָקַמְתָּ אֶת נִקְמָתָם, מָסַרְתָּ גִבּוֹרִים בְּיַד חַלָּשִׁים, וְרַבִּים בְּיַד מְעַטִּים, וּטְמֵאִים בְּיַד טְהוֹרִים, וּרְשָׁעִים בְּיַד צַדִּיקִים, וְזֵדִים בְּיַד עוֹסְקֵי תוֹרָתֶךָ, וּלְךָ עָשִׂיתָ שֵׁם גָּדוֹל וְקָדוֹשׁ בְּעוֹלָמֶךָ, וּלְעַמְּךָ יִשְׂרָאֵל עָשִׂיתָ תְּשׁוּעָה גְדוֹלָה וּפֻרְקָן כְּהַיּוֹם הַזֶּה. וְאַחַר כֵּן בָּאוּ בָנֶיךָ לִדְבִיר בֵּיתֶךָ, וּפִנּוּ אֶת הֵיכָלֶךָ, וְטִהֲרוּ אֶת מִקְדָּשֶׁךָ, וְהִדְלִיקוּ נֵרוֹת בְּחַצְרוֹת קָדְשֶׁךָ, וְקָבְעוּ שְׁמוֹנַת יְמֵי חֲנֻכָּה אֵלּוּ, לְהוֹדוֹת וּלְהַלֵּל לְשִׁמְךָ הַגָּדוֹל.

Continue with וְעַל כֻּלָּם.

בפורים:

עַל הַנִּסִּים וְעַל הַפֻּרְקָן וְעַל הַגְּבוּרוֹת וְעַל הַתְּשׁוּעוֹת וְעַל הַמִּלְחָמוֹת שֶׁעָשִׂיתָ לַאֲבוֹתֵינוּ בַּיָּמִים הָהֵם בַּזְּמַן הַזֶּה.

בִּימֵי מָרְדְּכַי וְאֶסְתֵּר בְּשׁוּשַׁן הַבִּירָה, כְּשֶׁעָמַד עֲלֵיהֶם הָמָן הָרָשָׁע, בִּקֵּשׁ לְהַשְׁמִיד לַהֲרֹג וּלְאַבֵּד אֶת־כָּל־הַיְּהוּדִים מִנַּעַר וְעַד־זָקֵן טַף וְנָשִׁים בְּיוֹם אֶחָד, בִּשְׁלוֹשָׁה עָשָׂר לְחֹדֶשׁ שְׁנֵים־עָשָׂר, הוּא־חֹדֶשׁ אֲדָר, וּשְׁלָלָם לָבוֹז: וְאַתָּה בְּרַחֲמֶיךָ הָרַבִּים הֵפַרְתָּ אֶת עֲצָתוֹ, וְקִלְקַלְתָּ אֶת מַחֲשַׁבְתּוֹ, וַהֲשֵׁבוֹתָ לּוֹ גְּמוּלוֹ בְּרֹאשׁוֹ, וְתָלוּ אוֹתוֹ וְאֶת בָּנָיו עַל הָעֵץ. אסתר ג

Continue with וְעַל כֻּלָּם.

וְעַל כֻּלָּם יִתְבָּרַךְ וְיִתְרוֹמַם שִׁמְךָ מַלְכֵּנוּ תָּמִיד לְעוֹלָם וָעֶד.

בעשרת ימי תשובה: וּכְתֹב לְחַיִּים טוֹבִים כָּל בְּנֵי בְרִיתֶךָ.

וְכֹל הַחַיִּים יוֹדוּךָ סֶּלָה, וִיהַלְלוּ אֶת שִׁמְךָ בֶּאֱמֶת
הָאֵל יְשׁוּעָתֵנוּ וְעֶזְרָתֵנוּ סֶלָה.
בָּרוּךְ אַתָּה יהוה, הַטּוֹב שִׁמְךָ וּלְךָ נָאֶה לְהוֹדוֹת.

The following is said by the Leader during the Repetition of the Amida, except in a house of mourning and on Tisha B'Av. In Israel, if Kohanim bless the congregation, *turn to page 386. See laws 62–69.*

Our God and God of our fathers, bless us with the threefold blessing in the Torah, written by the hand of Moses Your servant and pronounced by Aaron and his sons the priests, Your holy people, as it is said:

May the LORD bless you and protect you. *Cong:* May it be Your will. *Num. 6*
May the LORD make His face shine on you
and be gracious to you. *Cong:* May it be Your will.
May the LORD turn His face toward you,
and grant you peace. *Cong:* May it be Your will.

PEACE

שִׂים שָׁלוֹם Grant peace, goodness and blessing,
grace, loving-kindness and compassion to us and all Israel Your people.
Bless us, our Father, all as one, with the light of Your face,
for by the light of Your face You have given us, LORD our God,
the Torah of life and love of kindness,
righteousness, blessing, compassion, life and peace.
May it be good in Your eyes to bless Your people Israel
at every time, in every hour, with Your peace.

Between Rosh HaShana & Yom Kippur: In the book of life, blessing, peace and prosperity,
may we and all Your people the house of Israel
be remembered and written before You
for a good life, and for peace.*

Blessed are You, LORD, who blesses His people Israel with peace.

**Between Rosh HaShana and Yom Kippur outside Israel, many end the blessing:*
Blessed are You, LORD, who makes peace.

The following verse concludes the Leader's Repetition of the Amida. Some also say it here as part of the silent Amida. See law 60.

May the words of my mouth and the meditation of my heart *Ps. 19*
find favor before You, LORD, my Rock and Redeemer.

famously in the words of Isaiah: "Nation shall not lift up sword against nation; neither shall they learn war anymore" (Is. 2:4). Peace is the ultimate hope of monotheism, with its belief that the world is the product of a single will, not the blind clash of conflicting elements.

The following is said by the שליח ציבור *during* חזרת הש״ץ *except in a house of mourning and on* תשעה באב. *In* ארץ ישראל *if* כהנים *say* ברכת כהנים *turn to page 387. See laws 62–69.*

אֱלֹהֵינוּ וֵאלֹהֵי אֲבוֹתֵינוּ, בָּרְכֵנוּ בַּבְּרָכָה הַמְשֻׁלֶּשֶׁת בַּתּוֹרָה, הַכְּתוּבָה עַל יְדֵי מֹשֶׁה עַבְדֶּךָ, הָאֲמוּרָה מִפִּי אַהֲרֹן וּבָנָיו כֹּהֲנִים עַם קְדוֹשֶׁיךָ, כָּאָמוּר

יְבָרֶכְךָ יהוה וְיִשְׁמְרֶךָ: קהל: כֵּן יְהִי רָצוֹן — במדבר ו

יָאֵר יהוה פָּנָיו אֵלֶיךָ וִיחֻנֶּךָּ: קהל: כֵּן יְהִי רָצוֹן

יִשָּׂא יהוה פָּנָיו אֵלֶיךָ וְיָשֵׂם לְךָ שָׁלוֹם: קהל: כֵּן יְהִי רָצוֹן

שלום

שִׂים שָׁלוֹם טוֹבָה וּבְרָכָה
חֵן וָחֶסֶד וְרַחֲמִים עָלֵינוּ וְעַל כָּל יִשְׂרָאֵל עַמֶּךָ.
בָּרְכֵנוּ אָבִינוּ כֻּלָּנוּ כְּאֶחָד בְּאוֹר פָּנֶיךָ
כִּי בְאוֹר פָּנֶיךָ נָתַתָּ לָּנוּ יהוה אֱלֹהֵינוּ
תּוֹרַת חַיִּים וְאַהֲבַת חֶסֶד
וּצְדָקָה וּבְרָכָה וְרַחֲמִים וְחַיִּים וְשָׁלוֹם.
וְטוֹב בְּעֵינֶיךָ לְבָרֵךְ אֶת עַמְּךָ יִשְׂרָאֵל
בְּכָל עֵת וּבְכָל שָׁעָה בִּשְׁלוֹמֶךָ.

בעשרת ימי תשובה: בְּסֵפֶר חַיִּים, בְּרָכָה וְשָׁלוֹם, וּפַרְנָסָה טוֹבָה
נִזָּכֵר וְנִכָּתֵב לְפָנֶיךָ, אֲנַחְנוּ וְכָל עַמְּךָ בֵּית יִשְׂרָאֵל
לְחַיִּים טוֹבִים וּלְשָׁלוֹם.*

בָּרוּךְ אַתָּה יהוה, הַמְבָרֵךְ אֶת עַמּוֹ יִשְׂרָאֵל בַּשָּׁלוֹם.

**During the* עשרת ימי תשובה *in* חוץ לארץ, *many end the blessing:*

בָּרוּךְ אַתָּה יהוה, עוֹשֵׂה הַשָּׁלוֹם.

The following verse concludes the חזרת הש״ץ.
Some also say it here as part of the silent עמידה. *See law 60.*

יִהְיוּ לְרָצוֹן אִמְרֵי־פִי וְהֶגְיוֹן לִבִּי לְפָנֶיךָ, יהוה צוּרִי וְגֹאֲלִי: — תהלים יט

שלום *Blessing 19: Peace. Shalom* means more than the English word "peace": it also means "completeness, perfection, harmonious interaction." The prophets of Israel were the first in history to conceive of peace as an ideal, most

אֱלֹהַי My God, *Berakhot 17a*
guard my tongue from evil and my lips from deceitful speech.
To those who curse me, let my soul be silent;
may my soul be to all like the dust.
Open my heart to Your Torah and let my soul
pursue Your commandments.
As for all who plan evil against me,
swiftly thwart their counsel and frustrate their plans.
Act for the sake of Your name; act for the sake of Your right hand;
act for the sake of Your holiness; act for the sake of Your Torah.
That Your beloved ones may be delivered, *Ps. 60*
save with Your right hand and answer me.
May the words of my mouth and the meditation of my heart *Ps. 19*
find favor before You, LORD, my Rock and Redeemer.

Bow, take three steps back, then bow, first left, then right, then center, while saying:

May He who makes peace in His high places,
make peace for us and all Israel – and say: Amen.

יְהִי רָצוֹן May it be Your will, LORD our God and God of our ancestors,
that the Temple be rebuilt speedily in our days,
and grant us a share in Your Torah. And there we will serve You
with reverence, as in the days of old and as in former years.
Then the offering of Judah and Jerusalem will be pleasing to the LORD *Mal. 3*
as in the days of old and as in former years.

When praying with a minyan, the Amida is repeated aloud by the Leader.

On days when Tahanun is said (see page 144), start Tahanun on page 152.
On Mondays and Thursdays start Tahanun on page 144.
In Israel, on days on which Tahanun is said, some say Viduy and the Thirteen Attributes of Divine Compassion on page 136. See law 176a.

On fast days (except Tisha B'Av) most congregations say Selihot on page 466 before Avinu Malkenu on page 138.

Between Rosh HaShana and Yom Kippur (but not on Erev Yom Kippur, unless it falls on Friday), say Avinu Malkenu on page 138.

On Rosh Hodesh, Hanukka, Yom HaAtzma'ut and Yom Yerushalayim, say Hallel on page 360.

On other days when Tahanun is not said (see page 144), the Leader says Half Kaddish on page 156.

ברכות יז.

אֱלֹהַי
נְצֹר לְשׁוֹנִי מֵרָע וּשְׂפָתַי מִדַּבֵּר מִרְמָה
וְלִמְקַלְלַי נַפְשִׁי תִדֹּם, וְנַפְשִׁי כֶּעָפָר לַכֹּל תִּהְיֶה.
פְּתַח לִבִּי בְּתוֹרָתֶךָ, וּבְמִצְוֹתֶיךָ תִּרְדֹּף נַפְשִׁי.
וְכָל הַחוֹשְׁבִים עָלַי רָעָה
מְהֵרָה הָפֵר עֲצָתָם וְקַלְקֵל מַחֲשַׁבְתָּם.
עֲשֵׂה לְמַעַן שְׁמֶךָ, עֲשֵׂה לְמַעַן יְמִינֶךָ
עֲשֵׂה לְמַעַן קְדֻשָּׁתֶךָ, עֲשֵׂה לְמַעַן תּוֹרָתֶךָ.
לְמַעַן יֵחָלְצוּן יְדִידֶיךָ, הוֹשִׁיעָה יְמִינְךָ וַעֲנֵנִי: תהלים ס
יִהְיוּ לְרָצוֹן אִמְרֵי־פִי וְהֶגְיוֹן לִבִּי לְפָנֶיךָ, יהוה צוּרִי וְגֹאֲלִי: תהלים יט

Bow, take three steps back, then bow, first left, then right, then center, while saying:

עֹשֶׂה שָׁלוֹם/ בעשרת ימי תשובה: הַשָּׁלוֹם/ בִּמְרוֹמָיו
הוּא יַעֲשֶׂה שָׁלוֹם עָלֵינוּ וְעַל כָּל יִשְׂרָאֵל, וְאִמְרוּ אָמֵן.

יְהִי רָצוֹן מִלְּפָנֶיךָ יהוה אֱלֹהֵינוּ וֵאלֹהֵי אֲבוֹתֵינוּ
שֶׁיִּבָּנֶה בֵּית הַמִּקְדָּשׁ בִּמְהֵרָה בְיָמֵינוּ, וְתֵן חֶלְקֵנוּ בְּתוֹרָתֶךָ
וְשָׁם נַעֲבָדְךָ בְּיִרְאָה כִּימֵי עוֹלָם וּכְשָׁנִים קַדְמוֹנִיּוֹת.
וְעָרְבָה לַיהוה מִנְחַת יְהוּדָה וִירוּשָׁלָםִ כִּימֵי עוֹלָם וּכְשָׁנִים קַדְמוֹנִיּוֹת: מלאכי ג

When praying with a מנין*, the* עמידה *is repeated aloud by the* שליח ציבור*.*

On days when תחנון *is said (see page 145), start* תחנון *on page 153.*
On Mondays and Thursdays start תחנון *on page 145.*
In ארץ ישראל*, on days on which* תחנון *is said,*
some say וידוי *and the* י״ג מדות *on page 137. See law 176a.*

On fast days (except תשעה באב*) most congregations say*
סליחות *on page 467 before* אבינו מלכנו *on page 139.*

During the עשרת ימי תשובה *(but not on* ערב יום כיפור*,*
unless it falls on Friday), say אבינו מלכנו *on page 139.*

On ראש חודש*,* חנוכה*,* יום העצמאות *and* יום ירושלים*, say* הלל *on page 361.*

On other days when תחנון *is not said (see page 145),*
the שליח ציבור *says* חצי קדיש *on page 157.*

VIDUY

In Israel on days on which Taḥanun is said (see page 144), some say Viduy and the Thirteen Attributes of Divine Compassion. See law 176a. The congregation stands and says:

אֱלֹהֵינוּ Our God and God of our fathers, let our prayer come before You, and do not hide Yourself from our plea, for we are not so arrogant or obstinate as to say before You, LORD, our God and God of our fathers, we are righteous and have not sinned, for in truth, we and our fathers have sinned.

At each expression, strike the chest on the left side:

אָשַׁמְנוּ We have been guilty, we have acted treacherously, we have robbed, we have spoken slander. We have acted perversely, we have acted wickedly, we have acted presumptuously, we have been violent, we have framed lies. We have given bad advice, we have deceived, we have scorned, we have rebelled, we have provoked, we have turned away, we have committed iniquity, we have transgressed, we have persecuted, we have been obstinate. We have acted wickedly, we have corrupted, we have acted abominably, we have strayed, we have led others astray.

We have turned away from Your commandments and good laws, to no avail, for You are *Neh. 9*
just in all that has befallen us, for You have acted faithfully while we have done wickedly.

When praying without a minyan continue with "He is compassionate" on page 144.

THIRTEEN ATTRIBUTES OF DIVINE COMPASSION

אֵל אֶרֶךְ You are a God slow to anger, You are called Master of Compassion, and You have taught the way of repentance. May You remember today and every day the greatness of Your compassion and loving-kindness for the sake of the descendants of Your beloved ones. Turn toward us in compassion, for You are the Master of Compassion. We come before You in plea and prayer, as You in ancient times showed the humble one [Moses]. Turn from Your fierce anger, as is written in Your Torah. In the shadow of Your wings may we shelter and abide, as on the day when the LORD descended in the cloud. ▸ Disregard transgression and erase guilt as on the day You stood with him [Moses] there. Hear our cry and heed our word, as on the day You proclaimed in the name of the LORD, and there it is written:

All say aloud:

וַיַּעֲבֹר And the LORD passed by before him and proclaimed: *Ex. 34*

The LORD, the LORD, compassionate and gracious God, slow to anger,
abounding in loving-kindness and truth, extending loving-kindness to a
thousand generations, forgiving iniquity, rebellion and sin,
and absolving [the guilty who repent]. Forgive us our iniquity and our sin,
and take us as Your inheritance. Forgive us, our Father, for we have sinned.
Pardon us, our King, for we have transgressed. For You, LORD, are good *Ps. 86*
and forgiving, abounding in loving-kindness to all who call on You.

On Mondays and Thursdays continue with "He is compassionate" on page 144; on other days with "David said" on page 152.

וידוי

In ארץ ישראל *on days on which* תחנון *is said (see page 145), some say* וידוי *and the* י״ג מדות*. See law 176a. The* קהל *stands and says:*

אֱלֹהֵינוּ וֵאלֹהֵי אֲבוֹתֵינוּ, תָּבוֹא לְפָנֶיךָ תְּפִלָּתֵנוּ, וְאַל תִּתְעַלַּם מִתְּחִנָּתֵנוּ, שֶׁאֵין אֲנַחְנוּ עַזֵּי פָנִים וּקְשֵׁי עֹרֶף לוֹמַר לְפָנֶיךָ, יהוה אֱלֹהֵינוּ וֵאלֹהֵי אֲבוֹתֵינוּ, צַדִּיקִים אֲנַחְנוּ וְלֹא חָטָאנוּ, אֲבָל אֲנַחְנוּ וַאֲבוֹתֵינוּ חָטָאנוּ.

At each expression, strike the chest on the left side:

אָשַׁמְנוּ, בָּגַדְנוּ, גָּזַלְנוּ, דִּבַּרְנוּ דֹפִי, הֶעֱוִינוּ, וְהִרְשַׁעְנוּ, זַדְנוּ, חָמַסְנוּ, טָפַלְנוּ שֶׁקֶר, יָעַצְנוּ רָע, כִּזַּבְנוּ, לַצְנוּ, מָרַדְנוּ, נִאַצְנוּ, סָרַרְנוּ, עָוִינוּ, פָּשַׁעְנוּ, צָרַרְנוּ, קִשִּׁינוּ עֹרֶף, רָשַׁעְנוּ, שִׁחַתְנוּ, תִּעַבְנוּ, תָּעִינוּ, תִּעְתָּעְנוּ.

סַרְנוּ מִמִּצְוֹתֶיךָ וּמִמִּשְׁפָּטֶיךָ הַטּוֹבִים, וְלֹא שָׁוָה לָנוּ. וְאַתָּה צַדִּיק עַל כָּל־הַבָּא עָלֵינוּ, נחמיה ט
כִּי־אֱמֶת עָשִׂיתָ, וַאֲנַחְנוּ הִרְשָׁעְנוּ:

When praying without a מנין *continue with* וְהוּא רַחוּם *on page 145.*

י״ג מדות

אֵל אֶרֶךְ אַפַּיִם אַתָּה, וּבַעַל הָרַחֲמִים נִקְרֵאתָ, וְדֶרֶךְ תְּשׁוּבָה הוֹרֵיתָ. גְּדֻלַּת רַחֲמֶיךָ וַחֲסָדֶיךָ, תִּזְכֹּר הַיּוֹם וּבְכָל יוֹם לְזֶרַע יְדִידֶיךָ. תֵּפֶן אֵלֵינוּ בְּרַחֲמִים, כִּי אַתָּה הוּא בַּעַל הָרַחֲמִים. בְּתַחֲנוּן וּבִתְפִלָּה פָּנֶיךָ נְקַדֵּם, כְּהוֹדַעְתָּ לֶעָנָו מִקֶּדֶם. מֵחֲרוֹן אַפְּךָ שׁוּב, כְּמוֹ בְּתוֹרָתְךָ כָּתוּב. וּבְצֵל כְּנָפֶיךָ נֶחֱסֶה וְנִתְלוֹנָן, כְּיוֹם וַיֵּרֶד יהוה בֶּעָנָן. • תַּעֲבֹר עַל פֶּשַׁע וְתִמְחֶה אָשָׁם, כְּיוֹם וַיִּתְיַצֵּב עִמּוֹ שָׁם. תַּאֲזִין שַׁוְעָתֵנוּ וְתַקְשִׁיב מֶנּוּ מַאֲמָר, כְּיוֹם וַיִּקְרָא בְשֵׁם יהוה, וְשָׁם נֶאֱמַר:

All say aloud:

וַיַּעֲבֹר יהוה עַל־פָּנָיו וַיִּקְרָא שמות לד

יהוה, יהוה, אֵל רַחוּם וְחַנּוּן, אֶרֶךְ אַפַּיִם וְרַב־חֶסֶד וֶאֱמֶת:
נֹצֵר חֶסֶד לָאֲלָפִים, נֹשֵׂא עָוֹן וָפֶשַׁע וְחַטָּאָה, וְנַקֵּה:
וְסָלַחְתָּ לַעֲוֹנֵנוּ וּלְחַטָּאתֵנוּ, וּנְחַלְתָּנוּ:
סְלַח לָנוּ אָבִינוּ כִּי חָטָאנוּ, מְחַל לָנוּ מַלְכֵּנוּ כִּי פָשָׁעְנוּ
כִּי־אַתָּה אֲדֹנָי טוֹב וְסַלָּח וְרַב־חֶסֶד לְכָל־קֹרְאֶיךָ: תהלים פו

On Mondays and Thursdays continue with וְהוּא רַחוּם *on page 145; on other days with* וַיֹּאמֶר דָּוִד *on page 153.*

AVINU MALKENU

On fast days (except Tisha B'Av) most congregations say Seliḥot on page 466 before Avinu Malkenu.

Between Rosh HaShana and Yom Kippur (but not on Erev Yom Kippur, unless it falls on Friday), say Avinu Malkenu below.

The Ark is opened.

אָבִינוּ מַלְכֵּנוּ Our Father, our King, we have sinned before You.
Our Father, our King, we have no king but You.
Our Father, our King, deal kindly with us for the sake of Your name.
Our Father our King, /*bless us with / a good year.
/ *Between Rosh HaShana & Yom Kippur: renew for us/
Our Father, our King, nullify all harsh decrees against us.
Our Father, our King, nullify the plans of those who hate us.
Our Father, our King, thwart the counsel of our enemies.
Our Father, our King, rid us of every oppressor and adversary.
Our Father, our King, close the mouths of our adversaries and accusers.
Our Father, our King, eradicate pestilence, sword, famine, captivity and destruction, iniquity and eradication from the people of Your covenant.
Our Father, our King, withhold the plague from Your heritage.
Our Father, our King, forgive and pardon all our iniquities.
Our Father, our King, wipe away and remove our transgressions and sins from Your sight.
Our Father, our King, erase in Your abundant mercy all records of our sins.

The following nine sentences are said responsively, first by the Leader, then by the congregation:

Our Father, our King, bring us back to You in perfect repentance.
Our Father, our King, send a complete healing to the sick of Your people.
Our Father, our King, tear up the evil decree against us.
Our Father, our King, remember us with a memory of favorable deeds before You.

---

the second by love, compassion and forgiveness. By placing the words in the reverse order, we mirror both history and faith: history because God called us His children ("My child, My firstborn, Israel") at Mount Sinai before He became Israel's King; faith because we ask God to let His parental love temper the severity of justice.

אבינו מלכנו

On fast days (except תשעה באב*) most congregations say* סליחות *on page 467 before* אבינו מלכנו.

During the עשרת ימי תשובה *(but not on* ערב יום כיפור, *unless it falls on Friday), say* אבינו מלכנו *below.*

The ארון קודש *is opened.*

אָבִינוּ מַלְכֵּנוּ, חָטָאנוּ לְפָנֶיךָ.
אָבִינוּ מַלְכֵּנוּ, אֵין לָנוּ מֶלֶךְ אֶלָּא אָתָּה.
אָבִינוּ מַלְכֵּנוּ, עֲשֵׂה עִמָּנוּ לְמַעַן שְׁמֶךָ.
אָבִינוּ מַלְכֵּנוּ, בָּרֵךְ/ בעשרת ימי תשובה: חַדֵּשׁ/ עָלֵינוּ שָׁנָה טוֹבָה.
אָבִינוּ מַלְכֵּנוּ, בַּטֵּל מֵעָלֵינוּ כָּל גְּזֵרוֹת קָשׁוֹת.
אָבִינוּ מַלְכֵּנוּ, בַּטֵּל מַחְשְׁבוֹת שׂוֹנְאֵינוּ.
אָבִינוּ מַלְכֵּנוּ, הָפֵר עֲצַת אוֹיְבֵינוּ.
אָבִינוּ מַלְכֵּנוּ, כַּלֵּה כָּל צַר וּמַשְׂטִין מֵעָלֵינוּ.
אָבִינוּ מַלְכֵּנוּ, סְתֹם פִּיּוֹת מַשְׂטִינֵנוּ וּמְקַטְרְגֵנוּ.
אָבִינוּ מַלְכֵּנוּ, כַּלֵּה דֶּבֶר וְחֶרֶב וְרָעָב וּשְׁבִי וּמַשְׁחִית וְעָוֹן וּשְׁמַד מִבְּנֵי בְרִיתֶךָ.
אָבִינוּ מַלְכֵּנוּ, מְנַע מַגֵּפָה מִנַּחֲלָתֶךָ.
אָבִינוּ מַלְכֵּנוּ, סְלַח וּמְחַל לְכָל עֲוֹנוֹתֵינוּ.
אָבִינוּ מַלְכֵּנוּ, מְחֵה וְהַעֲבֵר פְּשָׁעֵינוּ וְחַטֹּאתֵינוּ מִנֶּגֶד עֵינֶיךָ.
אָבִינוּ מַלְכֵּנוּ, מְחֹק בְּרַחֲמֶיךָ הָרַבִּים כָּל שִׁטְרֵי חוֹבוֹתֵינוּ.

The following nine sentences are said responsively, first by the שליח ציבור*, then by the* קהל*:*

אָבִינוּ מַלְכֵּנוּ, הַחֲזִירֵנוּ בִּתְשׁוּבָה שְׁלֵמָה לְפָנֶיךָ.
אָבִינוּ מַלְכֵּנוּ, שְׁלַח רְפוּאָה שְׁלֵמָה לְחוֹלֵי עַמֶּךָ.
אָבִינוּ מַלְכֵּנוּ, קְרַע רֹעַ גְּזַר דִּינֵנוּ.
אָבִינוּ מַלְכֵּנוּ, זָכְרֵנוּ בְּזִכָּרוֹן טוֹב לְפָנֶיךָ.

אָבִינוּ מַלְכֵּנוּ *Our Father, our King:* A prayer attributed, in its earliest form, to Rabbi Akiva. The opening two words juxtapose the two aspects of our relationship with God. He is our King and we are His subjects; He is our Parent and we are His children. The first relationship is governed by justice,

Between Rosh HaShana and Yom Kippur:

Our Father, our King, write us in the book of good life.

Our Father, our King, write us in the book of redemption and salvation.

Our Father, our King, write us in the book of livelihood and sustenance.

Our Father, our King, write us in the book of merit.

Our Father, our King, write us in the book of pardon and forgiveness.

On Fast Days:

Our Father, our King, remember us for a good life.

Our Father, our King, remember us for redemption and salvation.

Our Father, our King, remember us for livelihood and sustenance.

Our Father, our King, remember us for merit.

Our Father, our King, remember us for pardon and forgiveness.

End of responsive reading.

Our Father, our King, let salvation soon flourish for us.

Our Father, our King, raise the honor of Your people Israel.

Our Father, our King, raise the honor of Your anointed.

Our Father, our King, fill our hands with Your blessings.

Our Father, our King, fill our storehouses with abundance.

Our Father, our King, hear our voice, pity and be compassionate to us.

Our Father, our King, accept, with compassion and favor, our prayer.

Our Father, our King, open the gates of heaven to our prayer.

Our Father, our King, remember that we are dust.

Our Father, our King, please do not turn us away from You empty-handed.

Our Father, our King, may this moment be a moment of compassion and a time of favor before You.

Our Father, our King, have pity on us, our children and our infants.

Our Father, our King, act for the sake of those who were killed for Your holy name.

Our Father, our King, act for the sake of those who were slaughtered for proclaiming Your Unity.

Our Father, our King, act for the sake of those who went through fire and water to sanctify Your name.

During the עשרת ימי תשובה:

אָבִינוּ מַלְכֵּנוּ, כָּתְבֵנוּ בְּסֵפֶר חַיִּים טוֹבִים.
אָבִינוּ מַלְכֵּנוּ, כָּתְבֵנוּ בְּסֵפֶר גְּאֻלָּה וִישׁוּעָה.
אָבִינוּ מַלְכֵּנוּ, כָּתְבֵנוּ בְּסֵפֶר פַּרְנָסָה וְכַלְכָּלָה.
אָבִינוּ מַלְכֵּנוּ, כָּתְבֵנוּ בְּסֵפֶר זְכֻיּוֹת.
אָבִינוּ מַלְכֵּנוּ, כָּתְבֵנוּ בְּסֵפֶר סְלִיחָה וּמְחִילָה.

On Fast Days:

אָבִינוּ מַלְכֵּנוּ, זָכְרֵנוּ לְחַיִּים טוֹבִים.
אָבִינוּ מַלְכֵּנוּ, זָכְרֵנוּ לִגְאֻלָּה וִישׁוּעָה.
אָבִינוּ מַלְכֵּנוּ, זָכְרֵנוּ לְפַרְנָסָה וְכַלְכָּלָה.
אָבִינוּ מַלְכֵּנוּ, זָכְרֵנוּ לִזְכֻיּוֹת.
אָבִינוּ מַלְכֵּנוּ, זָכְרֵנוּ לִסְלִיחָה וּמְחִילָה.

End of responsive reading.

אָבִינוּ מַלְכֵּנוּ, הַצְמַח לָנוּ יְשׁוּעָה בְּקָרוֹב.
אָבִינוּ מַלְכֵּנוּ, הָרֵם קֶרֶן יִשְׂרָאֵל עַמֶּךָ.
אָבִינוּ מַלְכֵּנוּ, הָרֵם קֶרֶן מְשִׁיחֶךָ.
אָבִינוּ מַלְכֵּנוּ, מַלֵּא יָדֵינוּ מִבִּרְכוֹתֶיךָ.
אָבִינוּ מַלְכֵּנוּ, מַלֵּא אֲסָמֵינוּ שָׂבָע.
אָבִינוּ מַלְכֵּנוּ, שְׁמַע קוֹלֵנוּ, חוּס וְרַחֵם עָלֵינוּ.
אָבִינוּ מַלְכֵּנוּ, קַבֵּל בְּרַחֲמִים וּבְרָצוֹן אֶת תְּפִלָּתֵנוּ.
אָבִינוּ מַלְכֵּנוּ, פְּתַח שַׁעֲרֵי שָׁמַיִם לִתְפִלָּתֵנוּ.
אָבִינוּ מַלְכֵּנוּ, זְכֹר כִּי עָפָר אֲנָחְנוּ.
אָבִינוּ מַלְכֵּנוּ, נָא אַל תְּשִׁיבֵנוּ רֵיקָם מִלְּפָנֶיךָ.
אָבִינוּ מַלְכֵּנוּ, תְּהֵא הַשָּׁעָה הַזֹּאת שְׁעַת רַחֲמִים וְעֵת רָצוֹן מִלְּפָנֶיךָ.
אָבִינוּ מַלְכֵּנוּ, חֲמֹל עָלֵינוּ וְעַל עוֹלָלֵינוּ וְטַפֵּנוּ.
אָבִינוּ מַלְכֵּנוּ, עֲשֵׂה לְמַעַן הֲרוּגִים עַל שֵׁם קָדְשֶׁךָ.
אָבִינוּ מַלְכֵּנוּ, עֲשֵׂה לְמַעַן טְבוּחִים עַל יִחוּדֶךָ.
אָבִינוּ מַלְכֵּנוּ, עֲשֵׂה לְמַעַן בָּאֵי בָאֵשׁ וּבַמַּיִם עַל קִדּוּשׁ שְׁמֶךָ.

Our Father, our King, avenge before our eyes
the spilt blood of Your servants.
Our Father, our King, act for Your sake, if not for ours.
Our Father, our King, act for Your sake, and save us.
Our Father, our King, act for the sake of Your abundant compassion.
Our Father, our King, act for the sake of Your great, mighty and awesome
name by which we are called.
▸ Our Father, our King, be gracious to us and answer us, though we have
no worthy deeds; act with us in charity and
loving-kindness and save us.

The Ark is closed.

During Minḥa continue with Taḥanun on page 252.

---

faces to the ground, even after the destruction of the Temple. We preserve a trace of that gesture by resting our heads on our arms and covering our faces as we say Psalm 6. The Leader's Repetition of the Amida stands in place of the daily sacrifice, which is why we subsequently "fall on our faces."

The custom of attaching special significance to Mondays and Thursdays is also ancient. Already in the Second Temple period, Mondays and Thursdays were days on which the pious would fast. According to tradition, Moses began his ascent of Mount Sinai to receive the second tablets on a Thursday and descended forty days later on a Monday (the 10th of Tishrei, Yom Kippur). The second tablets were a sign of God's forgiveness. Hence, these days were seen as "days of favor." They were also market days when people would come from villages to towns. Congregations were larger; the Torah was read; law courts were in session. The heightened atmosphere was the setting for more extended penitential prayer; therefore, on Mondays and Thursdays, *Taḥanun* is longer.

One of the classic biblical instances of supplication was Daniel's prayer on behalf of the exiles in Babylon (Daniel, chapter 9). Sections of that prayer, together with other verses from the prophetic books and Psalms, form the core of these paragraphs. There are three sections, each containing eighteen mentions of God's name; thus we say them quietly, standing, as if they were forms of the Amida.

A tradition, found in the Geonic literature, dates these prayers to the period of persecution under the Romans, when three exiles crossed the Mediterranean, found temporary refuge and then suffered renewed oppression.

אָבִינוּ מַלְכֵּנוּ, נְקֹם לְעֵינֵינוּ נִקְמַת דַּם עֲבָדֶיךָ הַשָּׁפוּךְ.
אָבִינוּ מַלְכֵּנוּ, עֲשֵׂה לְמַעַנְךָ אִם לֹא לְמַעֲנֵנוּ.
אָבִינוּ מַלְכֵּנוּ, עֲשֵׂה לְמַעַנְךָ וְהוֹשִׁיעֵנוּ.
אָבִינוּ מַלְכֵּנוּ, עֲשֵׂה לְמַעַן רַחֲמֶיךָ הָרַבִּים.
אָבִינוּ מַלְכֵּנוּ, עֲשֵׂה לְמַעַן שִׁמְךָ הַגָּדוֹל הַגִּבּוֹר וְהַנּוֹרָא, שֶׁנִּקְרָא עָלֵינוּ.
◂ אָבִינוּ מַלְכֵּנוּ, חָנֵּנוּ וַעֲנֵנוּ, כִּי אֵין בָּנוּ מַעֲשִׂים
עֲשֵׂה עִמָּנוּ צְדָקָה וָחֶסֶד וְהוֹשִׁיעֵנוּ.

The ארון קודש *is closed.*

During מנחה *continue with* סדר תחנון *on page 253.*

TAHANUN: PLEADING WITH GOD

This section of the prayers, known as *Taḥanun*, "plea," is a return to private prayer, which began with the silent Amida. The siddur preserves a careful balance between the two ways in which we address God: as individuals with our personal hopes and fears, and as members of a community whose fate and aspirations we share. First we pray individually (the silent Amida), then communally (the Leader's Repetition), then individually in *Taḥanun* again.

Knowing that our time in the direct presence of the Supreme King of kings is drawing to an end, we approach Him directly, seeking, as it were, a private audience. Our voices drop; we whisper our deepest thoughts; we express our feelings of inadequacy and vulnerability. We know we are unworthy: we say nothing in our defense except that we have absolute faith in God.

The word *Taḥanun* derives from the root *ḥ-n-n* meaning, "to show favor, to be gracious, to forgive." What differentiates *Taḥanun* from other modes of prayer is the extent to which we emphasize our failings and our lack of good deeds. We express our dependence on God's unconditional grace and mercy. *Taḥanun* is the chamber music rather than the symphony of the soul, and it has a unique intensity of tone.

The practice of following public prayer with private intercession goes back to Temple times. After the daily sacrifice, "The Levites sang the Psalm [of the day]. When they reached the end of each section [the psalm was divided into three parts] they blew the shofar and the people prostrated themselves" (*Tamid* 7:3). Some communities continued the custom of prostration, with

TAHANUN

On Mondays and Thursdays, when Taḥanun is said, begin with "He is compassionate" below. On other days when Taḥanun is said, begin with "David said" on page 152.
Taḥanun is not said on: Rosh Ḥodesh, Ḥanukka, Tu BiShvat, the 14th and 15th of Adar I, Purim and Shushan Purim, in the month of Nisan, Yom HaAtzma'ut, the 14th of Iyar (Pesaḥ Sheni), Lag BaOmer, Yom Yerushalayim, from Rosh Ḥodesh Sivan through the day after Shavuot (in Israel through 12th of Sivan), Tisha B'Av, Tu B'Av, Erev Rosh HaShana, and from Erev Yom Kippur through the day after Simḥat Torah (in Israel through Rosh Ḥodesh Marḥeshvan).
Taḥanun is also not said: on the morning of a Brit Mila, either where the brit will take place or where the father, Sandek or Mohel are present; if a groom is present (and some say a bride) on the day of his wedding or during the week of Sheva Berakhot; in a house of mourning.
In Israel on days on which Taḥanun is said, say Viduy and the Thirteen Attributes of Divine Compassion on page 136. See law 176a.

The following until "David said" on page 152 is said standing.

וְהוּא רַחוּם He is compassionate. He forgives iniquity and does not destroy. *Ps. 78*
Repeatedly He suppresses His anger, not rousing His full wrath. Lord, do
not withhold Your compassion from us. May Your loving-kindness and
truth always protect us. Save us, Lord our God, and gather us from among *Ps. 106*
the nations, that we may give thanks to Your holy name and glory in Your
praise. If You, Lord, should keep account of sins, O Lord, who could stand? *Ps. 130*
But with You is forgiveness, that You may be revered. Do not deal with us *Jer. 14*
according to our sins; do not repay us according to our iniquities. Though
our iniquities testify against us, Lord, act for Your name's sake. Remember, *Ps. 25*
Lord, Your compassion and loving-kindness, for they are everlasting. May *Ps. 20*
the Lord answer us when we are in distress; may the name of Jacob's God
protect us. Lord, save! May the King answer us when we call. Our Father,
our King, be gracious to us and answer us, though we have no worthy deeds;

---

hope defeats tragedy. In these profound and moving words, Jews found the strength to survive.

With its intense penitential mood, *Taḥanun* is not said on days of festive joy; nor is it said on the Ninth of Av or in the house of a mourner.

והוא רחום *He is compassionate:* Penitential prayers woven from a variety of biblical texts, from Genesis and Exodus, Isaiah, Jeremiah and Joel, Lamentations, Daniel and Psalms. Lacking a Temple and sacrifices, we offer God our tears in their place: "The sacrifices of God are a broken spirit; a broken and humbled heart, God, You will not despise" (Psalm 51:19).

סדר תחנון

On Mondays and Thursdays, when תחנון *is said, begin with* וְהוּא רַחוּם *below.*
On other days when תחנון *is said, begin with* וַיֹּאמֶר דָּוִד *on page 153.*

תחנון *is not said on:* ראש חודש, חנוכה, ט״ו בשבט, *the 14th and 15th of* אדר א׳, פורים *and* שושן פורים, *in the month of* ניסן, יום העצמאות, *the 14th of* אייר (פסח שני), ל״ג בעומר, יום ירושלים, *from* ראש חודש סיון *through the day after* שבועות (*in* ארץ ישראל *through* י״ב סיון), תשעה באב, ט״ו באב, ערב ראש השנה, *and from* ערב יום כיפור *through the day after* שמחת תורה (*in* ארץ ישראל *through* ראש חודש מרחשון).

תחנון *is also not said: on the morning of a* ברית מילה, *either where the* ברית *will take place or where the father,* סנדק *or* מוהל *are present; if a* חתן *is present (and some say a* כלה) *on the day of his wedding or during the week of* שבע ברכות; *in a house of mourning.*

In ארץ ישראל *on days on which* תחנון *is said, say* וידוי *and the* י״ג מדות *on page 137. See law 176a.*

The following until וַיֹּאמֶר דָּוִד *on page 153 is said standing.*

וְהוּא רַחוּם, יְכַפֵּר עָוֹן וְלֹא־יַשְׁחִית, וְהִרְבָּה לְהָשִׁיב אַפּוֹ וְלֹא־יָעִיר כָּל־ תהלים עח
חֲמָתוֹ: אַתָּה יהוה לֹא־תִכְלָא רַחֲמֶיךָ מִמֶּנּוּ, חַסְדְּךָ וַאֲמִתְּךָ תָּמִיד יִצְּרוּנוּ.
הוֹשִׁיעֵנוּ יהוה אֱלֹהֵינוּ וְקַבְּצֵנוּ מִן־הַגּוֹיִם, לְהוֹדוֹת לְשֵׁם קָדְשֶׁךָ, לְהִשְׁתַּבֵּחַ תהלים קו
בִּתְהִלָּתֶךָ: אִם־עֲוֹנוֹת תִּשְׁמָר־יָהּ, אֲדֹנָי מִי יַעֲמֹד: כִּי־עִמְּךָ הַסְּלִיחָה לְמַעַן תהלים קל
תִּוָּרֵא: לֹא כַחֲטָאֵינוּ תַּעֲשֶׂה לָּנוּ, וְלֹא כַעֲוֹנוֹתֵינוּ תִּגְמֹל עָלֵינוּ. אִם־עֲוֹנֵינוּ ירמיה יד
עָנוּ בָנוּ, יהוה עֲשֵׂה לְמַעַן שְׁמֶךָ: זְכֹר־רַחֲמֶיךָ יהוה וַחֲסָדֶיךָ, כִּי מֵעוֹלָם תהלים כה
הֵמָּה: יַעַנְנוּ יהוה בְּיוֹם צָרָה, יְשַׂגֶּבְנוּ שֵׁם אֱלֹהֵי יַעֲקֹב. יהוה הוֹשִׁיעָה, תהלים כ

Some passages may have been added in the wake of the Gothic and Frankish persecutions in the seventh century. Their mood bespeaks the tears of Jews throughout the centuries of exile who experienced persecution, expulsion, humiliation, and often bloodshed at the hands of those amongst whom they lived. Even in times of freedom, we continue to say these prayers, keeping faith with our ancestors and remembering their tears.

What is remarkable about the prayers is the absence of anger or despair. If we ever doubt the power of prayer to transform the human situation, here we find an answer. Despite being treated as a pariah people, Jews never allowed themselves to be defined by their enemies. They wept and gave voice to pain: "God, see how low our glory has sunk among the nations. They abhor us as if we were impure." Yet they remained the people of the covenant, children of the divine promise, unbroken and unbreakable. Prayer sustains hope, and act charitably with us for Your name's sake. LORD our God, hear the sound of our pleas. Remember for us the covenant of our ancestors, and save us for Your name's sake.

וְעַתָּה And now, My LORD, our God, who took Your people out of the land of Egypt with a mighty hand, creating for Yourself renown to this day: we have sinned and acted wrongly. LORD, in keeping with all Your righteousness, please turn Your wrath and anger away from Jerusalem, Your holy mountain. Because of our sins and the iniquities of our ancestors, Jerusalem and Your people have become the scorn of all those around us. And now, our God, heed Your servant's prayer and pleas, and let Your face shine on Your desolate Sanctuary, for Your sake, O LORD. Incline Your ear, my God, and hear. Open Your eyes and see our desolation and that of the city called by Your name. Not because of our righteousness do we lay our pleas before You, but because of Your great compassion. LORD, hear! LORD, forgive! LORD, listen and act! Do not delay – for Your sake, my God, because Your city and Your people are called by Your name. *Dan. 9*

אָבִינוּ Our Father, compassionate Father, show us a sign for good, and gather our scattered ones from the four quarters of the earth. Let all the nations recognize and know that You are the LORD our God. And now, LORD, You *Is. 64* are our Father. We are the clay and You are our Potter; we are all the work of Your hand. Save us for the sake of Your name, our Rock, our King and our Redeemer. Pity Your people, LORD. Let not Your heritage become an object *Joel 2* of scorn, a byword among nations. Why should they say among the peoples, "Where is their God?" We know we have sinned and that there is no one to stand up for us. Let Your great name stand up for us in time of trouble. We know we have no merits of our own: therefore deal with us charitably for Your name's sake. As a father has compassion on his children, so, LORD, have compassion on us, and save us for the sake of Your name. Have mercy on Your people; have compassion for Your heritage; take pity in Your great

---

The passage weaves together three appeals to God's compassion: (1) we are Your children and You our Parent: have mercy on us as a parent forgives a child; (2) we are Your creation and You are our Creator: save us as an artist saves his most precious works of art; (3) we are Your witnesses, bearers of Your name: therefore save us for the sake of Your name. Let not the nations say, seeing our suffering, "Where is God?"

הַמֶּלֶךְ יַעֲנֵנוּ בְיוֹם־קָרְאֵנוּ: אָבִינוּ מַלְכֵּנוּ, חָנֵּנוּ וַעֲנֵנוּ, כִּי אֵין בָּנוּ מַעֲשִׂים, צְדָקָה עֲשֵׂה עִמָּנוּ לְמַעַן שְׁמֶךָ. אֲדוֹנֵינוּ אֱלֹהֵינוּ, שְׁמַע קוֹל תַּחֲנוּנֵינוּ, וּזְכָר לָנוּ אֶת בְּרִית אֲבוֹתֵינוּ וְהוֹשִׁיעֵנוּ לְמַעַן שְׁמֶךָ.

וְעַתָּה אֲדֹנָי אֱלֹהֵינוּ, אֲשֶׁר הוֹצֵאתָ אֶת־עַמְּךָ מֵאֶרֶץ מִצְרַיִם בְּיָד חֲזָקָה דניאל ט
וַתַּעַשׂ־לְךָ שֵׁם כַּיּוֹם הַזֶּה, חָטָאנוּ רָשָׁעְנוּ: אֲדֹנָי, כְּכָל־צִדְקֹתֶךָ יָשָׁב־נָא
אַפְּךָ וַחֲמָתְךָ, מֵעִירְךָ יְרוּשָׁלַםִ הַר־קָדְשֶׁךָ, כִּי בַחֲטָאֵינוּ וּבַעֲוֺנוֹת אֲבֹתֵינוּ,
יְרוּשָׁלַםִ וְעַמְּךָ לְחֶרְפָּה לְכָל־סְבִיבֹתֵינוּ: וְעַתָּה שְׁמַע אֱלֹהֵינוּ אֶל־תְּפִלַּת
עַבְדְּךָ וְאֶל־תַּחֲנוּנָיו, וְהָאֵר פָּנֶיךָ עַל־מִקְדָּשְׁךָ הַשָּׁמֵם, לְמַעַן אֲדֹנָי: הַטֵּה
אֱלֹהַי אָזְנְךָ וּשְׁמָע, פְּקַח עֵינֶיךָ וּרְאֵה שֹׁמְמֹתֵינוּ וְהָעִיר אֲשֶׁר־נִקְרָא שִׁמְךָ
עָלֶיהָ, כִּי לֹא עַל־צִדְקֹתֵינוּ אֲנַחְנוּ מַפִּילִים תַּחֲנוּנֵינוּ לְפָנֶיךָ, כִּי עַל־רַחֲמֶיךָ
הָרַבִּים: אֲדֹנָי שְׁמָעָה, אֲדֹנָי סְלָחָה, אֲדֹנָי הַקְשִׁיבָה וַעֲשֵׂה אַל־תְּאַחַר,
לְמַעַנְךָ אֱלֹהַי, כִּי־שִׁמְךָ נִקְרָא עַל־עִירְךָ וְעַל־עַמֶּךָ:

אָבִינוּ הָאָב הָרַחֲמָן, הַרְאֵנוּ אוֹת לְטוֹבָה וְקַבֵּץ נְפוּצוֹתֵינוּ מֵאַרְבַּע כַּנְפוֹת
הָאָרֶץ. יַכִּירוּ וְיֵדְעוּ כָּל הַגּוֹיִם כִּי אַתָּה יהוה אֱלֹהֵינוּ: וְעַתָּה יהוה אָבִינוּ ישעיה סד
אָתָּה, אֲנַחְנוּ הַחֹמֶר וְאַתָּה יֹצְרֵנוּ וּמַעֲשֵׂה יָדְךָ כֻּלָּנוּ. הוֹשִׁיעֵנוּ לְמַעַן
שְׁמֶךָ, צוּרֵנוּ מַלְכֵּנוּ וְגוֹאֲלֵנוּ. חוּסָה יהוה עַל־עַמֶּךָ, וְאַל־תִּתֵּן נַחֲלָתְךָ יואל ב
לְחֶרְפָּה לִמְשָׁל־בָּם גּוֹיִם, לָמָּה יֹאמְרוּ בָעַמִּים אַיֵּה אֱלֹהֵיהֶם: יָדַעְנוּ כִּי
חָטָאנוּ וְאֵין מִי יַעֲמֹד בַּעֲדֵנוּ, שִׁמְךָ הַגָּדוֹל יַעֲמָד לָנוּ בְּעֵת צָרָה. יָדַעְנוּ
כִּי אֵין בָּנוּ מַעֲשִׂים, צְדָקָה עֲשֵׂה עִמָּנוּ לְמַעַן שְׁמֶךָ. כְּרַחֵם אָב עַל בָּנִים
כֵּן תְּרַחֵם יהוה עָלֵינוּ, וְהוֹשִׁיעֵנוּ לְמַעַן שְׁמֶךָ. חֲמֹל עַל עַמֶּךָ, רַחֵם עַל

וְעַתָּה *And now:* A prayer uttered by Daniel (9:15–19) in the first year of the reign of Xerxes, when he foresaw that the desolation of Jerusalem would last for seventy years. Fasting, dressed in sackcloth and ashes, he pleaded to God to forgive the people and bring an end to their suffering. These words play a key part in the Seliḥot (penitential prayers) on Fast Days.

אֲנַחְנוּ הַחֹמֶר *We are the clay and You are our Potter:* A verse from Isaiah (64:7) which became the basis of one of the liturgical poems on *Kol Nidrei* night.

compassion. Be gracious to us and answer us, for righteousness is Yours, LORD. Always You do wondrous things.

הַבֵּט נָא Please look, please swiftly have compassion for Your people for Your name's sake. In Your great compassion, LORD our God, have pity and compassion, and rescue the flock You tend. Let us not be ruled by wrath, for our eyes are turned toward You. Save us for Your name's sake. Have compassion on us for the sake of Your covenant. Look and answer us in time of trouble, for Yours, LORD, is the power to save. Our hope is in You, God of forgiveness. Please forgive, good and forgiving God, for You are a gracious, compassionate God and King.

אָנָּא מֶלֶךְ Please, gracious and compassionate King, remember and call to mind the Covenant between the Pieces [with Abraham] and let the binding of his only son [Isaac] appear before You for Israel's sake. Our Father, our King, be gracious to us and answer us, for we are called by Your great name. You who work miracles at all times, deal with us according to Your loving-kindness. Gracious and compassionate One, look and answer us in time of trouble, for salvation is Yours, LORD. Our Father, our King, our Refuge, do not act with us according to our evil deeds. Remember, LORD, Your tender mercies and Your love. Save us in Your great goodness, and have mercy on us, for we have no other god but You, our Rock. Do not abandon us, LORD our God, do not be distant from us, for we are worn out by the sword and captivity, pestilence and plague, and by every trouble and sorrow. Rescue us, for in You lies our hope. Put us not to shame, LORD our God. Let Your face shine upon us. Remember for us the covenant of our ancestors and save us for Your name's sake. See our troubles and heed the voice of our prayer, for You heed the prayer of every mouth.

אֵל רַחוּם וְחַנּוּן O Compassionate and gracious God, have compassion on us and on all Your works, for there is none like You, LORD our God. Please, we beg You, forgive our sins, our Father, our King, our Rock, our Redeemer, living and eternal God, mighty in strength, loving and good to all Your works, for You are the LORD our God. O God, slow to anger and full of compassion, act with us according to Your great compassion and save us for Your name's sake. Hear our prayer, our King, and save us from our enemies' hands. Heed our prayer, our King, and save us from all distress and sorrow. You are our Father, our King. We are called by Your name. Do not desert us. Do not abandon us, our Father. Do not cast us away, our Creator. Do not forget us, our Maker – for You are a gracious and compassionate God and King.

נַחֲלָתֶךָ, חוּסָה נָּא כְּרֹב רַחֲמֶיךָ, חָנֵּנוּ וַעֲנֵנוּ. כִּי לְךָ יהוה הַצְּדָקָה, עֹשֵׂה נִפְלָאוֹת בְּכָל עֵת.

הַבֶּט נָא, רַחֶם נָא עַל עַמְּךָ מְהֵרָה לְמַעַן שְׁמֶךָ בְּרַחֲמֶיךָ הָרַבִּים יהוה אֱלֹהֵינוּ. חוּס וְרַחֵם וְהוֹשִׁיעָה צֹאן מַרְעִיתֶךָ, וְאַל יִמְשָׁל בָּנוּ קֶצֶף, כִּי לְךָ עֵינֵינוּ תְלוּיוֹת. הוֹשִׁיעֵנוּ לְמַעַן שְׁמֶךָ. רַחֵם עָלֵינוּ לְמַעַן בְּרִיתֶךָ. הַבִּיטָה וַעֲנֵנוּ בְּעֵת צָרָה, כִּי לְךָ יהוה הַיְשׁוּעָה. בְּךָ תוֹחַלְתֵּנוּ אֱלוֹהַּ סְלִיחוֹת, אָנָּא סְלַח נָא אֵל טוֹב וְסַלָּח, כִּי אֵל מֶלֶךְ חַנּוּן וְרַחוּם אָתָּה.

אָנָּא מֶלֶךְ חַנּוּן וְרַחוּם, זְכֹר וְהַבֵּט לִבְרִית בֵּין הַבְּתָרִים, וְתֵרָאֶה לְפָנֶיךָ עֲקֵדַת יָחִיד לְמַעַן יִשְׂרָאֵל. אָבִינוּ מַלְכֵּנוּ, חָנֵּנוּ וַעֲנֵנוּ, כִּי שִׁמְךָ הַגָּדוֹל נִקְרָא עָלֵינוּ. עֹשֵׂה נִפְלָאוֹת בְּכָל עֵת, עֲשֵׂה עִמָּנוּ כְּחַסְדֶּךָ. חַנּוּן וְרַחוּם, הַבִּיטָה וַעֲנֵנוּ בְּעֵת צָרָה, כִּי לְךָ יהוה הַיְשׁוּעָה. אָבִינוּ מַלְכֵּנוּ מַחֲסֵנוּ, אַל תַּעַשׂ עִמָּנוּ כְּרֹעַ מַעֲלָלֵינוּ. זְכֹר רַחֲמֶיךָ יהוה וַחֲסָדֶיךָ, וּכְרֹב טוּבְךָ הוֹשִׁיעֵנוּ, וַחֲמָל נָא עָלֵינוּ, כִּי אֵין לָנוּ אֱלוֹהַּ אַחֵר מִבַּלְעָדֶיךָ צוּרֵנוּ. אַל תַּעַזְבֵנוּ יהוה אֱלֹהֵינוּ אַל תִּרְחַק מִמֶּנּוּ. כִּי נַפְשֵׁנוּ קְצָרָה, מֵחֶרֶב וּמִשְּׁבִי וּמִדֶּבֶר וּמִמַּגֵּפָה. וּמִכָּל צָרָה וְיָגוֹן הַצִּילֵנוּ, כִּי לְךָ קִוִּינוּ. וְאַל תַּכְלִימֵנוּ יהוה אֱלֹהֵינוּ, וְהָאֵר פָּנֶיךָ בָּנוּ, וּזְכָר לָנוּ אֶת בְּרִית אֲבוֹתֵינוּ וְהוֹשִׁיעֵנוּ לְמַעַן שְׁמֶךָ. רְאֵה בְצָרוֹתֵינוּ, וּשְׁמַע קוֹל תְּפִלָּתֵנוּ, כִּי אַתָּה שׁוֹמֵעַ תְּפִלַּת כָּל פֶּה.

אֵל רַחוּם וְחַנּוּן, רַחֵם עָלֵינוּ וְעַל כָּל מַעֲשֶׂיךָ, כִּי אֵין כָּמוֹךָ יהוה אֱלֹהֵינוּ. אָנָּא שָׂא נָא פְשָׁעֵינוּ, אָבִינוּ מַלְכֵּנוּ צוּרֵנוּ וְגוֹאֲלֵנוּ, אֵל חַי וְקַיָּם הַחֲסִין בַּכֹּחַ, חָסִיד וָטוֹב עַל כָּל מַעֲשֶׂיךָ, כִּי אַתָּה הוּא יהוה אֱלֹהֵינוּ. אֵל אֶרֶךְ אַפַּיִם וּמָלֵא רַחֲמִים, עֲשֵׂה עִמָּנוּ כְּרֹב רַחֲמֶיךָ, וְהוֹשִׁיעֵנוּ לְמַעַן שְׁמֶךָ. שְׁמַע מַלְכֵּנוּ תְּפִלָּתֵנוּ, וּמִיַּד אוֹיְבֵינוּ הַצִּילֵנוּ. שְׁמַע מַלְכֵּנוּ תְּפִלָּתֵנוּ, וּמִכָּל צָרָה וְיָגוֹן הַצִּילֵנוּ. אָבִינוּ מַלְכֵּנוּ אָתָּה, וְשִׁמְךָ עָלֵינוּ נִקְרָא. אַל תַּנִּחֵנוּ. אַל תַּעַזְבֵנוּ אָבִינוּ וְאַל תִּטְּשֵׁנוּ בּוֹרְאֵנוּ וְאַל תִּשְׁכָּחֵנוּ יוֹצְרֵנוּ, כִּי אֵל מֶלֶךְ חַנּוּן וְרַחוּם אָתָּה.

אֵין כָּמוֹךָ There is none like You in grace and compassion, LORD our God. There is none like You, God, slow to anger and abounding in loving-kindness and truth. Save us in Your great compassion; rescue us from storm and turmoil. Remember Your servants Abraham, Isaac and Jacob; do not attend to our stubbornness, wickedness and sinfulness. Turn from Your *Ex. 32*
fierce anger, and relent from the evil meant for Your people. Remove from us the scourge of death, for You are compassionate. This is Your way, to show unearned loving-kindness to every generation. Have pity on Your people, LORD, and save us from Your wrath. Remove from us the scourge of plague and the harsh decree, for You are the Guardian of Israel. You are *Dan. 9*
right, my LORD, and we are shamefaced. How can we complain? What can we say? What can we plead? How can we justify ourselves? Let us search our ways and examine them and return to You, for Your right hand is outstretched to receive those who return. Please, LORD, please save. Please, *Ps. 118*
LORD, please send success. Please, LORD, answer us when we call. For You, LORD, we wait. For You, LORD, we hope. For You, LORD, we long. Do not be silent while we suffer, for the nations are saying, "Their hope is lost." To You alone every knee must bend, and those who hold themselves high bow down.

הַפּוֹתֵחַ יָד You who hold out an open hand of repentance to receive transgressors and sinners – our soul is overwhelmed by our great sorrow. Do not forget us for ever. Arise and save us, for we seek refuge in You. Our Father, our King, though we lack righteousness and good deeds, remember for us the covenant of our fathers, and our testimonies daily that "The LORD is One." Look on our affliction, for many are our sufferings and heartaches. Have pity on us, LORD, in the land of our captivity. Do not pour out Your wrath on us, for we are Your people, the children of Your covenant. God, see how low our glory has sunk among the nations. They abhor us as if we were impure. How long will Your strength be captive, and Your glory in the hand of the foe? Arouse Your strength and zeal against Your enemies. Let them be shamed and deprived of power. Let not our hardships seem small to You. Swiftly may Your compassion reach us in the day of our distress. If not for our sake, act for Yours, so that the memory of our survivors be not destroyed. Be gracious to the nation who, in constant love, proclaim twice daily the unity of Your name, saying, "Listen, Israel, the LORD is our God, *Deut. 6*
the LORD is One."

אֵין כָּמְוֹךָ חַנּוּן וְרַחוּם יהוה אֱלֹהֵינוּ, אֵין כָּמְוֹךָ אֵל אֶרֶךְ אַפַּיִם וְרַב חֶסֶד
וֶאֱמֶת. הוֹשִׁיעֵנוּ בְּרַחֲמֶיךָ הָרַבִּים, מֵרַעַשׁ וּמֵרְגֶז הַצִּילֵנוּ. זְכֹר לַעֲבָדֶיךָ
לְאַבְרָהָם לְיִצְחָק וּלְיַעֲקֹב, אַל תֵּפֶן אֶל קָשְׁיֵנוּ וְאֶל רִשְׁעֵנוּ וְאֶל חַטָּאתֵנוּ.
שׁוּב מֵחֲרוֹן אַפֶּךָ, וְהִנָּחֵם עַל־הָרָעָה לְעַמֶּךָ: וְהָסֵר מִמֶּנּוּ מַכַּת הַמָּוֶת כִּי שמות לב
רַחוּם אָתָּה, כִּי כֵן דַּרְכֶּךָ, עֹשֶׂה חֶסֶד חִנָּם בְּכָל דּוֹר וָדוֹר. חוּסָה יהוה עַל
עַמֶּךָ וְהַצִּילֵנוּ מִזַּעְמֶךָ, וְהָסֵר מִמֶּנּוּ מַכַּת הַמַּגֵּפָה וּגְזֵרָה קָשָׁה, כִּי אַתָּה
שׁוֹמֵר יִשְׂרָאֵל. לְךָ אֲדֹנָי הַצְּדָקָה וְלָנוּ בֹּשֶׁת הַפָּנִים: מַה נִּתְאוֹנֵן, מַה נֹּאמַר, דניאל ט
מַה נְּדַבֵּר וּמַה נִּצְטַדָּק. נַחְפְּשָׂה דְרָכֵינוּ וְנַחְקֹרָה וְנָשׁוּבָה אֵלֶיךָ, כִּי יְמִינְךָ
פְשׁוּטָה לְקַבֵּל שָׁבִים. אָנָּא יהוה הוֹשִׁיעָה נָּא, אָנָּא יהוה הַצְלִיחָה נָא: תהלים קיח
אָנָּא יהוה עֲנֵנוּ בְיוֹם קָרְאֵנוּ. לְךָ יהוה חִכִּינוּ, לְךָ יהוה קִוִּינוּ, לְךָ יהוה
נְיַחֵל. אַל תֶּחֱשֶׁה וּתְעַנֵּנוּ, כִּי נָאֲמוּ גוֹיִם, אָבְדָה תִקְוָתָם. כָּל בֶּרֶךְ וְכָל
קוֹמָה, לְךָ לְבַד תִּשְׁתַּחֲוֶה.

הַפּוֹתֵחַ יָד בִּתְשׁוּבָה לְקַבֵּל פּוֹשְׁעִים וְחַטָּאִים, נִבְהֲלָה נַפְשֵׁנוּ מֵרֹב עִצְּבוֹנֵנוּ. אַל תִּשְׁכָּחֵנוּ נֶצַח, קוּמָה וְהוֹשִׁיעֵנוּ כִּי חָסִינוּ בָךְ. אָבִינוּ מַלְכֵּנוּ, אִם אֵין בָּנוּ צְדָקָה וּמַעֲשִׂים טוֹבִים, זְכָר לָנוּ אֶת בְּרִית אֲבוֹתֵינוּ וְעֵדוֹתֵינוּ בְּכָל יוֹם יהוה אֶחָד. הַבִּיטָה בְעָנְיֵנוּ, כִּי רַבּוּ מַכְאוֹבֵינוּ וְצָרוֹת לְבָבֵנוּ. חוּסָה יהוה עָלֵינוּ בְּאֶרֶץ שִׁבְיֵנוּ, וְאַל תִּשְׁפֹּךְ חֲרוֹנְךָ עָלֵינוּ, כִּי אֲנַחְנוּ עַמְּךָ בְּנֵי בְרִיתֶךָ. אֵל, הַבִּיטָה, דַּל כְּבוֹדֵנוּ בַּגּוֹיִם וְשִׁקְּצוּנוּ כְּטֻמְאַת הַנִּדָּה. עַד מָתַי עֻזְּךָ בַּשְּׁבִי, וְתִפְאַרְתְּךָ בְּיַד צָר. עוֹרְרָה גְבוּרָתְךָ וְקִנְאָתְךָ עַל אוֹיְבֶיךָ. הֵם יֵבֹשׁוּ וְיֵחַתּוּ מִגְּבוּרָתָם. וְאַל יִמְעֲטוּ לְפָנֶיךָ תְּלָאוֹתֵינוּ, מַהֵר יְקַדְּמוּנוּ רַחֲמֶיךָ בְּיוֹם צָרָתֵנוּ. וְאִם לֹא לְמַעֲנֵנוּ, לְמַעַנְךָ פְעַל, וְאַל תַּשְׁחִית זֵכֶר שְׁאֵרִיתֵנוּ, וְחֹן אֹם הַמְיַחֲדִים שִׁמְךָ פַּעֲמַיִם בְּכָל יוֹם תָּמִיד בְּאַהֲבָה,
וְאוֹמְרִים, שְׁמַע יִשְׂרָאֵל, יהוה אֱלֹהֵינוּ, יהוה אֶחָד: דברים ו

הַפּוֹתֵחַ יָד *You who hold out an open hand:* God's forgiveness stretches beyond strict retribution: "I do not desire the death of the wicked, but rather that they turn from their ways and live" (Ezek. 33:11).

LOWERING THE HEAD

On Sundays, Tuesdays, Wednesdays and Fridays, begin Taḥanun here. The following, until "We do not know" on page 156, is said sitting. When praying in a place where there is a Torah scroll, one should lean forward, resting one's head on the left arm (unless you are wearing tefillin on the left arm, in which case rest on the right arm out of respect for the tefillin), until in "sudden shame."

וַיֹּאמֶר דָּוִד David said to Gad, "I am in great distress. *II Sam. 24*
Let us fall into God's hand, for His mercy is great;
but do not let me fall into the hand of man."

Compassionate and gracious One, I have sinned before You.
LORD, full of compassion, have compassion on me and accept my pleas.

LORD, do not rebuke me in Your anger or chastise me in Your wrath. Be gracious to me, LORD, for I am weak. Heal me, LORD, for my bones are in agony. My soul is in anguish, and You, O LORD – how long? Turn, LORD, set my soul free; save me for the sake of Your love. For no one remembers You when he is dead. Who can praise You from the grave? I am weary with my sighing. Every night I drench my bed, I soak my couch with my tears. My eye grows dim from grief, worn out because of all my foes. Leave me, all you evildoers, for the LORD has heard the sound of my weeping. The LORD has heard my pleas. The LORD will accept my prayer. All my enemies will be shamed and utterly dismayed. They will turn back in sudden shame. *Ps. 6*

Sit upright. On Mondays and Thursdays, say the following. On other days, continue with "Guardian of Israel" on the next page.

LORD, God of Israel, turn away from Your fierce anger,
and relent from the evil against Your people.

Look down from heaven and see how we have become an object of scorn and derision among the nations. We are regarded as sheep led to the slaughter, to be killed, destroyed, beaten and humiliated. Yet, despite all this, we have not forgotten Your name. Please do not forget us.

LORD, God of Israel, turn away from Your fierce anger,
and relent from the evil against Your people.

Strangers say, "You have no hope or expectation." Be gracious to the nation whose hope is in Your name. O Pure One, bring our deliverance close. We are exhausted. We are given no rest. May Your compassion suppress Your anger against us. Please turn away from Your fierce anger, and have compassion on the people You chose as Your own.

---

when prayer becomes the ladder on which we climb from the pit of despair to the free air of hope.

הַבֵּט מִשָּׁמַיִם *Look down from heaven:* These heart-rending words were already known in Europe in the eleventh century, and recall the terrible persecutions Jews suffered during the early Middle Ages.

נפילת אפיים

On Sundays, Tuesdays, Wednesdays and Fridays, begin תחנון *here.*
The following, until וַאֲנַחְנוּ לֹא נֵדַע *on page 157, is said sitting. When praying in a place where there is a* ספר תורה*, one should lean forward, resting one's head on the arm on which the* תפילין *are not worn, until* יֵבֹשׁוּ רָגַע.

שמואל ב, כד
וַיֹּאמֶר דָּוִד אֶל־גָּד, צַר־לִי מְאֹד
נִפְּלָה־נָּא בְיַד־יהוה, כִּי רַבִּים רַחֲמָו, וּבְיַד־אָדָם אַל־אֶפֹּלָה:

רַחוּם וְחַנּוּן, חָטָאתִי לְפָנֶיךָ. יהוה מָלֵא רַחֲמִים, רַחֵם עָלַי וְקַבֵּל תַּחֲנוּנָי.

תהלים ו
יהוה, אַל־בְּאַפְּךָ תוֹכִיחֵנִי, וְאַל־בַּחֲמָתְךָ תְיַסְּרֵנִי: חָנֵּנִי יהוה, כִּי אֻמְלַל אָנִי, רְפָאֵנִי יהוה, כִּי נִבְהֲלוּ עֲצָמָי: וְנַפְשִׁי נִבְהֲלָה מְאֹד, וְאַתָּ יהוה, עַד־מָתָי: שׁוּבָה יהוה, חַלְּצָה נַפְשִׁי, הוֹשִׁיעֵנִי לְמַעַן חַסְדֶּךָ: כִּי אֵין בַּמָּוֶת זִכְרֶךָ, בִּשְׁאוֹל מִי יוֹדֶה־לָּךְ: יָגַעְתִּי בְּאַנְחָתִי, אַשְׂחֶה בְכָל־לַיְלָה מִטָּתִי, בְּדִמְעָתִי עַרְשִׂי אַמְסֶה: עָשְׁשָׁה מִכַּעַס עֵינִי, עָתְקָה בְּכָל־צוֹרְרָי: סוּרוּ מִמֶּנִּי כָּל־פֹּעֲלֵי אָוֶן, כִּי שָׁמַע יהוה קוֹל בִּכְיִי: שָׁמַע יהוה תְּחִנָּתִי, יהוה תְּפִלָּתִי יִקָּח: יֵבֹשׁוּ וְיִבָּהֲלוּ מְאֹד כָּל־אֹיְבָי, יָשֻׁבוּ יֵבֹשׁוּ רָגַע:

Sit upright. On Mondays and Thursdays, say the following.
On other days, continue with שׁוֹמֵר יִשְׂרָאֵל *on the next page.*

יהוה אֱלֹהֵי יִשְׂרָאֵל, שׁוּב מֵחֲרוֹן אַפֶּךָ וְהִנָּחֵם עַל הָרָעָה לְעַמֶּךָ.
הַבֵּט מִשָּׁמַיִם וּרְאֵה כִּי הָיִינוּ לַעַג וָקֶלֶס בַּגּוֹיִם, נֶחְשַׁבְנוּ כַּצֹּאן לַטֶּבַח יוּבָל, לַהֲרֹג וּלְאַבֵּד וּלְמַכָּה וּלְחֶרְפָּה. וּבְכָל זֹאת שִׁמְךָ לֹא שָׁכָחְנוּ, נָא אַל תִּשְׁכָּחֵנוּ.
יהוה אֱלֹהֵי יִשְׂרָאֵל, שׁוּב מֵחֲרוֹן אַפֶּךָ וְהִנָּחֵם עַל הָרָעָה לְעַמֶּךָ.
זָרִים אוֹמְרִים אֵין תּוֹחֶלֶת וְתִקְוָה, חֹן אֹם לְשִׁמְךָ מְקַוֶּה, טָהוֹר יְשׁוּעָתֵנוּ קָרְבָה, יָגַעְנוּ וְלֹא הוּנַח לָנוּ, רַחֲמֶיךָ יִכְבְּשׁוּ אֶת כַּעַסְךָ מֵעָלֵינוּ. אָנָּא שׁוּב מֵחֲרוֹנְךָ וְרַחֵם סְגֻלָּה אֲשֶׁר בָּחָרְתָּ.

וַיֹּאמֶר דָּוִד *David said to Gad:* Words spoken by David during a moment of crisis (II Sam. 24:14). The king had sinned by taking a census of the people. God, through the prophet Gad, offered him a choice: famine, war, or punishment directly from heaven. David replied: it is better to be punished by God than suffer the cruelty of man.

יהוה, אַל־בְּאַפְּךָ תוֹכִיחֵנִי *Lord, do not rebuke me in Your anger*: A psalm of intense emotional power, spoken out of fear's heart of darkness. שָׁמַע יהוה תְּחִנָּתִי *The Lord has heard my pleas:* from the deepest pain, strength is born,

Lord, God of Israel, turn away from Your fierce anger,
and relent from the evil against Your people.

Have pity on us, Lord, in Your compassion, and do not hand us over to cruel oppressors. Why should the nations say, "Where is their God now?" For Your own sake, deal kindly with us, and do not delay. Please turn away from Your fierce anger, and have compassion on the people You chose as Your own.

Lord, God of Israel, turn away from Your fierce anger,
and relent from the evil against Your people.

Heed our voice and be gracious. Do not abandon us into the hand of our enemies to blot out our name. Remember what You promised our fathers: "I will make your descendants as many as the stars of heaven" – yet now we are only a few left from many. Yet, despite all this, we have not forgotten Your name. Please do not forget us.

Lord, God of Israel, turn away from Your fierce anger,
and relent from the evil against Your people.

Help us, God of our salvation, for the sake of the glory of Your name. Save *Ps. 79*
us and pardon our sins for Your name's sake.

Lord, God of Israel, turn away from Your fierce anger,
and relent from the evil against Your people.

On all days continue here:

שׁוֹמֵר יִשְׂרָאֵל Guardian of Israel, guard the remnant of Israel,
and let not Israel perish, who declare, "Listen, Israel."
Guardian of a unique nation, guard the remnant of a unique people,
and let not that unique nation perish, who proclaim the unity
of Your name [saying], "The Lord is our God, the Lord is One."
Guardian of a holy nation, guard the remnant of that holy people,
and let not the holy nation perish, who three times repeat
the threefold declaration of holiness to the Holy One.
You who are conciliated by calls for compassion and placated by pleas,
be conciliated and placated toward an afflicted generation,
for there is no other help.
Our Father, our King, be gracious to us and answer us, though we have no
worthy deeds; act with us in charity and loving-kindness and save us.

שׁוֹמֵר יִשְׂרָאֵל *Guardian of Israel:* A three-verse prayer set in motion by a phrase from Psalm 121: "See: the Guardian of Israel neither slumbers nor sleeps." An example of early liturgical poetry, it has the same structure as

יהוה אֱלֹהֵי יִשְׂרָאֵל, שׁוּב מֵחֲרוֹן אַפֶּךָ וְהִנָּחֵם עַל הָרָעָה לְעַמֶּךָ.

חוּסָה יהוה עָלֵינוּ בְּרַחֲמֶיךָ, וְאַל תִּתְּנֵנוּ בִּידֵי אַכְזָרִים. לָמָּה יֹאמְרוּ הַגּוֹיִם אַיֵּה נָא אֱלֹהֵיהֶם, לְמַעַנְךָ עֲשֵׂה עִמָּנוּ חֶסֶד וְאַל תְּאַחַר. אָנָּא שׁוּב מֵחֲרוֹנְךָ וְרַחֵם סְגֻלָּה אֲשֶׁר בָּחָרְתָּ.

יהוה אֱלֹהֵי יִשְׂרָאֵל, שׁוּב מֵחֲרוֹן אַפֶּךָ וְהִנָּחֵם עַל הָרָעָה לְעַמֶּךָ.

קוֹלֵנוּ תִשְׁמַע וְתָחֹן, וְאַל תִּטְּשֵׁנוּ בְּיַד אֹיְבֵינוּ לִמְחוֹת אֶת שְׁמֵנוּ. זְכֹר אֲשֶׁר נִשְׁבַּעְתָּ לַאֲבוֹתֵינוּ כְּכוֹכְבֵי הַשָּׁמַיִם אַרְבֶּה אֶת זַרְעֲכֶם, וְעַתָּה נִשְׁאַרְנוּ מְעַט מֵהַרְבֵּה. וּבְכָל זֹאת שִׁמְךָ לֹא שָׁכָחְנוּ, נָא אַל תִּשְׁכָּחֵנוּ.

יהוה אֱלֹהֵי יִשְׂרָאֵל, שׁוּב מֵחֲרוֹן אַפֶּךָ וְהִנָּחֵם עַל הָרָעָה לְעַמֶּךָ.

עָזְרֵנוּ אֱלֹהֵי יִשְׁעֵנוּ עַל־דְּבַר כְּבוֹד־שְׁמֶךָ, וְהַצִּילֵנוּ וְכַפֵּר עַל־חַטֹּאתֵינוּ לְמַעַן שְׁמֶךָ: תהלים עט

יהוה אֱלֹהֵי יִשְׂרָאֵל, שׁוּב מֵחֲרוֹן אַפֶּךָ וְהִנָּחֵם עַל הָרָעָה לְעַמֶּךָ.

On all days continue here:

שׁוֹמֵר יִשְׂרָאֵל, שְׁמֹר שְׁאֵרִית יִשְׂרָאֵל, וְאַל יֹאבַד יִשְׂרָאֵל
הָאוֹמְרִים שְׁמַע יִשְׂרָאֵל.

שׁוֹמֵר גּוֹי אֶחָד, שְׁמֹר שְׁאֵרִית עַם אֶחָד, וְאַל יֹאבַד גּוֹי אֶחָד
הַמְיַחֲדִים שִׁמְךָ, יהוה אֱלֹהֵינוּ יהוה אֶחָד.

שׁוֹמֵר גּוֹי קָדוֹשׁ, שְׁמֹר שְׁאֵרִית עַם קָדוֹשׁ, וְאַל יֹאבַד גּוֹי קָדוֹשׁ
הַמְשַׁלְּשִׁים בְּשָׁלֹשׁ קְדֻשּׁוֹת לְקָדוֹשׁ.

מִתְרַצֶּה בְּרַחֲמִים וּמִתְפַּיֵּס בְּתַחֲנוּנִים, הִתְרַצֵּה וְהִתְפַּיֵּס לְדוֹר עָנִי
כִּי אֵין עוֹזֵר.

אָבִינוּ מַלְכֵּנוּ, חָנֵּנוּ וַעֲנֵנוּ, כִּי אֵין בָּנוּ מַעֲשִׂים
עֲשֵׂה עִמָּנוּ צְדָקָה וָחֶסֶד וְהוֹשִׁיעֵנוּ.

וּבְכָל זֹאת *Yet, despite all this:* After the Holocaust, the concentration camp at Theresienstadt was excavated. A hidden room was discovered, which had served as a secret place in which the prisoners would pray. On one of its walls were written the words: "Yet, despite all this, we have not forgotten Your name. Please do not forget us."

Stand at ▴.

וַאֲנַחְנוּ We do not know ▴what to do, but our eyes are turned to You. Remem- *II Chr. 12* *Ps. 25*
ber, Lord, Your compassion and loving-kindness, for they are everlasting.
May Your loving-kindness, Lord, be with us, for we have put our hope in *Ps. 33*
You. Do not hold against us the sins of those who came before us. May Your *Ps. 79*
mercies meet us swiftly, for we have been brought very low. Be gracious to us, *Ps. 123*
Lord, be gracious to us, for we are sated with contempt. In wrath, remember *Hab. 3*
mercy. He knows our nature; He remembers that we are dust. ▸ Help us, God *Ps. 103* *Ps. 79*
of our salvation, for the sake of the glory of Your name. Save us and grant
atonement for our sins for Your name's sake.

HALF KADDISH

Leader: יִתְגַּדַּל Magnified and sanctified
may His great name be,
in the world He created by His will.
May He establish His kingdom
in your lifetime and in your days,
and in the lifetime of all the house of Israel,
swiftly and soon – and say: Amen.

All: May His great name be blessed for ever and all time.

Leader: Blessed and praised, glorified and exalted,
raised and honored, uplifted and lauded
be the name of the Holy One,
blessed be He,
beyond any blessing, song, praise and consolation
uttered in the world – and say: Amen.

וַאֲנַחְנוּ לֹא נֵדַע *We do not know:* A line taken from the prayer of King Jehoshaphat when the nation was confronted by a coalition of hostile powers intent on war (II Chr. 20:12). Our custom is to stand after these words. Abudarham explains that this is because – like Moses pleading on behalf of the people – we have prayed in every posture, sitting (before the Amida), standing (during the Amida), and "falling on our faces" (during *Taḥanun*). We have exhausted the repertoire of prayer and do not know what else to do. We stand at this point to signal that our private supplications have come to an end.

Stand at ^.

^וַאֲנַחְנוּ לֹא נֵדַע ^מַה־נַּעֲשֶׂה, כִּי עָלֶיךָ עֵינֵינוּ: זְכֹר־רַחֲמֶיךָ יהוה וַחֲסָדֶיךָ, דברי הימים ב׳ כ / תהלים כה
כִּי מֵעוֹלָם הֵמָּה: יְהִי־חַסְדְּךָ יהוה עָלֵינוּ, כַּאֲשֶׁר יִחַלְנוּ לָךְ: אַל־תִּזְכָּר־לָנוּ תהלים לג / תהלים עט
עֲוֹנֹת רִאשֹׁנִים, מַהֵר יְקַדְּמוּנוּ רַחֲמֶיךָ, כִּי דַלּוֹנוּ מְאֹד: חָנֵּנוּ יהוה חָנֵּנוּ, תהלים קכג
כִּי־רַב שָׂבַעְנוּ בוּז: בְּרֹגֶז רַחֵם תִּזְכּוֹר: כִּי־הוּא יָדַע יִצְרֵנוּ, זָכוּר כִּי־עָפָר חבקוק ג / תהלים קג
אֲנָחְנוּ: ‹ עָזְרֵנוּ אֱלֹהֵי יִשְׁעֵנוּ עַל־דְּבַר כְּבוֹד־שְׁמֶךָ, וְהַצִּילֵנוּ וְכַפֵּר עַל־ תהלים עט
חַטֹּאתֵינוּ לְמַעַן שְׁמֶךָ:

חצי קדיש

ש״ץ: יִתְגַּדַּל וְיִתְקַדַּשׁ שְׁמֵהּ רַבָּא (קהל: אָמֵן)
בְּעָלְמָא דִּי בְרָא כִרְעוּתֵהּ
וְיַמְלִיךְ מַלְכוּתֵהּ
בְּחַיֵּיכוֹן וּבְיוֹמֵיכוֹן וּבְחַיֵּי דְכָל בֵּית יִשְׂרָאֵל
בַּעֲגָלָא וּבִזְמַן קָרִיב, וְאִמְרוּ אָמֵן. (קהל: אָמֵן)

קהל וש״ץ: יְהֵא שְׁמֵהּ רַבָּא מְבָרַךְ לְעָלַם וּלְעָלְמֵי עָלְמַיָּא.

ש״ץ: יִתְבָּרַךְ וְיִשְׁתַּבַּח וְיִתְפָּאַר וְיִתְרוֹמַם וְיִתְנַשֵּׂא
וְיִתְהַדָּר וְיִתְעַלֶּה וְיִתְהַלָּל
שְׁמֵהּ דְּקֻדְשָׁא בְּרִיךְ הוּא (קהל: בְּרִיךְ הוּא)
לְעֵלָּא מִן כָּל בִּרְכָתָא
/בעשרת ימי תשובה: לְעֵלָּא לְעֵלָּא מִכָּל בִּרְכָתָא/
וְשִׁירָתָא, תֻּשְׁבְּחָתָא וְנֶחֱמָתָא
דַּאֲמִירָן בְּעָלְמָא, וְאִמְרוּ אָמֵן. (קהל: אָמֵן)

---

the poem preceding the morning Amida, "Rock of Israel! Arise to the help of Israel…" and the prayer said on the Ten Days of Penitence, "Remember us for life, O King who desires life…" In each case every verse contains four phrases, all ending with the same word (Rabbi Jeffrey Cohen). The prayer was transferred from the penitential prayers known as Selihot to the Daily Service.

REMOVING THE TORAH FROM THE ARK

On Mondays and Thursdays, Rosh Hodesh, Hanukka, Purim and Fast Days, the Torah is read when a minyan is present. On all other days, continue with "Happy are those" on page 174.

Before taking the Torah out of the Ark, on Mondays and Thursdays, stand while reciting "God, slow to anger." It is not said on Rosh Hodesh, Erev Pesah, Hanukka, the 14th and 15th of Adar I, Purim and Shushan Purim, Yom HaAtzma'ut, Yom Yerushalayim, Tisha B'Av or in a house of mourning, and in Israel on Isru Hag. Most people say both paragraphs; some say only the first.

God, slow to anger, abounding
in loving-kindness and truth,
do not rebuke us in Your anger.
Have pity on Your people, LORD,
and save us from all evil.
We have sinned against You, LORD.
Please forgive in accordance with
Your great compassion, God.

God, slow to anger, full of compassion,
do not hide Your face from us.
Have pity on the remnant of Israel
Your people, LORD,
and deliver us from all evil.
We have sinned against You, LORD.
Please forgive in accordance with
Your great compassion, God.

The Ark is opened and the congregation stands. All say:

וַיְהִי בִּנְסֹעַ Whenever the Ark set out, Moses would say, "Arise, LORD, *Num. 10*
and may Your enemies be scattered. May those who hate You flee
before You." For the Torah shall come forth from Zion, and the word *Is. 2*
of the LORD from Jerusalem. Blessed is He who in His holiness gave
the Torah to His people Israel.

---

them the entire Book of the Covenant which had been found in the LORD's Temple" (II Chr. 34:30).

The book of Nehemiah (8:1–12) contains a graphic description of the return of the Babylonian exiles to Israel. Ezra gathered the people at the Temple and read the Torah to them "from dawn until midday," assisted by Levites who "interpreted it and explained its meaning, so that they understood the verses."

These were national occasions. At a more local level, tradition holds that Moses instituted the practice that the Torah be read on Shabbat, Yom Tov, Hol HaMo'ed, and Rosh Hodesh. Ezra ordained that it also be read on Mondays and Thursdays (market days in ancient times) and on Shabbat afternoons (Yerushalmi, *Megilla* 4:1). The public reading of the Torah is as ancient an institution as prayer itself.

The synagogue thus became not only a house of prayer but also a house of study. The result is a dynamic tension between speaking and listening. In

הוצאת ספר תורה

On Mondays and Thursdays, ראש חודש, חנוכה, פורים *and Fast Days,*
the תורה *is read when a* מנין *is present. On all other days, continue with* אשרי *on page 175.*

Before taking the תורה *out of the* ארון קודש*, on Mondays and Thursdays, stand while reciting* אֵל אֶרֶךְ אַפַּיִם*. It is not said on:* ראש חודש*,* ערב פסח*,* חנוכה*, the 14th and 15th of* אדר א׳*,* תשעה באב*,* יום ירושלים*,* יום העצמאות*,* שושן פורים *and* פורים *or in a house of mourning, and in* ארץ ישראל *on* אסרו חג*. Most people say both paragraphs, some say only the first.*

אֵל אֶֽרֶךְ אַפַּֽיִם וְרַב חֶֽסֶד וֶאֱמֶת
אַל בְּאַפְּךָ תוֹכִיחֵֽנוּ.
חֽוּסָה יהוה עַל עַמֶּֽךָ
וְהוֹשִׁיעֵֽנוּ מִכָּל רָע.
חָטָֽאנוּ לְךָ אָדוֹן
סְלַח נָא כְּרֹב רַחֲמֶֽיךָ אֵל.

אֵל אֶֽרֶךְ אַפַּֽיִם וּמָלֵא רַחֲמִים
אַל תַּסְתֵּר פָּנֶֽיךָ מִמֶּֽנּוּ.
חֽוּסָה יהוה עַל שְׁאֵרִית יִשְׂרָאֵל עַמֶּֽךָ
וְהַצִּילֵֽנוּ מִכָּל רָע.
חָטָֽאנוּ לְךָ אָדוֹן
סְלַח נָא כְּרֹב רַחֲמֶֽיךָ אֵל.

The ארון קודש *is opened and the* קהל *stands. All say:*

וַיְהִי בִּנְסֹֽעַ הָאָרֹן וַיֹּֽאמֶר מֹשֶׁה, קוּמָה יהוה וְיָפֻֽצוּ אֹיְבֶֽיךָ וְיָנֻֽסוּ במדבר י
מְשַׂנְאֶֽיךָ מִפָּנֶֽיךָ: כִּי מִצִּיּוֹן תֵּצֵא תוֹרָה וּדְבַר־יהוה מִירוּשָׁלָֽםִ: ישעיה ב
בָּרוּךְ שֶׁנָּתַן תּוֹרָה לְעַמּוֹ יִשְׂרָאֵל בִּקְדֻשָּׁתוֹ.

READING OF THE TORAH

From earliest times, the public reading of the Torah has been a constitutive element of the spiritual life of Israel. At Mount Sinai, to confirm the covenant between the people and God, Moses "took the Book of the Covenant and read it aloud to the people" (Ex. 24:7). The penultimate commandment of the Torah specifies that every seven years (on Sukkot following the sabbatical year) there should be a national assembly at which "the people, men, women, children and the strangers in your communities" are to hear the Torah proclaimed "so that they may listen and learn to fear the Lord your God and observe faithfully all the words of this Torah" (Deut. 31:12).

At critical moments during the biblical era, when the people had drifted from their faith, national renewal was marked by a public Torah reading. King Jehoshaphat sent out officers who "taught throughout Judah, having with them a scroll of the Lord's Torah. They circulated throughout the towns of Judah and taught the people" (II Chr. 17:9).

King Josiah assembled "all the men of Judah, the inhabitants of Jerusalem, the priests, the Levites, and all the people, young and old alike, and read to

Blessed is the name of the Master of the Universe. Blessed is Your crown and Your place. May Your favor always be with Your people Israel. Show Your people the salvation of Your right hand in Your Temple. Grant us the gift of Your good light, and accept our prayers in mercy. May it be Your will to prolong our life in goodness. May I be counted among the righteous, so that You will have compassion on me and protect me and all that is mine and all that is Your people Israel's. You feed all; You sustain all; You rule over all; You rule over kings, for sovereignty is Yours. I am a servant of the Holy One, blessed be He, before whom and before whose glorious Torah I bow at all times. Not in man do I trust, nor on any angel do I rely, but on the God of heaven who is the God of truth, whose Torah is truth, whose prophets speak truth, and who abounds in acts of love and truth. ▸ In Him I trust, and to His holy and glorious name I offer praises. May it be Your will to open my heart to the Torah, and to fulfill the wishes of my heart and of the hearts of all Your people Israel for good, for life, and for peace. *Zohar, Vayak-hel*

The Leader takes the Torah scroll in his right arm, bows toward the Ark and says:

Magnify the LORD with me, and let us exalt His name together. *Ps. 34*

The Ark is closed. The Leader carries the Torah scroll to the bima and the congregation says:

לְךָ Yours, LORD, are the greatness and the power, the glory and the majesty and splendor, for everything in heaven and earth is Yours. Yours, LORD, is the kingdom; You are exalted as Head over all. *1 Chr. 29*

רוֹמְמוּ Exalt the LORD our God and bow to His footstool; He is holy. Exalt the LORD our God, and bow at His holy mountain, for holy is the LORD our God. *Ps. 99*

אַב הָרַחֲמִים May the Father of compassion have compassion on the people borne by Him. May He remember the covenant with the mighty [patriarchs], and deliver us from evil times. May He reproach the evil instinct in the people carried by Him, and graciously grant that we be an everlasting remnant. May He fulfill in good measure our requests for salvation and compassion.

---

literacy and lifelong learning. The Torah is not just written on parchment; it is meant to be engraved on the Jewish soul.

Keriat HaTorah, translated as "the reading of the Torah," also means "the proclamation of the Torah." The public reading symbolically affirms the Torah as the written constitution of the Jewish people as a nation under the sovereignty of God. It is a reenactment of the revelation at Mount Sinai when the Israelites first became a nation, bound by the Torah's laws, summoned to translate its ideals into life.

זוהר ויקהל בְּרִיךְ שְׁמֵהּ דְּמָרֵא עָלְמָא, בְּרִיךְ כִּתְרָךְ וְאַתְרָךְ. יְהֵא רְעוּתָךְ עִם עַמָּךְ יִשְׂרָאֵל לְעָלַם, וּפֻרְקַן יְמִינָךְ אַחֲזֵי לְעַמָּךְ בְּבֵית מַקְדְּשָׁךְ, וּלְאַמְטוּיֵי לַנָא מִטּוּב נְהוֹרָךְ, וּלְקַבֵּל צְלוֹתַנָא בְּרַחֲמִין. יְהֵא רַעֲוָא קֳדָמָךְ דְּתוֹרִיךְ לַן חַיִּין בְּטִיבוּ, וְלֶהֱוֵי אֲנָא פְקִידָא בְּגוֹ צַדִּיקַיָּא, לְמִרְחַם עָלַי וּלְמִנְטַר יָתִי וְיַת כָּל דִּי לִי וְדִי לְעַמָּךְ יִשְׂרָאֵל. אַנְתְּ הוּא זָן לְכֹלָּא וּמְפַרְנֵס לְכֹלָּא, אַנְתְּ הוּא שַׁלִּיט עַל כֹּלָּא, אַנְתְּ הוּא דְּשַׁלִּיט עַל מַלְכַיָּא, וּמַלְכוּתָא דִּילָךְ הִיא. אֲנָא עַבְדָּא דְקֻדְשָׁא בְּרִיךְ הוּא, דְּסָגֶדְנָא קַמֵּהּ וּמִקַּמֵּי דִּיקַר אוֹרַיְתֵהּ בְּכָל עִדָּן וְעִדָּן. לָא עַל אֱנָשׁ רָחִיצְנָא וְלָא עַל בַּר אֱלָהִין סָמִיכְנָא, אֶלָּא בֶּאֱלָהָא דִשְׁמַיָּא, דְּהוּא אֱלָהָא קְשׁוֹט, וְאוֹרַיְתֵהּ קְשׁוֹט, וּנְבִיאוֹהִי קְשׁוֹט, וּמַסְגֵּא לְמֶעְבַּד טַבְוָן וּקְשׁוֹט. ‹ בֵּהּ אֲנָא רָחִיץ, וְלִשְׁמֵהּ קַדִּישָׁא יַקִּירָא אֲנָא אֵמַר תֻּשְׁבְּחָן. יְהֵא רַעֲוָא קֳדָמָךְ דְּתִפְתַּח לִבַּאי בְּאוֹרַיְתָא, וְתַשְׁלִים מִשְׁאֲלִין דְּלִבַּאי וְלִבָּא דְכָל עַמָּךְ יִשְׂרָאֵל לְטָב וּלְחַיִּין וְלִשְׁלָם.

The שליח ציבור *takes the* ספר תורה *in his right arm, bows toward the* ארון קודש *and says:*

תהלים לד **גַּדְּלוּ לַיהוה אִתִּי וּנְרוֹמְמָה שְׁמוֹ יַחְדָּו:**

The ארון קודש *is closed. The* שליח ציבור *carries the* ספר תורה *to the* בימה *and the* קהל *says:*

דברי הימים א, כט **לְךָ יהוה הַגְּדֻלָּה וְהַגְּבוּרָה וְהַתִּפְאֶרֶת וְהַנֵּצַח וְהַהוֹד, כִּי־כֹל בַּשָּׁמַיִם וּבָאָרֶץ, לְךָ יהוה הַמַּמְלָכָה וְהַמִּתְנַשֵּׂא לְכֹל לְרֹאשׁ:**

תהלים צט **רוֹמְמוּ יהוה אֱלֹהֵינוּ וְהִשְׁתַּחֲווּ לַהֲדֹם רַגְלָיו, קָדוֹשׁ הוּא: רוֹמְמוּ יהוה אֱלֹהֵינוּ וְהִשְׁתַּחֲווּ לְהַר קָדְשׁוֹ, כִּי־קָדוֹשׁ יהוה אֱלֹהֵינוּ:**

אַב הָרַחֲמִים הוּא יְרַחֵם עַם עֲמוּסִים, וְיִזְכֹּר בְּרִית אֵיתָנִים, וְיַצִּיל נַפְשׁוֹתֵינוּ מִן הַשָּׁעוֹת הָרָעוֹת, וְיִגְעַר בְּיֵצֶר הָרָע מִן הַנְּשׂוּאִים, וְיָחֹן אוֹתָנוּ לִפְלֵיטַת עוֹלָמִים, וִימַלֵּא מִשְׁאֲלוֹתֵינוּ בְּמִדָּה טוֹבָה יְשׁוּעָה וְרַחֲמִים.

---

prayer, we speak to God. In study we listen to God speaking to us, His word unchanged and undiminished across the centuries.

The assembly convened by Ezra, when the Torah was not only read but also explained, became the model for educational activities within the synagogue, of which the *derasha* ("sermon," or more precisely, "exposition") is only one of many forms. To an unparalleled degree, Judaism is predicated on universal

The Torah scroll is placed on the bima and the Gabbai calls a Kohen to the Torah. See laws 75–87.

May His kingship over us be soon revealed and made manifest. May He be gracious to our surviving remnant, the remnant of His people the house of Israel in grace, loving-kindness, compassion and favor, and let us say: Amen. Let us all render greatness to our God and give honor to the Torah. *Let the Kohen come forward. Arise (*name* son of *father's name*), the Kohen.

**If no Kohen is present, a Levi or Yisrael is called up as follows:*

/As there is no Kohen, arise (*name* son of *father's name*) in place of a Kohen./

Blessed is He who, in His holiness, gave the Torah to His people Israel.

Congregation followed by the Gabbai:

You who cling to the LORD your God are all alive today. *Deut. 4*

The appropriate Torah portions are to be found from page 614.

The Reader shows the oleh the section to be read. The oleh touches the scroll at that place with the tzitzit of his tallit, which he then kisses. Holding the handles of the scroll, he says:

Oleh: Bless the LORD, the blessed One.

Cong: Bless the LORD, the blessed One, for ever and all time.

Oleh: Bless the LORD, the blessed One, for ever and all time.
Blessed are You, LORD our God, King of the Universe,
who has chosen us from all peoples and has given us His Torah.
Blessed are You, LORD, Giver of the Torah.

After the reading, the oleh says:

Oleh: Blessed are You, LORD our God, King of the Universe, who has
given us the Torah of truth, planting everlasting life in our midst.
Blessed are You, LORD, Giver of the Torah.

One who has survived a situation of danger (see laws 88–89) says:

Blessed are You, LORD our God, King of the Universe,
who bestows good on the unworthy,
who has bestowed on me much good.

The congregation responds:

Amen. May He who bestowed much good on you continue to bestow on you much good, Selah.

After a Bar Mitzva boy has finished the Torah blessing, his father says aloud:

Blessed is He who has released me from the responsibility for this child.

The ספר תורה *is placed on the* שולחן *and the* גבאי *calls a* כהן *to the* תורה. *See laws 75–87.*

וְתִגָּלֶה וְתֵרָאֶה מַלְכוּתוֹ עָלֵינוּ בִּזְמַן קָרוֹב, וְיָחֹן פְּלֵיטָתֵנוּ וּפְלֵיטַת עַמּוֹ בֵּית יִשְׂרָאֵל לְחֵן וּלְחֶסֶד וּלְרַחֲמִים וּלְרָצוֹן וְנֹאמַר אָמֵן. הַכֹּל הָבוּ גֹדֶל לֵאלֹהֵינוּ וּתְנוּ כָבוֹד לַתּוֹרָה.
*כֹּהֵן קְרַב, יַעֲמֹד (פלוני בֶּן פלוני) הַכֹּהֵן.

**If no* כהן *is present, a* לוי *or* ישראל *is called up as follows:*

/אֵין כָּאן כֹּהֵן, יַעֲמֹד (פלוני בֶּן פלוני) בִּמְקוֹם כֹּהֵן./

בָּרוּךְ שֶׁנָּתַן תּוֹרָה לְעַמּוֹ יִשְׂרָאֵל בִּקְדֻשָּׁתוֹ.

קהל *followed by the* גבאי*:*

וְאַתֶּם הַדְּבֵקִים בַּיהוה אֱלֹהֵיכֶם חַיִּים כֻּלְּכֶם הַיּוֹם: דברים ד

The appropriate תורה *portions are to be found from page 614.*

The קורא *shows the* עולה *the section to be read. The* עולה *touches the* ספר תורה *at that place with the* ציצית *of his* טלית*, which he then kisses. Holding the handles of the* ספר תורה*, he says:*

עולה: בָּרְכוּ אֶת יהוה הַמְבֹרָךְ.

קהל: בָּרוּךְ יהוה הַמְבֹרָךְ לְעוֹלָם וָעֶד.

עולה: בָּרוּךְ יהוה הַמְבֹרָךְ לְעוֹלָם וָעֶד.
בָּרוּךְ אַתָּה יהוה, אֱלֹהֵינוּ מֶלֶךְ הָעוֹלָם
אֲשֶׁר בָּחַר בָּנוּ מִכָּל הָעַמִּים וְנָתַן לָנוּ אֶת תּוֹרָתוֹ.
בָּרוּךְ אַתָּה יהוה, נוֹתֵן הַתּוֹרָה.

After the קריאת התורה*, the* עולה *says:*

עולה: בָּרוּךְ אַתָּה יהוה אֱלֹהֵינוּ מֶלֶךְ הָעוֹלָם
אֲשֶׁר נָתַן לָנוּ תּוֹרַת אֱמֶת וְחַיֵּי עוֹלָם נָטַע בְּתוֹכֵנוּ.
בָּרוּךְ אַתָּה יהוה, נוֹתֵן הַתּוֹרָה.

One who has survived a situation of danger (see laws 88–89) says:

בָּרוּךְ אַתָּה יהוה אֱלֹהֵינוּ מֶלֶךְ הָעוֹלָם הַגּוֹמֵל לְחַיָּבִים טוֹבוֹת שֶׁגְּמָלַנִי כָּל טוֹב.

The קהל *responds:*

אָמֵן. מִי שֶׁגְּמָלְךָ כָּל טוֹב הוּא יִגְמָלְךָ כָּל טוֹב, סֶלָה.

After a בר מצווה *has finished the* תורה *blessing, his father says aloud:*

בָּרוּךְ שֶׁפְּטָרַנִי מֵעָנְשׁוֹ שֶׁלָּזֶה.

FOR AN OLEH

May He who blessed our fathers, Abraham, Isaac and Jacob, bless (*name*, son of *father's name*) who has been called up in honor of the All-Present, in honor of the Torah. As a reward for this, may the Holy One, blessed be He, protect and deliver him from all trouble and distress, all infection and illness, and send blessing and success to all the work of his hands, together with all Israel, his brethren, and let us say: Amen.

FOR A SICK MAN

May He who blessed our fathers, Abraham, Isaac and Jacob, Moses and Aaron, David and Solomon, bless and heal one who is ill, (*sick person's name*, son of *mother's name*), on whose behalf (*name of the one making the offering*) is making a contribution to charity. As a reward for this, may the Holy One, blessed be He, be filled with compassion for him, to restore his health, cure him, strengthen and revive him, sending him a swift and full recovery from heaven to all his 248 organs and 365 sinews, amongst the other sick ones in Israel, a healing of the spirit and a healing of the body, now, swiftly and soon, and let us say: Amen.

FOR A SICK WOMAN

May He who blessed our fathers, Abraham, Isaac and Jacob, Moses and Aaron, David and Solomon, bless and heal one who is ill, (*sick person's name*, daughter of *mother's name*), on whose behalf (*name of the one making the offering*) is making a contribution to charity. As a reward for this, may the Holy One, blessed be He, be filled with compassion for her, to restore her health, cure her, strengthen and revive her, sending her a swift and full recovery from heaven to all her organs and sinews, amongst the other sick ones in Israel, a healing of the spirit and a healing of the body, now, swiftly and soon, and let us say: Amen.

ON THE BIRTH OF A SON

May He who blessed our fathers, Abraham, Isaac and Jacob, Moses and Aaron, David and Solomon, Sarah, Rebecca, Rachel and Leah, bless the woman (*name*, daughter of *father's name*) who has given birth, and her son who has been born to her as an auspicious sign. Her husband, the child's father, is making a contribution to charity. As a reward for this, may father and mother merit to bring the child into the covenant of Abraham and to a life of Torah, to the marriage canopy and to good deeds, and let us say: Amen.

ON THE BIRTH OF A DAUGHTER

May He who blessed our fathers, Abraham, Isaac and Jacob, Moses and Aaron, David and Solomon, Sarah, Rebecca, Rachel and Leah, bless the woman (*name*, daughter of *father's name*) who has given birth, and her daughter who has been

מי שברך לעולה לתורה

מִי שֶׁבֵּרַךְ אֲבוֹתֵינוּ אַבְרָהָם יִצְחָק וְיַעֲקֹב, הוּא יְבָרֵךְ אֶת (פלוני בֶּן פלוני), בַּעֲבוּר שֶׁעָלָה לִכְבוֹד הַמָּקוֹם וְלִכְבוֹד הַתּוֹרָה. בִּשְׂכַר זֶה הַקָּדוֹשׁ בָּרוּךְ הוּא יִשְׁמְרֵהוּ וְיַצִּילֵהוּ מִכָּל צָרָה וְצוּקָה וּמִכָּל נֶגַע וּמַחֲלָה, וְיִשְׁלַח בְּרָכָה וְהַצְלָחָה בְּכָל מַעֲשֵׂה יָדָיו עִם כָּל יִשְׂרָאֵל אֶחָיו, וְנֹאמַר אָמֵן.

מי שברך לחולֶה

מִי שֶׁבֵּרַךְ אֲבוֹתֵינוּ אַבְרָהָם יִצְחָק וְיַעֲקֹב, מֹשֶׁה וְאַהֲרֹן דָּוִד וּשְׁלֹמֹה הוּא יְבָרֵךְ וִירַפֵּא אֶת הַחוֹלֶה (פלוני בֶּן פלונית) בַּעֲבוּר שֶׁ(פלוני בֶּן פלוני) נוֹדֵר צְדָקָה בַּעֲבוּרוֹ. בִּשְׂכַר זֶה הַקָּדוֹשׁ בָּרוּךְ הוּא יִמָּלֵא רַחֲמִים עָלָיו לְהַחֲלִימוֹ וּלְרַפֹּאתוֹ וּלְהַחֲזִיקוֹ וּלְהַחֲיוֹתוֹ וְיִשְׁלַח לוֹ מְהֵרָה רְפוּאָה שְׁלֵמָה מִן הַשָּׁמַיִם לְרמ״ח אֵבָרָיו וּשְׁסָ״ה גִּידָיו בְּתוֹךְ שְׁאָר חוֹלֵי יִשְׂרָאֵל, רְפוּאַת הַנֶּפֶשׁ וּרְפוּאַת הַגּוּף, הַשְׁתָּא בַּעֲגָלָא וּבִזְמַן קָרִיב, וְנֹאמַר אָמֵן.

מי שברך לחולָה

מִי שֶׁבֵּרַךְ אֲבוֹתֵינוּ אַבְרָהָם יִצְחָק וְיַעֲקֹב, מֹשֶׁה וְאַהֲרֹן דָּוִד וּשְׁלֹמֹה הוּא יְבָרֵךְ וִירַפֵּא אֶת הַחוֹלָה (פלונית בַּת פלונית) בַּעֲבוּר שֶׁ(פלוני בֶּן פלוני) נוֹדֵר צְדָקָה בַּעֲבוּרָהּ. בִּשְׂכַר זֶה הַקָּדוֹשׁ בָּרוּךְ הוּא יִמָּלֵא רַחֲמִים עָלֶיהָ לְהַחֲלִימָהּ וּלְרַפֹּאתָהּ וּלְהַחֲזִיקָהּ וּלְהַחֲיוֹתָהּ וְיִשְׁלַח לָהּ מְהֵרָה רְפוּאָה שְׁלֵמָה מִן הַשָּׁמַיִם לְכָל אֵבָרֶיהָ וּלְכָל גִּידֶיהָ בְּתוֹךְ שְׁאָר חוֹלֵי יִשְׂרָאֵל, רְפוּאַת הַנֶּפֶשׁ וּרְפוּאַת הַגּוּף, הַשְׁתָּא בַּעֲגָלָא וּבִזְמַן קָרִיב, וְנֹאמַר אָמֵן.

מי שברך ליולדת בן

מִי שֶׁבֵּרַךְ אֲבוֹתֵינוּ אַבְרָהָם יִצְחָק וְיַעֲקֹב, מֹשֶׁה וְאַהֲרֹן דָּוִד וּשְׁלֹמֹה, שָׂרָה רִבְקָה רָחֵל וְלֵאָה הוּא יְבָרֵךְ אֶת הָאִשָּׁה הַיּוֹלֶדֶת (פלונית בַּת פלוני) וְאֶת בְּנָהּ שֶׁנּוֹלַד לָהּ לְמַזָּל טוֹב בַּעֲבוּר שֶׁבַּעְלָהּ וְאָבִיו נוֹדֵר צְדָקָה בַּעֲדָם. בִּשְׂכַר זֶה יִזְכּוּ אָבִיו וְאִמּוֹ לְהַכְנִיסוֹ בִּבְרִיתוֹ שֶׁל אַבְרָהָם אָבִינוּ וּלְגַדְּלוֹ לְתוֹרָה וּלְחֻפָּה וּלְמַעֲשִׂים טוֹבִים, וְנֹאמַר אָמֵן.

מי שברך ליולדת בת

מִי שֶׁבֵּרַךְ אֲבוֹתֵינוּ אַבְרָהָם יִצְחָק וְיַעֲקֹב, מֹשֶׁה וְאַהֲרֹן דָּוִד וּשְׁלֹמֹה, שָׂרָה רִבְקָה רָחֵל וְלֵאָה הוּא יְבָרֵךְ אֶת הָאִשָּׁה הַיּוֹלֶדֶת (פלונית בַּת פלוני) וְאֶת בִּתָּהּ

born to her as an auspicious sign; and may her name be called in Israel (*baby's name*, daughter of *father's name*). Her husband, the child's father, is making a contribution to charity. As a reward for this, may father and mother merit to raise her to a life of Torah, to the marriage canopy, and to good deeds, and let us say: Amen.

FOR A BAR MITZVA

May He who blessed our fathers, Abraham, Isaac and Jacob, bless (*name*, son of *father's name*) who has completed thirteen years and attained the age of the commandments, who has been called to the Torah to give praise and thanks to God, may His name be blessed, for all the good He has bestowed on him. May the Holy One, blessed be He, protect and sustain him and direct his heart to be perfect with God, to walk in His ways and keep the commandments all the days of his life, and let us say: Amen.

FOR A BAT MITZVA

May He who blessed our fathers, Abraham, Isaac and Jacob, Sarah, Rebecca, Rachel and Leah, bless (*name*, daughter of *father's name*) who has completed twelve years and attained the age of the commandments, and gives praise and thanks to God, may His name be blessed, for all the good He has bestowed on her. May the Holy One, blessed be He, protect and sustain her and direct her heart to be perfect with God, to walk in His ways and keep the commandments all the days of her life, and let us say: Amen.

MEMORIAL (YAHRZEIT) PRAYER

For a male close relative:

אֵל מָלֵא רַחֲמִים God, full of mercy, who dwells on high, grant fitting rest on the wings of the Divine Presence, in the heights of the holy and the pure who shine like the radiance of heaven, to the soul of (*name*, son of *father's name*) who has gone to his eternal home, and to this I pledge (without formal vow) to give charity in his memory, may his resting place be in the Garden of Eden. Therefore, Master of compassion, shelter him in the shadow of Your wings forever and bind his soul in the bond of everlasting life. The Lord is his heritage; may he rest in peace, and let us say: Amen.

For a female close relative:

אֵל מָלֵא רַחֲמִים God, full of mercy, who dwells on high, grant fitting rest on the wings of the Divine Presence, in the heights of the holy and the pure who shine like the radiance of heaven, to the soul of (*name*, daughter of *father's name*) who has gone to her eternal home, and to this I pledge (without formal vow) to give charity in her memory, may her resting place be in the Garden of Eden. Therefore, Master of compassion, shelter her in the shadow of Your wings forever and bind her soul in the bond of everlasting life. The Lord is her heritage; may she rest in peace, and let us say: Amen.

שֶׁנּוֹלְדָה לָהּ לְמַזָּל טוֹב וְיִקָּרֵא שְׁמָהּ בְּיִשְׂרָאֵל (פלונית בַּת פלוני), בַּעֲבוּר שֶׁבַּעְלָהּ וְאָבִיהָ נוֹדֵר צְדָקָה בַּעֲדָהּ. בִּשְׂכַר זֶה יִזְכּוּ אָבִיהָ וְאִמָּהּ לְגַדְּלָהּ לְתוֹרָה וּלְחֻפָּה וּלְמַעֲשִׂים טוֹבִים, וְנֹאמַר אָמֵן.

מי שברך לבר מצווה

מִי שֶׁבֵּרַךְ אֲבוֹתֵינוּ אַבְרָהָם יִצְחָק וְיַעֲקֹב הוּא יְבָרֵךְ אֶת (פלוני בֶּן פלוני) שֶׁמָּלְאוּ לוֹ שְׁלֹשׁ עֶשְׂרֵה שָׁנָה וְהִגִּיעַ לְמִצְוֹת, וְעָלָה לַתּוֹרָה, לָתֵת שֶׁבַח וְהוֹדָיָה לְהַשֵּׁם יִתְבָּרַךְ עַל כָּל הַטּוֹבָה שֶׁגָּמַל אִתּוֹ. יִשְׁמְרֵהוּ הַקָּדוֹשׁ בָּרוּךְ הוּא וִיחַיֵּהוּ, וִיכוֹנֵן אֶת לִבּוֹ לִהְיוֹת שָׁלֵם עִם יהוה וְלָלֶכֶת בִּדְרָכָיו וְלִשְׁמֹר מִצְוֹתָיו כָּל הַיָּמִים, וְנֹאמַר אָמֵן.

מי שברך לבת מצווה

מִי שֶׁבֵּרַךְ אֲבוֹתֵינוּ אַבְרָהָם יִצְחָק וְיַעֲקֹב, שָׂרָה רִבְקָה רָחֵל וְלֵאָה, הוּא יְבָרֵךְ אֶת (פלונית בַּת פלוני) שֶׁמָּלְאוּ לָהּ שְׁתֵּים עֶשְׂרֵה שָׁנָה וְהִגִּיעָה לְמִצְוֹת, וְנוֹתֶנֶת שֶׁבַח וְהוֹדָיָה לְהַשֵּׁם יִתְבָּרַךְ עַל כָּל הַטּוֹבָה שֶׁגָּמַל אִתָּהּ. יִשְׁמְרֶהָ הַקָּדוֹשׁ בָּרוּךְ הוּא וִיחַיֶּהָ, וִיכוֹנֵן אֶת לִבָּהּ לִהְיוֹת שָׁלֵם עִם יהוה וְלָלֶכֶת בִּדְרָכָיו וְלִשְׁמֹר מִצְוֹתָיו כָּל הַיָּמִים, וְנֹאמַר אָמֵן.

הזכרת נשמות

For a male close relative:

אֵל מָלֵא רַחֲמִים, שׁוֹכֵן בַּמְּרוֹמִים, הַמְצֵא מְנוּחָה נְכוֹנָה עַל כַּנְפֵי הַשְּׁכִינָה, בְּמַעֲלוֹת קְדוֹשִׁים וּטְהוֹרִים, כְּזֹהַר הָרָקִיעַ מַזְהִירִים, לְנִשְׁמַת (פלוני בֶּן פלוני) שֶׁהָלַךְ לְעוֹלָמוֹ, בַּעֲבוּר שֶׁבְּלִי נֶדֶר אֶתֵּן צְדָקָה בְּעַד הַזְכָּרַת נִשְׁמָתוֹ, בְּגַן עֵדֶן תְּהֵא מְנוּחָתוֹ. לָכֵן, בַּעַל הָרַחֲמִים יַסְתִּירֵהוּ בְּסֵתֶר כְּנָפָיו לְעוֹלָמִים, וְיִצְרֹר בִּצְרוֹר הַחַיִּים אֶת נִשְׁמָתוֹ, יהוה הוּא נַחֲלָתוֹ, וְיָנוּחַ בְּשָׁלוֹם עַל מִשְׁכָּבוֹ, וְנֹאמַר אָמֵן.

For a female close relative:

אֵל מָלֵא רַחֲמִים, שׁוֹכֵן בַּמְּרוֹמִים, הַמְצֵא מְנוּחָה נְכוֹנָה עַל כַּנְפֵי הַשְּׁכִינָה, בְּמַעֲלוֹת קְדוֹשִׁים וּטְהוֹרִים, כְּזֹהַר הָרָקִיעַ מַזְהִירִים, לְנִשְׁמַת (פלונית בַּת פלוני) שֶׁהָלְכָה לְעוֹלָמָהּ, בַּעֲבוּר שֶׁבְּלִי נֶדֶר אֶתֵּן צְדָקָה בְּעַד הַזְכָּרַת נִשְׁמָתָהּ, בְּגַן עֵדֶן תְּהֵא מְנוּחָתָהּ. לָכֵן, בַּעַל הָרַחֲמִים יַסְתִּירָהּ בְּסֵתֶר כְּנָפָיו לְעוֹלָמִים, וְיִצְרֹר בִּצְרוֹר הַחַיִּים אֶת נִשְׁמָתָהּ, יהוה הוּא נַחֲלָתָהּ, וְתָנוּחַ בְּשָׁלוֹם עַל מִשְׁכָּבָהּ, וְנֹאמַר אָמֵן.

HALF KADDISH

After the Reading of the Torah, the Reader says Half Kaddish:

Reader: יִתְגַּדַּל Magnified and sanctified may His great name be,
in the world He created by His will.
May He establish His kingdom
in your lifetime and in your days,
and in the lifetime of all the house of Israel,
swiftly and soon –
and say: Amen.

All: May His great name be blessed for ever and all time.

Reader: Blessed and praised, glorified and exalted,
raised and honored, uplifted and lauded
be the name of the Holy One,
blessed be He,
beyond any blessing,
song, praise and consolation
uttered in the world –
and say: Amen.

The Torah scroll is lifted and the congregation says:

וְזֹאת הַתּוֹרָה This is the Torah *Deut. 4*
that Moses placed before the children of Israel,
at the Lord's commandment, by the hand of Moses. *Num. 9*

Some add:

It is a tree of life to those who grasp it, and those who uphold it are happy. *Prov. 3*
Its ways are ways of pleasantness, and all its paths are peace.
Long life is at its right hand; at its left, riches and honor.
It pleased the Lord for the sake of [Israel's] righteousness, *Is. 42*
to make the Torah great and glorious.

On those Mondays and Thursdays when Taḥanun is said,
the Leader says the following while the Torah scroll is being bound:

יְהִי רָצוֹן May it be the will of our Father in heaven to establish
(the Temple), home of our life,
and to restore His Presence to our midst,
swiftly in our days – and let us say: Amen.

חצי קדיש

After the קריאת התורה*, the* קורא *says* חצי קדיש:

קורא: יִתְגַּדַּל וְיִתְקַדַּשׁ שְׁמֵהּ רַבָּא (קהל: אָמֵן)
בְּעָלְמָא דִּי בְרָא כִרְעוּתֵהּ
וְיַמְלִיךְ מַלְכוּתֵהּ
בְּחַיֵּיכוֹן וּבְיוֹמֵיכוֹן וּבְחַיֵּי דְכָל בֵּית יִשְׂרָאֵל
בַּעֲגָלָא וּבִזְמַן קָרִיב, וְאִמְרוּ אָמֵן. (קהל: אָמֵן)

קורא וקהל: יְהֵא שְׁמֵהּ רַבָּא מְבָרַךְ לְעָלַם וּלְעָלְמֵי עָלְמַיָּא.

קורא: יִתְבָּרַךְ וְיִשְׁתַּבַּח וְיִתְפָּאַר וְיִתְרוֹמַם וְיִתְנַשֵּׂא
וְיִתְהַדָּר וְיִתְעַלֶּה וְיִתְהַלָּל
שְׁמֵהּ דְּקֻדְשָׁא בְּרִיךְ הוּא (קהל: בְּרִיךְ הוּא)
לְעֵלָּא מִן כָּל בִּרְכָתָא / בעשרת ימי תשובה: לְעֵלָּא לְעֵלָּא מִכָּל בִּרְכָתָא/
וְשִׁירָתָא, תֻּשְׁבְּחָתָא וְנֶחֱמָתָא
דַּאֲמִירָן בְּעָלְמָא, וְאִמְרוּ אָמֵן. (קהל: אָמֵן)

The ספר תורה *is lifted and the* קהל *says:*

וְזֹאת הַתּוֹרָה אֲשֶׁר־שָׂם מֹשֶׁה לִפְנֵי בְּנֵי יִשְׂרָאֵל: דברים ד
עַל־פִּי יהוה בְּיַד־מֹשֶׁה: במדבר ט

Some add:

עֵץ־חַיִּים הִיא לַמַּחֲזִיקִים בָּהּ וְתֹמְכֶיהָ מְאֻשָּׁר: משלי ג
דְּרָכֶיהָ דַרְכֵי־נֹעַם וְכָל־נְתִיבֹתֶיהָ שָׁלוֹם:
אֹרֶךְ יָמִים בִּימִינָהּ, בִּשְׂמֹאולָהּ עֹשֶׁר וְכָבוֹד:
יהוה חָפֵץ לְמַעַן צִדְקוֹ יַגְדִּיל תּוֹרָה וְיַאְדִּיר: ישעיה מב

On those Mondays and Thursdays when תחנון *is said,*
the שליח ציבור *says the following while the* ספר תורה *is being bound:*

יְהִי רָצוֹן מִלִּפְנֵי אָבִינוּ שֶׁבַּשָּׁמַיִם, לְכוֹנֵן אֶת בֵּית חַיֵּינוּ
וּלְהָשִׁיב אֶת שְׁכִינָתוֹ בְּתוֹכֵנוּ
בִּמְהֵרָה בְיָמֵינוּ, וְנֹאמַר אָמֵן.

יְהִי רָצוֹן May it be the will of our Father in heaven
to have compassion on us and our remnant,
and to keep destruction and plague away from us
and from all His people the house of Israel –
and let us say: Amen.

יְהִי רָצוֹן May it be the will of our Father in heaven
to preserve among us the sages of Israel:
them, their wives, their sons and daughters,
their disciples and their disciples' disciples,
in all their dwelling places – and let us say: Amen.

יְהִי רָצוֹן May it be the will of our Father in heaven
that we may hear and be given good tidings
of salvation and consolation,
and that our dispersed be gathered
from the four quarters of the earth – and let us say: Amen.

All:

אַחֵינוּ As for our brothers of the whole house of Israel who are in distress or captivity, on sea or land, may the All-Present have compassion on them and lead them from distress to relief, from darkness to light, and from oppression to freedom, now, swiftly and soon – and let us say: Amen.

RETURNING THE TORAH TO THE ARK

The Ark is opened. The Leader takes the Torah scroll and says:

יְהַלְלוּ Let them praise the name of the Lord, *Ps. 148*
for His name alone is sublime.

The congregation responds:

הוֹדוֹ His majesty is above earth and heaven.
He has raised the horn of His people,
for the glory of all His devoted ones,
the children of Israel, the people close to Him.
Halleluya!

יְהִי רָצוֹן מִלִּפְנֵי אָבִינוּ שֶׁבַּשָּׁמַיִם, לְרַחֵם עָלֵינוּ וְעַל פְּלֵיטָתֵנוּ
וְלִמְנֹעַ מַשְׁחִית וּמַגֵּפָה מֵעָלֵינוּ
וּמֵעַל כָּל עַמּוֹ בֵּית יִשְׂרָאֵל, וְנֹאמַר אָמֵן.

יְהִי רָצוֹן מִלִּפְנֵי אָבִינוּ שֶׁבַּשָּׁמַיִם, לְקַיֶּם בָּנוּ חַכְמֵי יִשְׂרָאֵל
הֵם וּנְשֵׁיהֶם וּבְנֵיהֶם וּבְנוֹתֵיהֶם
וְתַלְמִידֵיהֶם וְתַלְמִידֵי תַלְמִידֵיהֶם
בְּכָל מְקוֹמוֹת מוֹשְׁבוֹתֵיהֶם, וְנֹאמַר אָמֵן.

יְהִי רָצוֹן מִלִּפְנֵי אָבִינוּ שֶׁבַּשָּׁמַיִם
שֶׁנִּשְׁמַע וְנִתְבַּשֵּׂר בְּשׂוֹרוֹת טוֹבוֹת, יְשׁוּעוֹת וְנֶחָמוֹת
וִיקַבֵּץ נִדָּחֵינוּ מֵאַרְבַּע כַּנְפוֹת הָאָרֶץ, וְנֹאמַר אָמֵן.

All:

אַחֵינוּ כָּל בֵּית יִשְׂרָאֵל, הַנְּתוּנִים בַּצָּרָה וּבַשִּׁבְיָה, הָעוֹמְדִים בֵּין בַּיָּם וּבֵין בַּיַּבָּשָׁה, הַמָּקוֹם יְרַחֵם עֲלֵיהֶם וְיוֹצִיאֵם מִצָּרָה לִרְוָחָה, וּמֵאֲפֵלָה לְאוֹרָה, וּמִשִּׁעְבּוּד לִגְאֻלָּה, הַשְׁתָּא בַּעֲגָלָא וּבִזְמַן קָרִיב, וְנֹאמַר אָמֵן.

הכנסת ספר תורה

The ארון קודש *is opened. The* שליח ציבור *takes the* ספר תורה *and says:*

יְהַלְלוּ אֶת־שֵׁם יהוה, כִּי נִשְׂגָּב־שְׁמוֹ, לְבַדּוֹ תהלים קמח

The קהל *responds:*

הוֹדוֹ עַל־אֶרֶץ וְשָׁמָיִם:
וַיָּרֶם קֶרֶן לְעַמּוֹ
תְּהִלָּה לְכָל־חֲסִידָיו
לִבְנֵי יִשְׂרָאֵל עַם קְרֹבוֹ, הַלְלוּיָהּ:

As the Torah scroll is returned to the Ark, say:

לְדָוִד מִזְמוֹר A psalm of David. The earth is the LORD's and all it con- *Ps. 24*
tains, the world and all who live in it. For He founded it on the seas and established it on the streams. Who may climb the mountain of the LORD? Who may stand in His holy place? He who has clean hands and a pure heart, who has not taken My name in vain, or sworn deceitfully. He shall receive blessing from the LORD, and just reward from God, his salvation. This is a generation of those who seek Him, the descendants of Jacob who seek Your presence, Selah! Lift up your heads, O gates; be uplifted, eternal doors, so that the King of glory may enter. Who is the King of glory? It is the LORD, strong and mighty, the LORD mighty in battle. Lift up your heads, O gates; lift them up, eternal doors, so that the King of glory may enter. Who is He, the King of glory? The LORD of hosts, He is the King of glory, Selah!

As the Torah scroll is placed into the Ark, say:

וּבְנֻחֹה יֹאמַר When the Ark came to rest, Moses would say: "Return, *Num. 10*
O LORD, to the myriad thousands of Israel." Advance, LORD, to Your *Ps. 132*
resting place, You and Your mighty Ark. Your priests are clothed in righteousness, and Your devoted ones sing in joy. For the sake of
Your servant David, do not reject Your anointed one. For I give you *Prov. 4*
good instruction; do not forsake My Torah. It is a tree of life to those *Prov. 3*
who grasp it, and those who uphold it are happy. Its ways are ways of
pleasantness, and all its paths are peace. ▸ Turn us back, O LORD, to *Lam. 5*
You, and we will return. Renew our days as of old.

The Ark is closed.

וּבְנֻחֹה יֹאמַר *When the Ark came to rest:* These words, taken from Numbers 10:36, recall the journeys of the Israelites through the wilderness in the days of Moses. They parallel the words we say when the scroll is taken out, "Whenever the Ark set out" (page 158), said by the Israelites when they began a new journey. Throughout the centuries, wherever Jews went, they took the Torah with them: it became their "portable homeland." **עֵץ־חַיִּים הִיא לַמַּחֲזִיקִים בָּהּ** *It is a tree of life to those who grasp it:* though Adam and Eve were forbidden to eat the fruit of the tree of life (Gen. 3:22), the Torah is our intimation of eternity in the midst of time. Immortality is a matter, not of *how long* we live, but of *how* we live.

As the ספר תורה *is returned to the* ארון קודש*, say:*

תהלים כד לְדָוִד מִזְמוֹר, לַיהוה הָאָרֶץ וּמְלוֹאָהּ, תֵּבֵל וְיֹשְׁבֵי בָהּ: כִּי־הוּא
עַל־יַמִּים יְסָדָהּ, וְעַל־נְהָרוֹת יְכוֹנְנֶהָ: מִי־יַעֲלֶה בְהַר־יהוה,
וּמִי־יָקוּם בִּמְקוֹם קָדְשׁוֹ: נְקִי כַפַּיִם וּבַר־לֵבָב, אֲשֶׁר לֹא־נָשָׂא
לַשָּׁוְא נַפְשִׁי וְלֹא נִשְׁבַּע לְמִרְמָה: יִשָּׂא בְרָכָה מֵאֵת יהוה, וּצְדָקָה
מֵאֱלֹהֵי יִשְׁעוֹ: זֶה דּוֹר דֹּרְשָׁו, מְבַקְשֵׁי פָנֶיךָ, יַעֲקֹב, סֶלָה: שְׂאוּ
שְׁעָרִים רָאשֵׁיכֶם, וְהִנָּשְׂאוּ פִּתְחֵי עוֹלָם, וְיָבוֹא מֶלֶךְ הַכָּבוֹד:
מִי זֶה מֶלֶךְ הַכָּבוֹד, יהוה עִזּוּז וְגִבּוֹר, יהוה גִּבּוֹר מִלְחָמָה: שְׂאוּ
שְׁעָרִים רָאשֵׁיכֶם, וּשְׂאוּ פִּתְחֵי עוֹלָם, וְיָבֹא מֶלֶךְ הַכָּבוֹד: מִי הוּא
זֶה מֶלֶךְ הַכָּבוֹד, יהוה צְבָאוֹת הוּא מֶלֶךְ הַכָּבוֹד, סֶלָה:

As the ספר תורה *is placed into the* ארון קודש*, say:*

במדבר י וּבְנֻחֹה יֹאמַר, שׁוּבָה יהוה רִבְבוֹת אַלְפֵי יִשְׂרָאֵל: קוּמָה יהוה
תהלים קלב לִמְנוּחָתֶךָ, אַתָּה וַאֲרוֹן עֻזֶּךָ: כֹּהֲנֶיךָ יִלְבְּשׁוּ־צֶדֶק, וַחֲסִידֶיךָ יְרַנֵּנוּ:
משלי ד בַּעֲבוּר דָּוִד עַבְדֶּךָ אַל־תָּשֵׁב פְּנֵי מְשִׁיחֶךָ: כִּי לֶקַח טוֹב נָתַתִּי
משלי ג לָכֶם, תּוֹרָתִי אַל־תַּעֲזֹבוּ: עֵץ־חַיִּים הִיא לַמַּחֲזִיקִים בָּהּ, וְתֹמְכֶיהָ
איכה ה מְאֻשָּׁר: דְּרָכֶיהָ דַרְכֵי־נֹעַם וְכָל־נְתִיבוֹתֶיהָ שָׁלוֹם: ◄ הֲשִׁיבֵנוּ יהוה
אֵלֶיךָ וְנָשׁוּבָה, חַדֵּשׁ יָמֵינוּ כְּקֶדֶם:

The ארון קודש *is closed.*

לְדָוִד מִזְמוֹר *A psalm of David:* A psalm of joyous procession to the Temple. It begins with creation, "The earth is the LORD's," and moves directly to the moral requirements of the religious life: "Who may climb the mountain of the LORD?" Just as God created an orderly universe, so we are commanded to create an orderly society. Worshiping God at the Temple may not be divorced from honesty and integrity in everyday life. The latter part of the psalm, "Lift up your heads, O gates," was said by King Solomon when the Ark, containing the tablets of the covenant, was first brought into the Temple (*Shabbat* 30a). As the Torah scroll is returned to the Ark, we recall that historic scene.

CONCLUSION OF THE SERVICE

Some have the custom to touch the hand-tefillin at °, and the head-tefillin at °°.

אַשְׁרֵי Happy are those who dwell in Your House; Ps. 84
they shall continue to praise You, Selah!
Happy are the people for whom this is so; Ps. 144
happy are the people whose God is the LORD.
A song of praise by David. Ps. 145

I will exalt You, my God, the King, and bless Your name for ever and all time. Every day I will bless You, and praise Your name for ever and all time. Great is the LORD and greatly to be praised; His greatness is unfathomable. One generation will praise Your works to the next, and tell of Your mighty deeds. On the glorious splendor of Your majesty I will meditate, and on the acts of Your wonders. They shall talk of the power of Your awesome deeds, and I will tell of Your greatness. They shall recite the record of Your great goodness, and sing with joy of Your righteousness. The LORD is gracious and compassionate, slow to anger and great in loving-kindness. The LORD is good to all, and His compassion extends to all His works. All Your works shall thank You, LORD, and Your devoted ones shall bless You. They shall talk of the glory of Your kingship, and speak of Your might. To make known to mankind His mighty deeds

---

your mouth will not depart from your mouth, or from the mouth of your children"). Thus are joined study, the *internalization* of God's word, and redemption, the *externalization* of God's word as we prepare to enter the world of work, striving to live by the Torah's commandments.

אַשְׁרֵי *Happy are those:* Just as we say *Ashrei before* the Shema and the Amida, so do we say it *after*, following the custom of "the pious of old" who devoted time before prayer in preparation, and afterward in meditation. According to the Talmud, the practice was based on the first line of *Ashrei* itself: "Happy are those who dwell in Your House."

סיום התפילה

Some have the custom to touch the תפילין של יד *at* °*, and the* תפילין של ראש *at* °°*.*

אַשְׁרֵי יוֹשְׁבֵי בֵיתֶךָ, עוֹד יְהַלְלוּךָ סֶּלָה: תהלים פד

אַשְׁרֵי הָעָם שֶׁכָּכָה לּוֹ, אַשְׁרֵי הָעָם שֶׁיהוה אֱלֹהָיו: תהלים קמד

תְּהִלָּה לְדָוִד תהלים קמה

אֲרוֹמִמְךָ אֱלוֹהַי הַמֶּלֶךְ, וַאֲבָרְכָה שִׁמְךָ לְעוֹלָם וָעֶד:
בְּכָל־יוֹם אֲבָרְכֶךָּ, וַאֲהַלְלָה שִׁמְךָ לְעוֹלָם וָעֶד:
גָּדוֹל יהוה וּמְהֻלָּל מְאֹד, וְלִגְדֻלָּתוֹ אֵין חֵקֶר:
דּוֹר לְדוֹר יְשַׁבַּח מַעֲשֶׂיךָ, וּגְבוּרֹתֶיךָ יַגִּידוּ:
הֲדַר כְּבוֹד הוֹדֶךָ, וְדִבְרֵי נִפְלְאֹתֶיךָ אָשִׂיחָה:
וֶעֱזוּז נוֹרְאֹתֶיךָ יֹאמֵרוּ, וּגְדוּלָּתְךָ אֲסַפְּרֶנָּה:
זֵכֶר רַב־טוּבְךָ יַבִּיעוּ, וְצִדְקָתְךָ יְרַנֵּנוּ:
חַנּוּן וְרַחוּם יהוה, אֶרֶךְ אַפַּיִם וּגְדָל־חָסֶד:
טוֹב־יהוה לַכֹּל, וְרַחֲמָיו עַל־כָּל־מַעֲשָׂיו:
יוֹדְוּךָ יהוה כָּל־מַעֲשֶׂיךָ, וַחֲסִידֶיךָ יְבָרְכוּכָה:

CONCLUSION OF THE SERVICE

The final section of the prayers now begins. It interweaves two distinct elements: one is a formal conclusion to the morning service, including *Aleinu* and the Daily Psalm, with an emphasis on the theme of Redemption; and the other is study. It was the custom in ancient times, and in many places today, to devote time after prayer to Torah learning. This originally included texts from the prophetic books. The close of a study session was marked by a series of prayers beginning "You are the Holy One." The Kaddish had its origin in such sessions.

The link between these two ideas – redemption and Torah study – is created in an inspired fashion, by reading two consecutive verses from Isaiah, the first of which speaks of redemption ("A redeemer will come to Zion"), and the second of which talks of Torah study ("My words I have placed in and the glorious majesty of His kingship. Your kingdom is an everlasting kingdom, and Your reign is for all generations. The LORD supports all who fall, and raises all who are bowed down. All raise their eyes to You in hope, and You give them their food in due season. °You open Your hand, °°and satisfy every living thing with favor. The LORD is righteous in all His ways, and kind in all He does. The LORD is close to all who call on Him, to all who call on Him in truth. He fulfills the will of those who revere Him; He hears their cry and saves them. The LORD guards all who love Him, but all the wicked He will destroy. ▸ My mouth shall speak the praise of the LORD, and all creatures shall bless His holy name for ever and all time.

We will bless the LORD now and for ever. Halleluya! *Ps. 115*

Omit on Rosh Ḥodesh, Erev Pesaḥ, Erev Yom Kippur, Ḥanukka, the 14th and 15th of Adar I, Purim and Shushan Purim, Yom HaAtzma'ut, Yom Yerushalayim, Tisha B'Av, or in a house of mourning, and in Israel on Isru Ḥag.

לַמְנַצֵּחַ For the conductor of music. A psalm of David. May the LORD answer you when you are in distress; may the name of Jacob's God protect you. May He send you help from the Sanctuary and support from Zion. May He remember all your meal-offerings and accept your burnt-offerings, Selah! May He give you your heart's desire and make all your plans succeed. We will shout for joy at Your salvation and lift a banner in the name of our God. May the LORD grant all your requests. Now I know that the LORD saves His anointed; He answers him from His holy heaven with the saving power of His right hand. Some trust in chariots, others in horses, but we call on the name of the LORD our God. They were brought to their knees and fell, but we rose up and stood firm. ▸ LORD, save! May the King answer us on the day we call. *Ps. 20*

---

dangers, we ask God to keep us from harm. Because of the solemnity of its mood, this psalm is omitted on festivals or in a house of mourning, so as not to subtract from the joy of the former, or add to the grief of the latter.

כְּבוֹד מַלְכוּתְךָ יֹאמֵרוּ, וּגְבוּרָתְךָ יְדַבֵּרוּ:
לְהוֹדִיעַ לִבְנֵי הָאָדָם גְּבוּרֹתָיו, וּכְבוֹד הֲדַר מַלְכוּתוֹ:
מַלְכוּתְךָ מַלְכוּת כָּל־עֹלָמִים, וּמֶמְשַׁלְתְּךָ בְּכָל־דּוֹר וָדֹר:
סוֹמֵךְ יהוה לְכָל־הַנֹּפְלִים, וְזוֹקֵף לְכָל־הַכְּפוּפִים:
עֵינֵי־כֹל אֵלֶיךָ יְשַׂבֵּרוּ, וְאַתָּה נוֹתֵן־לָהֶם אֶת־אָכְלָם בְּעִתּוֹ:
°פּוֹתֵחַ אֶת־יָדֶךָ, °°וּמַשְׂבִּיעַ לְכָל־חַי רָצוֹן:
צַדִּיק יהוה בְּכָל־דְּרָכָיו, וְחָסִיד בְּכָל־מַעֲשָׂיו:
קָרוֹב יהוה לְכָל־קֹרְאָיו, לְכֹל אֲשֶׁר יִקְרָאֻהוּ בֶאֱמֶת:
רְצוֹן־יְרֵאָיו יַעֲשֶׂה, וְאֶת־שַׁוְעָתָם יִשְׁמַע, וְיוֹשִׁיעֵם:
שׁוֹמֵר יהוה אֶת־כָּל־אֹהֲבָיו, וְאֵת כָּל־הָרְשָׁעִים יַשְׁמִיד:
▸ תְּהִלַּת יהוה יְדַבֶּר פִּי, וִיבָרֵךְ כָּל־בָּשָׂר שֵׁם קָדְשׁוֹ לְעוֹלָם וָעֶד:
תהלים קטו וַאֲנַחְנוּ נְבָרֵךְ יָהּ מֵעַתָּה וְעַד־עוֹלָם, הַלְלוּיָהּ:

Omit on ראש חודש, ערב פסח, ערב יום כיפור, חנוכה,
the 14th and 15th of אדר א׳, פורים *and* שושן פורים, יום העצמאות,
יום ירושלים, תשעה באב, *or in a house of mourning, and in* ארץ ישראל *on* אסרו חג.

תהלים כ לַמְנַצֵּחַ מִזְמוֹר לְדָוִד: יַעַנְךָ יהוה בְּיוֹם צָרָה, יְשַׂגֶּבְךָ שֵׁם אֱלֹהֵי
יַעֲקֹב: יִשְׁלַח־עֶזְרְךָ מִקֹּדֶשׁ, וּמִצִּיּוֹן יִסְעָדֶךָּ: יִזְכֹּר כָּל־מִנְחֹתֶךָ,
וְעוֹלָתְךָ יְדַשְּׁנֶה סֶלָה: יִתֶּן־לְךָ כִלְבָבֶךָ, וְכָל־עֲצָתְךָ יְמַלֵּא: נְרַנְּנָה
בִּישׁוּעָתֶךָ, וּבְשֵׁם־אֱלֹהֵינוּ נִדְגֹּל, יְמַלֵּא יהוה כָּל־מִשְׁאֲלוֹתֶיךָ: עַתָּה
יָדַעְתִּי כִּי הוֹשִׁיעַ יהוה מְשִׁיחוֹ, יַעֲנֵהוּ מִשְּׁמֵי קָדְשׁוֹ, בִּגְבוּרוֹת יֵשַׁע
יְמִינוֹ: אֵלֶּה בָרֶכֶב וְאֵלֶּה בַסּוּסִים, וַאֲנַחְנוּ בְּשֵׁם־יהוה אֱלֹהֵינוּ
נַזְכִּיר: הֵמָּה כָּרְעוּ וְנָפָלוּ, וַאֲנַחְנוּ קַמְנוּ וַנִּתְעוֹדָד: ▸ יהוה הוֹשִׁיעָה,
הַמֶּלֶךְ יַעֲנֵנוּ בְיוֹם־קָרְאֵנוּ:

לַמְנַצֵּחַ *Psalm 20:* A prayer for protection from harm. As prayer reaches its close, and we prepare to reenter the outside world with its hazards and

In a house of mourning and on Tisha B'Av omit the verse beginning "As for Me" and continue with "You are the Holy One."

וּבָא לְצִיּוֹן גּוֹאֵל "A redeemer will come to Zion, to those in Jacob who repent of their sins," declares the LORD. "As for Me, this is My covenant with them," says the LORD. "My spirit, that is on you, and My words I have placed in your mouth will not depart from your mouth, or from the mouth of your children, or from the mouth of their descendants from this time on and for ever," says the LORD. *Is. 59*

▸ You are the Holy One, enthroned on the praises of Israel. *Ps. 22*
And (the angels) call to one another, saying, "Holy, holy, holy is the LORD of hosts; the whole world is filled with His glory." *Is. 6*
And they receive permission from one another, saying: "Holy in the highest heavens, home of His Presence; holy on earth, the work of His strength; holy for ever and all time is the LORD of hosts; the whole earth is full of His radiant glory." *Targum Yonatan Is. 6*

▸ Then a wind lifted me up and I heard behind me the sound of a great noise, saying, "Blessed is the LORD's glory from His place." *Ezek. 3*
Then a wind lifted me up and I heard behind me the sound of a great tempest of those who uttered praise, saying, "Blessed is the LORD's glory from the place of the home of His Presence." *Targum Yonatan Ezek. 3*

The LORD shall reign for ever and all time. *Ex. 15*
The LORD's kingdom is established for ever and all time. *Targum Onkelos Ex. 15*

יהוה LORD, God of Abraham, Isaac and Yisrael, our ancestors, may You keep this for ever so that it forms the thoughts in Your people's heart, and directs their heart toward You. He is compassionate. He forgives iniquity and does not destroy. Repeatedly He suppresses His anger, not rousing His full wrath. For You, my LORD, are good *1 Chr. 29* *Ps. 78* *Ps. 86*

---

service, known as *Kedusha deSidra*. Here, it is incorporated into an act of study. Hence the verses of the *Kedusha* are followed by their Aramaic translations and expansions (Aramaic was for a long time the language of study).

In a house of mourning and on תשעה באב *omit the verse beginning* וַאֲנִי זֹאת בְּרִיתִי *and continue with* וְאַתָּה קָדוֹשׁ.

ישעיה נט
וּבָא לְצִיּוֹן גּוֹאֵל, וּלְשָׁבֵי פֶשַׁע בְּיַעֲקֹב, נְאֻם יהוה:
וַאֲנִי זֹאת בְּרִיתִי אוֹתָם, אָמַר יהוה
רוּחִי אֲשֶׁר עָלֶיךָ וּדְבָרַי אֲשֶׁר־שַׂמְתִּי בְּפִיךָ
לֹא־יָמוּשׁוּ מִפִּיךָ וּמִפִּי זַרְעֲךָ וּמִפִּי זֶרַע זַרְעֲךָ
אָמַר יהוה, מֵעַתָּה וְעַד־עוֹלָם:

תהלים כב
ישעיה ו
◂ וְאַתָּה קָדוֹשׁ יוֹשֵׁב תְּהִלּוֹת יִשְׂרָאֵל: וְקָרָא זֶה אֶל־זֶה וְאָמַר
קָדוֹשׁ, קָדוֹשׁ, קָדוֹשׁ, יהוה צְבָאוֹת, מְלֹא כָל־הָאָרֶץ כְּבוֹדוֹ:

תרגום יונתן ישעיה ו
וּמְקַבְּלִין דֵּין מִן דֵּין וְאָמְרִין, קַדִּישׁ בִּשְׁמֵי מְרוֹמָא עִלָּאָה בֵּית שְׁכִינְתֵהּ
קַדִּישׁ עַל אַרְעָא עוֹבַד גְּבוּרְתֵהּ, קַדִּישׁ לְעָלַם וּלְעָלְמֵי עָלְמַיָּא
יהוה צְבָאוֹת, מַלְיָא כָל אַרְעָא זִיו יְקָרֵהּ.

יחזקאל ג
◂ וַתִּשָּׂאֵנִי רוּחַ, וָאֶשְׁמַע אַחֲרַי קוֹל רַעַשׁ גָּדוֹל
בָּרוּךְ כְּבוֹד־יהוה מִמְּקוֹמוֹ:

תרגום יונתן יחזקאל ג
וּנְטָלַתְנִי רוּחָא, וּשְׁמָעִית בַּתְרַי קָל זִיעַ סַגִּיא, דִּמְשַׁבְּחִין וְאָמְרִין
בְּרִיךְ יְקָרָא דַיהוה מֵאֲתַר בֵּית שְׁכִינְתֵהּ.

שמות טו
יהוה יִמְלֹךְ לְעֹלָם וָעֶד:

תרגום אונקלוס שמות טו
יהוה מַלְכוּתֵהּ קָאֵם לְעָלַם וּלְעָלְמֵי עָלְמַיָּא.

דברי הימים א׳ כט
יהוה אֱלֹהֵי אַבְרָהָם יִצְחָק וְיִשְׂרָאֵל אֲבֹתֵינוּ, שָׁמְרָה־זֹּאת לְעוֹלָם
תהלים עח
לְיֵצֶר מַחְשְׁבוֹת לְבַב עַמֶּךָ, וְהָכֵן לְבָבָם אֵלֶיךָ: וְהוּא רַחוּם יְכַפֵּר
עָוֹן וְלֹא־יַשְׁחִית, וְהִרְבָּה לְהָשִׁיב אַפּוֹ, וְלֹא־יָעִיר כָּל־חֲמָתוֹ:

וּבָא לְצִיּוֹן גּוֹאֵל *A redeemer will come to Zion:* These two verses (from Isaiah), are all that remain of the ancient custom of studying prophetic texts after prayer. **וְאַתָּה קָדוֹשׁ** *You are the Holy One:* the third and final *Kedusha* of the morning

and forgiving, abundantly kind to all who call on You. Your righ- *Ps. 119*
teousness is eternally righteous, and Your Torah is truth. Grant *Mic. 7*
truth to Jacob, loving-kindness to Abraham, as You promised our
ancestors in ancient times. Blessed is my LORD for day after day *Ps. 68*
He burdens us [with His blessings]; God is our salvation, Selah!
The LORD of hosts is with us; the God of Jacob is our refuge, Selah! *Ps. 46*
LORD of hosts, happy is the one who trusts in You. LORD, save! May *Ps. 84* *Ps. 20*
the King answer us on the day we call.

בָּרוּךְ Blessed is He, our God, who created us for His glory, separating us from those who go astray; who gave us the Torah of truth, planting within us eternal life. May He open our heart to His Torah, imbuing our heart with the love and awe of Him, that we may do His will and serve Him with a perfect heart, so that we neither toil in vain nor give birth to confusion.

יְהִי רָצוֹן May it be Your will, O LORD our God and God of our ancestors, that we keep Your laws in this world, and thus be worthy to live,
see and inherit goodness and blessing in the Messianic Age and in
the life of the World to Come. So that my soul may sing to You and *Ps. 30*
not be silent. LORD, my God, for ever I will thank You. Blessed is *Jer. 17*
the man who trusts in the LORD, whose trust is in the LORD alone.
Trust in the LORD for evermore, for God, the LORD, is an everlast- *Is. 26*
ing Rock. ▸ Those who know Your name trust in You, for You, LORD, *Ps. 9*
do not forsake those who seek You. The LORD desired, for the sake *Is. 42*
of Israel's merit, to make the Torah great and glorious.

On Rosh Ḥodesh the Leader says Half Kaddish, page 168.
The service then continues with Musaf for Rosh Ḥodesh on page 372.

On other days, the Leader continues with Full Kaddish on the next page.

The prayer, by contrast, looks forward to the future, personal and collective: personal – may God help us to keep His commandments, and collective – may we see the coming of the Messianic Age.

תהלים פו / תהלים קיט כִּי־אַתָּה אֲדֹנָי טוֹב וְסַלָּח, וְרַב־חֶסֶד לְכָל־קֹרְאֶיךָ: צִדְקָתְךָ
מיכה ז צֶדֶק לְעוֹלָם וְתוֹרָתְךָ אֱמֶת: תִּתֵּן אֱמֶת לְיַעֲקֹב, חֶסֶד לְאַבְרָהָם,
תהלים סח אֲשֶׁר־נִשְׁבַּעְתָּ לַאֲבֹתֵינוּ מִימֵי קֶדֶם: בָּרוּךְ אֲדֹנָי יוֹם יוֹם יַעֲמָס־
תהלים מו לָנוּ, הָאֵל יְשׁוּעָתֵנוּ סֶלָה: יהוה צְבָאוֹת עִמָּנוּ, מִשְׂגָּב לָנוּ אֱלֹהֵי
תהלים פד / תהלים כ יַעֲקֹב סֶלָה: יהוה צְבָאוֹת, אַשְׁרֵי אָדָם בֹּטֵחַ בָּךְ: יהוה הוֹשִׁיעָה,
הַמֶּלֶךְ יַעֲנֵנוּ בְיוֹם־קָרְאֵנוּ:

בָּרוּךְ הוּא אֱלֹהֵינוּ שֶׁבְּרָאָנוּ לִכְבוֹדוֹ, וְהִבְדִּילָנוּ מִן הַתּוֹעִים, וְנָתַן לָנוּ תּוֹרַת אֱמֶת, וְחַיֵּי עוֹלָם נָטַע בְּתוֹכֵנוּ. הוּא יִפְתַּח לִבֵּנוּ בְּתוֹרָתוֹ, וְיָשֵׂם בְּלִבֵּנוּ אַהֲבָתוֹ וְיִרְאָתוֹ וְלַעֲשׂוֹת רְצוֹנוֹ וּלְעָבְדוֹ בְּלֵבָב שָׁלֵם, לְמַעַן לֹא נִיגַע לָרִיק וְלֹא נֵלֵד לַבֶּהָלָה.

יְהִי רָצוֹן מִלְּפָנֶיךָ יהוה אֱלֹהֵינוּ וֵאלֹהֵי אֲבוֹתֵינוּ, שֶׁנִּשְׁמֹר חֻקֶּיךָ
בָּעוֹלָם הַזֶּה, וְנִזְכֶּה וְנִחְיֶה וְנִרְאֶה וְנִירַשׁ טוֹבָה וּבְרָכָה, לִשְׁנֵי
תהלים ל יְמוֹת הַמָּשִׁיחַ וּלְחַיֵּי הָעוֹלָם הַבָּא. לְמַעַן יְזַמֶּרְךָ כָבוֹד וְלֹא יִדֹּם,
ירמיה יז יהוה אֱלֹהַי, לְעוֹלָם אוֹדֶךָּ: בָּרוּךְ הַגֶּבֶר אֲשֶׁר יִבְטַח בַּיהוה,
ישעיה כו וְהָיָה יהוה מִבְטַחוֹ: בִּטְחוּ בַיהוה עֲדֵי־עַד, כִּי בְּיָהּ יהוה צוּר
תהלים ט עוֹלָמִים: ◂ וְיִבְטְחוּ בְךָ יוֹדְעֵי שְׁמֶךָ, כִּי לֹא־עָזַבְתָּ דֹרְשֶׁיךָ, יהוה:
ישעיה מב יהוה חָפֵץ לְמַעַן צִדְקוֹ, יַגְדִּיל תּוֹרָה וְיַאְדִּיר:

On ראש חודש *the* שליח ציבור *says* חצי קדיש, *page 169.*
The service then continues with מוסף *for* ראש חודש *on page 373.*

On other days the שליח ציבור *continues with* קדיש שלם *on the next page.*

בָּרוּךְ הוּא אֱלֹהֵינוּ *Blessed is He, our God:* There now follow a concluding blessing and a prayer. The blessing marks the end of a Torah study session (the counterpart of the two opening benedictions in the Blessings over the Torah).

FULL KADDISH

Leader: יִתְגַּדַּל Magnified and sanctified may His great name be,
in the world He created by His will.
May He establish His kingdom in your lifetime
and in your days,
and in the lifetime of all the house of Israel,
swiftly and soon –
and say: Amen.

All: May His great name be blessed for ever and all time.

Leader: Blessed and praised,
glorified and exalted,
raised and honored,
uplifted and lauded be
the name of the Holy One,
blessed be He,
beyond any blessing,
song, praise and consolation
uttered in the world –
and say: Amen.

On Tisha B'Av, omit the next verse and continue with "May there be great peace."

May the prayers and pleas of all Israel
be accepted by their Father in heaven –
and say: Amen.

May there be great peace from heaven,
and life for us and all Israel –
and say: Amen.

Bow, take three steps back, as if taking leave of the Divine Presence, then bow, first left, then right, then center, while saying:

May He who makes peace in His high places,
make peace for us and all Israel –
and say: Amen.

קדיש שלם

ש״ץ: יִתְגַּדַּל וְיִתְקַדַּשׁ שְׁמֵהּ רַבָּא (קהל: אָמֵן)
בְּעָלְמָא דִּי בְרָא כִרְעוּתֵהּ
וְיַמְלִיךְ מַלְכוּתֵהּ
בְּחַיֵּיכוֹן וּבְיוֹמֵיכוֹן וּבְחַיֵּי דְכָל בֵּית יִשְׂרָאֵל
בַּעֲגָלָא וּבִזְמַן קָרִיב, וְאִמְרוּ אָמֵן. (קהל: אָמֵן)

קהל וש״ץ: יְהֵא שְׁמֵהּ רַבָּא מְבָרַךְ לְעָלַם וּלְעָלְמֵי עָלְמַיָּא.

ש״ץ: יִתְבָּרַךְ וְיִשְׁתַּבַּח וְיִתְפָּאַר
וְיִתְרוֹמַם וְיִתְנַשֵּׂא וְיִתְהַדַּר וְיִתְעַלֶּה וְיִתְהַלָּל
שְׁמֵהּ דְּקֻדְשָׁא בְּרִיךְ הוּא (קהל: בְּרִיךְ הוּא)
לְעֵלָּא מִן כָּל בִּרְכָתָא
/בעשרת ימי תשובה: לְעֵלָּא לְעֵלָּא מִכָּל בִּרְכָתָא/
וְשִׁירָתָא, תֻּשְׁבְּחָתָא וְנֶחֱמָתָא
דַּאֲמִירָן בְּעָלְמָא, וְאִמְרוּ אָמֵן. (קהל: אָמֵן)

On תשעה באב, omit the next verse and continue with יְהֵא שְׁלָמָא.

תִּתְקַבַּל צְלוֹתְהוֹן וּבָעוּתְהוֹן דְּכָל יִשְׂרָאֵל
קֳדָם אֲבוּהוֹן דִּי בִשְׁמַיָּא, וְאִמְרוּ אָמֵן. (קהל: אָמֵן)

יְהֵא שְׁלָמָא רַבָּא מִן שְׁמַיָּא
וְחַיִּים, עָלֵינוּ וְעַל כָּל יִשְׂרָאֵל, וְאִמְרוּ אָמֵן. (קהל: אָמֵן)

Bow, take three steps back, as if taking leave of the Divine Presence, then bow, first left, then right, then center, while saying:

עֹשֶׂה שָׁלוֹם/בעשרת ימי תשובה: הַשָּׁלוֹם/ בִּמְרוֹמָיו
הוּא יַעֲשֶׂה שָׁלוֹם עָלֵינוּ וְעַל כָּל יִשְׂרָאֵל
וְאִמְרוּ אָמֵן. (קהל: אָמֵן)

Stand while saying Aleinu. Bow at ▾.

עָלֵינוּ It is our duty to praise the Master of all,
and ascribe greatness to the Author of creation,
who has not made us like the nations of the lands
nor placed us like the families of the earth;
who has not made our portion like theirs,
nor our destiny like all their multitudes.
(For they worship vanity and emptiness,
and pray to a god who cannot save.)
▾But we bow in worship and thank the Supreme King of kings,
the Holy One, blessed be He,
who extends the heavens and establishes the earth,
whose throne of glory is in the heavens above,
and whose power's Presence is in the highest of heights.
He is our God; there is no other.
Truly He is our King, there is none else,
as it is written in His Torah:
"You shall know and take to heart this day that the LORD is God, *Deut. 4*
in heaven above and on earth below. There is no other."

Therefore, we place our hope in You, LORD our God,
that we may soon see the glory of Your power,
when You will remove abominations from the earth,
and idols will be utterly destroyed,
when the world will be perfected under the sovereignty of the Almighty,
when all humanity will call on Your name,
to turn all the earth's wicked toward You.
All the world's inhabitants will realize and know
that to You every knee must bow and every tongue swear loyalty.
Before You, LORD our God, they will kneel and bow down
and give honor to Your glorious name.

---

statement of the particularity of Jewish faith and its universal aspiration for humanity.

The first paragraph, was originally used (and still is) as an introduction to the Blessing of Kingship in the *Musaf* of Rosh HaShana. Less a prayer than a declaration of faith, it speaks of the singular vocation of the Jewish people as bearers

Stand while saying עָלֵינוּ. *Bow at* ׳.

עָלֵינוּ לְשַׁבֵּחַ לַאֲדוֹן הַכֹּל, לָתֵת גְּדֻלָּה לְיוֹצֵר בְּרֵאשִׁית
שֶׁלֹּא עָשָׂנוּ כְּגוֹיֵי הָאֲרָצוֹת, וְלֹא שָׂמָנוּ כְּמִשְׁפְּחוֹת הָאֲדָמָה
שֶׁלֹּא שָׂם חֶלְקֵנוּ כָּהֶם וְגוֹרָלֵנוּ כְּכָל הֲמוֹנָם.
(שֶׁהֵם מִשְׁתַּחֲוִים לְהֶבֶל וָרִיק וּמִתְפַּלְּלִים אֶל אֵל לֹא יוֹשִׁיעַ.)
׳וַאֲנַחְנוּ כּוֹרְעִים וּמִשְׁתַּחֲוִים וּמוֹדִים
לִפְנֵי מֶלֶךְ מַלְכֵי הַמְּלָכִים, הַקָּדוֹשׁ בָּרוּךְ הוּא
שֶׁהוּא נוֹטֶה שָׁמַיִם וְיוֹסֵד אָרֶץ, וּמוֹשַׁב יְקָרוֹ בַּשָּׁמַיִם מִמַּעַל
וּשְׁכִינַת עֻזּוֹ בְּגָבְהֵי מְרוֹמִים.
הוּא אֱלֹהֵינוּ, אֵין עוֹד.
אֱמֶת מַלְכֵּנוּ, אֶפֶס זוּלָתוֹ
כַּכָּתוּב בְּתוֹרָתוֹ
וְיָדַעְתָּ הַיּוֹם וַהֲשֵׁבֹתָ אֶל־לְבָבֶךָ דברים ד
כִּי יהוה הוּא הָאֱלֹהִים בַּשָּׁמַיִם מִמַּעַל וְעַל־הָאָרֶץ מִתָּחַת, אֵין עוֹד:

עַל כֵּן נְקַוֶּה לְּךָ יהוה אֱלֹהֵינוּ, לִרְאוֹת מְהֵרָה בְּתִפְאֶרֶת עֻזֶּךָ
לְהַעֲבִיר גִּלּוּלִים מִן הָאָרֶץ, וְהָאֱלִילִים כָּרוֹת יִכָּרֵתוּן
לְתַקֵּן עוֹלָם בְּמַלְכוּת שַׁדַּי.
וְכָל בְּנֵי בָשָׂר יִקְרְאוּ בִשְׁמֶךָ לְהַפְנוֹת אֵלֶיךָ כָּל רִשְׁעֵי אָרֶץ.
יַכִּירוּ וְיֵדְעוּ כָּל יוֹשְׁבֵי תֵבֵל
כִּי לְךָ תִּכְרַע כָּל בֶּרֶךְ, תִּשָּׁבַע כָּל לָשׁוֹן.
לְפָנֶיךָ יהוה אֱלֹהֵינוּ יִכְרְעוּ וְיִפֹּלוּ, וְלִכְבוֹד שִׁמְךָ יְקָר יִתֵּנוּ
וִיקַבְּלוּ כֻלָּם אֶת עֹל מַלְכוּתֶךָ
וְתִמְלֹךְ עֲלֵיהֶם מְהֵרָה לְעוֹלָם וָעֶד.

עָלֵינוּ *It is our duty:* Since the twelfth or thirteenth century, it has become the custom to bring all services to a close with the magnificent prayer known as *Aleinu,* a construct of two paragraphs, which together make a striking

They will all accept the yoke of Your kingdom,
and You will reign over them soon and for ever.
For the kingdom is Yours, and to all eternity You will reign in glory,
as it is written in Your Torah: "The LORD will reign for ever and ever." *Ex. 15*
▸ And it is said: "Then the LORD shall be King over all the earth; *Zech. 14*
on that day the LORD shall be One and His name One."

Some add:
Have no fear of sudden terror or of the ruin when it overtakes the wicked. *Prov. 3*
Devise your strategy, but it will be thwarted; *Is. 8*
propose your plan, but it will not stand, for God is with us.
When you grow old, I will still be the same. *Is. 46*
When your hair turns gray, I will still carry you.
I made you, I will bear you, I will carry you, and I will rescue you.

MOURNER'S KADDISH

The following prayer, said by mourners, requires the presence of a minyan. A transliteration can be found on page 699.

Mourner: יִתְגַּדַּל Magnified and sanctified
may His great name be,
in the world He created by His will.
May He establish His kingdom
in your lifetime and in your days,
and in the lifetime of all the house of Israel,
swiftly and soon – and say: Amen.

All: May His great name be blessed for ever and all time.

Mourner: Blessed and praised, glorified and exalted,
raised and honored, uplifted and lauded
be the name of the Holy One,
blessed be He,

No prayer more eloquently expresses the dual nature of the Jewish people: its singular history as the nation chosen to be God's witnesses on earth, and its universal aspiration for the time when all the inhabitants of earth will recognize the God in whose image we are formed.

כִּי הַמַּלְכוּת שֶׁלְּךָ הִיא וּלְעוֹלְמֵי עַד תִּמְלֹךְ בְּכָבוֹד

שמות טו כַּכָּתוּב בְּתוֹרָתֶךָ, יהוה יִמְלֹךְ לְעֹלָם וָעֶד:

זכריה יד ◂ וְנֶאֱמַר, וְהָיָה יהוה לְמֶלֶךְ עַל־כָּל־הָאָרֶץ

בַּיּוֹם הַהוּא יִהְיֶה יהוה אֶחָד וּשְׁמוֹ אֶחָד:

Some add:

משלי ג אַל־תִּירָא מִפַּחַד פִּתְאֹם וּמִשֹּׁאַת רְשָׁעִים כִּי תָבֹא:

ישעיה ח עֻצוּ עֵצָה וְתֻפָר, דַּבְּרוּ דָבָר וְלֹא יָקוּם, כִּי עִמָּנוּ אֵל:

ישעיה מו וְעַד־זִקְנָה אֲנִי הוּא, וְעַד־שֵׂיבָה אֲנִי אֶסְבֹּל, אֲנִי עָשִׂיתִי וַאֲנִי אֶשָּׂא וַאֲנִי אֶסְבֹּל וַאֲמַלֵּט:

קדיש יתום

The following prayer, said by mourners, requires the presence of a מנין.
A transliteration can be found on page 699.

אבל: יִתְגַּדַּל וְיִתְקַדַּשׁ שְׁמֵהּ רַבָּא (קהל: אָמֵן)

בְּעָלְמָא דִּי בְרָא כִרְעוּתֵהּ

וְיַמְלִיךְ מַלְכוּתֵהּ

בְּחַיֵּיכוֹן וּבְיוֹמֵיכוֹן וּבְחַיֵּי דְכָל בֵּית יִשְׂרָאֵל

בַּעֲגָלָא וּבִזְמַן קָרִיב, וְאִמְרוּ אָמֵן. (קהל: אָמֵן)

קהל ואבל: יְהֵא שְׁמֵהּ רַבָּא מְבָרַךְ לְעָלַם וּלְעָלְמֵי עָלְמַיָּא.

אבל: יִתְבָּרַךְ וְיִשְׁתַּבַּח וְיִתְפָּאַר

וְיִתְרוֹמַם וְיִתְנַשֵּׂא וְיִתְהַדָּר וְיִתְעַלֶּה וְיִתְהַלָּל

שְׁמֵהּ דְּקֻדְשָׁא בְּרִיךְ הוּא (קהל: בְּרִיךְ הוּא)

---

of the message of monotheism. Twice, the prayer uses the expression, "There is no other," forcefully expressed in Hebrew by two monosyllabic words, *ein od*.

The second paragraph turns to God and to the future, to a time when all humanity will acknowledge the One God, a vision eloquently spoken of by the prophet Zechariah, from whose book the final verse is taken. It contains a phrase – "to perfect the world under the sovereignty of God" – which became a leading theme of Lurianic mysticism in the sixteenth century (*tikkun olam*).

beyond any blessing, song, praise and consolation
uttered in the world – and say: Amen.

May there be great peace from heaven,
and life for us and all Israel – and say: Amen.

Bow, take three steps back, as if taking leave of the Divine Presence, then bow, first left, then right, then center, while saying:

May He who makes peace in His high places,
make peace for us and all Israel – and say: Amen.

THE DAILY PSALM

One of the following psalms is said on the appropriate day of the week as indicated.

After the Daily Psalm, on Rosh Ḥodesh, add Barekhi Nafshi, page 194 (in Israel, some only say Barekhi Nafshi). On Ḥanukka, add Psalm 30, page 58 followed by Mourner's Kaddish. From the second day of Rosh Ḥodesh Elul through Shemini Atzeret (in Israel, through Hoshana Raba), add Psalm 27 on page 196. In a house of mourning the service concludes on page 602.

Sunday: Today is the first day of the week,
on which the Levites used to say this psalm in the Temple:

לְדָוִד מִזְמוֹר A psalm of David. The earth is the LORD's and all it contains, the world and all who live in it. For He founded it on the seas and established it on the streams. Who may climb the mountain of the LORD? Who may stand in His holy place? He who has clean hands and a pure heart, who has not taken My name in vain or sworn deceitfully. He shall receive a blessing from the LORD, and just reward from the God of his salvation. This is a generation of those who seek Him, the descendants of Jacob who seek Your presence, Selah! Lift up your heads, O gates; be uplifted, eternal doors, so that the King of glory may enter. Who is the King of glory? It is the LORD, strong and mighty, the LORD mighty in battle. Lift up your heads, O gates; lift them up, eternal doors, that the King of glory may enter. ▸ Who is He, the King of glory? The LORD of hosts, He is the King of glory, Selah! *Ps. 24*

Mourner's Kaddish (previous page)

לְדָוִד מִזְמוֹר *Sunday: Psalm 24.* The opening verses mirror the act of creation, reminding us that each week mirrors the seven days of creation itself. The ·salm also alludes to the Temple, built on "the mountain of the LORD." The nnection between the two is based on the idea that the Temple was a ocosm of the universe, and its construction a human counterpart to the creation of the cosmos.

Monday הַיּוֹם יוֹם שֵׁנִי בְּשַׁבָּת, שֶׁבּוֹ הָיוּ הַלְוִיִּם אוֹמְרִים בְּבֵית הַמִּקְדָּשׁ:

שִׁיר מִזְמוֹר לִבְנֵי־קֹֽרַח: גָּדוֹל יהוה וּמְהֻלָּל מְאֹד, בְּעִיר אֱלֹהֵֽינוּ, הַר־קָדְשׁוֹ: תהלים מח
יְפֵה נוֹף מְשׂוֹשׂ כָּל־הָאָֽרֶץ, הַר־צִיּוֹן יַרְכְּתֵי צָפוֹן, קִרְיַת מֶֽלֶךְ רָב: אֱלֹהִים
בְּאַרְמְנוֹתֶֽיהָ נוֹדַע לְמִשְׂגָּב: כִּי־הִנֵּה הַמְּלָכִים נוֹעֲדוּ, עָבְרוּ יַחְדָּו: הֵֽמָּה
רָאוּ כֵּן תָּמָֽהוּ, נִבְהֲלוּ נֶחְפָּֽזוּ: רְעָדָה אֲחָזָֽתַם שָׁם, חִיל כַּיּוֹלֵדָה: בְּרֽוּחַ
קָדִים תְּשַׁבֵּר אֳנִיּוֹת תַּרְשִׁישׁ: כַּאֲשֶׁר שָׁמַֽעְנוּ כֵּן רָאִֽינוּ, בְּעִיר־יהוה צְבָאוֹת,
בְּעִיר אֱלֹהֵֽינוּ, אֱלֹהִים יְכוֹנְנֶֽהָ עַד־עוֹלָם סֶֽלָה: דִּמִּֽינוּ אֱלֹהִים חַסְדֶּֽךָ, בְּקֶֽרֶב
הֵיכָלֶֽךָ: כְּשִׁמְךָ אֱלֹהִים כֵּן תְּהִלָּתְךָ עַל־קַצְוֵי־אֶֽרֶץ, צֶֽדֶק מָלְאָה יְמִינֶֽךָ:
יִשְׂמַח הַר־צִיּוֹן, תָּגֵֽלְנָה בְּנוֹת יְהוּדָה, לְמַֽעַן מִשְׁפָּטֶֽיךָ: סֹֽבּוּ צִיּוֹן וְהַקִּיפֽוּהָ,
סִפְרוּ מִגְדָּלֶֽיהָ: שִׁיתוּ לִבְּכֶם לְחֵילָה, פַּסְּגוּ אַרְמְנוֹתֶֽיהָ, לְמַֽעַן תְּסַפְּרוּ לְדוֹר
אַחֲרוֹן: › כִּי זֶה אֱלֹהִים אֱלֹהֵֽינוּ עוֹלָם וָעֶד, הוּא יְנַהֲגֵֽנוּ עַל־מוּת:

קדיש יתום (*page 187*)

Tuesday הַיּוֹם יוֹם שְׁלִישִׁי בְּשַׁבָּת, שֶׁבּוֹ הָיוּ הַלְוִיִּם אוֹמְרִים בְּבֵית הַמִּקְדָּשׁ:

מִזְמוֹר לְאָסָף, אֱלֹהִים נִצָּב בַּעֲדַת־אֵל, בְּקֶֽרֶב אֱלֹהִים יִשְׁפֹּט: עַד־מָתַי תהלים פב
תִּשְׁפְּטוּ־עָֽוֶל, וּפְנֵי רְשָׁעִים תִּשְׂאוּ־סֶֽלָה: שִׁפְטוּ־דָל וְיָתוֹם, עָנִי וָרָשׁ
הַצְדִּֽיקוּ: פַּלְּטוּ־דַל וְאֶבְיוֹן, מִיַּד רְשָׁעִים הַצִּֽילוּ: לֹא יָדְעוּ וְלֹא יָבִֽינוּ,
בַּחֲשֵׁכָה יִתְהַלָּֽכוּ, יִמּֽוֹטוּ כָּל־מֽוֹסְדֵי אָֽרֶץ: אֲנִי־אָמַֽרְתִּי אֱלֹהִים אַתֶּם, וּבְנֵי
עֶלְיוֹן כֻּלְּכֶם: אָכֵן כְּאָדָם תְּמוּתוּן, וּכְאַחַד הַשָּׂרִים תִּפֹּֽלוּ: › קוּמָה אֱלֹהִים
שָׁפְטָה הָאָֽרֶץ, כִּי־אַתָּה תִנְחַל בְּכָל־הַגּוֹיִם:

קדיש יתום (*page 187*)

שִׁיר מִזְמוֹר לִבְנֵי־קֹֽרַח *Monday: Psalm 48.* A hymn of praise to the beauty and endurance of Jerusalem, the city that outlived all those who sought to conquer it.

A score of conquerors have held it as their choicest prize; and more than a dozen times has it been utterly destroyed. The Babylonians burnt it, and deported its population; the Romans slew a million of its inhabitants, razed it to the ground, passed the ploughshare over it, and strewed its furrows with salt; Hadrian banished its very name from the lips of men, changed it to *Aelia Capitolina*, and prohibited any Jew from entering its precincts on pain of death. Persians and Arabs, Barbarians and Crusaders and Turks took it and retook it, ravaged it and burnt it; and yet, marvelous

Wednesday: Today is the fourth day of the week,
on which the Levites used to say this psalm in the Temple:

אֵל־נְקָמוֹת God of retribution, LORD, God of retribution, appear! Rise up, Judge of the earth. Repay to the arrogant what they deserve. How long shall the wicked, LORD, how long shall the wicked triumph? They pour out insolent words. All the evildoers are full of boasting. They crush Your people, LORD, and oppress Your inheritance. They kill the widow and the stranger. They murder the orphaned. They say, "The LORD does not see. The God of Jacob pays no heed." Take heed, you most brutish people. You fools, when will you grow wise? Will He who implants the ear not hear? Will He who formed the eye not see? Will He who disciplines nations – He who teaches man knowledge – not punish? The LORD knows that the thoughts of man are a mere fleeting breath. Happy is the man whom You discipline, LORD, the one You instruct in Your Torah, giving him tranquility in days of trouble, until a pit is dug for the wicked. For the LORD will not forsake His people, nor abandon His heritage. Judgment shall again accord with justice, and all the upright in heart will follow it. Who will rise up for me against the wicked? Who will stand up for me against wrongdoers? Had the LORD not been my help, I would soon have dwelt in death's silence. When I thought my foot was slipping, Your loving-kindness, LORD, gave me support. When I was filled with anxiety, Your consolations soothed my soul. Can a corrupt throne be allied with You? Can injustice be framed into law? They join forces against the life of the righteous, and condemn the innocent to death. But the LORD is my stronghold, my God is the Rock of my refuge. He will bring back on them their wickedness, and destroy them for their evil deeds. The LORD our God will destroy them. *Ps. 94*

▸ Come, let us sing for joy to the LORD; let us shout aloud to the Rock of our salvation. Let us greet Him with thanksgiving, shout aloud to Him with songs of praise. For the LORD is the great God, the King great above all powers. *Ps. 95*

Mourner's Kaddish (page 186)

Thursday: Today is the fifth day of the week,
on which the Levites used to say this psalm in the Temple:

לַמְנַצֵּחַ For the conductor of music. On the Gittit. By Asaph. Sing for joy to God, our strength. Shout aloud to the God of Jacob. Raise a song, beat the drum, play the sweet harp and lyre. Sound the shofar on the new moon, on our feast *Ps. 81*

לַמְנַצֵּחַ *Thursday: Psalm 81.* God pleads with His people: a classic expression of one of the great themes of the prophetic literature, the divine pathos – God's love for, but exasperation with, His children. "If only My people would listen to Me."

Wednesday הַיּוֹם יוֹם רְבִיעִי בְּשַׁבָּת, שֶׁבּוֹ הָיוּ הַלְוִיִּם אוֹמְרִים בְּבֵית הַמִּקְדָּשׁ:

תהלים צד אֵל־נְקָמוֹת יהוה, אֵל נְקָמוֹת הוֹפִיעַ: הִנָּשֵׂא שֹׁפֵט הָאָרֶץ, הָשֵׁב גְּמוּל עַל־גֵּאִים: עַד־מָתַי רְשָׁעִים, יהוה, עַד־מָתַי רְשָׁעִים יַעֲלֹזוּ: יַבִּיעוּ יְדַבְּרוּ עָתָק, יִתְאַמְּרוּ כׇּל־פֹּעֲלֵי אָוֶן: עַמְּךָ יהוה יְדַכְּאוּ, וְנַחֲלָתְךָ יְעַנּוּ: אַלְמָנָה וְגֵר יַהֲרֹגוּ, וִיתוֹמִים יְרַצֵּחוּ: וַיֹּאמְרוּ לֹא יִרְאֶה־יָּהּ, וְלֹא־יָבִין אֱלֹהֵי יַעֲקֹב: בִּינוּ בֹּעֲרִים בָּעָם, וּכְסִילִים מָתַי תַּשְׂכִּילוּ: הֲנֹטַע אֹזֶן הֲלֹא יִשְׁמָע, אִם־יֹצֵר עַיִן הֲלֹא יַבִּיט: הֲיֹסֵר גּוֹיִם הֲלֹא יוֹכִיחַ, הַמְלַמֵּד אָדָם דָּעַת: יהוה יֹדֵעַ מַחְשְׁבוֹת אָדָם, כִּי־הֵמָּה הָבֶל: אַשְׁרֵי הַגֶּבֶר אֲשֶׁר־תְּיַסְּרֶנּוּ יָּהּ, וּמִתּוֹרָתְךָ תְלַמְּדֶנּוּ: לְהַשְׁקִיט לוֹ מִימֵי רָע, עַד יִכָּרֶה לָרָשָׁע שָׁחַת: כִּי לֹא־יִטֹּשׁ יהוה עַמּוֹ, וְנַחֲלָתוֹ לֹא יַעֲזֹב: כִּי־עַד־צֶדֶק יָשׁוּב מִשְׁפָּט, וְאַחֲרָיו כׇּל־יִשְׁרֵי־לֵב: מִי־יָקוּם לִי עִם־מְרֵעִים, מִי־יִתְיַצֵּב לִי עִם־פֹּעֲלֵי אָוֶן: לוּלֵי יהוה עֶזְרָתָה לִּי, כִּמְעַט שָׁכְנָה דוּמָה נַפְשִׁי: אִם־אָמַרְתִּי מָטָה רַגְלִי, חַסְדְּךָ יהוה יִסְעָדֵנִי: בְּרֹב שַׂרְעַפַּי בְּקִרְבִּי, תַּנְחוּמֶיךָ יְשַׁעַשְׁעוּ נַפְשִׁי: הַיְחָבְרְךָ כִּסֵּא הַוּוֹת, יֹצֵר עָמָל עֲלֵי־חֹק: יָגוֹדּוּ עַל־נֶפֶשׁ צַדִּיק, וְדָם נָקִי יַרְשִׁיעוּ: וַיְהִי יהוה לִי לְמִשְׂגָּב, וֵאלֹהַי לְצוּר מַחְסִי: וַיָּשֶׁב עֲלֵיהֶם אֶת־אוֹנָם, וּבְרָעָתָם יַצְמִיתֵם, יַצְמִיתֵם יהוה אֱלֹהֵינוּ:

תהלים צה ◂ לְכוּ נְרַנְּנָה לַיהוה, נָרִיעָה לְצוּר יִשְׁעֵנוּ: נְקַדְּמָה פָנָיו בְּתוֹדָה, בִּזְמִרוֹת נָרִיעַ לוֹ: כִּי אֵל גָּדוֹל יהוה, וּמֶלֶךְ גָּדוֹל עַל־כׇּל־אֱלֹהִים:

קדיש יתום (*page 187*)

Thursday הַיּוֹם יוֹם חֲמִישִׁי בְּשַׁבָּת, שֶׁבּוֹ הָיוּ הַלְוִיִּם אוֹמְרִים בְּבֵית הַמִּקְדָּשׁ:

תהלים פא לַמְנַצֵּחַ עַל־הַגִּתִּית לְאָסָף: הַרְנִינוּ לֵאלֹהִים עוּזֵּנוּ, הָרִיעוּ לֵאלֹהֵי יַעֲקֹב: שְׂאוּ־זִמְרָה וּתְנוּ־תֹף, כִּנּוֹר נָעִים עִם־נָבֶל: תִּקְעוּ בַחֹדֶשׁ שׁוֹפָר, בַּכֶּסֶה לְיוֹם חַגֵּנוּ: כִּי חֹק לְיִשְׂרָאֵל הוּא, מִשְׁפָּט לֵאלֹהֵי יַעֲקֹב: עֵדוּת בִּיהוֹסֵף

אֵל־נְקָמוֹת יהוה *Wednesday: Psalm 94.* Marking the midweek, this is a psalm of intense power about the connection between religious faith and ethical conduct and their opposite: lack of faith and a failure of humanity. When man begins to worship himself, he dreams of becoming a god but ends by becoming lower than the beasts. Appropriately, some communities recite this psalm on Yom HaSho'a, Holocaust Memorial Day (27 Nisan).

day when the moon is hidden. For it is a statute for Israel, an ordinance of the God of Jacob. He established it as a testimony for Joseph when He went forth against the land of Egypt, where I heard a language that I did not know. I relieved his shoulder of the burden. His hands were freed from the builder's basket. In distress you called and I rescued you. I answered you from the secret place of thunder; I tested you at the waters of Meribah, Selah! Hear, My people, and I will warn you. Israel, if you would only listen to Me! Let there be no strange god among you. Do not bow down to an alien god. I am the LORD your God who brought you out of the land of Egypt. Open your mouth wide and I will fill it. But My people would not listen to Me. Israel would have none of Me. So I left them to their stubborn hearts, letting them follow their own devices. If only My people would listen to Me, if Israel would walk in My ways, I would soon subdue their enemies, and turn My hand against their foes. Those who hate the LORD would cower before Him and their doom would last for ever. ▸ He would feed Israel with the finest wheat – with honey from the rock I would satisfy you.

Mourner's Kaddish (page 186)

Friday: Today is the sixth day of the week,
on which the Levites used to say this psalm in the Temple:

יהוה מָלָךְ The LORD reigns. He is robed in majesty. The LORD is robed, girded with strength. The world is firmly established; it cannot be moved. Your throne stands firm as of old; You are eternal. Rivers lift up, LORD, rivers lift up their voice, rivers lift up their crashing waves. Mightier than the noise of many waters, than the mighty waves of the sea is the LORD on high. ▸ Your testimonies are very sure; holiness adorns Your House, LORD, for evermore. *Ps. 93*

Mourner's Kaddish (page 186)

On Rosh Ḥodesh, the following psalm is said:

בָּרְכִי נַפְשִׁי Bless the LORD, my soul. LORD, my God, You are very great, clothed in majesty and splendor, wrapped in a robe of light. You have spread out the heavens like a tent. He has laid the beams of His lofts in the waters. He makes the clouds His chariot, riding on the wings of the wind. He makes the winds His messengers, flames of fire His ministers. He has fixed the earth on its foundations so that it will never be shaken. You covered it with the deep like a cloak; the waters stood above the mountains. At Your rebuke they fled; at the sound of Your thunder they rushed away, flowing over the hills, pouring down into the valleys to the place You appointed for them. You fixed a boundary they were not to pass, so that they would never cover the earth again. He makes springs flow in the valleys; they make their way between the hills, giving drink to all *Ps. 104*

שְׁמוֹ, בְּצֵאתוֹ עַל־אֶרֶץ מִצְרָיִם, שְׂפַת לֹא־יָדַעְתִּי אֶשְׁמָע: הֲסִירוֹתִי מִסֵּבֶל
שִׁכְמוֹ, כַּפָּיו מִדּוּד תַּעֲבֹרְנָה: בַּצָּרָה קָרָאתָ וָאֲחַלְּצֶךָּ, אֶעֶנְךָ בְּסֵתֶר רַעַם,
אֶבְחָנְךָ עַל־מֵי מְרִיבָה סֶלָה: שְׁמַע עַמִּי וְאָעִידָה בָּךְ, יִשְׂרָאֵל אִם־תִּשְׁמַע־
לִי: לֹא־יִהְיֶה בְךָ אֵל זָר, וְלֹא תִשְׁתַּחֲוֶה לְאֵל נֵכָר: אָנֹכִי יהוה אֱלֹהֶיךָ,
הַמַּעַלְךָ מֵאֶרֶץ מִצְרָיִם, הַרְחֶב־פִּיךָ וַאֲמַלְאֵהוּ: וְלֹא־שָׁמַע עַמִּי לְקוֹלִי,
וְיִשְׂרָאֵל לֹא־אָבָה לִי: וָאֲשַׁלְּחֵהוּ בִּשְׁרִירוּת לִבָּם, יֵלְכוּ בְּמוֹעֲצוֹתֵיהֶם: לוּ
עַמִּי שֹׁמֵעַ לִי, יִשְׂרָאֵל בִּדְרָכַי יְהַלֵּכוּ: כִּמְעַט אוֹיְבֵיהֶם אַכְנִיעַ, וְעַל־צָרֵיהֶם
אָשִׁיב יָדִי: מְשַׂנְאֵי יהוה יְכַחֲשׁוּ־לוֹ, וִיהִי עִתָּם לְעוֹלָם: ‹ וַיַּאֲכִילֵהוּ מֵחֵלֶב
חִטָּה, וּמִצּוּר, דְּבַשׁ אַשְׂבִּיעֶךָ:

קדיש יתום (*page 187*)

Friday הַיּוֹם יוֹם שִׁשִּׁי בְּשַׁבָּת, שֶׁבּוֹ הָיוּ הַלְוִיִּם אוֹמְרִים בְּבֵית הַמִּקְדָּשׁ

יהוה מָלָךְ, גֵּאוּת לָבֵשׁ, לָבֵשׁ יהוה עֹז הִתְאַזָּר, אַף־תִּכּוֹן תֵּבֵל בַּל־תִּמּוֹט: תהלים צג
נָכוֹן כִּסְאֲךָ מֵאָז, מֵעוֹלָם אָתָּה: נָשְׂאוּ נְהָרוֹת יהוה, נָשְׂאוּ נְהָרוֹת קוֹלָם,
יִשְׂאוּ נְהָרוֹת דָּכְיָם: מִקֹּלוֹת מַיִם רַבִּים, אַדִּירִים מִשְׁבְּרֵי־יָם, אַדִּיר בַּמָּרוֹם
יהוה: ‹ עֵדֹתֶיךָ נֶאֶמְנוּ מְאֹד, לְבֵיתְךָ נַאֲוָה־קֹדֶשׁ, יהוה לְאֹרֶךְ יָמִים:

קדיש יתום (*page 187*)

On ראש חודש*, the following psalm is said:*

בָּרְכִי נַפְשִׁי אֶת־יהוה, יהוה אֱלֹהַי גָּדַלְתָּ מְּאֹד, הוֹד וְהָדָר לָבָשְׁתָּ: עֹטֶה־אוֹר תהלים קד
כַּשַּׂלְמָה, נוֹטֶה שָׁמַיִם כַּיְרִיעָה: הַמְקָרֶה בַמַּיִם עֲלִיּוֹתָיו, הַשָּׂם־עָבִים רְכוּבוֹ,
הַמְהַלֵּךְ עַל־כַּנְפֵי־רוּחַ: עֹשֶׂה מַלְאָכָיו רוּחוֹת, מְשָׁרְתָיו אֵשׁ לֹהֵט: יָסַד־אֶרֶץ
עַל־מְכוֹנֶיהָ, בַּל־תִּמּוֹט עוֹלָם וָעֶד: תְּהוֹם כַּלְּבוּשׁ כִּסִּיתוֹ, עַל־הָרִים יַעַמְדוּ־
מָיִם: מִן־גַּעֲרָתְךָ יְנוּסוּן, מִן־קוֹל רַעַמְךָ יֵחָפֵזוּן: יַעֲלוּ הָרִים, יֵרְדוּ בְקָעוֹת,
אֶל־מְקוֹם זֶה יָסַדְתָּ לָהֶם: גְּבוּל־שַׂמְתָּ בַּל־יַעֲבֹרוּן, בַּל־יְשׁוּבוּן לְכַסּוֹת הָאָרֶץ:
הַמְשַׁלֵּחַ מַעְיָנִים בַּנְּחָלִים, בֵּין הָרִים יְהַלֵּכוּן: יַשְׁקוּ כָּל־חַיְתוֹ שָׂדָי, יִשְׁבְּרוּ
פְרָאִים צְמָאָם: עֲלֵיהֶם עוֹף־הַשָּׁמַיִם יִשְׁכּוֹן, מִבֵּין עֳפָאיִם יִתְּנוּ־קוֹל: מַשְׁקֶה

יהוה מָלָךְ *Friday: Psalm 93.* Speaking as it does of the completion of creation ("the world is firmly established"), this psalm is appropriate for the sixth day, when "the heavens and the earth were completed, and all their array."

the beasts of the field; the wild donkeys quench their thirst. The birds of the sky dwell beside them, singing among the foliage. He waters the mountains from His lofts: the earth is sated with the fruit of Your work. He makes grass grow for the cattle, and plants for the use of man, that he may produce bread from the earth, wine to cheer the heart of man, oil to make the face shine, and bread to sustain man's heart. The trees of the LORD drink their fill, the cedars of Lebanon which He planted. There, birds build their nests; the stork makes its home in the cypresses. High hills are for the wild goats; crags are shelter for the badgers. He made the moon to mark the seasons, and makes the sun know when to set. You bring darkness and it is night; then all the beasts of the forests stir. The young lions roar for prey, seeking their food from God. When the sun rises, they slink away and seek rest in their lairs. Man goes out to his work and his labor until evening. How numerous are Your works, LORD; You made them all in wisdom; the earth is full of Your creations. There is the vast, immeasurable sea with its countless swarming creatures, living things great and small. There ships sail. There is Leviathan You formed to sport there. All of them look to You in hope, to give them their food when it is due. What You give them, they gather up. When You open Your hand, they are sated with good. When You hide Your face, they are dismayed. When You take away their breath, they die and return to dust. When You send back Your breath, they are created, giving new life to the earth. May the glory of the LORD be for ever; may the LORD rejoice in His works. When He looks at the earth, it trembles. When He touches the mountains, they pour forth smoke. I will sing to the LORD as long as I live; I will sing psalms to my God all my life. ▸ May my meditation be pleasing to Him; I shall rejoice in the LORD. May sinners vanish from the earth, and the wicked be no more. Bless the LORD, my soul. Halleluya!

Mourner's Kaddish *(page 186)*

During the month of Elul (except Erev Rosh HaShana), the shofar is sounded (some sound the shofar after the psalm below). From the second day of Rosh Ḥodesh Elul through Shemini Atzeret, the following psalm is said:

לְדָוִד By David. The LORD is my light and my salvation – whom then shall I fear? *Ps. 27*
The LORD is the stronghold of my life – of whom shall I be afraid? When evil men close in on me to devour my flesh, it is they, my enemies and foes, who stumble and fall. Should an army besiege me, my heart would not fear. Should war break out against me, still I would be confident. One thing I ask of the LORD, only this do I seek: to live in the House of the LORD all the days of my life, to gaze on the beauty of the LORD and worship in His Temple. For He will keep me safe in His pavilion on the day of trouble. He will hide me under the cover of His tent. He will set me high upon a rock. Now my head is high above my enemies who surround me. I will sacrifice in His tent with shouts of joy. I will sing and chant praises to the LORD. LORD, hear my voice when I call. Be

הָרִים מֵעֲלִיּוֹתָיו, מִפְּרִי מַעֲשֶׂיךָ תִּשְׂבַּע הָאָרֶץ: מַצְמִיחַ חָצִיר לַבְּהֵמָה, וְעֵשֶׂב לַעֲבֹדַת הָאָדָם, לְהוֹצִיא לֶחֶם מִן־הָאָרֶץ: וְיַיִן יְשַׂמַּח לְבַב־אֱנוֹשׁ, לְהַצְהִיל פָּנִים מִשָּׁמֶן, וְלֶחֶם לְבַב־אֱנוֹשׁ יִסְעָד: יִשְׂבְּעוּ עֲצֵי יהוה, אַרְזֵי לְבָנוֹן אֲשֶׁר נָטָע: אֲשֶׁר־שָׁם צִפֳּרִים יְקַנֵּנוּ, חֲסִידָה בְּרוֹשִׁים בֵּיתָהּ: הָרִים הַגְּבֹהִים לַיְּעֵלִים, סְלָעִים מַחְסֶה לַשְׁפַנִּים: עָשָׂה יָרֵחַ לְמוֹעֲדִים, שֶׁמֶשׁ יָדַע מְבוֹאוֹ: תָּשֶׁת־חֹשֶׁךְ וִיהִי לָיְלָה, בּוֹ־תִרְמֹשׂ כָּל־חַיְתוֹ־יָעַר: הַכְּפִירִים שֹׁאֲגִים לַטָּרֶף, וּלְבַקֵּשׁ מֵאֵל אָכְלָם: תִּזְרַח הַשֶּׁמֶשׁ יֵאָסֵפוּן, וְאֶל־מְעוֹנֹתָם יִרְבָּצוּן: יֵצֵא אָדָם לְפָעֳלוֹ, וְלַעֲבֹדָתוֹ עֲדֵי־עָרֶב: מָה־רַבּוּ מַעֲשֶׂיךָ יהוה, כֻּלָּם בְּחָכְמָה עָשִׂיתָ, מָלְאָה הָאָרֶץ קִנְיָנֶךָ: זֶה הַיָּם גָּדוֹל וּרְחַב יָדָיִם, שָׁם־רֶמֶשׂ וְאֵין מִסְפָּר, חַיּוֹת קְטַנּוֹת עִם־גְּדֹלוֹת: שָׁם אֳנִיּוֹת יְהַלֵּכוּן, לִוְיָתָן זֶה־יָצַרְתָּ לְשַׂחֶק־בּוֹ: כֻּלָּם אֵלֶיךָ יְשַׂבֵּרוּן, לָתֵת אָכְלָם בְּעִתּוֹ: תִּתֵּן לָהֶם יִלְקֹטוּן, תִּפְתַּח יָדְךָ יִשְׂבְּעוּן טוֹב: תַּסְתִּיר פָּנֶיךָ יִבָּהֵלוּן, תֹּסֵף רוּחָם יִגְוָעוּן, וְאֶל־עֲפָרָם יְשׁוּבוּן: תְּשַׁלַּח רוּחֲךָ יִבָּרֵאוּן, וּתְחַדֵּשׁ פְּנֵי אֲדָמָה: יְהִי כְבוֹד יהוה לְעוֹלָם, יִשְׂמַח יהוה בְּמַעֲשָׂיו: הַמַּבִּיט לָאָרֶץ וַתִּרְעָד, יִגַּע בֶּהָרִים וְיֶעֱשָׁנוּ: אָשִׁירָה לַיהוה בְּחַיָּי, אֲזַמְּרָה לֵאלֹהַי בְּעוֹדִי: ◂ יֶעֱרַב עָלָיו שִׂיחִי, אָנֹכִי אֶשְׂמַח בַּיהוה: יִתַּמּוּ חַטָּאִים מִן־הָאָרֶץ, וּרְשָׁעִים עוֹד אֵינָם, בָּרְכִי נַפְשִׁי אֶת־יהוה, הַלְלוּיָהּ:

קדיש יתום (*page 187*)

During the month of אלול (*except* ערב ראש השנה), *the* שופר *is sounded (some sound the* שופר *after the psalm below). From the second day of* ראש חודש אלול *through* שמיני עצרת, *the following psalm is said:*

תהלים כז

לְדָוִד, יהוה אוֹרִי וְיִשְׁעִי, מִמִּי אִירָא, יהוה מָעוֹז־חַיַּי, מִמִּי אֶפְחָד: בִּקְרֹב עָלַי מְרֵעִים לֶאֱכֹל אֶת־בְּשָׂרִי, צָרַי וְאֹיְבַי לִי, הֵמָּה כָשְׁלוּ וְנָפָלוּ: אִם־תַּחֲנֶה עָלַי מַחֲנֶה, לֹא־יִירָא לִבִּי, אִם־תָּקוּם עָלַי מִלְחָמָה, בְּזֹאת אֲנִי בוֹטֵחַ: אַחַת שָׁאַלְתִּי מֵאֵת־יהוה, אוֹתָהּ אֲבַקֵּשׁ, שִׁבְתִּי בְּבֵית־יהוה כָּל־יְמֵי חַיַּי, לַחֲזוֹת בְּנֹעַם־יהוה, וּלְבַקֵּר בְּהֵיכָלוֹ: כִּי יִצְפְּנֵנִי בְּסֻכֹּה בְּיוֹם רָעָה, יַסְתִּרֵנִי בְּסֵתֶר

לְדָוִד *Psalm 27*: A magnificent expression of trust in God's protection and unfailing love. An early Midrash (*Vayikra Raba* 21:4) relates it to the festivals of Tishrei: "*The Lord is my light* – on Rosh HaShana, *and my salvation* – on Yom Kippur." The phrase, "He will keep me safe in His pavilion [*beSukko*]" suggested Sukkot. It was accordingly adopted as a prayer for the penitential period up to and including these holy days, beginning on Rosh Ḥodesh Elul.

gracious to me and answer me. On Your behalf my heart says, "Seek My face." Your face, LORD, will I seek. Do not hide Your face from me. Do not turn Your servant away in anger. You have been my help. Do not reject or forsake me, God, my Savior. Were my father and my mother to forsake me, the LORD would take me in. Teach me Your way, LORD, and lead me on a level path, because of my oppressors. Do not abandon me to the will of my foes, for false witnesses have risen against me, breathing violence. ▸ Were it not for my faith that I shall see the LORD's goodness in the land of the living. Hope in the LORD. Be strong and of good courage, and hope in the LORD!

Mourner's Kaddish (page 186)

In Israel the following through "Bless the LORD," on the next page, is said:

אֵין כֵּאלֹהֵינוּ There is none like our God, none like our LORD, none like our King, none like our Savior. Who is like our God? Like our LORD? Like our King? Like our Savior? We will thank our God, thank our LORD, thank our King, thank our Savior. Blessed is our God, blessed our LORD, blessed our King, blessed our Savior. You are our God, You are our LORD, You are our King, You are our Savior. You are He to whom our ancestors offered the fragrant incense.

פִּטּוּם הַקְּטֹרֶת The incense mixture consisted of balsam, onycha, galbanum and frankincense, each weighing seventy manehs; myrrh, cassia, spikenard and saffron, each weighing sixteen manehs; twelve manehs of costus, three of aromatic bark; nine of cinnamon; nine kabs of Carsina lye; three seahs and three kabs of Cyprus wine. If Cyprus wine was not available, old white wine might be used. A quarter of a kab of Sodom salt, and a minute amount of a smoke-raising herb. Rabbi Nathan says: Also a minute amount of Jordan amber. If one added honey to the mixture, he rendered it unfit for sacred use. If he omitted any one of its ingredients, he is guilty of a capital offence. *Keritot 6a*

Rabban Shimon ben Gamliel says: "Balsam" refers to the sap that drips from the balsam tree. The Carsina lye was used for bleaching the onycha to improve it. The Cyprus wine was used to soak the onycha in it to make it pungent. Though urine is suitable for this purpose, it is not brought into the Temple out of respect.

It was taught in the Academy of Elijah: Whoever studies [Torah] laws every day is assured that he will be destined for the World to Come, as it is said, "The ways of the world are His" – read not, "ways" [*halikhot*] but "laws" [*halakhot*]. *Megilla 28b* *Hab. 3*

Rabbi Elazar said in the name of Rabbi Ḥanina: The disciples of the sages increase peace in the world, as it is said, "And all your children shall be taught of the LORD, and great shall be the peace of your children [*banayikh*]." Read not *banayikh*, "your children," but *bonayikh*, "your builders." Those who love Your Torah have great peace; there is no stumbling block for them. May there be peace within your ramparts, prosperity in your palaces. For the sake of my brothers and friends, I shall say, "Peace be within you." For the sake of the House of the LORD our God, I will seek your good. ▸ May the LORD grant strength to His people; may the LORD bless His people with peace. *Berakhot 64a* *Is. 54* *Ps. 119* *Ps. 122* *Ps. 29*

אָהֳלוֹ, בְּצוּר יְרוֹמְמֵנִי: וְעַתָּה יָרוּם רֹאשִׁי עַל אֹיְבַי סְבִיבוֹתַי, וְאֶזְבְּחָה בְאָהֳלוֹ זִבְחֵי תְרוּעָה, אָשִׁירָה וַאֲזַמְּרָה לַיהוה: שְׁמַע־יהוה קוֹלִי אֶקְרָא, וְחָנֵּנִי וַעֲנֵנִי: לְךָ אָמַר לִבִּי בַּקְּשׁוּ פָנָי, אֶת־פָּנֶיךָ יהוה אֲבַקֵּשׁ: אַל־תַּסְתֵּר פָּנֶיךָ מִמֶּנִּי, אַל תַּט־בְּאַף עַבְדֶּךָ, עֶזְרָתִי הָיִיתָ, אַל־תִּטְּשֵׁנִי וְאַל־תַּעַזְבֵנִי, אֱלֹהֵי יִשְׁעִי: כִּי־אָבִי וְאִמִּי עֲזָבוּנִי, וַיהוה יַאַסְפֵנִי: הוֹרֵנִי יהוה דַּרְכֶּךָ, וּנְחֵנִי בְּאֹרַח מִישׁוֹר, לְמַעַן שׁוֹרְרָי: אַל־תִּתְּנֵנִי בְּנֶפֶשׁ צָרָי, כִּי קָמוּ־בִי עֵדֵי־שֶׁקֶר, וִיפֵחַ חָמָס: › לוּלֵא הֶאֱמַנְתִּי לִרְאוֹת בְּטוּב־יהוה בְּאֶרֶץ חַיִּים: קַוֵּה אֶל־יהוה, חֲזַק וְיַאֲמֵץ לִבֶּךָ, וְקַוֵּה אֶל־יהוה:

קדיש יתום (page 187)

In ארץ ישראל *the following through* בָּרְכוּ*, on the next page, is said:*

אֵין כֵּאלֹהֵינוּ, אֵין כַּאדוֹנֵינוּ, אֵין כְּמַלְכֵּנוּ, אֵין כְּמוֹשִׁיעֵנוּ. מִי כֵאלֹהֵינוּ, מִי כַאדוֹנֵינוּ, מִי כְמַלְכֵּנוּ, מִי כְמוֹשִׁיעֵנוּ. נוֹדֶה לֵאלֹהֵינוּ, נוֹדֶה לַאדוֹנֵינוּ, נוֹדֶה לְמַלְכֵּנוּ, נוֹדֶה לְמוֹשִׁיעֵנוּ. בָּרוּךְ אֱלֹהֵינוּ, בָּרוּךְ אֲדוֹנֵינוּ, בָּרוּךְ מַלְכֵּנוּ, בָּרוּךְ מוֹשִׁיעֵנוּ. אַתָּה הוּא אֱלֹהֵינוּ, אַתָּה הוּא אֲדוֹנֵינוּ, אַתָּה הוּא מַלְכֵּנוּ, אַתָּה הוּא מוֹשִׁיעֵנוּ. אַתָּה הוּא שֶׁהִקְטִירוּ אֲבוֹתֵינוּ לְפָנֶיךָ אֶת קְטֹרֶת הַסַּמִּים.

פִּטּוּם הַקְּטֹרֶת: הַצֳּרִי, וְהַצִּפֹּרֶן, וְהַחֶלְבְּנָה, וְהַלְּבוֹנָה מִשְׁקַל שִׁבְעִים שִׁבְעִים מָנֶה, מֹר, וּקְצִיעָה, שִׁבֹּלֶת נֵרְדְּ, וְכַרְכֹּם מִשְׁקַל שִׁשָּׁה עָשָׂר שִׁשָּׁה עָשָׂר מָנֶה, הַקֹּשְׁטְ שְׁנֵים עָשָׂר, קִלּוּפָה שְׁלֹשָׁה, וְקִנָּמוֹן תִּשְׁעָה, בֹּרִית כַּרְשִׁינָה תִּשְׁעָה קַבִּין, יֵין קַפְרִיסִין סְאִין תְּלָת וְקַבִּין תְּלָתָא, וְאִם אֵין לוֹ יֵין קַפְרִיסִין, מֵבִיא חֲמַר חִוַּרְיָן עַתִּיק. מֶלַח סְדוֹמִית רֹבַע, מַעֲלֶה עָשָׁן כָּל שֶׁהוּא. רַבִּי נָתָן הַבַּבְלִי אוֹמֵר: אַף כִּפַּת הַיַּרְדֵּן כָּל שֶׁהוּא, וְאִם נָתַן בָּהּ דְּבַשׁ פְּסָלָהּ, וְאִם חִסֵּר אֶחָד מִכָּל סַמָּנֶיהָ, חַיָּב מִיתָה. כריתות ו.

רַבָּן שִׁמְעוֹן בֶּן גַּמְלִיאֵל אוֹמֵר: הַצֳּרִי אֵינוֹ אֶלָּא שְׂרָף הַנּוֹטֵף מֵעֲצֵי הַקְּטָף. בֹּרִית כַּרְשִׁינָה שֶׁשָּׁפִין בָּהּ אֶת הַצִּפֹּרֶן כְּדֵי שֶׁתְּהֵא נָאָה, יֵין קַפְרִיסִין שֶׁשּׁוֹרִין בּוֹ אֶת הַצִּפֹּרֶן כְּדֵי שֶׁתְּהֵא עַזָּה, וַהֲלֹא מֵי רַגְלַיִם יָפִין לָהּ, אֶלָּא שֶׁאֵין מַכְנִיסִין מֵי רַגְלַיִם בַּמִּקְדָּשׁ מִפְּנֵי הַכָּבוֹד.

תָּנָא דְבֵי אֵלִיָּהוּ: כָּל הַשּׁוֹנֶה הֲלָכוֹת בְּכָל יוֹם, מֻבְטָח לוֹ שֶׁהוּא בֶּן עוֹלָם הַבָּא, שֶׁנֶּאֱמַר מגילה כח:
הֲלִיכוֹת עוֹלָם לוֹ: אַל תִּקְרֵי הֲלִיכוֹת אֶלָּא הֲלָכוֹת. חבקוק ג

אָמַר רַבִּי אֶלְעָזָר, אָמַר רַבִּי חֲנִינָא: תַּלְמִידֵי חֲכָמִים מַרְבִּים שָׁלוֹם בָּעוֹלָם, שֶׁנֶּאֱמַר ברכות סד.
וְכָל־בָּנַיִךְ לִמּוּדֵי יהוה, וְרַב שְׁלוֹם בָּנָיִךְ: אַל תִּקְרֵי בָּנָיִךְ, אֶלָּא בּוֹנָיִךְ. שָׁלוֹם רָב לְאֹהֲבֵי ישעיה נד / תהלים קיט
תוֹרָתֶךָ, וְאֵין־לָמוֹ מִכְשׁוֹל: יְהִי־שָׁלוֹם בְּחֵילֵךְ, שַׁלְוָה בְּאַרְמְנוֹתָיִךְ: לְמַעַן אַחַי וְרֵעָי תהלים קכב
אֲדַבְּרָה־נָּא שָׁלוֹם בָּךְ: לְמַעַן בֵּית־יהוה אֱלֹהֵינוּ אֲבַקְשָׁה טוֹב לָךְ: › יהוה עֹז לְעַמּוֹ תהלים כט
יִתֵּן, יהוה יְבָרֵךְ אֶת־עַמּוֹ בַשָּׁלוֹם:

THE RABBIS' KADDISH

The following prayer, said by mourners, requires the presence of a minyan.
A transliteration can be found on page 698.

Mourner: יִתְגַּדַּל Magnified and sanctified
may His great name be, in the world He created by His will.
May He establish His kingdom in your lifetime
and in your days, and in the lifetime of all the house of Israel,
swiftly and soon – and say: Amen.

All: May His great name be blessed for ever and all time.

Mourner: Blessed and praised, glorified and exalted,
raised and honored, uplifted and lauded be
the name of the Holy One, blessed be He,
beyond any blessing,
song, praise and consolation
uttered in the world – and say: Amen.

To Israel, to the teachers,
their disciples and their disciples' disciples,
and to all who engage in the study of Torah,
in this (*in Israel add:* holy) place or elsewhere,
may there come to them and you great peace,
grace, kindness and compassion, long life, ample sustenance
and deliverance, from their Father in Heaven – and say: Amen.

May there be great peace from heaven,
and (good) life for us and all Israel – and say: Amen.

Bow, take three steps back, as if taking leave of the Divine Presence,
then bow, first left, then right, then center, while saying:

May He who makes peace in His high places,
in His compassion make peace for us
and all Israel – and say: Amen.

In Israel, on days when the Torah is not read, the person saying Kaddish adds:

Bless the LORD, the blessed One.

and the congregation responds:

Bless the LORD, the blessed One, for ever and all time.

In Israel during Elul, some congregations blow shofar and say Psalm 27 (page 196) at this point. In a house of mourning the service continues on page 602.

קדיש דרבנן

The following prayer, said by mourners, requires the presence of a מנין.
A transliteration can be found on page 698.

אבל: יִתְגַּדַּל וְיִתְקַדַּשׁ שְׁמֵהּ רַבָּא (קהל: אָמֵן)
בְּעָלְמָא דִּי בְרָא כִרְעוּתֵהּ
וְיַמְלִיךְ מַלְכוּתֵהּ
בְּחַיֵּיכוֹן וּבְיוֹמֵיכוֹן וּבְחַיֵּי דְכָל בֵּית יִשְׂרָאֵל
בַּעֲגָלָא וּבִזְמַן קָרִיב, וְאִמְרוּ אָמֵן. (קהל: אָמֵן)

קהל ואבל: יְהֵא שְׁמֵהּ רַבָּא מְבָרַךְ לְעָלַם וּלְעָלְמֵי עָלְמַיָּא.

אבל: יִתְבָּרַךְ וְיִשְׁתַּבַּח וְיִתְפָּאַר וְיִתְרוֹמַם וְיִתְנַשֵּׂא
וְיִתְהַדָּר וְיִתְעַלֶּה וְיִתְהַלָּל, שְׁמֵהּ דְּקֻדְשָׁא בְּרִיךְ הוּא (קהל: בְּרִיךְ הוּא)
לְעֵלָּא מִן כָּל בִּרְכָתָא / בעשרת ימי תשובה: לְעֵלָּא לְעֵלָּא מִכָּל בִּרְכָתָא /
וְשִׁירָתָא, תֻּשְׁבְּחָתָא וְנֶחֱמָתָא, דַּאֲמִירָן בְּעָלְמָא, וְאִמְרוּ אָמֵן. (קהל: אָמֵן)

עַל יִשְׂרָאֵל וְעַל רַבָּנָן, וְעַל תַּלְמִידֵיהוֹן וְעַל כָּל תַּלְמִידֵי תַלְמִידֵיהוֹן
וְעַל כָּל מָאן דְּעָסְקִין בְּאוֹרַיְתָא
דִּי בְאַתְרָא (בארץ ישראל: קַדִּישָׁא) הָדֵין וְדִי בְכָל אֲתַר וַאֲתַר
יְהֵא לְהוֹן וּלְכוֹן שְׁלָמָא רַבָּא, חִנָּא וְחִסְדָּא, וְרַחֲמֵי, וְחַיֵּי אֲרִיכֵי, וּמְזוֹנֵי רְוִיחֵי
וּפֻרְקָנָא מִן קֳדָם אֲבוּהוֹן דִּי בִשְׁמַיָּא, וְאִמְרוּ אָמֵן. (קהל: אָמֵן)

יְהֵא שְׁלָמָא רַבָּא מִן שְׁמַיָּא
וְחַיִּים (טוֹבִים) עָלֵינוּ וְעַל כָּל יִשְׂרָאֵל, וְאִמְרוּ אָמֵן. (קהל: אָמֵן)

Bow, take three steps back, as if taking leave of the Divine Presence, then bow, first left, then right, then center, while saying:

עֹשֶׂה שָׁלוֹם/ בעשרת ימי תשובה: הַשָּׁלוֹם/ בִּמְרוֹמָיו
הוּא יַעֲשֶׂה בְרַחֲמָיו שָׁלוֹם, עָלֵינוּ וְעַל כָּל יִשְׂרָאֵל, וְאִמְרוּ אָמֵן. (קהל: אָמֵן)

In ארץ ישראל*, on days when the* תורה *is not read, the person saying* קדיש *adds:*

בָּרְכוּ אֶת יהוה הַמְבֹרָךְ.

and the קהל *responds:*

בָּרוּךְ יהוה הַמְבֹרָךְ לְעוֹלָם וָעֶד.

In ארץ ישראל *during* אלול*, some congregations blow* שופר *and say* לְדָוִד, יהוה אוֹרִי *(page 197) at this point. In a house of mourning the service continues on page 603.*

READINGS AFTER THE SERVICE

Over the centuries, some communities have added various readings and personal supplications to the end of the service. The following is based on the text as compiled in Siddur Otzar HaTefillot (Vilna, 1911).

THE SIX REMEMBRANCES

The Exodus from Egypt

That you may remember the day you left the land of Egypt all the days of your life. *Deut. 16*

The Revelation at Mount Sinai

Only be careful and watch yourself very closely lest you forget the things your eyes have seen or let them slip from your heart all the days of your life. You shall make them known to your children and your children's children – the day you stood before the LORD your God at Horeb when the LORD said to me, "Assemble the people before Me and I will let them hear My words, so that they may learn to be in awe of Me as long as they live on earth, and they will teach them to their children." *Deut. 4*

Amalek

Remember what Amalek did to you on your way out of Egypt, how he met you on the way, cutting off those who were lagging behind, when you were tired and exhausted, and he did not fear God. So, when the LORD your God grants you rest from all your enemies around you in the land the LORD your God is about to give you to possess as an inheritance, you shall wipe out the memory of Amalek from under the heavens: you shall not forget. *Deut. 25*

The Golden Calf

Remember, and do not forget, how you provoked the LORD your God in the wilderness. *Deut. 9*

Miriam

Remember what the LORD your God did to Miriam on the way when you came out of Egypt. *Deut. 24*

The Shabbat

Remember the Sabbath day to hallow it. *Ex. 20*

---

golden calf reminds us of sins against God; Miriam's fate reminds us of sins against our fellows, especially through evil speech. Amalek's attack on the Israelites showed how a failure to fear God leads to cruelty against human beings.

אמירות לאחר התפילה

Over the centuries, some communities have added various readings and personal supplications to the end of the service. The following is based on the text as compiled in סידור אוצר התפילות *(Vilna, 1911).*

שש זכירות

יציאת מצרים

לְמַעַן תִּזְכֹּר אֶת־יוֹם צֵאתְךָ מֵאֶרֶץ מִצְרַיִם כֹּל יְמֵי חַיֶּיךָ׃ דברים טז

מעמד הר סיני

רַק הִשָּׁמֶר לְךָ וּשְׁמֹר נַפְשְׁךָ מְאֹד פֶּן־תִּשְׁכַּח אֶת־הַדְּבָרִים אֲשֶׁר־רָאוּ עֵינֶיךָ דברים ד
וּפֶן־יָסוּרוּ מִלְּבָבְךָ כֹּל יְמֵי חַיֶּיךָ וְהוֹדַעְתָּם לְבָנֶיךָ וְלִבְנֵי בָנֶיךָ׃ יוֹם אֲשֶׁר עָמַדְתָּ
לִפְנֵי יהוה אֱלֹהֶיךָ בְּחֹרֵב בֶּאֱמֹר יהוה אֵלַי הַקְהֶל־לִי אֶת־הָעָם וְאַשְׁמִעֵם
אֶת־דְּבָרָי אֲשֶׁר יִלְמְדוּן לְיִרְאָה אֹתִי כָּל־הַיָּמִים אֲשֶׁר הֵם חַיִּים עַל־הָאֲדָמָה
וְאֶת־בְּנֵיהֶם יְלַמֵּדוּן׃

מעשה עמלק ומחייתו

זָכוֹר אֵת אֲשֶׁר־עָשָׂה לְךָ עֲמָלֵק בַּדֶּרֶךְ בְּצֵאתְכֶם מִמִּצְרָיִם׃ אֲשֶׁר קָרְךָ בַּדֶּרֶךְ דברים כה
וַיְזַנֵּב בְּךָ כָּל־הַנֶּחֱשָׁלִים אַחֲרֶיךָ וְאַתָּה עָיֵף וְיָגֵעַ וְלֹא יָרֵא אֱלֹהִים׃ וְהָיָה
בְּהָנִיחַ יהוה אֱלֹהֶיךָ ׀ לְךָ מִכָּל־אֹיְבֶיךָ מִסָּבִיב בָּאָרֶץ אֲשֶׁר־יהוה אֱלֹהֶיךָ
נֹתֵן לְךָ נַחֲלָה לְרִשְׁתָּהּ תִּמְחֶה אֶת־זֵכֶר עֲמָלֵק מִתַּחַת הַשָּׁמָיִם לֹא תִּשְׁכָּח׃

מעשי אבותינו במדבר

זְכֹר אַל־תִּשְׁכַּח אֵת אֲשֶׁר־הִקְצַפְתָּ אֶת־יהוה אֱלֹהֶיךָ בַּמִּדְבָּר דברים ט

מעשה מרים

זָכוֹר אֵת אֲשֶׁר־עָשָׂה יהוה אֱלֹהֶיךָ לְמִרְיָם בַּדֶּרֶךְ בְּצֵאתְכֶם מִמִּצְרָיִם׃ דברים כד

שבת

זָכוֹר אֶת־יוֹם הַשַּׁבָּת לְקַדְּשׁוֹ׃ שמות כ

THE SIX REMEMBRANCES

These acts of remembrance define three positive and three negative parameters of Jewish faith and life. Positively, the exodus reminds us of divine redemption, Sinai of revelation, and the Sabbath of creation. Negatively, the

THE TEN COMMANDMENTS

God spoke all these words, saying: *Ex. 20*

1. אָנֹכִי I am the LORD your God who brought you out of the land of Egypt, from the slave-house.
2. לֹא־יִהְיֶה Have no other gods besides Me. Do not make a sculptured image for yourself, or any likeness of what is in the heavens above, or on the earth below, or in the waters under the earth. Do not bow down to them or worship them, for I am the LORD your God, a zealous God, visiting the guilt of the parents on the children to the third and fourth generation, if they also reject Me; but showing kindness to thousands of generations of those who love Me and keep My commandments.
3. לֹא תִשָּׂא Do not take the name of the LORD your God in vain. The LORD will not leave unpunished one who utters His name in vain.
4. זָכוֹר Remember the Sabbath and keep it holy. Six days you shall labor and do all your work, but the seventh day is a Sabbath of the LORD your God; on it you shall not do any work – you, your son or daughter, your male or female slaves, your cattle, or the stranger within your gates. For in six days the LORD made heaven and earth and sea, and all that is in them, and rested on the seventh day; therefore the LORD blessed the Sabbath day and made it holy.
5. כַּבֵּד Honor your father and your mother, so that you may live long in the land that the LORD your God is giving you.
6. לֹא תִרְצָח Do not murder.
7. לֹא תִנְאָף Do not commit adultery.
8. לֹא תִגְנֹב Do not steal.
9. לֹא־תַעֲנֶה Do not testify as a false witness against your neighbor.
10. לֹא תַחְמֹד Do not be envious of your neighbor's house. Do not be envious of your neighbor's wife, his male or female slave, his ox, his ass, or anything else that is your neighbor's.

---

when sectarians maintained that only these, and not the other commandments, were from God (*Berakhot* 12a). So deep was the attachment of Jews to this "sublime summary of human duties" (Rabbi J.H. Hertz), however, that the custom developed to say it privately after the end of the morning service.

עשרת הדברות

וַיְדַבֵּר אֱלֹהִים אֵת כָּל־הַדְּבָרִים הָאֵלֶּה לֵאמֹר׃ שמות כ

א אָנֹכִי יהוה אֱלֹהֶיךָ אֲשֶׁר הוֹצֵאתִיךָ מֵאֶרֶץ מִצְרַיִם מִבֵּית עֲבָדִים׃

ב לֹא־יִהְיֶה לְךָ אֱלֹהִים אֲחֵרִים עַל־פָּנָי׃ לֹא־תַעֲשֶׂה לְךָ פֶסֶל וְכָל־תְּמוּנָה
אֲשֶׁר בַּשָּׁמַיִם מִמַּעַל וַאֲשֶׁר בָּאָרֶץ מִתַּחַת וַאֲשֶׁר בַּמַּיִם מִתַּחַת לָאָרֶץ׃
לֹא־תִשְׁתַּחֲוֶה לָהֶם וְלֹא תָעָבְדֵם כִּי אָנֹכִי יהוה אֱלֹהֶיךָ אֵל קַנָּא פֹּקֵד עֲוֹן
אָבֹת עַל־בָּנִים עַל־שִׁלֵּשִׁים וְעַל־רִבֵּעִים לְשֹׂנְאָי׃ וְעֹשֶׂה חֶסֶד לַאֲלָפִים
לְאֹהֲבַי וּלְשֹׁמְרֵי מִצְוֺתָי׃

ג לֹא תִשָּׂא אֶת־שֵׁם־יהוה אֱלֹהֶיךָ לַשָּׁוְא כִּי לֹא יְנַקֶּה יהוה אֵת אֲשֶׁר־יִשָּׂא
אֶת־שְׁמוֹ לַשָּׁוְא׃

ד זָכוֹר אֶת־יוֹם הַשַּׁבָּת לְקַדְּשׁוֹ׃ שֵׁשֶׁת יָמִים תַּעֲבֹד וְעָשִׂיתָ כָּל־מְלַאכְתֶּךָ׃
וְיוֹם הַשְּׁבִיעִי שַׁבָּת לַיהוה אֱלֹהֶיךָ לֹא־תַעֲשֶׂה כָל־מְלָאכָה אַתָּה ׀ וּבִנְךָ
וּבִתֶּךָ עַבְדְּךָ וַאֲמָתְךָ וּבְהֶמְתֶּךָ וְגֵרְךָ אֲשֶׁר בִּשְׁעָרֶיךָ׃ כִּי שֵׁשֶׁת־יָמִים עָשָׂה
יהוה אֶת־הַשָּׁמַיִם וְאֶת־הָאָרֶץ אֶת־הַיָּם וְאֶת־כָּל־אֲשֶׁר־בָּם וַיָּנַח בַּיּוֹם
הַשְּׁבִיעִי עַל־כֵּן בֵּרַךְ יהוה אֶת־יוֹם הַשַּׁבָּת וַיְקַדְּשֵׁהוּ׃

ה כַּבֵּד אֶת־אָבִיךָ וְאֶת־אִמֶּךָ לְמַעַן יַאֲרִכוּן יָמֶיךָ עַל הָאֲדָמָה אֲשֶׁר־יהוה
אֱלֹהֶיךָ נֹתֵן לָךְ׃

ו לֹא תִרְצָח

ז לֹא תִנְאָף

ח לֹא תִגְנֹב

ט לֹא־תַעֲנֶה בְרֵעֲךָ עֵד שָׁקֶר׃

י לֹא תַחְמֹד בֵּית רֵעֶךָ לֹא־תַחְמֹד אֵשֶׁת רֵעֶךָ וְעַבְדּוֹ וַאֲמָתוֹ וְשׁוֹרוֹ וַחֲמֹרוֹ
וְכֹל אֲשֶׁר לְרֵעֶךָ׃

THE TEN COMMANDMENTS

In Temple times, the Ten Commandments were recited as part of the daily prayers, immediately prior to the Shema. The practice was discontinued

THE THIRTEEN PRINCIPLES OF JEWISH FAITH

1. I believe with perfect faith
   that the Creator,
   blessed be His name,
   creates and rules all creatures,
   and that He alone made, makes, and will make, all things.

2. I believe with perfect faith
   that the Creator,
   blessed be His name, is One;
   that there is no oneness like His in any way;
   and that He alone is our God who was, is, and ever will be.

3. I believe with perfect faith
   that the Creator,
   blessed be His name, is not physical,
   that no physical attributes can apply to Him,
   and that there is nothing whatsoever to compare to Him.

4. I believe with perfect faith
   that the Creator,
   blessed be His name, is first and last.

5. I believe with perfect faith
   that the Creator,
   blessed be His name,
   is the only one to whom it is proper to pray,
   and that it is improper to pray to anyone else.

6. I believe with perfect faith
   that all the words of the prophets are true.

7. I believe with perfect faith
   that the prophecy of Moses our teacher,
   peace be to him, was true,
   and that he was the father of the prophets –
   those who preceded him and those who followed him.

---

and (5) the belief that He alone is to be worshiped. The next four are about revelation: (6) belief in prophecy; (7) the unique status of Moses as the

שלושה עשר עיקרים

א אֲנִי מַאֲמִין בֶּאֱמוּנָה שְׁלֵמָה
שֶׁהַבּוֹרֵא יִתְבָּרַךְ שְׁמוֹ הוּא בּוֹרֵא וּמַנְהִיג לְכָל הַבְּרוּאִים
וְהוּא לְבַדּוֹ עָשָׂה וְעוֹשֶׂה וְיַעֲשֶׂה לְכָל הַמַּעֲשִׂים.

ב אֲנִי מַאֲמִין בֶּאֱמוּנָה שְׁלֵמָה
שֶׁהַבּוֹרֵא יִתְבָּרַךְ שְׁמוֹ הוּא יָחִיד
וְאֵין יְחִידוּת כָּמוֹהוּ בְּשׁוּם פָּנִים
וְהוּא לְבַדּוֹ אֱלֹהֵינוּ, הָיָה הֹוֶה וְיִהְיֶה.

ג אֲנִי מַאֲמִין בֶּאֱמוּנָה שְׁלֵמָה
שֶׁהַבּוֹרֵא יִתְבָּרַךְ שְׁמוֹ אֵינוֹ גוּף
וְלֹא יַשִּׂיגוּהוּ מַשִּׂיגֵי הַגּוּף
וְאֵין לוֹ שׁוּם דִּמְיוֹן כְּלָל.

ד אֲנִי מַאֲמִין בֶּאֱמוּנָה שְׁלֵמָה
שֶׁהַבּוֹרֵא יִתְבָּרַךְ שְׁמוֹ הוּא רִאשׁוֹן וְהוּא אַחֲרוֹן.

ה אֲנִי מַאֲמִין בֶּאֱמוּנָה שְׁלֵמָה
שֶׁהַבּוֹרֵא יִתְבָּרַךְ שְׁמוֹ לוֹ לְבַדּוֹ רָאוּי לְהִתְפַּלֵּל
וְאֵין רָאוּי לְהִתְפַּלֵּל לְזוּלָתוֹ.

ו אֲנִי מַאֲמִין בֶּאֱמוּנָה שְׁלֵמָה
שֶׁכָּל דִּבְרֵי נְבִיאִים אֱמֶת.

ז אֲנִי מַאֲמִין בֶּאֱמוּנָה שְׁלֵמָה
שֶׁנְּבוּאַת מֹשֶׁה רַבֵּנוּ עָלָיו הַשָּׁלוֹם הָיְתָה אֲמִתִּית
וְשֶׁהוּא הָיָה אָב לַנְּבִיאִים, לַקּוֹדְמִים לְפָנָיו וְלַבָּאִים אַחֲרָיו.

THE THIRTEEN PRINCIPLES OF JEWISH FAITH

A prose counterpart to the poetic Yigdal, both of which summarize the principles set out by Moses Maimonides (1135–1204). The first five are about God: (1) His existence; (2) His unity; (3) His incorporeality; (4) His eternity;

8. I believe with perfect faith
that the entire Torah now in our hands
is the same one that was given to Moses our teacher,
peace be upon him.

9. I believe with perfect faith
that this Torah will not be changed,
nor will there be any other Torah from the Creator,
blessed be His name.

10. I believe with perfect faith
that the Creator, blessed be His name,
knows all the deeds and thoughts of humanity,
as it is said, "He fashions the hearts of them all, *Ps. 33*
comprehending all their deeds."

11. I believe with perfect faith
that the Creator, blessed be His name,
rewards those who keep His commandments,
and punishes those who transgress them.

12. I believe with perfect faith
in the coming of the Messiah,
and though he may delay,
I wait daily for his coming.

13. I believe with perfect faith
that the dead will live again
at a time of the Creator's choosing:
blessed be His name and exalted be His mention
for ever and all time.

---

ishes; (12) He will send the Messiah; and (13) in time to come, He will bring the dead back to life again. The presence of this passage is a reminder that the siddur is not just a book of prayer but also of faith.

ח אֲנִי מַאֲמִין בֶּאֱמוּנָה שְׁלֵמָה
שֶׁכָּל הַתּוֹרָה הַמְּצוּיָה עַתָּה בְיָדֵינוּ
הִיא הַנְּתוּנָה לְמֹשֶׁה רַבֵּנוּ עָלָיו הַשָּׁלוֹם.

ט אֲנִי מַאֲמִין בֶּאֱמוּנָה שְׁלֵמָה
שֶׁזֹּאת הַתּוֹרָה לֹא תְהֵא מֻחְלֶפֶת
וְלֹא תְהֵא תּוֹרָה אַחֶרֶת מֵאֵת הַבּוֹרֵא יִתְבָּרַךְ שְׁמוֹ.

י אֲנִי מַאֲמִין בֶּאֱמוּנָה שְׁלֵמָה
שֶׁהַבּוֹרֵא יִתְבָּרַךְ שְׁמוֹ
יוֹדֵעַ כָּל מַעֲשֵׂה בְנֵי אָדָם וְכָל מַחְשְׁבוֹתָם.
שֶׁנֶּאֱמַר: הַיֹּצֵר יַחַד לִבָּם, הַמֵּבִין אֶל־כָּל־מַעֲשֵׂיהֶם: תהלים לג

יא אֲנִי מַאֲמִין בֶּאֱמוּנָה שְׁלֵמָה
שֶׁהַבּוֹרֵא יִתְבָּרַךְ שְׁמוֹ גּוֹמֵל טוֹב לְשׁוֹמְרֵי מִצְוֹתָיו
וּמַעֲנִישׁ לְעוֹבְרֵי מִצְוֹתָיו.

יב אֲנִי מַאֲמִין בֶּאֱמוּנָה שְׁלֵמָה
בְּבִיאַת הַמָּשִׁיחַ
וְאַף עַל פִּי שֶׁיִּתְמַהְמֵהַּ עִם כָּל זֶה אֲחַכֶּה לּוֹ
בְּכָל יוֹם שֶׁיָּבוֹא.

יג אֲנִי מַאֲמִין בֶּאֱמוּנָה שְׁלֵמָה
שֶׁתִּהְיֶה תְּחִיַּת הַמֵּתִים
בְּעֵת שֶׁיַּעֲלֶה רָצוֹן מֵאֵת הַבּוֹרֵא
יִתְבָּרַךְ שְׁמוֹ וְיִתְעַלֶּה זִכְרוֹ לָעַד וּלְנֵצַח נְצָחִים.

---

greatest of the prophets; (8) the divine authorship of the Torah; and (9) the immutability of the Torah. The last four are about reward, punishment and justice: (10) God knows our thoughts and deeds; (11) He rewards and pun-

The following is said after morning and evening prayers:

יְהִי יהוה May the LORD our God be with us, as He was with our ancestors. *I Kings 8*
May He never abandon us or forsake us, ever; as He turns our hearts toward Him, to follow all His paths and to keep His commands and His statutes and laws, as He charged our ancestors. And may these words with which I have pleaded before the LORD be close to the LORD our God, day and night, that He do justice for Your servant, and for Your people Israel, day by day. That all the peoples of the earth shall know that the LORD is God; there is no other.

יהוה נְחֵנִי Lead me, LORD, in Your righteousness, because of my foes; make *Ps. 5*
Your way straight before me. As for me, I lead a blameless life; redeem me and *Ps. 26*
show me favor. Turn to me and show me favor, for I am lonely and afflicted. *Ps. 25*
My foot stands on level ground: in the assemblies I will bless the LORD. The *Ps. 26*
LORD is my Guardian; the LORD is my Shade at my right hand. My help comes *Ps. 121*
from the LORD, Maker of heaven and earth. The LORD will guard my coming
and going, for life and for peace, now and for evermore. Gaze down from Your *Deut. 26*
holy dwelling place, from the heavens, and bless Your people Israel, and the land that You have given us, as You promised our ancestors: a land flowing with milk and honey.

אֵל הַכָּבוֹד Glorious God, I bring before You song and praise; I shall worship You day and night. Blessed be the One and Only One – who was, who is and who will always be. LORD God, God of Israel, King, King of kings, Holy One, blessed be He. He is the living God, the living and ever, forever enduring King.
Blessed be the name of His glorious kingdom for ever and ever. I long for Your *Gen. 49*
salvation, LORD. All the nations will walk, each in the name of its god; and
I will walk in the name of the LORD, the living God and eternal King. My help *Ps. 121*
comes from the LORD, Maker of heaven and earth. The LORD will reign for *Ex. 15*
ever and all time.

לַמְנַצֵּחַ For the Chief Musician; with stringed instruments. A psalm. A song. *Ps. 67*
May God be gracious to us and bless us; may He cause His face to shine upon us, Selah, that Your way may be known on earth, Your salvation, among all nations. May the peoples praise You, God; may all the peoples praise You! The nations will rejoice and break into song; for You judge the peoples with equity and guide the nations of the earth, Selah. May the peoples praise You, God; may all the peoples praise You! The earth has yielded its produce; may God, our God, bless us. May God bless us, and may all the ends of the earth fear Him!

Some say Adon Olam (page 22) at this point.

The following is said after morning and evening prayers:

יְהִי יהוה אֱלֹהֵינוּ עִמָּנוּ כַּאֲשֶׁר הָיָה עִם־אֲבֹתֵינוּ, אַל־יַעַזְבֵנוּ וְאַל־יִטְּשֵׁנוּ: מלכים א׳ ח
לְהַטּוֹת לְבָבֵנוּ אֵלָיו, לָלֶכֶת בְּכָל־דְּרָכָיו וְלִשְׁמֹר מִצְוֹתָיו וְחֻקָּיו וּמִשְׁפָּטָיו
אֲשֶׁר צִוָּה אֶת־אֲבֹתֵינוּ: וְיִהְיוּ דְבָרַי אֵלֶּה אֲשֶׁר הִתְחַנַּנְתִּי לִפְנֵי יהוה,
קְרֹבִים אֶל־יהוה אֱלֹהֵינוּ יוֹמָם וָלָיְלָה, לַעֲשׂוֹת מִשְׁפַּט עַבְדּוֹ וּמִשְׁפַּט
עַמּוֹ יִשְׂרָאֵל דְּבַר־יוֹם בְּיוֹמוֹ: לְמַעַן דַּעַת כָּל־עַמֵּי הָאָרֶץ כִּי יהוה הוּא
הָאֱלֹהִים, אֵין עוֹד:

יהוה נְחֵנִי בְצִדְקָתֶךָ לְמַעַן שׁוֹרְרָי, הַיְשַׁר לְפָנַי דַּרְכֶּךָ: וַאֲנִי בְּתֻמִּי אֵלֵךְ, פְּדֵנִי תהלים ה תהלים כו
וְחָנֵּנִי: פְּנֵה־אֵלַי וְחָנֵּנִי כִּי־יָחִיד וְעָנִי אָנִי: רַגְלִי עָמְדָה בְמִישׁוֹר, בְּמַקְהֵלִים תהלים כה תהלים כו
אֲבָרֵךְ יהוה: יהוה שֹׁמְרִי, יהוה צִלִּי עַל יַד יְמִינִי. עֶזְרִי מֵעִם יהוה, עֹשֵׂה תהלים קכא
שָׁמַיִם וָאָרֶץ: יהוה יִשְׁמָר צֵאתִי וּבוֹאִי לְחַיִּים וּלְשָׁלוֹם, מֵעַתָּה וְעַד עוֹלָם.
הַשְׁקִיפָה מִמְּעוֹן קָדְשְׁךָ מִן־הַשָּׁמַיִם, וּבָרֵךְ אֶת־עַמְּךָ אֶת־יִשְׂרָאֵל, וְאֵת דברים כו
הָאֲדָמָה אֲשֶׁר נָתַתָּה לָנוּ כַּאֲשֶׁר נִשְׁבַּעְתָּ לַאֲבֹתֵינוּ, אֶרֶץ זָבַת חָלָב
וּדְבָשׁ:

אֵל הַכָּבוֹד, אֶתֵּן לְךָ שִׁיר וְהַלֵּל וְאֶעֱבֹד לְךָ יוֹם וָלֵיל. בָּרוּךְ יָחִיד וּמְיֻחָד,
הָיָה הֹוֶה וְיִהְיֶה, יהוה אֱלֹהִים אֱלֹהֵי יִשְׂרָאֵל, מֶלֶךְ מַלְכֵי הַמְּלָכִים, הַקָּדוֹשׁ
בָּרוּךְ הוּא. הוּא אֱלֹהִים חַיִּים, מֶלֶךְ חַי וְקַיָּם לָעַד וּלְעוֹלְמֵי עַד. בָּרוּךְ שֵׁם
כְּבוֹד מַלְכוּתוֹ לְעוֹלָם וָעֶד. לִישׁוּעָתְךָ קִוִּיתִי יהוה: כִּי כָּל הָעַמִּים יֵלְכוּ בראשית מט
אִישׁ בְּשֵׁם אֱלֹהָיו, וַאֲנִי אֵלֵךְ בְּשֵׁם יהוה אֱלֹהִים חַיִּים וּמֶלֶךְ עוֹלָם. עֶזְרִי תהלים קכא
מֵעִם יהוה, עֹשֵׂה שָׁמַיִם וָאָרֶץ: יהוה יִמְלֹךְ לְעֹלָם וָעֶד: שמות טו

לַמְנַצֵּחַ בִּנְגִינֹת, מִזְמוֹר שִׁיר: אֱלֹהִים יְחָנֵּנוּ וִיבָרְכֵנוּ, יָאֵר פָּנָיו אִתָּנוּ סֶלָה: תהלים סז
לָדַעַת בָּאָרֶץ דַּרְכֶּךָ, בְּכָל־גּוֹיִם יְשׁוּעָתֶךָ: יוֹדוּךָ עַמִּים אֱלֹהִים, יוֹדוּךָ עַמִּים
כֻּלָּם: יִשְׂמְחוּ וִירַנְּנוּ לְאֻמִּים, כִּי־תִשְׁפֹּט עַמִּים מִישֹׁר, וּלְאֻמִּים בָּאָרֶץ
תַּנְחֵם סֶלָה: יוֹדוּךָ עַמִּים אֱלֹהִים, יוֹדוּךָ עַמִּים כֻּלָּם: אֶרֶץ נָתְנָה יְבוּלָהּ,
יְבָרְכֵנוּ אֱלֹהִים אֱלֹהֵינוּ: יְבָרְכֵנוּ אֱלֹהִים, וְיִירְאוּ אוֹתוֹ כָּל־אַפְסֵי־אָרֶץ:

Some say אדון עולם *(page 23) at this point.*

PRAYER UPON LEAVING THE SYNAGOGUE

Say while seated:

אַךְ Surely the righteous will praise Your name; Ps. 104
the upright shall live in Your presence.

Stand and say:

כִּי All the nations will walk, each in the name of its god;
and I will walk in the name of the Lord, the living God and eternal King.
My help comes from the Lord, Maker of heaven and earth. Ps. 121
The Lord will reign for ever and all time. Ex. 15

Walk toward the door of the synagogue, respectfully, without turning one's back, as one taking leave of the Divine Presence.

At the door, bow toward the Ark and say:

יהוה נְחֵנִי Lead me, Lord, in Your righteousness, Ps. 5
because of my foes; make Your way straight before me.

While leaving, say the following three verses:

גָּד Invaders may invade Gad, but he will invade at their heels. Gen. 49
David was wise in all that he did, and the Lord was with him. 1 Sam. 18
And Noah found favor in the eyes of the Lord. Gen. 6

One who will conduct business says:

עֶזְרִי My help comes from the Lord, Maker of heaven and earth. Cast your Ps. 121 Ps. 55
cares upon the Lord and He will sustain you. Watch the blameless, observe Ps. 37
the upright, for there is a future for the peace-loving man. Trust in the Lord Ibid.
and do good, settle the land and cherish faithfulness. Behold, God is my sal- Is. 12
vation. I will trust and not be afraid. The Lord, the Lord, is my strength and my song. He has become my salvation. Master of the Universe, it is written
in Your holy scriptures: "Love surrounds him who trusts in the Lord"; and Ps. 32
it is written: "You give life to them all." Lord, God of truth, grant blessing Neh. 9
and success to all the works of my hands. For I place my trust in You, that through my trade, through my profession, You will send me blessing, allowing me to sustain myself and the people of my household with ease, without suffering, by legal and not by forbidden means, for life and for peace. And
may what is written be fulfilled in me: "Cast your cares upon the Lord and Ps. 55
He will sustain you." Amen.

תפילה כשיוצא מבית הכנסת

Say while seated:

אַךְ צַדִּיקִים יוֹדוּ לִשְׁמֶךָ, יֵשְׁבוּ יְשָׁרִים אֶת־פָּנֶיךָ: תהלים קמ

Stand and say:

כִּי כָּל הָעַמִּים יֵלְכוּ אִישׁ בְּשֵׁם אֱלֹהָיו,
וַאֲנִי אֵלֵךְ בְּשֵׁם יהוה אֱלֹהִים חַיִּים וּמֶלֶךְ עוֹלָם.
עֶזְרִי מֵעִם יהוה, עֹשֵׂה שָׁמַיִם וָאָרֶץ: תהלים קכא
יהוה יִמְלֹךְ לְעֹלָם וָעֶד: שמות טו

Walk toward the door of the בית כנסת*, respectfully, without turning one's back, as one taking leave of the Divine Presence.*
At the door, bow toward the ארון קדש *and say:*

יהוה נְחֵנִי בְצִדְקָתֶךָ לְמַעַן שׁוֹרְרָי, הַיְשַׁר לְפָנַי דַּרְכֶּךָ: תהלים ה

While leaving, say the following three verses:

גָּד גְּדוּד יְגוּדֶנּוּ, וְהוּא יָגֻד עָקֵב: בראשית מט
וַיְהִי דָוִד לְכָל־דְּרָכָו מַשְׂכִּיל, וַיהוה עִמּוֹ: שמואל א׳ יח
וְנֹחַ מָצָא חֵן בְּעֵינֵי יהוה: בראשית ו

One who will conduct business says:

עֶזְרִי מֵעִם יהוה, עֹשֵׂה שָׁמַיִם וָאָרֶץ: הַשְׁלֵךְ עַל־יהוה יְהָבְךָ וְהוּא יְכַלְכְּלֶךָ: תהלים קכא תהלים נה
שְׁמָר־תָּם וּרְאֵה יָשָׁר, כִּי־אַחֲרִית לְאִישׁ שָׁלוֹם: בְּטַח בַּיהוה וַעֲשֵׂה־ תהלים לז שם
טוֹב, שְׁכָן־אֶרֶץ וּרְעֵה אֱמוּנָה: הִנֵּה אֵל יְשׁוּעָתִי אֶבְטַח וְלֹא אֶפְחָד, כִּי־עָזִּי ישעיה יב
וְזִמְרָת יָהּ יהוה וַיְהִי־לִי לִישׁוּעָה: רִבּוֹנוֹ שֶׁל עוֹלָם, בְּדִבְרֵי קָדְשְׁךָ כָּתוּב
לֵאמֹר, הַבּוֹטֵחַ בַּיהוה חֶסֶד יְסוֹבְבֶנּוּ: וּכְתִיב, וְאַתָּה מְחַיֶּה אֶת־כֻּלָּם: תהלים לב נחמיה ט
יהוה אֱלֹהִים אֱמֶת, תֵּן בְּרָכָה וְהַצְלָחָה בְּכָל מַעֲשֵׂה יָדַי, כִּי בָטַחְתִּי
בְךָ שֶׁעַל יְדֵי מַשָּׂא וּמַתָּן וַעֲסָקִים שֶׁלִּי תִּשְׁלַח לִי בְּרָכָה, כְּדֵי שֶׁאוּכַל
לְפַרְנֵס אֶת עַצְמִי וּבְנֵי בֵיתִי בְּנַחַת וְלֹא בְצַעַר, בְּהֶתֵּר וְלֹא בְאִסּוּר,
לְחַיִּים וּלְשָׁלוֹם. וִיקֻיַּם בִּי מִקְרָא שֶׁכָּתוּב: הַשְׁלֵךְ עַל־יהוה יְהָבְךָ וְהוּא תהלים נה
יְכַלְכְּלֶךָ, אָמֵן.

PERSONAL SUPPLICATIONS

Some have the custom to read on a daily basis certain passages from the Torah, either in supplication to God that He may grant us our daily needs (both material and spiritual), or as a reminder that all our blessings come ultimately from Him.

THE CHAPTER OF THE MANNA

After the exodus from Egypt, the Israelites depended each day on the manna for their survival. Nowadays, we risk living under the illusion of self-reliance, and forgetting the true source of our sustenance. As early as the thirteenth century, the pupils of the Maharam of Rothenburg recommended reciting the verses which describe the miracle of the manna, as a declaration of faith and an expression of trust and gratitude.

יְהִי רָצוֹן May it be Your will, LORD our God, God of our ancestors, that you call forth sustenance for all Your people Israel, and among them, for me and for the people of my household. May it come with ease, without suffering, honorably, without shame, by legal and not by forbidden means, that we may perform Your service and learn Your Torah; just as You nourished our ancestors in the wilderness, in an arid, desert land.

וַיֹּאמֶר The LORD said to Moses: I shall rain bread down upon you from the sky. And the people shall go out and gather, each day their daily needs, so that I may test whether they will follow My Law or not. And on the sixth day, as they prepare what they bring home, it shall be twice what they gather every day. And so Moses and Aaron told all the people of Israel, "By evening you shall know that it was the LORD who brought you out of the land of Egypt, and in the morning you shall see the glory of God, who has heard all your protest against Him – as for us, who are we that you should stir up protest against us?" Moses said, "The LORD shall give you meat to eat in the evening, and bread in the morning to satisfy your hunger, when the LORD heeds the protest you have stirred up against Him – as for us, who are we? Your protest is not for us but for the LORD." Then Moses said to Aaron, "Tell all the congregation of Israel: Draw near to the LORD, for He has heard your protest." And when Aaron spoke to all the congregation of Israel, they turned toward the desert and there was the glory of God, revealed in a cloud. *Ex. 16*

The LORD said to Moses, "I have heard the protest of the people of Israel. Speak to them, tell them, by evening you shall eat meat, and in the morning, bread will satisfy you, and you shall know that I am the LORD your God." When evening came, quail rose up and covered the camp, and in the morning, a layer of dew surrounded the camp. And as the layer of dew lifted – there on the surface of the desert was a fine, round substance, fine as frost upon the land. And the

בקשות אישיות

Some have the custom to read on a daily basis certain passages from the תורה*, either in supplication to God that He may grant us our daily needs (both material and spiritual), or as a reminder that all our blessings come ultimately from Him.*

פרשת המן

After the exodus from Egypt, the Israelites depended each day on the manna for their survival. Nowadays, we risk living under the illusion of self-reliance, and forgetting the true source of our sustenance. As early as the thirteenth century, the pupils of the Maharam of Rothenburg recommended reciting the verses which describe the miracle of the manna, as a declaration of faith and an expression of trust and gratitude.

יְהִי רָצוֹן מִלְּפָנֶיךָ, יהוה אֱלֹהֵינוּ וֵאלֹהֵי אֲבוֹתֵינוּ, שֶׁתַּזְמִין פַּרְנָסָה לְכָל עַמְּךָ בֵּית יִשְׂרָאֵל, וּפַרְנָסָתִי וּפַרְנָסַת אַנְשֵׁי בֵיתִי בִּכְלָלָם, בְּנַחַת וְלֹא בְצַעַר, בְּכָבוֹד וְלֹא בְבִזּוּי, בְּהֶתֵּר וְלֹא בְאִסּוּר, כְּדֵי שֶׁנּוּכַל לַעֲבֹד עֲבוֹדָתֶךָ וְלִלְמֹד תּוֹרָתֶךָ, כְּמוֹ שֶׁזַּנְתָּ לַאֲבוֹתֵינוּ מָן בַּמִּדְבָּר, בְּאֶרֶץ צִיָּה וַעֲרָבָה.

שמות טז וַיֹּאמֶר יהוה אֶל־מֹשֶׁה, הִנְנִי מַמְטִיר לָכֶם לֶחֶם מִן־הַשָּׁמָיִם, וְיָצָא הָעָם וְלָקְטוּ דְּבַר־יוֹם בְּיוֹמוֹ, לְמַעַן אֲנַסֶּנּוּ הֲיֵלֵךְ בְּתוֹרָתִי אִם־לֹא: וְהָיָה בַּיּוֹם הַשִּׁשִּׁי, וְהֵכִינוּ אֵת אֲשֶׁר־יָבִיאוּ, וְהָיָה מִשְׁנֶה עַל אֲשֶׁר־יִלְקְטוּ יוֹם יוֹם: וַיֹּאמֶר מֹשֶׁה וְאַהֲרֹן אֶל־כָּל־בְּנֵי יִשְׂרָאֵל, עֶרֶב וִידַעְתֶּם כִּי יהוה הוֹצִיא אֶתְכֶם מֵאֶרֶץ מִצְרָיִם: וּבֹקֶר וּרְאִיתֶם אֶת־כְּבוֹד יהוה, בְּשָׁמְעוֹ אֶת־תְּלֻנֹּתֵיכֶם עַל־יהוה, וְנַחְנוּ מָה כִּי תַלִּינוּ עָלֵינוּ: וַיֹּאמֶר מֹשֶׁה, בְּתֵת יהוה לָכֶם בָּעֶרֶב בָּשָׂר לֶאֱכֹל וְלֶחֶם בַּבֹּקֶר לִשְׂבֹּעַ, בִּשְׁמֹעַ יהוה אֶת־תְּלֻנֹּתֵיכֶם אֲשֶׁר־אַתֶּם מַלִּינִם עָלָיו, וְנַחְנוּ מָה, לֹא־עָלֵינוּ תְלֻנֹּתֵיכֶם כִּי עַל־יהוה: וַיֹּאמֶר מֹשֶׁה אֶל־אַהֲרֹן, אֱמֹר אֶל־כָּל־עֲדַת בְּנֵי יִשְׂרָאֵל, קִרְבוּ לִפְנֵי יהוה כִּי שָׁמַע אֵת תְּלֻנֹּתֵיכֶם: וַיְהִי כְּדַבֵּר אַהֲרֹן אֶל־כָּל־עֲדַת בְּנֵי־יִשְׂרָאֵל, וַיִּפְנוּ אֶל־הַמִּדְבָּר, וְהִנֵּה כְּבוֹד יהוה נִרְאָה בֶּעָנָן:

וַיְדַבֵּר יהוה אֶל־מֹשֶׁה לֵּאמֹר: שָׁמַעְתִּי אֶת־תְּלוּנֹּת בְּנֵי יִשְׂרָאֵל, דַּבֵּר אֲלֵהֶם לֵאמֹר בֵּין הָעַרְבַּיִם תֹּאכְלוּ בָשָׂר וּבַבֹּקֶר תִּשְׂבְּעוּ־לָחֶם, וִידַעְתֶּם כִּי אֲנִי יהוה אֱלֹהֵיכֶם: וַיְהִי בָעֶרֶב, וַתַּעַל הַשְּׂלָו וַתְּכַס אֶת־הַמַּחֲנֶה, וּבַבֹּקֶר הָיְתָה שִׁכְבַת הַטַּל סָבִיב לַמַּחֲנֶה: וַתַּעַל שִׁכְבַת הַטָּל, וְהִנֵּה עַל־פְּנֵי הַמִּדְבָּר דַּק מְחֻסְפָּס, דַּק כַּכְּפֹר עַל־הָאָרֶץ: וַיִּרְאוּ בְנֵי־יִשְׂרָאֵל וַיֹּאמְרוּ

children of Israel saw it and said one to another, "What is this?" not knowing what it could be. And Moses said, "This is the bread that the LORD has given you to eat. This is what the LORD has commanded: gather it, each person as much as he eats, an omer a head, as many as you are; let each man bring enough for the people in his tent." And so the people of Israel did; they each gathered; some much and some but little. And they measured what they had taken by the omer, and the ones who took much had no more, and the ones who took little had no less; each man had gathered as much as he would eat. Moses told them, "Let no man leave any of this behind until the morning." But they did not heed Moses, and some left some until the morning, and it became infested with worms and rotted, and Moses was furious with them. They gathered it early in the morning, each man as much as he would eat; and as the sun grew hot, it melted away. On the sixth day they gathered double bread, two omarim for each person, and all the princes of the congregation came and told Moses of it. And he said, "This is what the LORD has said: Tomorrow is a holy Sabbath of utter rest to the LORD – whatever you will bake, bake now, and whatever you will cook, cook; and all that is left over, save until the morning." So they left it for the morning as Moses had charged them; and it did not rot, and no worm was found in it. And Moses said, "Eat it today, for today is the Sabbath of the LORD; today you shall not find it outside. Six days shall you gather it, and on the seventh, the Sabbath, it will not be there." There were those of the people who went out on the seventh day to gather; but no manna did they find.

And the LORD said to Moses, "How long will you refuse to keep My commands and My Law? Look – the LORD has given you the Sabbath; and so He gave you two days' bread on the sixth day; each of you, sit in your places, and let no man leave his home on the seventh day." And so the people rested on the seventh day. The people of Israel named that substance, "Manna." And it looked like coriander seeds, but white, and its taste was that of flatbread made with honey. And Moses said, "This is what the LORD has commanded: An omer measure of this shall be kept down your generations, that you may see the bread that I fed you with in the desert when I brought you out of the land of Egypt." And Moses said to Aaron, "Take a jar and fill it with an omer of manna, and place it in the LORD's presence to be kept through the generations." So, as the LORD commanded Moses, Aaron placed it before the Testimony to be kept there. And the children of Israel ate the manna for forty years, until they arrived in settled land; they ate manna until they came to the borders of the Land of Canaan. An omer is the tenth of an ephah measure.

אִישׁ אֶל־אָחִיו מָן הוּא, כִּי לֹא יָדְעוּ מַה־הוּא, וַיֹּאמֶר מֹשֶׁה אֲלֵהֶם, הוּא
הַלֶּחֶם אֲשֶׁר נָתַן יהוה לָכֶם לְאׇכְלָה: זֶה הַדָּבָר אֲשֶׁר צִוָּה יהוה, לִקְטוּ
מִמֶּנּוּ אִישׁ לְפִי אׇכְלוֹ, עֹמֶר לַגֻּלְגֹּלֶת מִסְפַּר נַפְשֹׁתֵיכֶם, אִישׁ לַאֲשֶׁר בְּאׇהֳלוֹ
תִּקָּחוּ: וַיַּעֲשׂוּ־כֵן בְּנֵי יִשְׂרָאֵל, וַיִּלְקְטוּ הַמַּרְבֶּה וְהַמַּמְעִיט: וַיָּמֹדּוּ בָעֹמֶר,
וְלֹא הֶעְדִּיף הַמַּרְבֶּה וְהַמַּמְעִיט לֹא הֶחְסִיר, אִישׁ לְפִי־אׇכְלוֹ לָקָטוּ: וַיֹּאמֶר
מֹשֶׁה אֲלֵהֶם, אִישׁ אַל־יוֹתֵר מִמֶּנּוּ עַד־בֹּקֶר: וְלֹא־שָׁמְעוּ אֶל־מֹשֶׁה, וַיּוֹתִרוּ
אֲנָשִׁים מִמֶּנּוּ עַד־בֹּקֶר, וַיָּרֻם תּוֹלָעִים וַיִּבְאַשׁ, וַיִּקְצֹף עֲלֵהֶם מֹשֶׁה: וַיִּלְקְטוּ
אֹתוֹ בַּבֹּקֶר בַּבֹּקֶר אִישׁ כְּפִי אׇכְלוֹ, וְחַם הַשֶּׁמֶשׁ וְנָמָס: וַיְהִי בַּיּוֹם הַשִּׁשִּׁי
לָקְטוּ לֶחֶם מִשְׁנֶה, שְׁנֵי הָעֹמֶר לָאֶחָד, וַיָּבֹאוּ כׇּל־נְשִׂיאֵי הָעֵדָה וַיַּגִּידוּ
לְמֹשֶׁה: וַיֹּאמֶר אֲלֵהֶם, הוּא אֲשֶׁר דִּבֶּר יהוה, שַׁבָּתוֹן שַׁבַּת־קֹדֶשׁ לַיהוה
מָחָר, אֵת אֲשֶׁר־תֹּאפוּ אֵפוּ וְאֵת אֲשֶׁר־תְּבַשְּׁלוּ בַּשֵּׁלוּ, וְאֵת כׇּל־הָעֹדֵף
הַנִּיחוּ לָכֶם לְמִשְׁמֶרֶת עַד־הַבֹּקֶר: וַיַּנִּיחוּ אֹתוֹ עַד־הַבֹּקֶר כַּאֲשֶׁר צִוָּה מֹשֶׁה,
וְלֹא הִבְאִישׁ וְרִמָּה לֹא־הָיְתָה־בּוֹ: וַיֹּאמֶר מֹשֶׁה אִכְלֻהוּ הַיּוֹם כִּי־שַׁבָּת
הַיּוֹם לַיהוה, הַיּוֹם לֹא תִמְצָאֻהוּ בַּשָּׂדֶה: שֵׁשֶׁת יָמִים תִּלְקְטֻהוּ, וּבַיּוֹם
הַשְּׁבִיעִי שַׁבָּת לֹא יִהְיֶה־בּוֹ: וַיְהִי בַּיּוֹם הַשְּׁבִיעִי יָצְאוּ מִן־הָעָם לִלְקֹט, וְלֹא
מָצָאוּ: וַיֹּאמֶר יהוה אֶל־מֹשֶׁה, עַד־אָנָה מֵאַנְתֶּם לִשְׁמֹר מִצְוֺתַי
וְתוֹרֹתָי: רְאוּ כִּי־יהוה נָתַן לָכֶם הַשַּׁבָּת, עַל־כֵּן הוּא נֹתֵן לָכֶם בַּיּוֹם הַשִּׁשִּׁי
לֶחֶם יוֹמָיִם, שְׁבוּ אִישׁ תַּחְתָּיו, אַל־יֵצֵא אִישׁ מִמְּקֹמוֹ בַּיּוֹם הַשְּׁבִיעִי:
וַיִּשְׁבְּתוּ הָעָם בַּיּוֹם הַשְּׁבִעִי: וַיִּקְרְאוּ בֵית־יִשְׂרָאֵל אֶת־שְׁמוֹ מָן, וְהוּא כְּזֶרַע
גַּד לָבָן, וְטַעְמוֹ כְּצַפִּיחִת בִּדְבָשׁ: וַיֹּאמֶר מֹשֶׁה זֶה הַדָּבָר אֲשֶׁר צִוָּה יהוה,
מְלֹא הָעֹמֶר מִמֶּנּוּ לְמִשְׁמֶרֶת לְדֹרֹתֵיכֶם, לְמַעַן יִרְאוּ אֶת־הַלֶּחֶם אֲשֶׁר
הֶאֱכַלְתִּי אֶתְכֶם בַּמִּדְבָּר, בְּהוֹצִיאִי אֶתְכֶם מֵאֶרֶץ מִצְרָיִם: וַיֹּאמֶר מֹשֶׁה
אֶל־אַהֲרֹן, קַח צִנְצֶנֶת אַחַת וְתֶן־שָׁמָּה מְלֹא־הָעֹמֶר מָן, וְהַנַּח אֹתוֹ לִפְנֵי
יהוה לְמִשְׁמֶרֶת לְדֹרֹתֵיכֶם: כַּאֲשֶׁר צִוָּה יהוה אֶל־מֹשֶׁה, וַיַּנִּיחֵהוּ אַהֲרֹן
לִפְנֵי הָעֵדֻת לְמִשְׁמָרֶת: וּבְנֵי יִשְׂרָאֵל אָכְלוּ אֶת־הַמָּן אַרְבָּעִים שָׁנָה, עַד־
בֹּאָם אֶל־אֶרֶץ נוֹשָׁבֶת, אֶת־הַמָּן אָכְלוּ עַד־בֹּאָם אֶל־קְצֵה אֶרֶץ כְּנָעַן:
וְהָעֹמֶר עֲשִׂרִית הָאֵיפָה הוּא:

PRAYER FOR SUSTENANCE

אָנָּא Please, LORD who prepares sustenance for every creation, and calls forth clothing for all who have been made, and sends them their nourishment – grant me nourishment in plenty, provide for me and sustain me, and grant me and all the members of my household, and all of Israel, sustenance in plenty, honorable and obtained in serenity, without suffering, in legal ways and not forbidden ones, with honor and without disgrace, a sustenance with no shame or humiliation. A sustenance by which You will never make me needy of the gifts of other people, but only of Your full, broad hand; a sustenance that will allow me to engage in study of Your holy, pure and perfect Torah, pure meat, easily prepared; my bread and the bread of the people of my household – all our needs before we come to need them – so that my mind may be free of all worry to engage in study of the words of the Torah and to fulfill the commands, and to dwell in peace at my table, honorable, with all my household, without waiting to be invited to the tables of others. So that I will not be subject to any man, and that I will have the yoke of no man upon my shoulders, but only the yoke of Your kingship, making me serve You wholeheartedly, wearing clothes of honor; let our clothing be costly and not shameful. And save us from poverty, from vulnerability and shame, and allow me the merit of welcoming guests and dealing generously with every person. Send opportunities for me to give charity to those who deserve it, and let me not fall at the hands of dishonest people. Amen.

THE CHAPTER OF REVERENCE

In his final address before his death, Moses charges the people of Israel with loving God and holding Him in reverence, reminding them of God's combined majesty and humility (see "May God give you," page 324), and recounting the miracles He has done for them.

וְעַתָּה And now, Israel, what does the LORD your God ask of you, but that you hold the LORD your God in awe, walk in His ways and love Him, serving the LORD your God with all your heart and all your soul; keeping the commands of the LORD and His laws, as I charge you on this day, as a blessing. The sky, the highest heavens, the earth and all that fills it, belong to the LORD. Yet the LORD delighted in your ancestors, and loved them, and He chose their children after them – chose you – from all the other nations, as you see this day. Now, open your hearts, and stiffen your necks no longer. For the LORD your God is the God of gods, the LORD of lords, the great, mighty and awesome God, who does not favor the powerful, or accept any bribe. He does justice for the orphan and the widow, and loves the stranger, giving him bread and clothing. And you shall love the stranger, for you were strangers in the land of Egypt. Hold the LORD your God in awe and serve Him, cling to Him and swear by His name. For He

Deut. 10

תפילה על הפרנסה

אָנָּא הָאֵל הַמֵּכִין פַּרְנָסָה לְכָל בְּרִיָּה, וּמַזְמִין מַלְבּוּשׁ לְכָל נִבְרָא, וְשׁוֹלֵחַ לָהֶם מִחְיָה, שֶׁתִּתֵּן לִי מִחְיָתִי בְּשֶׁפַע, שֶׁתְּכַלְכְּלֵנִי וּתְפַרְנְסֵנִי לִי וּלְכָל אַנְשֵׁי בֵיתִי וּלְכָל יִשְׂרָאֵל פַּרְנָסָה טוֹבָה שֶׁל כָּבוֹד, בְּנַחַת וְלֹא בְּצַעַר, בְּהֶתֵּר וְלֹא בְאִסּוּר, בְּכָבוֹד וְלֹא בְּבִזּוּי. פַּרְנָסָה שֶׁלֹּא תִהְיֶה בָהּ שׁוּם בּוּשָׁה וּכְלִמָּה, פַּרְנָסָה שֶׁלֹּא תַצְרִיכֵנִי בָּהּ לִידֵי מַתְּנַת בָּשָׂר וָדָם, כִּי אִם לְיָדְךָ הַמְּלֵאָה וְהָרְחָבָה, פַּרְנָסָה שֶׁאוּכַל לַעֲסֹק בְּתוֹרָתְךָ הַקְּדוֹשָׁה וְהַטְּהוֹרָה וְהַתְּמִימָה, וְטֶרֶף נָקִי וּמְזֻמָּן וּמְזוֹנוֹתַי וּמְזוֹנוֹת אַנְשֵׁי בֵיתִי וְכָל צְרָכֵינוּ קֹדֶם שֶׁנִּצְטָרֵךְ לָהֶם, כְּדֵי שֶׁיִּהְיֶה לִבִּי פָּנוּי בְּלִי טִרְדָּה לַעֲסֹק בְּדִבְרֵי תוֹרָה וּלְקַיֵּם הַמִּצְוֹת, וְלֵישֵׁב בְּשָׁלוֹם עַל שֻׁלְחָנִי בְּכָבוֹד עִם כָּל בְּנֵי בֵיתִי. וְשֶׁלֹּא אֲצַפֶּה לְשֻׁלְחָן שֶׁל אֲחֵרִים, וְשֶׁלֹּא אֶצְטָרֵךְ לְהִשְׁתַּעְבֵּד לְשׁוּם אָדָם, וְשֶׁלֹּא יְהֵא עָלַי שׁוּם עֹל בָּשָׂר וָדָם, כִּי אִם עֹל מַלְכוּתְךָ לְעָבְדְּךָ בְּלֵבָב שָׁלֵם. וּבִגְדֵי כָבוֹד יִהְיוּ לְבוּשֵׁינוּ, בְּיֹקֶר וְלֹא בְּבֹשֶׁת פָּנִים. וְהַצִּילֵנוּ מִן עֲנִיּוּת וּמִדַּלּוּת וְשִׁפְלוּת, וְאֶזְכֶּה לְהַכְנִיס אוֹרְחִים וְלִגְמֹל חֶסֶד לְכָל אָדָם. וְהַזְמֵן לִי לַעֲשׂוֹת צְדָקָה לְהָרְאוּיִים לָהּ, וְלֹא אֶכָּשֵׁל בִּבְנֵי אָדָם שֶׁאֵינָם הֲגוּנִים, אָמֵן.

פרשת היראה

In his final address before his death, Moses charges the people of Israel with loving God and holding Him in reverence, reminding them of God's combined majesty and humility (see וַיִּתֶּן־לְךָ*, page 325), and recounting the miracles He has done for them.*

וְעַתָּה יִשְׂרָאֵל, מָה יהוה אֱלֹהֶיךָ שֹׁאֵל מֵעִמָּךְ, כִּי אִם־לְיִרְאָה אֶת־יהוה דברים י
אֱלֹהֶיךָ לָלֶכֶת בְּכָל־דְּרָכָיו וּלְאַהֲבָה אֹתוֹ, וְלַעֲבֹד אֶת־יהוה אֱלֹהֶיךָ בְּכָל־
לְבָבְךָ וּבְכָל־נַפְשֶׁךָ: לִשְׁמֹר אֶת־מִצְוֹת יהוה וְאֶת־חֻקֹּתָיו, אֲשֶׁר אָנֹכִי מְצַוְּךָ
הַיּוֹם, לְטוֹב לָךְ: הֵן לַיהוה אֱלֹהֶיךָ הַשָּׁמַיִם וּשְׁמֵי הַשָּׁמָיִם, הָאָרֶץ וְכָל־אֲשֶׁר־
בָּהּ: רַק בַּאֲבֹתֶיךָ חָשַׁק יהוה לְאַהֲבָה אוֹתָם, וַיִּבְחַר בְּזַרְעָם אַחֲרֵיהֶם, בָּכֶם
מִכָּל־הָעַמִּים, כַּיּוֹם הַזֶּה: וּמַלְתֶּם אֵת עָרְלַת לְבַבְכֶם, וְעָרְפְּכֶם לֹא תַקְשׁוּ
עוֹד: כִּי יהוה אֱלֹהֵיכֶם הוּא אֱלֹהֵי הָאֱלֹהִים וַאֲדֹנֵי הָאֲדֹנִים, הָאֵל הַגָּדֹל
הַגִּבֹּר וְהַנּוֹרָא, אֲשֶׁר לֹא־יִשָּׂא פָנִים וְלֹא יִקַּח שֹׁחַד: עֹשֶׂה מִשְׁפַּט יָתוֹם
וְאַלְמָנָה, וְאֹהֵב גֵּר לָתֶת לוֹ לֶחֶם וְשִׂמְלָה: וַאֲהַבְתֶּם אֶת־הַגֵּר, כִּי־גֵרִים
הֱיִיתֶם בְּאֶרֶץ מִצְרָיִם: אֶת־יהוה אֱלֹהֶיךָ תִּירָא, אֹתוֹ תַעֲבֹד, וּבוֹ תִדְבָּק

is your glory and He is the God who performed with you these great and awesome things that your eyes have witnessed. Your ancestors were but seventy souls when they went down to Egypt, and now the LORD your God has made you as many as the stars of the sky.

You shall love the LORD your God, and keep what He gives you to guard, His statutes, His laws and His commands, every day of your lives. And know this day – for your children do not know and did not see what the LORD your God has taught you – His greatness, His mighty hand and His outstretched arm; His signs and the acts He has performed in Egypt, against Pharaoh, king of Egypt and all his land; and what He did to all the army of Egypt, its horses and its chariots, which He drowned in the waters of the Sea of Reeds before their eyes, as they chased after you – and the LORD destroyed them, gone to this very day; and what He did for you in the desert, until you came to this place; and what He did to Datan and to Aviram, the sons of Eliav, son of Reuben, when the earth opened her mouth and swallowed them, their families and their tents and everything that was theirs, in the very midst of all Israel – it is your eyes that have seen all the great work of the LORD that He has done. And you shall keep all the command that I charge you with on this day, that you may be strong and come and inherit the land that you are soon to cross over to and inherit; and so that you may live long upon the land that the LORD promised to give your ancestors and their descendants; a land flowing with milk and honey.

יְהִי רָצוֹן May it be Your will, LORD my God and God of my ancestors, that You plant the love and the awe of You in my heart, and in the hearts of all Israel, Your people, that we may revere Your great, mighty and awesome name, with all our heart and soul – in awe of the sublimity of the Infinite One; may Your name be blessed and raised high, for You are great and Your name is awesome, Amen, Selah.

THE CHAPTER OF REPENTANCE

This passage comes from the end of Moses' final address. After describing the blessings which might be conferred by keeping the covenant and the repercussions of breaking it, Moses promises the people that the punishment incurred will not be irrevocable; the gates of repentance are always open, and by returning to God the people might yet be redeemed. These verses were later interwoven into the prayer for the State of Israel (*page 462*) *to express the hope that this first stage of redemption will lead to its full flowering, with the ingathering of all exiles and the opening of our hearts to truly loving and revering God.*

וְהָיָה And when all these things come upon you, the blessing and the curse that *Deut. 30*
I have laid before you now – you shall take this to heart, as you dwell with all the nations among whom the LORD your God has scattered you. And you will

וּבִשְׁמוֹ תִּשָּׁבֵעַ: הוּא תְהִלָּתְךָ וְהוּא אֱלֹהֶיךָ, אֲשֶׁר־עָשָׂה אִתְּךָ אֶת־הַגְּדֹלֹת וְאֶת־הַנּוֹרָאֹת הָאֵלֶּה אֲשֶׁר רָאוּ עֵינֶיךָ: בְּשִׁבְעִים נֶפֶשׁ יָרְדוּ אֲבֹתֶיךָ מִצְרָיְמָה, וְעַתָּה שָׂמְךָ יהוה אֱלֹהֶיךָ כְּכוֹכְבֵי הַשָּׁמַיִם לָרֹב: וְאָהַבְתָּ אֵת יהוה אֱלֹהֶיךָ, וְשָׁמַרְתָּ מִשְׁמַרְתּוֹ וְחֻקֹּתָיו וּמִשְׁפָּטָיו וּמִצְוֹתָיו כָּל־הַיָּמִים: וִידַעְתֶּם הַיּוֹם, כִּי לֹא אֶת־בְּנֵיכֶם אֲשֶׁר לֹא־יָדְעוּ וַאֲשֶׁר לֹא־רָאוּ אֶת־מוּסַר יהוה אֱלֹהֵיכֶם, אֶת־גָּדְלוֹ אֶת־יָדוֹ הַחֲזָקָה וּזְרֹעוֹ הַנְּטוּיָה: וְאֶת־אֹתֹתָיו וְאֶת־מַעֲשָׂיו אֲשֶׁר עָשָׂה בְּתוֹךְ מִצְרָיִם, לְפַרְעֹה מֶלֶךְ־מִצְרַיִם וּלְכָל־אַרְצוֹ: וַאֲשֶׁר עָשָׂה לְחֵיל מִצְרַיִם לְסוּסָיו וּלְרִכְבּוֹ, אֲשֶׁר הֵצִיף אֶת־מֵי יַם־סוּף עַל־פְּנֵיהֶם בְּרָדְפָם אַחֲרֵיכֶם, וַיְאַבְּדֵם יהוה עַד הַיּוֹם הַזֶּה: וַאֲשֶׁר עָשָׂה לָכֶם בַּמִּדְבָּר, עַד־בֹּאֲכֶם עַד־הַמָּקוֹם הַזֶּה: וַאֲשֶׁר עָשָׂה לְדָתָן וְלַאֲבִירָם בְּנֵי אֱלִיאָב בֶּן־רְאוּבֵן, אֲשֶׁר פָּצְתָה הָאָרֶץ אֶת־פִּיהָ וַתִּבְלָעֵם וְאֶת־בָּתֵּיהֶם וְאֶת־אָהֳלֵיהֶם, וְאֵת כָּל־הַיְקוּם אֲשֶׁר בְּרַגְלֵיהֶם בְּקֶרֶב כָּל־יִשְׂרָאֵל: כִּי עֵינֵיכֶם הָרֹאֹת אֶת כָּל־מַעֲשֵׂה יהוה הַגָּדֹל, אֲשֶׁר עָשָׂה: וּשְׁמַרְתֶּם אֶת־כָּל־הַמִּצְוָה אֲשֶׁר אָנֹכִי מְצַוְּךָ הַיּוֹם, לְמַעַן תֶּחֶזְקוּ וּבָאתֶם וִירִשְׁתֶּם אֶת־הָאָרֶץ אֲשֶׁר אַתֶּם עֹבְרִים שָׁמָּה לְרִשְׁתָּהּ: וּלְמַעַן תַּאֲרִיכוּ יָמִים עַל־הָאֲדָמָה אֲשֶׁר נִשְׁבַּע יהוה לַאֲבֹתֵיכֶם לָתֵת לָהֶם וּלְזַרְעָם, אֶרֶץ זָבַת חָלָב וּדְבָשׁ:

יְהִי רָצוֹן מִלְּפָנֶיךָ, יהוה אֱלֹהַי וֵאלֹהֵי אֲבוֹתַי, שֶׁתִּטַּע אַהֲבָתְךָ וְיִרְאָתְךָ בְּלִבִּי וּבְלֵב כָּל יִשְׂרָאֵל עַמֶּךָ, לְיִרְאָה אֶת שִׁמְךָ הַגָּדוֹל הַגִּבּוֹר וְהַנּוֹרָא בְּכָל לְבָבֵנוּ וּבְכָל נַפְשֵׁנוּ, יִרְאַת הָרוֹמְמוּת שֶׁל אֵין סוֹף בָּרוּךְ הוּא, וְיִתְעַלֶּה שִׁמְךָ. כִּי גָדוֹל אַתָּה וְנוֹרָא שְׁמֶךָ, אָמֵן סֶלָה.

פרשת התשובה

This passage comes from the end of Moses' final address. After describing the blessings which might be conferred by keeping the covenant and the repercussions of breaking it, Moses promises the people that the punishment incurred will not be irrevocable; the gates of repentance are always open, and by returning to God the people might yet be redeemed. These verses were later interwoven into the תפילה לשלום מדינת ישראל *(page 463) to express the hope that this first stage of redemption will lead to its full flowering, with the ingathering of all exiles and the opening of our hearts to truly loving and revering God.*

וְהָיָה כִּי־יָבֹאוּ עָלֶיךָ כָּל־הַדְּבָרִים הָאֵלֶּה, הַבְּרָכָה וְהַקְּלָלָה אֲשֶׁר נָתַתִּי דברים ל
לְפָנֶיךָ, וַהֲשֵׁבֹתָ אֶל־לְבָבֶךָ בְּכָל־הַגּוֹיִם אֲשֶׁר הִדִּיחֲךָ יהוה אֱלֹהֶיךָ שָׁמָּה:

return to the LORD your God, and you will listen to His voice, just as I charge you on this day, you and your children, with all your heart and all your soul. And the LORD shall restore your fortunes, and have compassion for you, and will return and gather you in from all the nations among whom the LORD has dispersed you. Even if you are scattered to the furthermost lands under the heavens, from there the LORD your God will gather you and take you back. The LORD your God will bring you to the land your ancestors possessed and you will possess it; and He will make you more prosperous and numerous than your ancestors. Then the LORD your God will open up your heart and the heart of your descendants, to love the LORD your God with all your heart and with all your soul, that you may live. And as for all these curses the LORD your God will place them upon your enemies, upon those who hate you and who persecute you. And you will return and listen again to the voice of the LORD, and will fulfill all the commands that I charge you with this day. And the LORD your God will give you plenty in all the works of your hand, your young, the young of your cattle, the fruits of the land, for the good, for the LORD will come back to rejoice in you for the good, just as He rejoiced in your ancestors. For you shall listen to the voice of the LORD your God, keeping His commands and His statutes, as they are written in this scroll of the Torah, for you shall return to the LORD your God with all your heart and with all your soul.

יְהִי רָצוֹן May it be Your will, LORD my God and God of my ancestors, that You dig a passage for us beneath the walls to tunnel through to the throne of Your glory, returning all the sinners of Your people in full repentance – for Your right hand is outstretched to receive those who return, and You desire our repentance, Amen, Selah.

וְשַׁבְתָּ עַד־יהוה אֱלֹהֶיךָ וְשָׁמַעְתָּ בְקֹלוֹ, כְּכֹל אֲשֶׁר־אָנֹכִי מְצַוְּךָ הַיּוֹם, אַתָּה וּבָנֶיךָ בְּכָל־לְבָבְךָ וּבְכָל־נַפְשֶׁךָ: וְשָׁב יהוה אֱלֹהֶיךָ אֶת־שְׁבוּתְךָ וְרִחֲמֶךָ, וְשָׁב וְקִבֶּצְךָ מִכָּל־הָעַמִּים אֲשֶׁר הֱפִיצְךָ יהוה אֱלֹהֶיךָ שָׁמָּה: אִם־יִהְיֶה נִדַּחֲךָ בִּקְצֵה הַשָּׁמָיִם, מִשָּׁם יְקַבֶּצְךָ יהוה אֱלֹהֶיךָ וּמִשָּׁם יִקָּחֶךָ: וֶהֱבִיאֲךָ יהוה אֱלֹהֶיךָ אֶל־הָאָרֶץ אֲשֶׁר־יָרְשׁוּ אֲבֹתֶיךָ וִירִשְׁתָּהּ, וְהֵיטִבְךָ וְהִרְבְּךָ מֵאֲבֹתֶיךָ: וּמָל יהוה אֱלֹהֶיךָ אֶת־לְבָבְךָ וְאֶת־לְבַב זַרְעֶךָ, לְאַהֲבָה אֶת־יהוה אֱלֹהֶיךָ בְּכָל־לְבָבְךָ וּבְכָל־נַפְשְׁךָ, לְמַעַן חַיֶּיךָ: וְנָתַן יהוה אֱלֹהֶיךָ אֵת כָּל־הָאָלוֹת הָאֵלֶּה עַל־אֹיְבֶיךָ וְעַל־שֹׂנְאֶיךָ אֲשֶׁר רְדָפוּךָ: וְאַתָּה תָשׁוּב וְשָׁמַעְתָּ בְּקוֹל יהוה, וְעָשִׂיתָ אֶת־כָּל־מִצְוֹתָיו אֲשֶׁר אָנֹכִי מְצַוְּךָ הַיּוֹם: וְהוֹתִירְךָ יהוה אֱלֹהֶיךָ בְּכֹל מַעֲשֵׂה יָדֶךָ, בִּפְרִי בִטְנְךָ וּבִפְרִי בְהֶמְתְּךָ וּבִפְרִי אַדְמָתְךָ, לְטֹבָה, כִּי יָשׁוּב יהוה לָשׂוּשׂ עָלֶיךָ לְטוֹב כַּאֲשֶׁר־שָׂשׂ עַל־אֲבֹתֶיךָ: כִּי תִשְׁמַע בְּקוֹל יהוה אֱלֹהֶיךָ, לִשְׁמֹר מִצְוֹתָיו וְחֻקֹּתָיו הַכְּתוּבָה בְּסֵפֶר הַתּוֹרָה הַזֶּה, כִּי תָשׁוּב אֶל־יהוה אֱלֹהֶיךָ בְּכָל־לְבָבְךָ וּבְכָל־נַפְשֶׁךָ:

יְהִי רָצוֹן מִלְּפָנֶיךָ, יהוה אֱלֹהַי וֵאלֹהֵי אֲבוֹתַי, שֶׁתַּחְתֹּר חֲתִירָה מִתַּחַת כִּסֵּא כְבוֹדֶךָ לְהַחֲזִיר בִּתְשׁוּבָה שְׁלֵמָה לְכָל פּוֹשְׁעֵי עַמְּךָ בֵּית יִשְׂרָאֵל, וּבִכְלָלָם תַּחֲזִירֵנִי בִּתְשׁוּבָה שְׁלֵמָה לְפָנֶיךָ, כִּי יְמִינְךָ פְּשׁוּטָה לְקַבֵּל שָׁבִים וְרוֹצֶה אַתָּה בִּתְשׁוּבָה, אָמֵן סֶלָה.

FOR PROTECTION FROM THE EVIL EYE

The following prayer, based on Rabbi Tzvi Hirsch Kaidanover's Kav HaYashar (Frankfurt, 1705), incorporates biblical verses as a segula (charm) for God's protection.

When the plague of tzara'at is found in a man, *Lev. 13*
he shall be brought before the priest.
We will pass over armed before the LORD into the land of Canaan, *Num. 32*
and possess our inheritance here on this side of the Jordan.
The LORD your God will raise up a prophet from your midst for you, *Deut. 18*
one of your brethren, like me; and it is him that you shall heed.
There is a river whose streams bring joy to the city of God, *Ps. 46*
the holy dwelling-place of the Most High.
You led Your people like a flock by the hand of Moses and Aaron. *Ps. 77*
He performed wonders in the sight of their fathers, in the land of Egypt, *Ps. 78*
in the fields of Tzo'an.
I have perfumed my bed with myrrh, aloes, and cinnamon. *Prov. 7*
The spirit of man is the candle of the LORD, *Prov. 20*
searching out all his inner chambers.
Your lips drip nectar, my bride; honey and milk lie under your tongue, *Song. 4*
and on your dress lingers Lebanon's scent.
Flee out of the midst of Babylonia; depart from the land of the Kasdim; *Jer. 50*
and be as the he-goats running before the flocks.
They were armed with bows, and could use both the right hand *1 Chr. 12*
and the left, slinging stones and shooting arrows from their bows;
they were Saul's brethren, from Benjamin.

רִבּוֹנוֹ Master of the Universe, shelter Your people Israel from every kind of sorcery, from every evil eye. And just as You spread Your wings over our ancestors in the desert, and did not allow the evil eye of Balaam son of Beor to have hold over them, so may You spread Your wings over us, in Your great compassion, that we may be protected (protected and guided,) by Your holy names, from every evil eye.

You are my shelter, You will shield me from distress; *Ps. 32*
You will surround me with songs of deliverance. Selah.

שמירה נגד עין הרע

The following prayer, based on Rabbi Tzvi Hirsch Kaidanover's קב הישר *(Frankfurt, 1705), incorporates biblical verses as a* סגולה *(charm) for God's protection.*

נֶגַע צָרַעַת כִּי תִהְיֶה בְּאָדָם וְהוּבָא אֶל־הַכֹּהֵן: ויקרא יג

נַחְנוּ נַעֲבֹר חֲלוּצִים לִפְנֵי יהוה אֶרֶץ כְּנָעַן במדבר לב
וְאִתָּנוּ אֲחֻזַּת נַחֲלָתֵנוּ מֵעֵבֶר לַיַּרְדֵּן:

נָבִיא מִקִּרְבְּךָ מֵאַחֶיךָ כָּמֹנִי יָקִים לְךָ יהוה אֱלֹהֶיךָ, אֵלָיו תִּשְׁמָעוּן: דברים יח

נָהָר פְּלָגָיו יְשַׂמְּחוּ עִיר־אֱלֹהִים, קְדֹשׁ מִשְׁכְּנֵי עֶלְיוֹן: תהלים מו

נָחִיתָ כַצֹּאן עַמֶּךָ בְּיַד־מֹשֶׁה וְאַהֲרֹן: תהלים עז

נֶגֶד אֲבוֹתָם עָשָׂה פֶלֶא בְּאֶרֶץ מִצְרַיִם שְׂדֵה־צֹעַן: תהלים עח

נַפְתִּי מִשְׁכָּבִי מֹר אֲהָלִים וְקִנָּמוֹן: משלי ז

נֵר יהוה נִשְׁמַת אָדָם חֹפֵשׂ כָּל־חַדְרֵי־בָטֶן: משלי כ

נֹפֶת תִּטֹּפְנָה שִׂפְתוֹתַיִךְ כַּלָּה שיר השירים ד
דְּבַשׁ וְחָלָב תַּחַת לְשׁוֹנֵךְ וְרֵיחַ שַׂלְמֹתַיִךְ כְּרֵיחַ לְבָנוֹן:

נֻדוּ מִתּוֹךְ בָּבֶל וּמֵאֶרֶץ כַּשְׂדִּים צֵאוּ, וִהְיוּ כְּעַתּוּדִים לִפְנֵי־צֹאן: ירמיה נ

נֹשְׁקֵי קֶשֶׁת מַיְמִינִים וּמַשְׂמְאִלִים בָּאֲבָנִים וּבַחִצִּים בַּקָּשֶׁת דברי הימים א יב
מֵאֲחֵי שָׁאוּל מִבִּנְיָמִן:

רִבּוֹנוֹ שֶׁל עוֹלָם, הַצֵּל עַמְּךָ בֵּית יִשְׂרָאֵל מִכָּל מִינֵי כְשׁוּפִים וּמִכָּל מִינֵי עַיִן הָרָע, וּכְשֵׁם שֶׁפָּרַשְׂתָּ כְּנָפֶיךָ עַל אֲבוֹתֵינוּ שֶׁבַּמִּדְבָּר, שֶׁלֹּא שָׁלַט עֲלֵיהֶם עֵינָא בִּישָׁא דְּבִלְעָם בֶּן בְּעוֹר, כֵּן תִּפְרֹס כְּנָפֶיךָ עָלֵינוּ בְּרַחֲמֶיךָ הָרַבִּים לִהְיוֹתֵנוּ מְכֻסִּים (בְּמִכְסֶה וּבְהַנְהָגָה) בְּשְׁמוֹתֶיךָ הַקְּדוֹשִׁים מִכָּל עֵינָא בִּישָׁא.

אַתָּה סֵתֶר לִי מִצַּר תִּצְּרֵנִי רָנֵּי פַלֵּט תְּסוֹבְבֵנִי סֶלָה: תהלים לב

Minḥa for Weekdays

אַשְׁרֵי Happy are those who dwell in Your House; Ps. 84
they shall continue to praise You, Selah!
Happy are the people for whom this is so; Ps. 144
happy are the people whose God is the LORD.
A song of praise by David. Ps. 145

I will exalt You, my God, the King, and bless Your name for ever and all time. Every day I will bless You, and praise Your name for ever and all time. Great is the LORD and greatly to be praised; His greatness is unfathomable. One generation will praise Your works to the next, and tell of Your mighty deeds. On the glorious splendor of Your majesty I will meditate, and on the acts of Your wonders. They shall talk of the power of Your awesome deeds, and I will tell of Your greatness. They shall recite the record of Your great goodness, and sing with joy of Your righteousness. The LORD is gracious and compassionate, slow to anger and great in loving-kindness. The LORD is good to all, and His compassion extends to all His works. All Your works shall thank You, LORD, and Your devoted ones shall bless You. They shall talk of the glory of Your kingship, and speak of Your might. To make known to mankind His mighty deeds and the

---

Its form is simple. It begins with *Ashrei* as a prelude to prayer, the third of three daily recitals. The Amida is the same as in the morning with two changes. In the Leader's Repetition, the passage referring to the priestly blessing is not said, since in the Temple the priests did not bless the congregation in the afternoon. Likewise, a shorter form of the final blessing (associated with the priestly blessing in the Temple) is said. *Taḥanun* is also said at Minḥa, on days when it is said in the morning, except on the afternoon before Shabbat and Yom Tov and certain other occasions (see page 253). The service ends with *Aleinu*.

מנחה לחול

אַשְׁרֵי יוֹשְׁבֵי בֵיתֶךָ, עוֹד יְהַלְלְוּךָ סֶּלָה: תהלים פד
אַשְׁרֵי הָעָם שֶׁכָּכָה לּוֹ, אַשְׁרֵי הָעָם שֶׁיהוה אֱלֹהָיו: תהלים קמד
תְּהִלָּה לְדָוִד תהלים קמה
אֲרוֹמִמְךָ אֱלוֹהַי הַמֶּלֶךְ, וַאֲבָרְכָה שִׁמְךָ לְעוֹלָם וָעֶד:
בְּכָל־יוֹם אֲבָרְכֶךָּ, וַאֲהַלְלָה שִׁמְךָ לְעוֹלָם וָעֶד:
גָּדוֹל יהוה וּמְהֻלָּל מְאֹד, וְלִגְדֻלָּתוֹ אֵין חֵקֶר:
דּוֹר לְדוֹר יְשַׁבַּח מַעֲשֶׂיךָ, וּגְבוּרֹתֶיךָ יַגִּידוּ:
הֲדַר כְּבוֹד הוֹדֶךָ, וְדִבְרֵי נִפְלְאֹתֶיךָ אָשִׂיחָה:
וֶעֱזוּז נוֹרְאֹתֶיךָ יֹאמֵרוּ, וּגְדוּלָּתְךָ אֲסַפְּרֶנָּה:
זֵכֶר רַב־טוּבְךָ יַבִּיעוּ, וְצִדְקָתְךָ יְרַנֵּנוּ:
חַנּוּן וְרַחוּם יהוה, אֶרֶךְ אַפַּיִם וּגְדָל־חָסֶד:
טוֹב־יהוה לַכֹּל, וְרַחֲמָיו עַל־כָּל־מַעֲשָׂיו:
יוֹדְוּךָ יהוה כָּל־מַעֲשֶׂיךָ, וַחֲסִידֶיךָ יְבָרְכוּכָה:
כְּבוֹד מַלְכוּתְךָ יֹאמֵרוּ, וּגְבוּרָתְךָ יְדַבֵּרוּ:
לְהוֹדִיעַ לִבְנֵי הָאָדָם גְּבוּרֹתָיו, וּכְבוֹד הֲדַר מַלְכוּתוֹ:
מַלְכוּתְךָ מַלְכוּת כָּל־עֹלָמִים, וּמֶמְשַׁלְתְּךָ בְּכָל־דּוֹר וָדֹר:

AFTERNOON SERVICE

The afternoon service corresponds to the daily afternoon sacrifice (Num. 28:4). *Minḥa*, the "meal-offering," was not unique to the afternoon. The prayer may have acquired this name because of the verse in Psalms (141:2): "May my prayer be like incense before You, the lifting up of my hands like the afternoon offering (*minḥat arev*)." The sages attached special significance to this prayer, noting that Elijah's prayer was answered at this time (1 Kings 18:36).

glorious majesty of His kingship. Your kingdom is an everlasting kingdom, and Your reign is for all generations. The LORD supports all who fall, and raises all who are bowed down. All raise their eyes to You in hope, and You give them their food in due season. You open Your hand, and satisfy every living thing with favor. The LORD is righteous in all His ways, and kind in all He does. The LORD is close to all who call on Him, to all who call on Him in truth. He fulfills the will of those who revere Him; He hears their cry and saves them. The LORD guards all who love Him, but all the wicked He will destroy. ▸ My mouth shall speak the praise of the LORD, and all creatures shall bless His holy name for ever and all time.

We will bless the LORD now and for ever. Halleluya! *Ps. 115*

HALF KADDISH

Leader: יִתְגַּדַּל Magnified and sanctified may His great name be,
in the world He created by His will.
May He establish His kingdom
in your lifetime and in your days,
and in the lifetime of all the house of Israel,
swiftly and soon –
and say: Amen.

All: May His great name be blessed for ever and all time.

Leader: Blessed and praised, glorified and exalted,
raised and honored, uplifted and lauded
be the name of the Holy One, blessed be He,
beyond any blessing,
song, praise and consolation
uttered in the world –
and say: Amen.

On fast days, go to Removing the Torah from the Ark on page 158. The Torah reading and Haftara for fast days are on page 654. After the Torah is returned to the Ark, the Leader says Half Kaddish.

סוֹמֵךְ יהוה לְכָל־הַנֹּפְלִים, וְזוֹקֵף לְכָל־הַכְּפוּפִים:
עֵינֵי־כֹל אֵלֶיךָ יְשַׂבֵּרוּ, וְאַתָּה נוֹתֵן־לָהֶם אֶת־אָכְלָם בְּעִתּוֹ:
פּוֹתֵחַ אֶת־יָדֶךָ, וּמַשְׂבִּיעַ לְכָל־חַי רָצוֹן:
צַדִּיק יהוה בְּכָל־דְּרָכָיו, וְחָסִיד בְּכָל־מַעֲשָׂיו:
קָרוֹב יהוה לְכָל־קֹרְאָיו, לְכֹל אֲשֶׁר יִקְרָאֻהוּ בֶאֱמֶת:
רְצוֹן־יְרֵאָיו יַעֲשֶׂה, וְאֶת־שַׁוְעָתָם יִשְׁמַע, וְיוֹשִׁיעֵם:
שׁוֹמֵר יהוה אֶת־כָּל־אֹהֲבָיו, וְאֵת כָּל־הָרְשָׁעִים יַשְׁמִיד:
◂ תְּהִלַּת יהוה יְדַבֶּר פִּי, וִיבָרֵךְ כָּל־בָּשָׂר שֵׁם קָדְשׁוֹ לְעוֹלָם וָעֶד:
וַאֲנַחְנוּ נְבָרֵךְ יָהּ מֵעַתָּה וְעַד־עוֹלָם, הַלְלוּיָהּ: תהלים קטו

חצי קדיש

ש״ץ: יִתְגַּדַּל וְיִתְקַדַּשׁ שְׁמֵהּ רַבָּא (קהל: אָמֵן)
בְּעָלְמָא דִּי בְרָא כִרְעוּתֵהּ
וְיַמְלִיךְ מַלְכוּתֵהּ
בְּחַיֵּיכוֹן וּבְיוֹמֵיכוֹן וּבְחַיֵּי דְכָל בֵּית יִשְׂרָאֵל
בַּעֲגָלָא וּבִזְמַן קָרִיב, וְאִמְרוּ אָמֵן. (קהל: אָמֵן)

קהל וש״ץ: יְהֵא שְׁמֵהּ רַבָּא מְבָרַךְ לְעָלַם וּלְעָלְמֵי עָלְמַיָּא.

ש״ץ: יִתְבָּרַךְ וְיִשְׁתַּבַּח וְיִתְפָּאַר וְיִתְרוֹמַם וְיִתְנַשֵּׂא
וְיִתְהַדָּר וְיִתְעַלֶּה וְיִתְהַלָּל
שְׁמֵהּ דְּקֻדְשָׁא בְּרִיךְ הוּא (קהל: בְּרִיךְ הוּא)
לְעֵלָּא מִן כָּל בִּרְכָתָא / בעשרת ימי תשובה: לְעֵלָּא לְעֵלָּא מִכָּל בִּרְכָתָא/
וְשִׁירָתָא, תֻּשְׁבְּחָתָא וְנֶחֱמָתָא
דַּאֲמִירָן בְּעָלְמָא, וְאִמְרוּ אָמֵן. (קהל: אָמֵן)

On fast days, go to הוצאת ספר תורה *on page 159. The* תורה *reading and* הפטרה *for fast days are on page 654. After the* תורה *is returned to the* ארון קודש, *the* שליח ציבור *says* חצי קדיש.

THE AMIDA

The following prayer, until "in former years" on page 250, is said silently, standing with feet together. If there is a minyan, the Amida is repeated aloud by the Leader. Take three steps forward and at the points indicated by ˅, bend the knees at the first word, bow at the second, and stand straight before saying God's name.

When I proclaim the LORD's name, give glory to our God. *Deut. 32*
O LORD, open my lips, so that my mouth may declare Your praise. *Ps. 51*

PATRIARCHS

˅בָּרוּךְ Blessed are You, LORD our God and God of our fathers,
God of Abraham, God of Isaac and God of Jacob;
the great, mighty and awesome God, God Most High,
who bestows acts of loving-kindness and creates all,
who remembers the loving-kindness of the fathers
and will bring a Redeemer to their children's children
for the sake of His name, in love.

Between Rosh HaShana & Yom Kippur: Remember us for life, O King who desires life,
and write us in the book of life –
for Your sake, O God of life.

King, Helper, Savior, Shield:
˅Blessed are You, LORD, Shield of Abraham.

DIVINE MIGHT

אַתָּה גִּבּוֹר You are eternally mighty, LORD.
You give life to the dead and have great power to save.

The phrase "He makes the wind blow and the rain fall" is added from Simḥat Torah until Pesaḥ. In Israel the phrase "He causes the dew to fall" is added from Pesaḥ until Shemini Atzeret. See laws 49–51.

In fall & winter: He makes the wind blow and the rain fall.
In Israel, in spring & summer: He causes the dew to fall.

"I am not a man of words … I am heavy of speech and tongue." Isaiah said, "I am a man of unclean lips." Jeremiah said, "I cannot speak for I am a child." So our first prayer is for divine help in the act of prayer itself.

עמידה

The following prayer, until קַדְמֹנִיּוֹת *on page 251, is said silently, standing with feet together. If there is a* מנין*, the* עמידה *is repeated aloud by the* שליח ציבור*. Take three steps forward and at the points indicated by* ׳*, bend the knees at the first word, bow at the second, and stand straight before saying God's name.*

כִּי שֵׁם יהוה אֶקְרָא, הָבוּ גֹדֶל לֵאלֹהֵינוּ: דברים לב

אֲדֹנָי, שְׂפָתַי תִּפְתָּח, וּפִי יַגִּיד תְּהִלָּתֶךָ: תהלים נא

אבות

׳בָּרוּךְ אַתָּה יהוה, אֱלֹהֵינוּ וֵאלֹהֵי אֲבוֹתֵינוּ
אֱלֹהֵי אַבְרָהָם, אֱלֹהֵי יִצְחָק, וֵאלֹהֵי יַעֲקֹב
הָאֵל הַגָּדוֹל הַגִּבּוֹר וְהַנּוֹרָא, אֵל עֶלְיוֹן
גּוֹמֵל חֲסָדִים טוֹבִים, וְקוֹנֵה הַכֹּל
וְזוֹכֵר חַסְדֵי אָבוֹת
וּמֵבִיא גוֹאֵל לִבְנֵי בְנֵיהֶם לְמַעַן שְׁמוֹ בְּאַהֲבָה.

בעשרת ימי תשובה: זָכְרֵנוּ לְחַיִּים, מֶלֶךְ חָפֵץ בַּחַיִּים
וְכָתְבֵנוּ בְּסֵפֶר הַחַיִּים, לְמַעַנְךָ אֱלֹהִים חַיִּים.

מֶלֶךְ עוֹזֵר וּמוֹשִׁיעַ וּמָגֵן.
׳בָּרוּךְ אַתָּה יהוה, מָגֵן אַבְרָהָם.

גבורות

אַתָּה גִּבּוֹר לְעוֹלָם, אֲדֹנָי
מְחַיֵּה מֵתִים אַתָּה, רַב לְהוֹשִׁיעַ

The phrase מַשִּׁיב הָרְוּחַ *is added from* שמחת תורה *until* פסח*.*
In ארץ ישראל *the phrase* מוֹרִיד הַטָּל *is added from* פסח *until* שמיני עצרת*. See laws 49–51.*

בחורף: מַשִּׁיב הָרְוּחַ וּמוֹרִיד הַגֶּשֶׁם / בארץ ישראל בקיץ: מוֹרִיד הַטָּל

אֲדֹנָי, שְׂפָתַי תִּפְתָּח *O Lord, open my lips:* Standing in the presence of God, we feel our inadequacy. The greatest of the prophets felt tongue-tied. Moses said,

He sustains the living with loving-kindness,
and with great compassion revives the dead.
He supports the fallen, heals the sick,
sets captives free,
and keeps His faith with those who sleep in the dust.
Who is like You, Master of might,
and to whom can You be compared,
O King who brings death and gives life,
and makes salvation grow?

Between Rosh HaShana & Yom Kippur: Who is like You, compassionate Father,
who remembers His creatures in compassion, for life?

Faithful are You to revive the dead.
Blessed are You, LORD, who revives the dead.

When saying the Amida silently, continue with "You are holy" on the next page.

KEDUSHA

During the Leader's Repetition, the following is said standing with feet together, rising on the toes at the words indicated by ▲.

Cong. then Leader: נְקַדֵּשׁ We will sanctify Your name on earth,
as they sanctify it in the highest heavens,
as is written by Your prophet,
"And they [the angels] call to one another saying: *Is. 6*

Cong. then Leader: ▲Holy, ▲holy, ▲holy is the LORD of hosts
the whole world is filled with His glory."
Those facing them say "Blessed – "

Cong. then Leader: ▲"Blessed is the LORD's glory from His place." *Ezek. 3*
And in Your holy Writings it is written thus:

Cong. then Leader: ▲"The LORD shall reign for ever. He is your God, Zion, *Ps. 146*
from generation to generation, Halleluya!"

Leader: From generation to generation we will declare Your greatness,
and we will proclaim Your holiness for evermore.
Your praise, our God, shall not leave our mouth forever,
for You, God, are a great and holy King. Blessed are You, LORD,
the holy God. / *Between Rosh HaShana & Yom Kippur:* the holy King./

The Leader continues with "You grace humanity" on the next page.

מְכַלְכֵּל חַיִּים בְּחֶסֶד, מְחַיֵּה מֵתִים בְּרַחֲמִים רַבִּים
סוֹמֵךְ נוֹפְלִים, וְרוֹפֵא חוֹלִים, וּמַתִּיר אֲסוּרִים
וּמְקַיֵּם אֱמוּנָתוֹ לִישֵׁנֵי עָפָר.
מִי כָמְוֹךָ, בַּעַל גְּבוּרוֹת
וּמִי דּוֹמֶה לָּךְ
מֶלֶךְ, מֵמִית וּמְחַיֶּה וּמַצְמִיחַ יְשׁוּעָה.

בעשרת ימי תשובה: מִי כָמְוֹךָ אַב הָרַחֲמִים
זוֹכֵר יְצוּרָיו לְחַיִּים בְּרַחֲמִים.

וְנֶאֱמָן אַתָּה לְהַחֲיוֹת מֵתִים.
בָּרוּךְ אַתָּה יהוה, מְחַיֵּה הַמֵּתִים.

When saying the עמידה silently, continue with אַתָּה קָדוֹשׁ on the next page.

קדושה

*During the חזרת הש״ץ, the following is said standing with feet together, rising on the toes at the words indicated by *.*

then קהל ש״ץ: נְקַדֵּשׁ אֶת שִׁמְךָ בָּעוֹלָם, כְּשֵׁם שֶׁמַּקְדִּישִׁים אוֹתוֹ בִּשְׁמֵי מָרוֹם
כַּכָּתוּב עַל יַד נְבִיאֶךָ: וְקָרָא זֶה אֶל־זֶה וְאָמַר ישעיה ו

then קהל ש״ץ: *קָדוֹשׁ, *קָדוֹשׁ, *קָדוֹשׁ, יהוה צְבָאוֹת, מְלֹא כָל־הָאָרֶץ כְּבוֹדוֹ:
לְעֻמָּתָם בָּרוּךְ יֹאמֵרוּ

then קהל ש״ץ: *בָּרוּךְ כְּבוֹד־יהוה מִמְּקוֹמוֹ: יחזקאל ג
וּבְדִבְרֵי קָדְשְׁךָ כָּתוּב לֵאמֹר

then קהל ש״ץ: *יִמְלֹךְ יהוה לְעוֹלָם, אֱלֹהַיִךְ צִיּוֹן לְדֹר וָדֹר, הַלְלוּיָהּ: תהלים קמו

ש״ץ: לְדוֹר וָדוֹר נַגִּיד גָּדְלֶךָ, וּלְנֵצַח נְצָחִים קְדֻשָּׁתְךָ נַקְדִּישׁ
וְשִׁבְחֲךָ אֱלֹהֵינוּ מִפִּינוּ לֹא יָמוּשׁ לְעוֹלָם וָעֶד
כִּי אֵל מֶלֶךְ גָּדוֹל וְקָדוֹשׁ אָתָּה.
בָּרוּךְ אַתָּה יהוה, הָאֵל הַקָּדוֹשׁ./ בעשרת ימי תשובה: הַמֶּלֶךְ הַקָּדוֹשׁ./

The שליח ציבור continues with אַתָּה חוֹנֵן on the next page.

HOLINESS

אַתָּה קָדוֹשׁ You are holy and Your name is holy,
and holy ones praise You daily, Selah!
Blessed are You, LORD,
the holy God. / *Between Rosh HaShana & Yom Kippur:* the holy King./
(If forgotten, repeat the Amida.)

KNOWLEDGE

אַתָּה חוֹנֵן You grace humanity with knowledge
and teach mortals understanding.
Grace us with the knowledge, understanding
and discernment that come from You.
Blessed are You, LORD,
who graciously grants knowledge.

REPENTANCE

הֲשִׁיבֵנוּ Bring us back, our Father, to Your Torah.
Draw us near, our King, to Your service.
Lead us back to You in perfect repentance.
Blessed are You, LORD,
who desires repentance.

FORGIVENESS

Strike the left side of the chest at °.

סְלַח לָנוּ Forgive us, our Father, for we have °sinned.
Pardon us, our King, for we have °transgressed;
for You pardon and forgive.
Blessed are You, LORD,
the gracious One who repeatedly forgives.

REDEMPTION

רְאֵה Look on our affliction, plead our cause,
and redeem us soon for Your name's sake,
for You are a powerful Redeemer.
Blessed are You, LORD,
the Redeemer of Israel.

קדושת השם

אַתָּה קָדוֹשׁ וְשִׁמְךָ קָדוֹשׁ
וּקְדוֹשִׁים בְּכָל יוֹם יְהַלְלוּךָ סֶּלָה.
בָּרוּךְ אַתָּה יהוה, הָאֵל הַקָּדוֹשׁ./ בעשרת ימי תשובה: הַמֶּלֶךְ הַקָּדוֹשׁ./
(*If forgotten, repeat the* עמידה.)

דעת

אַתָּה חוֹנֵן לְאָדָם דַּעַת, וּמְלַמֵּד לֶאֱנוֹשׁ בִּינָה.
חָנֵּנוּ מֵאִתְּךָ דֵּעָה בִּינָה וְהַשְׂכֵּל.
בָּרוּךְ אַתָּה יהוה, חוֹנֵן הַדָּעַת.

תשובה

הֲשִׁיבֵנוּ אָבִינוּ לְתוֹרָתֶךָ, וְקָרְבֵנוּ מַלְכֵּנוּ לַעֲבוֹדָתֶךָ
וְהַחֲזִירֵנוּ בִּתְשׁוּבָה שְׁלֵמָה לְפָנֶיךָ.
בָּרוּךְ אַתָּה יהוה, הָרוֹצֶה בִּתְשׁוּבָה.

סליחה

Strike the left side of the chest at °.

סְלַח לָנוּ אָבִינוּ כִּי °חָטָאנוּ
מְחַל לָנוּ מַלְכֵּנוּ כִּי °פָשָׁעְנוּ
כִּי מוֹחֵל וְסוֹלֵחַ אָתָּה.
בָּרוּךְ אַתָּה יהוה, חַנּוּן הַמַּרְבֶּה לִסְלֹחַ.

גאולה

רְאֵה בְעָנְיֵנוּ, וְרִיבָה רִיבֵנוּ
וּגְאָלֵנוּ מְהֵרָה לְמַעַן שְׁמֶךָ
כִּי גּוֹאֵל חָזָק אָתָּה.
בָּרוּךְ אַתָּה יהוה, גּוֹאֵל יִשְׂרָאֵל.

On fast days the Leader adds:

עֲנֵנוּ Answer us, Lord, answer us on our Fast Day, for we are in great distress. Look not at our wickedness. Do not hide Your face from us and do not ignore our plea. Be near to our cry; please let Your loving-kindness comfort us. Even before we call to You, answer us, as it is said, "Before they call, I will answer. *Is. 65*
While they are still speaking, I will hear." For You, Lord, are the One who answers in time of distress, redeems and rescues in all times of trouble and anguish. Blessed are You, Lord, who answers in time of distress.

HEALING

רְפָאֵנוּ Heal us, Lord, and we shall be healed.
Save us and we shall be saved,
for You are our praise.
Bring complete recovery for all our ailments,

The following prayer for a sick person may be said here:

May it be Your will, O Lord my God and God of my ancestors, that You speedily send a complete recovery from heaven, a healing of both soul and body, to the patient (*name*), son/daughter of (*mother's name*) among the other afflicted of Israel.

for You, God, King, are a faithful and compassionate Healer.
Blessed are You, Lord, Healer of the sick of His people Israel.

PROSPERITY

The phrase "Grant dew and rain as a blessing" is said from December 5th (in the year before a civil leap year, December 6th) until Pesaḥ. In Israel, it is said from the 7th of Marḥeshvan. The phrase "Grant blessing" is said from Ḥol HaMo'ed Pesaḥ until December 4th (in the year before a civil leap year, December 5th). In Israel it is said through the 6th of Marḥeshvan. See laws 52–54.

בָּרֵךְ Bless this year for us, Lord our God,
and all its types of produce for good.

In winter: Grant dew and rain as a blessing
In other seasons: Grant blessing

on the face of the earth,
and from its goodness satisfy us,
blessing our year as the best of years.
Blessed are You, Lord, who blesses the years.

On fast days the שליח ציבור *adds:*

עֲנֵנוּ יהוה עֲנֵנוּ בְּיוֹם צוֹם תַּעֲנִיתֵנוּ, כִּי בְצָרָה גְדוֹלָה אֲנָחְנוּ. אַל תֵּפֶן אֶל רִשְׁעֵנוּ, וְאַל תַּסְתֵּר פָּנֶיךָ מִמֶּנּוּ, וְאַל תִּתְעַלַּם מִתְּחִנָּתֵנוּ. הֱיֵה נָא קָרוֹב לְשַׁוְעָתֵנוּ, יְהִי נָא חַסְדְּךָ לְנַחֲמֵנוּ, טֶרֶם נִקְרָא אֵלֶיךָ עֲנֵנוּ, כַּדָּבָר שֶׁנֶּאֱמַר:
ישעיה סה וְהָיָה טֶרֶם יִקְרָאוּ וַאֲנִי אֶעֱנֶה, עוֹד הֵם מְדַבְּרִים וַאֲנִי אֶשְׁמָע: כִּי אַתָּה יהוה הָעוֹנֶה בְּעֵת צָרָה, פּוֹדֶה וּמַצִּיל בְּכָל עֵת צָרָה וְצוּקָה. בָּרוּךְ אַתָּה יהוה, הָעוֹנֶה בְּעֵת צָרָה.

רפואה

רְפָאֵנוּ יהוה וְנֵרָפֵא, הוֹשִׁיעֵנוּ וְנִוָּשֵׁעָה, כִּי תְהִלָּתֵנוּ אָתָּה וְהַעֲלֵה רְפוּאָה שְׁלֵמָה לְכָל מַכּוֹתֵינוּ

The following prayer for a sick person may be said here:

יְהִי רָצוֹן מִלְּפָנֶיךָ יהוה אֱלֹהַי וֵאלֹהֵי אֲבוֹתַי, שֶׁתִּשְׁלַח מְהֵרָה רְפוּאָה שְׁלֵמָה מִן הַשָּׁמַיִם רְפוּאַת הַנֶּפֶשׁ וּרְפוּאַת הַגּוּף לַחוֹלֶה/לַחוֹלָה *name of patient* בֶּן/בַּת *mother's name* בְּתוֹךְ שְׁאָר חוֹלֵי יִשְׂרָאֵל.

כִּי אֵל מֶלֶךְ רוֹפֵא נֶאֱמָן וְרַחֲמָן אָתָּה.
בָּרוּךְ אַתָּה יהוה, רוֹפֵא חוֹלֵי עַמּוֹ יִשְׂרָאֵל.

ברכת השנים

The phrase וְתֵן טַל וּמָטָר לִבְרָכָה *is said from December 5th (in the year before a civil leap year, December 6th) until* פסח*. In* ארץ ישראל*, it is said from* ז׳ מרחשון*. The phrase* וְתֵן בְּרָכָה *is said from* חול המועד פסח *until December 4th (in the year before a civil leap year, December 5th). In* ארץ ישראל *it is said through* ו׳ מרחשון*. See laws 52–54.*

בָּרֵךְ עָלֵינוּ יהוה אֱלֹהֵינוּ אֶת הַשָּׁנָה הַזֹּאת
וְאֶת כָּל מִינֵי תְבוּאָתָהּ, לְטוֹבָה
בחורף: **וְתֵן טַל וּמָטָר לִבְרָכָה** / בקיץ: **וְתֵן בְּרָכָה**
עַל פְּנֵי הָאֲדָמָה, וְשַׂבְּעֵנוּ מִטּוּבָהּ
וּבָרֵךְ שְׁנָתֵנוּ כַּשָּׁנִים הַטּוֹבוֹת.
בָּרוּךְ אַתָּה יהוה, מְבָרֵךְ הַשָּׁנִים.

INGATHERING OF EXILES

תְּקַע Sound the great shofar for our freedom,
raise high the banner to gather our exiles,
and gather us together from the four quarters of the earth.
Blessed are You, LORD,
who gathers the dispersed of His people Israel.

JUSTICE

הָשִׁיבָה Restore our judges as at first,
and our counselors as at the beginning,
and remove from us sorrow and sighing.
May You alone, LORD,
reign over us with loving-kindness and compassion,
and vindicate us in justice.
Blessed are You, LORD,
the King who loves righteousness and justice.
/ *Between Rosh HaShana & Yom Kippur, end the blessing:* the King of justice./

AGAINST INFORMERS

וְלַמַּלְשִׁינִים For the slanderers let there be no hope,
and may all wickedness perish in an instant.
May all Your people's enemies swiftly be cut down.
May You swiftly uproot, crush, cast down
and humble the arrogant swiftly in our days.
Blessed are You, LORD,
who destroys enemies and humbles the arrogant.

THE RIGHTEOUS

עַל הַצַּדִּיקִים To the righteous, the pious,
the elders of Your people the house of Israel,
the remnant of their scholars,
the righteous converts, and to us,
may Your compassion be aroused, LORD our God.

קבוץ גלויות

תְּקַע בְּשׁוֹפָר גָּדוֹל לְחֵרוּתֵנוּ
וְשָׂא נֵס לְקַבֵּץ גָּלֻיּוֹתֵינוּ
וְקַבְּצֵנוּ יַחַד מֵאַרְבַּע כַּנְפוֹת הָאָרֶץ.
בָּרוּךְ אַתָּה יהוה, מְקַבֵּץ נִדְחֵי עַמּוֹ יִשְׂרָאֵל.

השבת המשפט

הָשִׁיבָה שׁוֹפְטֵינוּ כְּבָרִאשׁוֹנָה וְיוֹעֲצֵינוּ כְּבַתְּחִלָּה
וְהָסֵר מִמֶּנּוּ יָגוֹן וַאֲנָחָה
וּמְלֹךְ עָלֵינוּ אַתָּה יהוה לְבַדְּךָ בְּחֶסֶד וּבְרַחֲמִים
וְצַדְּקֵנוּ בַּמִּשְׁפָּט.
בָּרוּךְ אַתָּה יהוה
מֶלֶךְ אוֹהֵב צְדָקָה וּמִשְׁפָּט. / בעשרת ימי תשובה: הַמֶּלֶךְ הַמִּשְׁפָּט./

ברכת המינים

וְלַמַּלְשִׁינִים אַל תְּהִי תִקְוָה, וְכָל הָרִשְׁעָה כְּרֶגַע תֹּאבֵד
וְכָל אוֹיְבֵי עַמְּךָ מְהֵרָה יִכָּרֵתוּ
וְהַזֵּדִים מְהֵרָה תְעַקֵּר וּתְשַׁבֵּר וּתְמַגֵּר וְתַכְנִיעַ בִּמְהֵרָה בְיָמֵינוּ.
בָּרוּךְ אַתָּה יהוה, שׁוֹבֵר אוֹיְבִים וּמַכְנִיעַ זֵדִים.

על הצדיקים

עַל הַצַּדִּיקִים וְעַל הַחֲסִידִים
וְעַל זִקְנֵי עַמְּךָ בֵּית יִשְׂרָאֵל
וְעַל פְּלֵיטַת סוֹפְרֵיהֶם
וְעַל גֵּרֵי הַצֶּדֶק, וְעָלֵינוּ
יֶהֱמוּ רַחֲמֶיךָ יהוה אֱלֹהֵינוּ

Grant a good reward to all who sincerely trust in Your name.
Set our lot with them,
so that we may never be ashamed, for in You we trust.
Blessed are You, Lord,
who is the support and trust of the righteous.

REBUILDING JERUSALEM

וְלִירוּשָׁלַיִם To Jerusalem, Your city, may You return in compassion,
and may You dwell in it as You promised.
May You rebuild it rapidly in our days as an everlasting structure,
and install within it soon the throne of David.
*Blessed are You, Lord,
who builds Jerusalem.

**On Tisha B'Av all conclude as follows:*

נַחֵם Console, O Lord our God, the mourners of Zion and the mourners of Jerusalem, and the city that is in sorrow, laid waste, scorned and desolate; that grieves for the loss of its children, that is laid waste of its dwellings, robbed of its glory, desolate without inhabitants. She sits with her head covered like a barren childless woman. Legions have devoured her; idolaters have taken possession of her; they have put Your people Israel to the sword and deliberately killed the devoted followers of the Most High. Therefore Zion weeps bitterly, and Jerusalem raises her voice. My heart, my heart grieves for those they killed; I am in anguish, I am in anguish for those they killed. For You, O Lord, consumed it with fire, and with fire You will rebuild it in the future, as is said, "And I Myself will be a wall of fire around it, says the Lord, *Zech. 2*
and I will be its glory within." Blessed are You, Lord, who consoles Zion and rebuilds Jerusalem.

Continue with "May the offshoot" below.

KINGDOM OF DAVID

אֶת צֶמַח May the offshoot of Your servant David soon flower,
and may his pride be raised high by Your salvation,
for we wait for Your salvation all day.
Blessed are You, Lord,
who makes the glory of salvation flourish.

וְתֵן שָׂכָר טוֹב לְכָל הַבּוֹטְחִים בְּשִׁמְךָ בֶּאֱמֶת
וְשִׂים חֶלְקֵנוּ עִמָּהֶם
וּלְעוֹלָם לֹא נֵבוֹשׁ כִּי בְךָ בָּטָחְנוּ.
בָּרוּךְ אַתָּה יהוה, מִשְׁעָן וּמִבְטָח לַצַּדִּיקִים.

בניין ירושלים
וְלִירוּשָׁלַיִם עִירְךָ בְּרַחֲמִים תָּשׁוּב
וְתִשְׁכֹּן בְּתוֹכָהּ כַּאֲשֶׁר דִּבַּרְתָּ
וּבְנֵה אוֹתָהּ בְּקָרוֹב בְּיָמֵינוּ בִּנְיַן עוֹלָם
וְכִסֵּא דָוִד מְהֵרָה לְתוֹכָהּ תָּכִין.
*בָּרוּךְ אַתָּה יהוה, בּוֹנֵה יְרוּשָׁלָיִם.

**On תשעה באב, all conclude as follows:*

נַחֵם יהוה אֱלֹהֵינוּ אֶת אֲבֵלֵי צִיּוֹן וְאֶת אֲבֵלֵי יְרוּשָׁלָיִם, וְאֶת הָעִיר הָאֲבֵלָה וְהֶחֲרֵבָה וְהַבְּזוּיָה וְהַשּׁוֹמֵמָה. הָאֲבֵלָה מִבְּלִי בָנֶיהָ, וְהֶחֲרֵבָה מִמְּעוֹנוֹתֶיהָ, וְהַבְּזוּיָה מִכְּבוֹדָהּ, וְהַשּׁוֹמֵמָה מֵאֵין יוֹשֵׁב. וְהִיא יוֹשֶׁבֶת וְרֹאשָׁהּ חָפוּי, כְּאִשָּׁה עֲקָרָה שֶׁלֹּא יָלָדָה. וַיְבַלְּעוּהָ לִגְיוֹנוֹת, וַיִּירָשׁוּהָ עוֹבְדֵי פְסִילִים, וַיָּטִילוּ אֶת עַמְּךָ יִשְׂרָאֵל לֶחָרֶב, וַיַּהַרְגוּ בְזָדוֹן חֲסִידֵי עֶלְיוֹן. עַל כֵּן צִיּוֹן בְּמַר תִּבְכֶּה, וִירוּשָׁלַיִם תִּתֵּן קוֹלָהּ. לִבִּי לִבִּי עַל חַלְלֵיהֶם, מֵעַי מֵעַי עַל חַלְלֵיהֶם, כִּי אַתָּה
יהוה בָּאֵשׁ הִצַּתָּהּ, וּבָאֵשׁ אַתָּה עָתִיד לִבְנוֹתָהּ. כָּאָמוּר: וַאֲנִי אֶהְיֶה־לָּהּ, זכריה ב
נְאֻם־יהוה, חוֹמַת אֵשׁ סָבִיב, וּלְכָבוֹד אֶהְיֶה בְתוֹכָהּ: בָּרוּךְ אַתָּה יהוה, מְנַחֵם צִיּוֹן וּבוֹנֵה יְרוּשָׁלָיִם.

Continue with אֶת צֶמַח *below.*

משיח בן דוד
אֶת צֶמַח דָּוִד עַבְדְּךָ מְהֵרָה תַצְמִיחַ
וְקַרְנוֹ תָּרוּם בִּישׁוּעָתֶךָ, כִּי לִישׁוּעָתְךָ קִוִּינוּ כָּל הַיּוֹם.
בָּרוּךְ אַתָּה יהוה, מַצְמִיחַ קֶרֶן יְשׁוּעָה.

RESPONSE TO PRAYER

שְׁמַע קוֹלֵנוּ Listen to our voice, LORD our God.
Spare us and have compassion on us,
and in compassion and favor accept our prayer,
for You, God, listen to prayers and pleas.
Do not turn us away, O our King,
empty-handed from Your presence,*
for You listen with compassion
to the prayer of Your people Israel.
Blessed are You, LORD, who listens to prayer.

**At this point on fast days, the congregation adds "Answer us" below.*
In times of drought in Israel, say "And answer us" on page 124.

עֲנֵנוּ Answer us, LORD, answer us on our Fast Day, for we are in great distress. Look not at our wickedness. Do not hide Your face from us and do not ignore our plea. Be near to our cry; please let Your loving-kindness comfort us. Even before we call to You, answer us, as is said, "Before they call, I will answer. While they are still speaking, I will hear." For You, LORD, are the One who answers in time of distress, redeems and rescues in all times of trouble and anguish.

Continue with "for You listen" above.

TEMPLE SERVICE

רְצֵה Find favor, LORD our God,
in Your people Israel and their prayer.
Restore the service to Your most holy House,
and accept in love and favor
the fire-offerings of Israel and their prayer.
May the service of Your people Israel always find favor with You.

On Rosh Ḥodesh, say:

אֱלֹהֵינוּ Our God and God of our ancestors, may there rise, come, reach, appear, be favored, heard, regarded and remembered before You, our recollection and remembrance, as well as the remembrance of our ancestors, and of the Messiah son of David Your servant, and of Jerusalem Your holy city, and of all Your people the house of Israel – for deliverance and

שומע תפלה

שְׁמַע קוֹלֵנוּ יהוה אֱלֹהֵינוּ
חוּס וְרַחֵם עָלֵינוּ
וְקַבֵּל בְּרַחֲמִים וּבְרָצוֹן אֶת תְּפִלָּתֵנוּ
כִּי אֵל שׁוֹמֵעַ תְּפִלּוֹת וְתַחֲנוּנִים אָתָּה
וּמִלְּפָנֶיךָ מַלְכֵּנוּ רֵיקָם אַל תְּשִׁיבֵנוּ*
כִּי אַתָּה שׁוֹמֵעַ תְּפִלַּת עַמְּךָ יִשְׂרָאֵל בְּרַחֲמִים.
בָּרוּךְ אַתָּה יהוה, שׁוֹמֵעַ תְּפִלָּה.

**At this point on fast days, the* קהל *adds* עֲנֵנוּ *below.*
In times of drought in ארץ ישראל*, say* וַעֲנֵנוּ *on page 125.*

עֲנֵנוּ יהוה עֲנֵנוּ בְּיוֹם צוֹם תַּעֲנִיתֵנוּ, כִּי בְצָרָה גְדוֹלָה אֲנָחְנוּ. אַל תֵּפֶן אֶל רִשְׁעֵנוּ, וְאַל תַּסְתֵּר פָּנֶיךָ מִמֶּנּוּ, וְאַל תִּתְעַלַּם מִתְּחִנָּתֵנוּ. הֱיֵה נָא קָרוֹב לְשַׁוְעָתֵנוּ, יְהִי נָא חַסְדְּךָ לְנַחֲמֵנוּ, טֶרֶם נִקְרָא אֵלֶיךָ עֲנֵנוּ, כַּדָּבָר שֶׁנֶּאֱמַר: וְהָיָה טֶרֶם יִקְרָאוּ וַאֲנִי אֶעֱנֶה, עוֹד הֵם מְדַבְּרִים וַאֲנִי אֶשְׁמָע: כִּי אַתָּה יהוה הָעוֹנֶה בְּעֵת צָרָה, פּוֹדֶה וּמַצִּיל בְּכָל עֵת צָרָה וְצוּקָה.

Continue with כִּי אַתָּה שׁוֹמֵעַ *above.*

עבודה

רְצֵה יהוה אֱלֹהֵינוּ בְּעַמְּךָ יִשְׂרָאֵל, וּבִתְפִלָּתָם
וְהָשֵׁב אֶת הָעֲבוֹדָה לִדְבִיר בֵּיתֶךָ
וְאִשֵּׁי יִשְׂרָאֵל וּתְפִלָּתָם בְּאַהֲבָה תְקַבֵּל בְּרָצוֹן
וּתְהִי לְרָצוֹן תָּמִיד עֲבוֹדַת יִשְׂרָאֵל עַמֶּךָ.

On ראש חודש*, say:*

אֱלֹהֵינוּ וֵאלֹהֵי אֲבוֹתֵינוּ, יַעֲלֶה וְיָבוֹא וְיַגִּיעַ, וְיֵרָאֶה וְיֵרָצֶה וְיִשָּׁמַע, וְיִפָּקֵד וְיִזָּכֵר זִכְרוֹנֵנוּ וּפִקְדוֹנֵנוּ וְזִכְרוֹן אֲבוֹתֵינוּ, וְזִכְרוֹן מָשִׁיחַ בֶּן דָּוִד עַבְדֶּךָ, וְזִכְרוֹן יְרוּשָׁלַיִם עִיר קָדְשֶׁךָ, וְזִכְרוֹן כָּל עַמְּךָ

well-being, grace, loving-kindness and compassion, life and peace, on this day of Rosh Ḥodesh. On it remember us, LORD our God, for good; recollect us for blessing, and deliver us for life. In accord with Your promise of salvation and compassion, spare us and be gracious to us; have compassion on us and deliver us, for our eyes are turned to You because You, God, are a gracious and compassionate King.

וְתֶחֱזֶינָה And may our eyes witness Your return
to Zion in compassion.
Blessed are You, LORD, who restores His Presence to Zion.

THANKSGIVING

Bow at the first nine words.

מוֹדִים We give thanks to You,
for You are the LORD our God
and God of our ancestors
for ever and all time.
You are the Rock of our lives,
Shield of our salvation
from generation to generation.
We will thank You and
declare Your praise for our lives,
which are entrusted into Your hand;
for our souls,
which are placed in Your charge;
for Your miracles
which are with us every day;
and for Your wonders and favors
at all times, evening,
morning and midday.
You are good –
for Your compassion never fails.
You are compassionate –
for Your loving-kindnesses never cease.
We have always placed our hope in You.

During the Leader's Repetition, the congregation says quietly:

מוֹדִים We give thanks to You,
for You are the LORD our God
and God of our ancestors,
God of all flesh,
who formed us
and formed the universe.
Blessings and thanks
are due to Your great
and holy name for giving us
life and sustaining us.
May You continue
to give us life
and sustain us;
and may You gather our
exiles to Your holy courts,
to keep Your decrees,
do Your will and serve You
with a perfect heart,
for it is for us
to give You thanks.
Blessed be God to whom
thanksgiving is due.

בֵּית יִשְׂרָאֵל, לְפָנֶיךָ, לִפְלֵיטָה לְטוֹבָה, לְחֵן וּלְחֶסֶד וּלְרַחֲמִים, לְחַיִּים וּלְשָׁלוֹם בְּיוֹם רֹאשׁ הַחֹדֶשׁ הַזֶּה. זָכְרֵנוּ יהוה אֱלֹהֵינוּ בּוֹ לְטוֹבָה, וּפָקְדֵנוּ בוֹ לִבְרָכָה, וְהוֹשִׁיעֵנוּ בוֹ לְחַיִּים. וּבִדְבַר יְשׁוּעָה וְרַחֲמִים, חוּס וְחָנֵּנוּ וְרַחֵם עָלֵינוּ וְהוֹשִׁיעֵנוּ, כִּי אֵלֶיךָ עֵינֵינוּ, כִּי אֵל מֶלֶךְ חַנּוּן וְרַחוּם אָתָּה.

וְתֶחֱזֶינָה עֵינֵינוּ בְּשׁוּבְךָ לְצִיּוֹן בְּרַחֲמִים.
בָּרוּךְ אַתָּה יהוה, הַמַּחֲזִיר שְׁכִינָתוֹ לְצִיּוֹן.

הודאה

Bow at the first five words.

ˈמוֹדִים אֲנַחְנוּ לָךְ
שָׁאַתָּה הוּא יהוה אֱלֹהֵינוּ
וֵאלֹהֵי אֲבוֹתֵינוּ לְעוֹלָם וָעֶד.
צוּר חַיֵּינוּ, מָגֵן יִשְׁעֵנוּ
אַתָּה הוּא לְדוֹר וָדוֹר.
נוֹדֶה לְּךָ וּנְסַפֵּר תְּהִלָּתֶךָ
עַל חַיֵּינוּ הַמְּסוּרִים בְּיָדֶךָ
וְעַל נִשְׁמוֹתֵינוּ הַפְּקוּדוֹת לָךְ
וְעַל נִסֶּיךָ שֶׁבְּכָל יוֹם עִמָּנוּ
וְעַל נִפְלְאוֹתֶיךָ וְטוֹבוֹתֶיךָ
שֶׁבְּכָל עֵת
עֶרֶב וָבֹקֶר וְצָהֳרָיִם.
הַטּוֹב, כִּי לֹא כָלוּ רַחֲמֶיךָ
וְהַמְרַחֵם, כִּי לֹא תַמּוּ חֲסָדֶיךָ
מֵעוֹלָם קִוִּינוּ לָךְ.

During the חזרת הש״ץ, *the* קהל *says quietly:*

ˈמוֹדִים אֲנַחְנוּ לָךְ
שָׁאַתָּה הוּא יהוה אֱלֹהֵינוּ
וֵאלֹהֵי אֲבוֹתֵינוּ
אֱלֹהֵי כָל בָּשָׂר
יוֹצְרֵנוּ, יוֹצֵר בְּרֵאשִׁית.
בְּרָכוֹת וְהוֹדָאוֹת
לְשִׁמְךָ הַגָּדוֹל וְהַקָּדוֹשׁ
עַל שֶׁהֶחֱיִיתָנוּ וְקִיַּמְתָּנוּ.
כֵּן תְּחַיֵּנוּ וּתְקַיְּמֵנוּ
וְתֶאֱסֹף גָּלֻיּוֹתֵינוּ
לְחַצְרוֹת קָדְשֶׁךָ
לִשְׁמֹר חֻקֶּיךָ
וְלַעֲשׂוֹת רְצוֹנֶךָ וּלְעָבְדְּךָ
בְּלֵבָב שָׁלֵם
עַל שֶׁאֲנַחְנוּ מוֹדִים לָךְ.
בָּרוּךְ אֵל הַהוֹדָאוֹת.

On Ḥanukka:

עַל הַנִּסִּים [We thank You also] for the miracles, the redemption, the mighty deeds, the salvations, and the victories in battle which You performed for our ancestors in those days, at this time.

בִּימֵי מַתִּתְיָהוּ In the days of Mattityahu, son of Yoḥanan, the High Priest, the Hasmonean, and his sons, the wicked Greek kingdom rose up against Your people Israel to make them forget Your Torah and to force them to transgress the statutes of Your will. It was then that You in Your great compassion stood by them in the time of their distress. You championed their cause, judged their claim, and avenged their wrong. You delivered the strong into the hands of the weak, the many into the hands of the few, the impure into the hands of the pure, the wicked into the hands of the righteous, and the arrogant into the hands of those who were engaged in the study of Your Torah. You made for Yourself great and holy renown in Your world, and for Your people Israel You performed a great salvation and redemption as of this very day. Your children then entered the holiest part of Your House, cleansed Your Temple, purified Your Sanctuary, kindled lights in Your holy courts, and designated these eight days of Ḥanukka for giving thanks and praise to Your great name.

Continue with "For all these things."

On Purim:

עַל הַנִּסִּים [We thank You also] for the miracles, the redemption, the mighty deeds, the salvations, and the victories in battle which You performed for our ancestors in those days, at this time.

בִּימֵי מָרְדְּכַי In the days of Mordekhai and Esther, in Shushan the capital, the wicked Haman rose up against them and sought to destroy, slay and exterminate *Esther 3* all the Jews, young and old, children and women, on one day, the thirteenth day of the twelfth month, which is the month of Adar, and to plunder their possessions. Then You in Your great compassion thwarted his counsel, frustrated his plans, and caused his scheme to recoil on his own head, so that they hanged him and his sons on the gallows.

Continue with "For all these things."

וְעַל כֻּלָּם For all these things may Your name be blessed and exalted, our King, continually, for ever and all time.

Between Rosh HaShana & Yom Kippur: And write, for a good life,
all the children of Your covenant.

Let all that lives thank You, Selah! and praise Your name in truth,
God, our Savior and Help, Selah!
▾Blessed are You, LORD, whose name is "the Good"
and to whom thanks are due.

בחנוכה:

עַל הַנִּסִּים וְעַל הַפֻּרְקָן וְעַל הַגְּבוּרוֹת וְעַל הַתְּשׁוּעוֹת וְעַל הַמִּלְחָמוֹת שֶׁעָשִׂיתָ לַאֲבוֹתֵינוּ בַּיָּמִים הָהֵם בַּזְּמַן הַזֶּה.

בִּימֵי מַתִּתְיָהוּ בֶּן יוֹחָנָן כֹּהֵן גָּדוֹל חַשְׁמוֹנַאי וּבָנָיו, כְּשֶׁעָמְדָה מַלְכוּת יָוָן הָרְשָׁעָה עַל עַמְּךָ יִשְׂרָאֵל לְהַשְׁכִּיחָם תּוֹרָתֶךָ וּלְהַעֲבִירָם מֵחֻקֵּי רְצוֹנֶךָ, וְאַתָּה בְּרַחֲמֶיךָ הָרַבִּים עָמַדְתָּ לָהֶם בְּעֵת צָרָתָם, רַבְתָּ אֶת רִיבָם, דַּנְתָּ אֶת דִּינָם, נָקַמְתָּ אֶת נִקְמָתָם, מָסַרְתָּ גִבּוֹרִים בְּיַד חַלָּשִׁים, וְרַבִּים בְּיַד מְעַטִּים, וּטְמֵאִים בְּיַד טְהוֹרִים, וּרְשָׁעִים בְּיַד צַדִּיקִים, וְזֵדִים בְּיַד עוֹסְקֵי תוֹרָתֶךָ, וּלְךָ עָשִׂיתָ שֵׁם גָּדוֹל וְקָדוֹשׁ בְּעוֹלָמֶךָ, וּלְעַמְּךָ יִשְׂרָאֵל עָשִׂיתָ תְּשׁוּעָה גְדוֹלָה וּפֻרְקָן כְּהַיּוֹם הַזֶּה. וְאַחַר כֵּן בָּאוּ בָנֶיךָ לִדְבִיר בֵּיתֶךָ, וּפִנּוּ אֶת הֵיכָלֶךָ, וְטִהֲרוּ אֶת מִקְדָּשֶׁךָ, וְהִדְלִיקוּ נֵרוֹת בְּחַצְרוֹת קָדְשֶׁךָ, וְקָבְעוּ שְׁמוֹנַת יְמֵי חֲנֻכָּה אֵלּוּ, לְהוֹדוֹת וּלְהַלֵּל לְשִׁמְךָ הַגָּדוֹל.

Continue with וְעַל כֻּלָּם.

בפורים:

עַל הַנִּסִּים וְעַל הַפֻּרְקָן וְעַל הַגְּבוּרוֹת וְעַל הַתְּשׁוּעוֹת וְעַל הַמִּלְחָמוֹת שֶׁעָשִׂיתָ לַאֲבוֹתֵינוּ בַּיָּמִים הָהֵם בַּזְּמַן הַזֶּה.

בִּימֵי מָרְדְּכַי וְאֶסְתֵּר בְּשׁוּשַׁן הַבִּירָה, כְּשֶׁעָמַד עֲלֵיהֶם הָמָן הָרָשָׁע, בִּקֵּשׁ
לְהַשְׁמִיד לַהֲרֹג וּלְאַבֵּד אֶת־כָּל־הַיְּהוּדִים מִנַּעַר וְעַד־זָקֵן טַף וְנָשִׁים בְּיוֹם אסתר ג
אֶחָד, בִּשְׁלוֹשָׁה עָשָׂר לְחֹדֶשׁ שְׁנֵים־עָשָׂר, הוּא־חֹדֶשׁ אֲדָר, וּשְׁלָלָם
לָבוֹז: וְאַתָּה בְּרַחֲמֶיךָ הָרַבִּים הֵפַרְתָּ אֶת עֲצָתוֹ, וְקִלְקַלְתָּ אֶת מַחֲשַׁבְתּוֹ, וַהֲשֵׁבוֹתָ לּוֹ גְּמוּלוֹ בְּרֹאשׁוֹ, וְתָלוּ אוֹתוֹ וְאֶת בָּנָיו עַל הָעֵץ.

Continue with וְעַל כֻּלָּם.

וְעַל כֻּלָּם יִתְבָּרַךְ וְיִתְרוֹמַם שִׁמְךָ מַלְכֵּנוּ תָּמִיד לְעוֹלָם וָעֶד.

בעשרת ימי תשובה: וּכְתֹב לְחַיִּים טוֹבִים כָּל בְּנֵי בְרִיתֶךָ.

וְכֹל הַחַיִּים יוֹדְוּךָ סֶּלָה, וִיהַלְלוּ אֶת שִׁמְךָ בֶּאֱמֶת
הָאֵל יְשׁוּעָתֵנוּ וְעֶזְרָתֵנוּ סֶלָה.

בָּרוּךְ אַתָּה יהוה, הַטּוֹב שִׁמְךָ וּלְךָ נָאֶה לְהוֹדוֹת.

On public fast days only, the following is said by the Leader during the Repetition of the Amida, except in a house of mourning. In Israel, on Fast Days, if Kohanim bless the congregation, turn to page 386. See laws 62–69.

Our God and God of our fathers, bless us with the threefold blessing in the Torah, written by the hand of Moses Your servant and pronounced by Aaron and his sons the priests, Your holy people, as it is said:

May the LORD bless you and protect you. *Cong:* May it be Your will. *Num. 6*
May the LORD make His face shine on you
and be gracious to you. *Cong:* May it be Your will.
May the LORD turn His face toward you,
and grant you peace. *Cong:* May it be Your will.

PEACE

שָׁלוֹם רָב Grant great peace to Your people Israel for ever, for You are the sovereign LORD of all peace; and may it be good in Your eyes to bless Your people Israel at every time, at every hour, with Your peace.

On fast days:
שִׂים שָׁלוֹם Grant peace,
goodness and blessing,
grace, loving-kindness and compassion
to us and all Israel Your people.
Bless us, our Father, all as one,
with the light of Your face,
for by the light of Your face
You have given us, LORD our God,
the Torah of life and love of kindness,
righteousness, blessing, compassion,
life and peace.
May it be good in Your eyes
to bless Your people Israel
at every time, in every hour,
with Your peace.

Between Rosh HaShana & Yom Kippur: In the book of life, blessing, peace and prosperity, may we and all Your people the house of Israel be remembered and written before You for a good life, and for peace.*

Blessed are You, LORD, who blesses His people Israel with peace.

**Between Rosh HaShana and Yom Kippur outside Israel, many end the blessing:*

Blessed are You, LORD, who makes peace.

The following verse concludes the Leader's Repetition of the Amida. Some also say it here as part of the silent Amida. See law 60.

May the words of my mouth and the meditation of my heart *Ps. 19*
find favor before You, LORD, my Rock and Redeemer.

On public fast days only, the following is said by the שליח ציבור *during the* חזרת הש״ץ *except in a house of mourning. In* ארץ ישראל*, on Fast Days, if* כהנים *say* ברכת כהנים *turn to page 387. See laws 62–69.*

אֱלֹהֵינוּ וֵאלֹהֵי אֲבוֹתֵינוּ, בָּרְכֵנוּ בַּבְּרָכָה הַמְשֻׁלֶּשֶׁת בַּתּוֹרָה, הַכְּתוּבָה עַל יְדֵי מֹשֶׁה עַבְדֶּךָ, הָאֲמוּרָה מִפִּי אַהֲרֹן וּבָנָיו כֹּהֲנִים עַם קְדוֹשֶׁךָ, כָּאָמוּר

במדבר ו יְבָרֶכְךָ יהוה וְיִשְׁמְרֶךָ: קהל: כֵּן יְהִי רָצוֹן

יָאֵר יהוה פָּנָיו אֵלֶיךָ וִיחֻנֶּךָּ: קהל: כֵּן יְהִי רָצוֹן

יִשָּׂא יהוה פָּנָיו אֵלֶיךָ וְיָשֵׂם לְךָ שָׁלוֹם: קהל: כֵּן יְהִי רָצוֹן

ברכת שלום

שָׁלוֹם רָב עַל יִשְׂרָאֵל
עַמְּךָ תָּשִׂים לְעוֹלָם
כִּי אַתָּה הוּא
מֶלֶךְ אָדוֹן לְכָל הַשָּׁלוֹם.
וְטוֹב בְּעֵינֶיךָ
לְבָרֵךְ אֶת עַמְּךָ יִשְׂרָאֵל
בְּכָל עֵת וּבְכָל שָׁעָה
בִּשְׁלוֹמֶךָ.

On fast days:

שִׂים שָׁלוֹם טוֹבָה וּבְרָכָה
חֵן וָחֶסֶד וְרַחֲמִים
עָלֵינוּ וְעַל כָּל יִשְׂרָאֵל עַמֶּךָ.
בָּרְכֵנוּ אָבִינוּ כֻּלָּנוּ כְּאֶחָד בְּאוֹר פָּנֶיךָ
כִּי בְאוֹר פָּנֶיךָ נָתַתָּ לָּנוּ יהוה אֱלֹהֵינוּ
תּוֹרַת חַיִּים וְאַהֲבַת חֶסֶד
וּצְדָקָה וּבְרָכָה וְרַחֲמִים וְחַיִּים וְשָׁלוֹם.
וְטוֹב בְּעֵינֶיךָ לְבָרֵךְ אֶת עַמְּךָ יִשְׂרָאֵל
בְּכָל עֵת וּבְכָל שָׁעָה בִּשְׁלוֹמֶךָ.

בעשרת ימי תשובה: בְּסֵפֶר חַיִּים, בְּרָכָה וְשָׁלוֹם, וּפַרְנָסָה טוֹבָה
נִזָּכֵר וְנִכָּתֵב לְפָנֶיךָ, אֲנַחְנוּ וְכָל עַמְּךָ בֵּית יִשְׂרָאֵל
לְחַיִּים טוֹבִים וּלְשָׁלוֹם.*

בָּרוּךְ אַתָּה יהוה, הַמְבָרֵךְ אֶת עַמּוֹ יִשְׂרָאֵל בַּשָּׁלוֹם.

*During the עשרת ימי תשובה in חוץ לארץ, many end the blessing:

בָּרוּךְ אַתָּה יהוה, עוֹשֵׂה הַשָּׁלוֹם.

The following verse concludes the חזרת הש״ץ.
Some also say it here as part of the silent עמידה. *See law 60.*

תהלים יט יִהְיוּ לְרָצוֹן אִמְרֵי־פִי וְהֶגְיוֹן לִבִּי לְפָנֶיךָ, יהוה צוּרִי וְגֹאֲלִי:

אֱלֹהַי My God, *Berakhot 17a*
guard my tongue from evil and my lips from deceitful speech.
To those who curse me, let my soul be silent;
may my soul be to all like the dust.
Open my heart to Your Torah and let my soul
pursue Your commandments. As for all who plan evil against me,
swiftly thwart their counsel and frustrate their plans.
Act for the sake of Your name; act for the sake of Your right hand;
act for the sake of Your holiness; act for the sake of Your Torah.
That Your beloved ones may be delivered, *Ps. 60*
save with Your right hand and answer me.
*May the words of my mouth and the meditation of my heart *Ps. 19*
find favor before You, LORD, my Rock and Redeemer.

Bow, take three steps back, then bow, first left, then right, then center, while saying:

May He who makes peace in His high places,
make peace for us and all Israel – and say: Amen.

יְהִי רָצוֹן May it be Your will, LORD our God and God of our ancestors,
that the Temple be rebuilt speedily in our days,
and grant us a share in Your Torah.
And there we will serve You with reverence,
as in the days of old and as in former years.
Then the offering of Judah and Jerusalem will be pleasing to the LORD *Mal. 3*
as in the days of old and as in former years.

On days when Taḥanun is not said, the Leader says Full Kaddish on page 254.

**A person undertaking a personal fast says the following at Minḥa before the fast:*

Master of all worlds, I hereby take upon myself before You a voluntary fast tomorrow. May it be Your will, LORD my God and God of my ancestors, that You accept me in love and favor, that my prayer may come before You, and that You may answer my entreaty in Your great compassion, for You hear the prayer of every mouth.

On the afternoon of the fast, the following is said:

Master of all worlds, it is revealed and known to You that when the Temple stood, a person who sinned would offer a sacrifice, of which were offered only the fat and blood, yet You in Your great compassion granted atonement. Now I have fasted, and my fat and blood have been diminished. May it be Your will that this diminution today of my fat and blood be as if I had offered them before You on the altar, and may You show me favor.

ברכות יז.

אֱלֹהַי

נְצֹר לְשׁוֹנִי מֵרָע וּשְׂפָתַי מִדַּבֵּר מִרְמָה

וְלִמְקַלְלַי נַפְשִׁי תִדֹּם, וְנַפְשִׁי כֶּעָפָר לַכֹּל תִּהְיֶה.

פְּתַח לִבִּי בְּתוֹרָתֶךָ, וּבְמִצְוֹתֶיךָ תִּרְדֹּף נַפְשִׁי.

וְכָל הַחוֹשְׁבִים עָלַי רָעָה

מְהֵרָה הָפֵר עֲצָתָם וְקַלְקֵל מַחֲשַׁבְתָּם.

עֲשֵׂה לְמַעַן שְׁמֶךָ, עֲשֵׂה לְמַעַן יְמִינֶךָ

עֲשֵׂה לְמַעַן קְדֻשָּׁתֶךָ, עֲשֵׂה לְמַעַן תּוֹרָתֶךָ.

תהלים ס

לְמַעַן יֵחָלְצוּן יְדִידֶיךָ, הוֹשִׁיעָה יְמִינְךָ וַעֲנֵנִי:

תהלים יט

*יִהְיוּ לְרָצוֹן אִמְרֵי־פִי וְהֶגְיוֹן לִבִּי לְפָנֶיךָ, יהוה צוּרִי וְגוֹאֲלִי:

Bow, take three steps back, then bow, first left, then right, then center, while saying:

עֹשֶׂה שָׁלוֹם/ בעשרת ימי תשובה: הַשָּׁלוֹם/ בִּמְרוֹמָיו

הוּא יַעֲשֶׂה שָׁלוֹם עָלֵינוּ וְעַל כָּל יִשְׂרָאֵל, וְאִמְרוּ אָמֵן.

יְהִי רָצוֹן מִלְּפָנֶיךָ יהוה אֱלֹהֵינוּ וֵאלֹהֵי אֲבוֹתֵינוּ

שֶׁיִּבָּנֶה בֵּית הַמִּקְדָּשׁ בִּמְהֵרָה בְיָמֵינוּ, וְתֵן חֶלְקֵנוּ בְּתוֹרָתֶךָ

וְשָׁם נַעֲבָדְךָ בְּיִרְאָה כִּימֵי עוֹלָם וּכְשָׁנִים קַדְמוֹנִיּוֹת.

מלאכי ג

וְעָרְבָה לַיהוה מִנְחַת יְהוּדָה וִירוּשָׁלָיִם כִּימֵי עוֹלָם וּכְשָׁנִים קַדְמֹנִיּוֹת:

On days when תחנון *is not said, the* שליח ציבור *says* קדיש שלם *on page 255.*

**A person undertaking a personal fast says the following at* מנחה *before the fast:*

רִבּוֹן כָּל הָעוֹלָמִים, הֲרֵי אֲנִי לְפָנֶיךָ בְּתַעֲנִית נְדָבָה לְמָחָר. יְהִי רָצוֹן מִלְּפָנֶיךָ יהוה אֱלֹהַי וֵאלֹהֵי אֲבוֹתַי, שֶׁתְּקַבְּלֵנִי בְּאַהֲבָה וּבְרָצוֹן, וְתָבֹא לְפָנֶיךָ תְּפִלָּתִי, וְתַעֲנֶה עֲתִירָתִי בְּרַחֲמֶיךָ הָרַבִּים, כִּי אַתָּה שׁוֹמֵעַ תְּפִלַּת כָּל־פֶּה.

On the afternoon of the fast, the following is said:

רִבּוֹן כָּל הָעוֹלָמִים, גָּלוּי וְיָדוּעַ לְפָנֶיךָ, בִּזְמַן שֶׁבֵּית הַמִּקְדָּשׁ קַיָּם, אָדָם חוֹטֵא וּמַקְרִיב קָרְבָּן, וְאֵין מַקְרִיבִין מִמֶּנּוּ אֶלָּא חֶלְבּוֹ וְדָמוֹ, וְאַתָּה בְּרַחֲמֶיךָ הָרַבִּים מְכַפֵּר. וְעַכְשָׁו יָשַׁבְתִּי בְּתַעֲנִית, וְנִתְמַעֵט חֶלְבִּי וְדָמִי. יְהִי רָצוֹן מִלְּפָנֶיךָ, שֶׁיְּהֵא מִעוּט חֶלְבִּי וְדָמִי שֶׁנִּתְמַעֵט הַיּוֹם, כְּאִלּוּ הִקְרַבְתִּיו עַל־גַּבֵּי הַמִּזְבֵּחַ, וְתִרְצֵנִי.

Between Rosh HaShana and Yom Kippur and on fast days, except days when Taḥanun is not said (see list below), Avinu Malkenu (on page 138) is said here.

TAḤANUN

Taḥanun is not said on Erev Shabbat and Erev Yom Tov. It is also not said on the following days: Rosh Ḥodesh, Ḥanukka, Tu BiShvat, the 14th and 15th of Adar I, Purim and Shushan Purim, Yom HaAtzma'ut, Lag BaOmer, Yom Yerushalayim, Tisha B'Av, Tu B'Av, and the preceding afternoons, the month of Nisan, the 14th of Iyar (Pesaḥ Sheni), from Rosh Ḥodesh Sivan through the day after Shavuot (in Israel through 12th of Sivan), and from Erev Yom Kippur through the day after Simḥat Torah (in Israel through Rosh Ḥodesh Marḥeshvan). Taḥanun is also not said: on the occasion of a Brit Mila, either where the brit will take place or where the father, Sandek or Mohel are present; if a groom is present (and some say, a bride) on the day of his wedding or during the week of Sheva Berakhot; in a house of mourning.

LOWERING THE HEAD

Say while sitting; in the presence of a Torah scroll say until "in sudden shame," leaning forward and resting one's head on the left arm.

וַיֹּאמֶר דָּוִד David said to Gad, "I am in great distress. *II Sam. 24*
Let us fall into God's hand, for His mercy is great;
but do not let me fall into the hand of man."

Compassionate and gracious One, I have sinned before You.
LORD, full of compassion, have compassion on me and accept my pleas.

LORD, do not rebuke me in Your anger or chastise me in Your wrath. *Ps. 6*
Be gracious to me, LORD, for I am weak.
Heal me, LORD, for my bones are in agony.
My soul is in anguish, and You, O LORD – how long?
Turn, LORD, set my soul free; save me for the sake of Your love.
For no one remembers You when he is dead.
Who can praise You from the grave? I am weary with my sighing.
Every night I drench my bed, I soak my couch with my tears.
My eye grows dim from grief, worn out because of all my foes.
Leave me, all you evildoers,
for the LORD has heard the sound of my weeping.
The LORD has heard my pleas. The LORD will accept my prayer.
All my enemies will be shamed and utterly dismayed.
They will turn back in sudden shame.

Sit upright.

During the עשרת ימי תשובה *and on fast days, except days when* תחנון *is not said (see list below),* אבינו מלכנו *(on page 139) is said here.*

סדר תחנון

תחנון *is not said on* ערב שבת *and* ערב יום טוב*. It is also not said on the following days:* ראש חודש, חנוכה, ט״ו בשבט*, the 14th and 15th of* אדר א׳, פורים *and* שושן פורים, יום העצמאות, ל״ג בעומר, יום ירושלים, תשעה באב, ט״ו באב*, and the preceding afternoons, the month of* ניסן*, the 14th of* אייר (פסח שני)*, from* ראש חודש סיון *through the day after* שבועות *(in* ארץ ישראל *through* י״ב סיון*), and from* ערב יום כיפור *through the day after* שמחת תורה *(in* ארץ ישראל *through* ראש חודש מרחשון*).* תחנון *is also not said: on the occasion of a* ברית מילה*, either where the* ברית *will take place or where the father,* סנדק *or* מוהל *are present; if a* חתן *is present (and some say, a* כלה*) on the day of his wedding or during the week of* שבע ברכות*; in a house of mourning.*

נפילת אפיים

Say while sitting; in the presence of a ספר תורה *say until* יֵבֹשׁוּ רָגַע*, leaning forward and resting one's head on the left arm.*

וַיֹּאמֶר דָּוִד אֶל־גָּד, צַר־לִי מְאֹד שמואל ב׳ כד
נִפְּלָה־נָּא בְיַד־יהוה, כִּי רַבִּים רַחֲמָו, וּבְיַד־אָדָם אַל־אֶפֹּלָה:

רַחוּם וְחַנּוּן, חָטָאתִי לְפָנֶיךָ.
יהוה מָלֵא רַחֲמִים, רַחֵם עָלַי וְקַבֵּל תַּחֲנוּנָי.

יהוה, אַל־בְּאַפְּךָ תוֹכִיחֵנִי, וְאַל־בַּחֲמָתְךָ תְיַסְּרֵנִי: תהלים ו
חָנֵּנִי יהוה, כִּי אֻמְלַל אָנִי, רְפָאֵנִי יהוה, כִּי נִבְהֲלוּ עֲצָמָי:
וְנַפְשִׁי נִבְהֲלָה מְאֹד, וְאַתָּה יהוה, עַד־מָתָי:
שׁוּבָה יהוה, חַלְּצָה נַפְשִׁי, הוֹשִׁיעֵנִי לְמַעַן חַסְדֶּךָ:
כִּי אֵין בַּמָּוֶת זִכְרֶךָ, בִּשְׁאוֹל מִי יוֹדֶה־לָּךְ:
יָגַעְתִּי בְּאַנְחָתִי, אַשְׂחֶה בְכָל־לַיְלָה מִטָּתִי, בְּדִמְעָתִי עַרְשִׂי אַמְסֶה:
עָשְׁשָׁה מִכַּעַס עֵינִי, עָתְקָה בְּכָל־צוֹרְרָי:
סוּרוּ מִמֶּנִּי כָּל־פֹּעֲלֵי אָוֶן, כִּי־שָׁמַע יהוה קוֹל בִּכְיִי:
שָׁמַע יהוה תְּחִנָּתִי, יהוה תְּפִלָּתִי יִקָּח:
יֵבֹשׁוּ וְיִבָּהֲלוּ מְאֹד כָּל־אֹיְבָי, יָשֻׁבוּ יֵבֹשׁוּ רָגַע:

Sit upright.

שׁוֹמֵר יִשְׂרָאֵל Guardian of Israel,
guard the remnant of Israel,
and let not Israel perish, who declare, "Listen, Israel."
Guardian of a unique nation, guard the remnant of a unique people,
and let not that unique nation perish, who proclaim the unity of Your name [saying], "The LORD is our God, the LORD is One."
Guardian of a holy nation, guard the remnant of that holy people,
and let not the holy nation perish, who three times repeat the threefold declaration of holiness to the Holy One.
You who are conciliated by calls for compassion and placated by pleas,
be conciliated and placated toward an afflicted generation,
for there is no other help.
Our Father, our King, be gracious to us and answer us,
though we have no worthy deeds;
act with us in charity and loving-kindness and save us.

Stand at ▴.

וַאֲנַחְנוּ We do not know ▴what to do, but our eyes are turned to You. *II Chr. 12*
Remember, LORD, Your compassion and loving-kindness, for they are *Ps. 25*
everlasting. May Your loving-kindness, LORD, be with us, for we have put *Ps. 33*
our hope in You. Do not hold against us the sins of those who came before *Ps. 79*
us. May Your mercies meet us swiftly, for we have been brought very low.
Be gracious to us, LORD, be gracious to us, for we are sated with contempt. *Ps. 123*
In wrath, remember mercy. He knows our nature; He remembers that *Hab. 3* *Ps. 103*
we are dust. ▸ Help us, God of our salvation, for the sake of the glory of *Ps. 79*
Your name. Save us and grant atonement for our sins for Your name's sake.

FULL KADDISH

Leader: יִתְגַּדַּל Magnified and sanctified may His great name be,
in the world He created by His will.
May He establish His kingdom
in your lifetime and in your days,
and in the lifetime of all the house of Israel,
swiftly and soon – and say: Amen.

All: May His great name be blessed for ever and all time.

שׁוֹמֵר יִשְׂרָאֵל, שְׁמֹר שְׁאֵרִית יִשְׂרָאֵל, וְאַל יֹאבַד יִשְׂרָאֵל
הָאוֹמְרִים שְׁמַע יִשְׂרָאֵל.
שׁוֹמֵר גּוֹי אֶחָד, שְׁמֹר שְׁאֵרִית עַם אֶחָד, וְאַל יֹאבַד גּוֹי אֶחָד
הַמְיַחֲדִים שִׁמְךָ, יהוה אֱלֹהֵינוּ יהוה אֶחָד.
שׁוֹמֵר גּוֹי קָדוֹשׁ, שְׁמֹר שְׁאֵרִית עַם קָדוֹשׁ, וְאַל יֹאבַד גּוֹי קָדוֹשׁ
הַמְשַׁלְּשִׁים בְּשָׁלֹשׁ קְדֻשּׁוֹת לְקָדוֹשׁ.
מִתְרַצֶּה בְּרַחֲמִים וּמִתְפַּיֵּס בְּתַחֲנוּנִים, הִתְרַצֵּה וְהִתְפַּיֵּס לְדוֹר עָנִי
כִּי אֵין עוֹזֵר.
אָבִינוּ מַלְכֵּנוּ, חָנֵּנוּ וַעֲנֵנוּ, כִּי אֵין בָּנוּ מַעֲשִׂים
עֲשֵׂה עִמָּנוּ צְדָקָה וָחֶסֶד וְהוֹשִׁיעֵנוּ.

Stand at ▴.

וַאֲנַחְנוּ לֹא נֵדַע ▴מַה־נַּעֲשֶׂה, כִּי עָלֶיךָ עֵינֵינוּ: זְכֹר־רַחֲמֶיךָ יהוה דברי הימים ב׳ יב, תהלים כה
וַחֲסָדֶיךָ, כִּי מֵעוֹלָם הֵמָּה: יְהִי־חַסְדְּךָ יהוה עָלֵינוּ, כַּאֲשֶׁר יִחַלְנוּ לָךְ: תהלים לג
אַל־תִּזְכָּר־לָנוּ עֲוֹנֹת רִאשֹׁנִים, מַהֵר יְקַדְּמוּנוּ רַחֲמֶיךָ, כִּי דַלּוֹנוּ מְאֹד: תהלים עט
חָנֵּנוּ יהוה חָנֵּנוּ, כִּי־רַב שָׂבַעְנוּ בוּז: בְּרֹגֶז רַחֵם תִּזְכּוֹר: כִּי־הוּא יָדַע תהלים קכג, חבקוק ג, תהלים קג
יִצְרֵנוּ, זָכוּר כִּי־עָפָר אֲנָחְנוּ: ◂ עָזְרֵנוּ אֱלֹהֵי יִשְׁעֵנוּ עַל־דְּבַר כְּבוֹד־ תהלים עט
שְׁמֶךָ, וְהַצִּילֵנוּ וְכַפֵּר עַל־חַטֹּאתֵינוּ לְמַעַן שְׁמֶךָ:

קדיש שלם

ש״ץ: יִתְגַּדַּל וְיִתְקַדַּשׁ שְׁמֵהּ רַבָּא (קהל: אָמֵן)
בְּעָלְמָא דִּי בְרָא כִרְעוּתֵהּ
וְיַמְלִיךְ מַלְכוּתֵהּ
בְּחַיֵּיכוֹן וּבְיוֹמֵיכוֹן וּבְחַיֵּי דְכָל בֵּית יִשְׂרָאֵל
בַּעֲגָלָא וּבִזְמַן קָרִיב, וְאִמְרוּ אָמֵן. (קהל: אָמֵן)

קהל וש״ץ: יְהֵא שְׁמֵהּ רַבָּא מְבָרַךְ לְעָלַם וּלְעָלְמֵי עָלְמַיָּא.

Leader: Blessed and praised,
glorified and exalted, raised and honored,
uplifted and lauded be
the name of the Holy One, blessed be He,
beyond any blessing,
song, praise and consolation
uttered in the world –
and say: Amen.

May the prayers and pleas of all Israel
be accepted by their Father in heaven –
and say: Amen.

May there be great peace from heaven,
and life for us and all Israel –
and say: Amen.

Bow, take three steps back, as if taking leave of the Divine Presence, then bow, first left, then right, then center, while saying:

May He who makes peace in His high places,
make peace for us and all Israel –
and say: Amen.

Stand while saying Aleinu. Bow at ▾.

עָלֵינוּ It is our duty to praise the Master of all,
and ascribe greatness to the Author of creation,
who has not made us like the nations of the lands
nor placed us like the families of the earth;
who has not made our portion like theirs,
nor our destiny like all their multitudes.
(For they worship vanity and emptiness,
and pray to a god who cannot save.)
▾But we bow in worship
and thank the Supreme King of kings,
the Holy One, blessed be He,
who extends the heavens and establishes the earth,

ש״ץ: יִתְבָּרַךְ וְיִשְׁתַּבַּח וְיִתְפָּאַר
וְיִתְרוֹמַם וְיִתְנַשֵּׂא וְיִתְהַדָּר וְיִתְעַלֶּה וְיִתְהַלָּל
שְׁמֵהּ דְּקֻדְשָׁא בְּרִיךְ הוּא (קהל: בְּרִיךְ הוּא)
לְעֵלָּא מִן כָּל בִּרְכָתָא / בעשרת ימי תשובה: לְעֵלָּא לְעֵלָּא מִכָּל בִּרְכָתָא/
וְשִׁירָתָא, תֻּשְׁבְּחָתָא וְנֶחֱמָתָא, דַּאֲמִירָן בְּעָלְמָא
וְאִמְרוּ אָמֵן. (קהל: אָמֵן)

תִּתְקַבַּל צְלוֹתְהוֹן וּבָעוּתְהוֹן דְּכָל יִשְׂרָאֵל
קֳדָם אֲבוּהוֹן דִּי בִשְׁמַיָּא
וְאִמְרוּ אָמֵן. (קהל: אָמֵן)

יְהֵא שְׁלָמָא רַבָּא מִן שְׁמַיָּא
וְחַיִּים, עָלֵינוּ וְעַל כָּל יִשְׂרָאֵל
וְאִמְרוּ אָמֵן. (קהל: אָמֵן)

Bow, take three steps back, as if taking leave of the Divine Presence, then bow, first left, then right, then center, while saying:

עֹשֶׂה שָׁלוֹם/ בעשרת ימי תשובה: הַשָּׁלוֹם/ בִּמְרוֹמָיו
הוּא יַעֲשֶׂה שָׁלוֹם עָלֵינוּ וְעַל כָּל יִשְׂרָאֵל
וְאִמְרוּ אָמֵן. (קהל: אָמֵן)

Stand while saying עָלֵינוּ*. Bow at* ׳.

עָלֵינוּ לְשַׁבֵּחַ לַאֲדוֹן הַכֹּל, לָתֵת גְּדֻלָּה לְיוֹצֵר בְּרֵאשִׁית
שֶׁלֹּא עָשָׂנוּ כְּגוֹיֵי הָאֲרָצוֹת, וְלֹא שָׂמָנוּ כְּמִשְׁפְּחוֹת הָאֲדָמָה
שֶׁלֹּא שָׂם חֶלְקֵנוּ כָּהֶם וְגוֹרָלֵנוּ כְּכָל הֲמוֹנָם.
(שֶׁהֵם מִשְׁתַּחֲוִים לְהֶבֶל וָרִיק וּמִתְפַּלְּלִים אֶל אֵל לֹא יוֹשִׁיעַ.)
׳וַאֲנַחְנוּ כּוֹרְעִים וּמִשְׁתַּחֲוִים וּמוֹדִים
לִפְנֵי מֶלֶךְ מַלְכֵי הַמְּלָכִים, הַקָּדוֹשׁ בָּרוּךְ הוּא
שֶׁהוּא נוֹטֶה שָׁמַיִם וְיוֹסֵד אָרֶץ

whose throne of glory is in the heavens above,
and whose power's Presence is in the highest of heights.
He is our God; there is no other.
Truly He is our King, there is none else,
as it is written in His Torah:
"You shall know and take to heart this day *Deut. 4*
that the LORD is God,
in heaven above and on earth below. There is no other."

Therefore, we place our hope in You, LORD our God,
that we may soon see the glory of Your power,
when You will remove abominations from the earth,
and idols will be utterly destroyed,
when the world will be perfected
under the sovereignty of the Almighty,
when all humanity will call on Your name,
to turn all the earth's wicked toward You.
All the world's inhabitants will realize and know
that to You every knee must bow and every tongue swear loyalty.
Before You, LORD our God, they will kneel and bow down
and give honor to Your glorious name.
They will all accept the yoke of Your kingdom,
and You will reign over them soon and for ever.
For the kingdom is Yours,
and to all eternity You will reign in glory,
as it is written in Your Torah:
"The LORD will reign for ever and ever." *Ex. 15*
▸ And it is said: "Then the LORD shall be King over all the earth; *Zech. 14*
on that day the LORD shall be One and His name One."

Some add:
Have no fear of sudden terror or of the ruin when it overtakes the wicked. *Prov. 3*
Devise your strategy, but it will be thwarted; *Is. 8*
propose your plan, but it will not stand, for God is with us.
When you grow old, I will still be the same. *Is. 46*
When your hair turns gray, I will still carry you.
I made you, I will bear you, I will carry you, and I will rescue you.

וּמוֹשַׁב יְקָרוֹ בַּשָּׁמַיִם מִמַּעַל
וּשְׁכִינַת עֻזּוֹ בְּגָבְהֵי מְרוֹמִים.
הוּא אֱלֹהֵינוּ, אֵין עוֹד.
אֱמֶת מַלְכֵּנוּ, אֶפֶס זוּלָתוֹ
כַּכָּתוּב בְּתוֹרָתוֹ
וְיָדַעְתָּ הַיּוֹם וַהֲשֵׁבֹתָ אֶל־לְבָבֶךָ דברים ד
כִּי יהוה הוּא הָאֱלֹהִים בַּשָּׁמַיִם מִמַּעַל וְעַל־הָאָרֶץ מִתָּחַת, אֵין עוֹד:

עַל כֵּן נְקַוֶּה לְּךָ יהוה אֱלֹהֵינוּ, לִרְאוֹת מְהֵרָה בְּתִפְאֶרֶת עֻזֶּךָ
לְהַעֲבִיר גִּלּוּלִים מִן הָאָרֶץ, וְהָאֱלִילִים כָּרוֹת יִכָּרֵתוּן
לְתַקֵּן עוֹלָם בְּמַלְכוּת שַׁדַּי.
וְכָל בְּנֵי בָשָׂר יִקְרְאוּ בִשְׁמֶךָ לְהַפְנוֹת אֵלֶיךָ כָּל רִשְׁעֵי אָרֶץ.
יַכִּירוּ וְיֵדְעוּ כָּל יוֹשְׁבֵי תֵבֵל
כִּי לְךָ תִּכְרַע כָּל בֶּרֶךְ, תִּשָּׁבַע כָּל לָשׁוֹן.
לְפָנֶיךָ יהוה אֱלֹהֵינוּ יִכְרְעוּ וְיִפֹּלוּ, וְלִכְבוֹד שִׁמְךָ יְקָר יִתֵּנוּ
וִיקַבְּלוּ כֻלָּם אֶת עֹל מַלְכוּתֶךָ
וְתִמְלֹךְ עֲלֵיהֶם מְהֵרָה לְעוֹלָם וָעֶד.
כִּי הַמַּלְכוּת שֶׁלְּךָ הִיא וּלְעוֹלְמֵי עַד תִּמְלֹךְ בְּכָבוֹד
כַּכָּתוּב בְּתוֹרָתֶךָ, יהוה יִמְלֹךְ לְעֹלָם וָעֶד: שמות טו
◂ וְנֶאֱמַר, וְהָיָה יהוה לְמֶלֶךְ עַל־כָּל־הָאָרֶץ זכריה יד
בַּיּוֹם הַהוּא יִהְיֶה יהוה אֶחָד וּשְׁמוֹ אֶחָד:

Some add:

אַל־תִּירָא מִפַּחַד פִּתְאֹם וּמִשֹּׁאַת רְשָׁעִים כִּי תָבֹא: משלי ג
עֻצוּ עֵצָה וְתֻפָר, דַּבְּרוּ דָבָר וְלֹא יָקוּם, כִּי עִמָּנוּ אֵל: ישעיה ח
וְעַד־זִקְנָה אֲנִי הוּא, וְעַד־שֵׂיבָה אֲנִי אֶסְבֹּל ישעיה מו
אֲנִי עָשִׂיתִי וַאֲנִי אֶשָּׂא וַאֲנִי אֶסְבֹּל וַאֲמַלֵּט:

MOURNER'S KADDISH

The following prayer, said by mourners, requires the presence of a minyan. A transliteration can be found on page 699.

Mourner: יִתְגַּדַּל Magnified and sanctified
may His great name be,
in the world He created by His will.
May He establish His kingdom
in your lifetime
and in your days,
and in the lifetime
of all the house of Israel,
swiftly and soon –
and say: Amen.

All: May His great name be blessed for ever and all time.

Mourner: Blessed and praised,
glorified and exalted,
raised and honored,
uplifted and lauded
be the name of the Holy One,
blessed be He,
beyond any blessing,
song, praise and consolation
uttered in the world –
and say: Amen.

May there be great peace from heaven,
and life for us and all Israel –
and say: Amen.

Bow, take three steps back, as if taking leave of the Divine Presence, then bow, first left, then right, then center, while saying:

May He who makes peace in His high places,
make peace for us and all Israel –
and say: Amen.

קדיש יתום

The following prayer, said by mourners, requires the presence of a מנין.
A transliteration can be found on page 699.

אבל: יִתְגַּדַּל וְיִתְקַדַּשׁ שְׁמֵהּ רַבָּא (קהל: אָמֵן)
בְּעָלְמָא דִּי בְרָא כִרְעוּתֵהּ
וְיַמְלִיךְ מַלְכוּתֵהּ
בְּחַיֵּיכוֹן וּבְיוֹמֵיכוֹן
וּבְחַיֵּי דְכָל בֵּית יִשְׂרָאֵל
בַּעֲגָלָא וּבִזְמַן קָרִיב
וְאִמְרוּ אָמֵן. (קהל: אָמֵן)

קהל ואבל: יְהֵא שְׁמֵהּ רַבָּא מְבָרַךְ לְעָלַם וּלְעָלְמֵי עָלְמַיָּא.

אבל: יִתְבָּרַךְ וְיִשְׁתַּבַּח וְיִתְפָּאַר
וְיִתְרוֹמַם וְיִתְנַשֵּׂא וְיִתְהַדָּר וְיִתְעַלֶּה וְיִתְהַלָּל
שְׁמֵהּ דְּקֻדְשָׁא בְּרִיךְ הוּא (קהל: בְּרִיךְ הוּא)
לְעֵלָּא מִן כָּל בִּרְכָתָא
/בעשרת ימי תשובה: לְעֵלָּא לְעֵלָּא מִכָּל בִּרְכָתָא/
וְשִׁירָתָא, תֻּשְׁבְּחָתָא וְנֶחֱמָתָא
דַּאֲמִירָן בְּעָלְמָא
וְאִמְרוּ אָמֵן. (קהל: אָמֵן)

יְהֵא שְׁלָמָא רַבָּא מִן שְׁמַיָּא
וְחַיִּים, עָלֵינוּ וְעַל כָּל יִשְׂרָאֵל, וְאִמְרוּ אָמֵן. (קהל: אָמֵן)

Bow, take three steps back, as if taking leave of the Divine Presence, then bow, first left, then right, then center, while saying:

עֹשֶׂה שָׁלוֹם/ בעשרת ימי תשובה: הַשָּׁלוֹם/ בִּמְרוֹמָיו
הוּא יַעֲשֶׂה שָׁלוֹם עָלֵינוּ וְעַל כָּל יִשְׂרָאֵל
וְאִמְרוּ אָמֵן. (קהל: אָמֵן)

Ma'ariv for Weekdays

On Motza'ei Shabbat some have the custom to sing Psalm 144 and Psalm 67 before the Ma'ariv Service (page 314).

וְהוּא רַחוּם He is compassionate. Ps. 78
He forgives iniquity and does not destroy.
Repeatedly He suppresses His anger, not rousing His full wrath.
LORD, save! May the King, answer us on the day we call. Ps. 20

BLESSINGS OF THE SHEMA

The Leader says the following, bowing at "Bless," standing straight at "the LORD"; the congregation, followed by the Leader, responds, bowing at "Bless," standing straight at "the LORD":

Leader: **BLESS**
the LORD, the blessed One.

Congregation: Bless the LORD, the blessed One,
for ever and all time.

Leader: Bless the LORD, the blessed One,
for ever and all time.

---

prayer: the ladder stretching from earth to heaven on which angels ascended and descended. During that vision, God promised Jacob that "I will protect you wherever you go" (Gen. 28:15). The evening service represents our trust in God during the dark and dangers of night.

וְהוּא רַחוּם *He is compassionate:* A prelude to prayer, from the book of Psalms, that serves as a brief equivalent to the Verses of Praise in the morning service. The verse (Psalm 78:38) contains thirteen words that are reminiscent of the thirteen attributes of divine mercy.

בָּרְכוּ אֶת יהוה *Bless the LORD:* As in the morning service, a call to the congregation to join in communal prayer, derived from the verse: "Magnify the LORD with me; let us exalt His name together" (Psalm 34:4).

מעריב לחול

On מוצאי שבת *some have the custom to sing* לְדָוִד, בָּרוּךְ יהוה צוּרִי *and* מִזְמוֹר שִׁיר לַמְנַצֵּחַ בִּנְגִינֹת *before* תפילת ערבית *(page 315).*

תהלים עח וְהוּא רַחוּם, יְכַפֵּר עָוֹן וְלֹא־יַשְׁחִית
וְהִרְבָּה לְהָשִׁיב אַפּוֹ, וְלֹא־יָעִיר כָּל־חֲמָתוֹ:
תהלים כ יהוה הוֹשִׁיעָה, הַמֶּלֶךְ יַעֲנֵנוּ בְיוֹם־קָרְאֵנוּ:

קריאת שמע וברכותיה

The שליח ציבור *says the following, bowing at* בָּרְכוּ*, standing straight at* ה'*; the* קהל*, followed by the* שליח ציבור*, responds, bowing at* בָּרוּךְ*, standing straight at* ה'*:*

ש״ץ: **בָּרְכוּ**
אֶת יהוה הַמְבֹרָךְ.
קהל: בָּרוּךְ יהוה הַמְבֹרָךְ לְעוֹלָם וָעֶד.
ש״ץ: בָּרוּךְ יהוה הַמְבֹרָךְ לְעוֹלָם וָעֶד.

EVENING SERVICE

The saying of Shema at night ("when you lie down") is a biblical imperative. In early post-Temple times there were some who held that the evening Amida was non-obligatory since – unlike the morning and afternoon services – there was no daily sacrifice to which it corresponded (*Berakhot* 27b–28a). So wide-spread was its observance, however, that it was eventually deemed obligatory. Notwithstanding, since the Amida at night does not correspond to a sacrifice, it is not repeated by the Leader.

Tradition identifies the evening prayer with Jacob, who had his most intense religious experiences at night, especially the vision most associated with

בָּרוּךְ Blessed are You, LORD our God, King of the Universe,
who by His word brings on evenings,
by His wisdom opens the gates of heaven,
with understanding makes time change and the seasons rotate,
and by His will
orders the stars in their constellations in the sky.
He creates day and night,
rolling away the light before the darkness,
and darkness before the light.
▸ He makes the day pass and brings on night,
distinguishing day from night:
the LORD of hosts is His name.
May the living and forever enduring God rule over us for all time.
Blessed are You, LORD, who brings on evenings.

אַהֲבַת עוֹלָם With everlasting love
have You loved Your people, the house of Israel.
You have taught us Torah and commandments,
decrees and laws of justice.
Therefore, LORD our God, when we lie down and when we rise up
we will speak of Your decrees, rejoicing in the words of Your Torah
and Your commandments for ever.
▸ For they are our life and the length of our days;
on them will we meditate day and night.
May You never take away Your love from us.
Blessed are You, LORD, who loves His people Israel.

---

revelation: God's gift to Israel of the Torah and its commandments. In the same way that God binds Himself to His people through word and deed, so do we bind ourselves to Him by the words of Torah and the deeds of the commandments. No simpler or more profound statement exists of the love of Jews for the life of the commandments than the phrase, "For they are our life and the length of our days."

בָּרוּךְ אַתָּה יהוה אֱלֹהֵינוּ מֶלֶךְ הָעוֹלָם
אֲשֶׁר בִּדְבָרוֹ מַעֲרִיב עֲרָבִים
בְּחָכְמָה פּוֹתֵחַ שְׁעָרִים
וּבִתְבוּנָה מְשַׁנֶּה עִתִּים וּמַחֲלִיף אֶת הַזְּמַנִּים
וּמְסַדֵּר אֶת הַכּוֹכָבִים בְּמִשְׁמְרוֹתֵיהֶם בָּרָקִיעַ כִּרְצוֹנוֹ.
בּוֹרֵא יוֹם וָלָיְלָה, גּוֹלֵל אוֹר מִפְּנֵי חֹשֶׁךְ וְחֹשֶׁךְ מִפְּנֵי אוֹר
‹ וּמַעֲבִיר יוֹם וּמֵבִיא לָיְלָה
וּמַבְדִּיל בֵּין יוֹם וּבֵין לָיְלָה
יהוה צְבָאוֹת שְׁמוֹ.
אֵל חַי וְקַיָּם תָּמִיד, יִמְלֹךְ עָלֵינוּ לְעוֹלָם וָעֶד.
בָּרוּךְ אַתָּה יהוה, הַמַּעֲרִיב עֲרָבִים.

אַהֲבַת עוֹלָם בֵּית יִשְׂרָאֵל עַמְּךָ אָהָבְתָּ
תּוֹרָה וּמִצְוֹת, חֻקִּים וּמִשְׁפָּטִים, אוֹתָנוּ לִמַּדְתָּ
עַל כֵּן יהוה אֱלֹהֵינוּ בְּשָׁכְבֵנוּ וּבְקוּמֵנוּ נָשִׂיחַ בְּחֻקֶּיךָ
וְנִשְׂמַח בְּדִבְרֵי תוֹרָתֶךָ וּבְמִצְוֹתֶיךָ לְעוֹלָם וָעֶד
‹ כִּי הֵם חַיֵּינוּ וְאֹרֶךְ יָמֵינוּ, וּבָהֶם נֶהְגֶּה יוֹמָם וָלָיְלָה.
וְאַהֲבָתְךָ אַל תָּסִיר מִמֶּנּוּ לְעוֹלָמִים.
בָּרוּךְ אַתָּה יהוה, אוֹהֵב עַמּוֹ יִשְׂרָאֵל.

הַמַּעֲרִיב עֲרָבִים *Who brings on evenings:* Praise of God as Creator of the universe, and hence of time itself. As with the morning service, the two blessings before the Shema, and the one immediately following, speak in turn of the three key elements of Jewish faith: creation, revelation and redemption.

אַהֲבַת עוֹלָם *With everlasting love:* A counterpart to the morning blessing, "You have loved us with great love." Both speak of divine love in terms of

The Shema must be said with intense concentration. See laws 35–39.

When not with a minyan, say:

God, faithful King!

The following verse should be said aloud, while covering the eyes with the right hand:

Listen, Israel: the LORD is our God, the LORD is One. *Deut. 6*

Quietly: Blessed be the name of His glorious kingdom for ever and all time.

וְאָהַבְתָּ Love the LORD your God with all your heart, with all your soul, and with all your might. These words which I command you today shall be on your heart. Teach them repeatedly to your children, speaking of them when you sit at home and when you travel on the way, when you lie down and when you rise. Bind them as a sign on your hand, and they shall be an emblem between your eyes. Write them on the doorposts of your house and gates. *Deut. 6*

וְהָיָה If you indeed heed My commandments with which I charge you today, to love the LORD your God and worship Him with all your heart and with all your soul, I will give rain in your land in its season, the early and late rain; and you shall gather in your grain, wine and oil. I will give grass in your field for your cattle, and you shall eat and be satisfied. Be careful lest your heart be tempted and you go astray and worship other gods, bowing down to them. Then the LORD's anger will flare against you and He will close the heavens so that there will be no rain. The land will not yield its crops, and you will perish swiftly from the good land that the LORD is giving you. Therefore, set these, My words, on your heart and soul. Bind them as a sign on your hand, and they shall be an emblem between your eyes. Teach them to your children, speaking of them when you sit at home and when you travel on the way, when you lie down and when you rise. Write them on the doorposts of your house and gates, so that you and your children may live long in the land that the LORD swore to your ancestors to give them, for as long as the heavens are above the earth. *Deut. 11*

The שמע *must be said with intense concentration. See laws 35–39.*

When not with a מנין*, say:*

אֵל מֶלֶךְ נֶאֱמָן

The following verse should be said aloud, while covering the eyes with the right hand:

שְׁמַע יִשְׂרָאֵל, יהוה אֱלֹהֵינוּ, יהוה אֶחָד׃ דברים ו

Quietly בָּרוּךְ שֵׁם כְּבוֹד מַלְכוּתוֹ לְעוֹלָם וָעֶד.

וְאָהַבְתָּ אֵת יהוה אֱלֹהֶיךָ, בְּכָל־לְבָבְךָ וּבְכָל־נַפְשְׁךָ וּבְכָל־מְאֹדֶךָ׃ דברים ו
וְהָיוּ הַדְּבָרִים הָאֵלֶּה, אֲשֶׁר אָנֹכִי מְצַוְּךָ הַיּוֹם, עַל־לְבָבֶךָ׃ וְשִׁנַּנְתָּם
לְבָנֶיךָ וְדִבַּרְתָּ בָּם, בְּשִׁבְתְּךָ בְּבֵיתֶךָ וּבְלֶכְתְּךָ בַדֶּרֶךְ, וּבְשָׁכְבְּךָ
וּבְקוּמֶךָ׃ וּקְשַׁרְתָּם לְאוֹת עַל־יָדֶךָ וְהָיוּ לְטֹטָפֹת בֵּין עֵינֶיךָ׃
וּכְתַבְתָּם עַל־מְזֻזוֹת בֵּיתֶךָ וּבִשְׁעָרֶיךָ׃

וְהָיָה אִם־שָׁמֹעַ תִּשְׁמְעוּ אֶל־מִצְוֹתַי אֲשֶׁר אָנֹכִי מְצַוֶּה אֶתְכֶם דברים יא
הַיּוֹם, לְאַהֲבָה אֶת־יהוה אֱלֹהֵיכֶם וּלְעָבְדוֹ, בְּכָל־לְבַבְכֶם וּבְכָל־
נַפְשְׁכֶם׃ וְנָתַתִּי מְטַר־אַרְצְכֶם בְּעִתּוֹ, יוֹרֶה וּמַלְקוֹשׁ, וְאָסַפְתָּ דְגָנֶךָ
וְתִירֹשְׁךָ וְיִצְהָרֶךָ׃ וְנָתַתִּי עֵשֶׂב בְּשָׂדְךָ לִבְהֶמְתֶּךָ, וְאָכַלְתָּ וְשָׂבָעְתָּ׃
הִשָּׁמְרוּ לָכֶם פֶּן־יִפְתֶּה לְבַבְכֶם, וְסַרְתֶּם וַעֲבַדְתֶּם אֱלֹהִים אֲחֵרִים
וְהִשְׁתַּחֲוִיתֶם לָהֶם׃ וְחָרָה אַף־יהוה בָּכֶם, וְעָצַר אֶת־הַשָּׁמַיִם
וְלֹא־יִהְיֶה מָטָר, וְהָאֲדָמָה לֹא תִתֵּן אֶת־יְבוּלָהּ, וַאֲבַדְתֶּם מְהֵרָה
מֵעַל הָאָרֶץ הַטֹּבָה אֲשֶׁר יהוה נֹתֵן לָכֶם׃ וְשַׂמְתֶּם אֶת־דְּבָרַי
אֵלֶּה עַל־לְבַבְכֶם וְעַל־נַפְשְׁכֶם, וּקְשַׁרְתֶּם אֹתָם לְאוֹת עַל־יֶדְכֶם,
וְהָיוּ לְטוֹטָפֹת בֵּין עֵינֵיכֶם׃ וְלִמַּדְתֶּם אֹתָם אֶת־בְּנֵיכֶם לְדַבֵּר בָּם,
בְּשִׁבְתְּךָ בְּבֵיתֶךָ וּבְלֶכְתְּךָ בַדֶּרֶךְ, וּבְשָׁכְבְּךָ וּבְקוּמֶךָ׃ וּכְתַבְתָּם
עַל־מְזוּזוֹת בֵּיתֶךָ וּבִשְׁעָרֶיךָ׃ לְמַעַן יִרְבּוּ יְמֵיכֶם וִימֵי בְנֵיכֶם עַל
הָאֲדָמָה אֲשֶׁר נִשְׁבַּע יהוה לַאֲבֹתֵיכֶם לָתֵת לָהֶם, כִּימֵי הַשָּׁמַיִם
עַל־הָאָרֶץ׃

וַיֹּאמֶר The Lord spoke to Moses, saying: Speak to the Israelites *Num. 15*
and tell them to make tassels on the corners of their garments for all generations. They shall attach to the tassel at each corner a thread of blue. This shall be your tassel, and you shall see it and remember all of the Lord's commandments and keep them, not straying after your heart and after your eyes, following your own sinful desires. Thus you will be reminded to keep all My commandments, and be holy to your God. I am the Lord your God, who brought you out of the land of Egypt to be your God. I am the Lord your God.

True –

The Leader repeats:

▸ The Lord your God is true –

וֶאֱמוּנָה – and faithful is all this,
and firmly established for us
that He is the Lord our God,
and there is none besides Him,
and that we, Israel, are His people.
He is our King, who redeems us from the hand of kings
and delivers us from the grasp of all tyrants.
He is our God,
who on our behalf repays our foes
and brings just retribution on our mortal enemies;
who performs great deeds beyond understanding
and wonders beyond number;
who kept us alive, not letting our foot slip; *Ps. 66*
who led us on the high places of our enemies,
raising our pride above all our foes;

---

faithfulness at night echoes the phrase from Psalm 92: "to tell of Your love in the morning, and Your faithfulness at night."

וַיֹּאמֶר יהוה אֶל־מֹשֶׁה לֵּאמֹר: דַּבֵּר אֶל־בְּנֵי יִשְׂרָאֵל וְאָמַרְתָּ במדבר טו
אֲלֵהֶם, וְעָשׂוּ לָהֶם צִיצִת עַל־כַּנְפֵי בִגְדֵיהֶם לְדֹרֹתָם, וְנָתְנוּ עַל־
צִיצִת הַכָּנָף פְּתִיל תְּכֵלֶת: וְהָיָה לָכֶם לְצִיצִת, וּרְאִיתֶם אֹתוֹ
וּזְכַרְתֶּם אֶת־כָּל־מִצְוֹת יהוה וַעֲשִׂיתֶם אֹתָם, וְלֹא תָתֻרוּ אַחֲרֵי
לְבַבְכֶם וְאַחֲרֵי עֵינֵיכֶם, אֲשֶׁר־אַתֶּם זֹנִים אַחֲרֵיהֶם: לְמַעַן תִּזְכְּרוּ
וַעֲשִׂיתֶם אֶת־כָּל־מִצְוֹתָי, וִהְיִיתֶם קְדֹשִׁים לֵאלֹהֵיכֶם: אֲנִי יהוה
אֱלֹהֵיכֶם, אֲשֶׁר הוֹצֵאתִי אֶתְכֶם מֵאֶרֶץ מִצְרַיִם, לִהְיוֹת לָכֶם
לֵאלֹהִים, אֲנִי יהוה אֱלֹהֵיכֶם:

אֱמֶת

The שליח ציבור *repeats:*

› יהוה אֱלֹהֵיכֶם אֱמֶת

וֶאֱמוּנָה כָּל זֹאת וְקַיָּם עָלֵינוּ
כִּי הוּא יהוה אֱלֹהֵינוּ וְאֵין זוּלָתוֹ
וַאֲנַחְנוּ יִשְׂרָאֵל עַמּוֹ.
הַפּוֹדֵנוּ מִיַּד מְלָכִים
מַלְכֵּנוּ הַגּוֹאֲלֵנוּ מִכַּף כָּל הֶעָרִיצִים.
הָאֵל הַנִּפְרָע לָנוּ מִצָּרֵינוּ
וְהַמְשַׁלֵּם גְּמוּל לְכָל אוֹיְבֵי נַפְשֵׁנוּ.
הָעוֹשֶׂה גְדוֹלוֹת עַד אֵין חֵקֶר, וְנִפְלָאוֹת עַד אֵין מִסְפָּר
הַשָּׂם נַפְשֵׁנוּ בַּחַיִּים, וְלֹא־נָתַן לַמּוֹט רַגְלֵנוּ: תהלים סו
הַמַּדְרִיכֵנוּ עַל בָּמוֹת אוֹיְבֵינוּ
וַיָּרֶם קַרְנֵנוּ עַל כָּל שׂוֹנְאֵינוּ.

אֱמֶת וֶאֱמוּנָה *True and faithful:* A blessing about redemption, parallel to the blessing **אֱמֶת וְיַצִּיב**, "True and firm," in the morning. The special emphasis on

who did miracles for us
and brought vengeance against Pharaoh;
who performed signs and wonders
in the land of Ham's children;
who smote in His wrath all the firstborn of Egypt,
and brought out His people Israel from their midst
into everlasting freedom;
who led His children through the divided Reed Sea,
plunging their pursuers and enemies into the depths.
When His children saw His might,
they gave praise and thanks to His name,
▸ and willingly accepted His Sovereignty.
Moses and the children of Israel
then sang a song to You with great joy,
and they all exclaimed:

מִי־כָמֹכָה "Who is like You, LORD, among the mighty? *Ex. 15*
Who is like You, majestic in holiness,
awesome in praises, doing wonders?"

▸ Your children beheld Your majesty
as You parted the sea before Moses.
"This is my God!" they responded,
and then said:

"The LORD shall reign for ever and ever." *Ex. 15*

▸ And it is said, "For the LORD has redeemed Jacob *Jer. 31*
and rescued him from a power stronger than his own."
Blessed are You, LORD, who redeemed Israel.

הַשְׁכִּיבֵנוּ Help us lie down, O LORD our God, in peace,
and rise up, O our King, to life.
Spread over us Your canopy of peace.
Direct us with Your good counsel,
and save us for the sake of Your name.

הָעוֹשֶׂה לָנוּ נִסִּים וּנְקָמָה בְּפַרְעֹה
אוֹתוֹת וּמוֹפְתִים בְּאַדְמַת בְּנֵי חָם.
הַמַּכֶּה בְעֶבְרָתוֹ כָּל בְּכוֹרֵי מִצְרָיִם
וַיּוֹצֵא אֶת עַמּוֹ יִשְׂרָאֵל מִתּוֹכָם לְחֵרוּת עוֹלָם.
הַמַּעֲבִיר בָּנָיו בֵּין גִּזְרֵי יַם סוּף
אֶת רוֹדְפֵיהֶם וְאֶת שׂוֹנְאֵיהֶם בִּתְהוֹמוֹת טִבַּע
וְרָאוּ בָנָיו גְּבוּרָתוֹ, שִׁבְּחוּ וְהוֹדוּ לִשְׁמוֹ
‹ וּמַלְכוּתוֹ בְּרָצוֹן קִבְּלוּ עֲלֵיהֶם.
מֹשֶׁה וּבְנֵי יִשְׂרָאֵל, לְךָ עָנוּ שִׁירָה בְּשִׂמְחָה רַבָּה
וְאָמְרוּ כֻלָּם

מִי־כָמֹכָה בָּאֵלִם יהוה שמות טו
מִי כָּמֹכָה נֶאְדָּר בַּקֹּדֶשׁ
נוֹרָא תְהִלֹּת עֹשֵׂה פֶלֶא:

‹ מַלְכוּתְךָ רָאוּ בָנֶיךָ, בּוֹקֵעַ יָם לִפְנֵי מֹשֶׁה
זֶה אֵלִי עָנוּ, וְאָמְרוּ
יהוה יִמְלֹךְ לְעֹלָם וָעֶד: שמות טו
‹ וְנֶאֱמַר
כִּי־פָדָה יהוה אֶת־יַעֲקֹב, וּגְאָלוֹ מִיַּד חָזָק מִמֶּנּוּ: ירמיהו לא
בָּרוּךְ אַתָּה יהוה, גָּאַל יִשְׂרָאֵל.

הַשְׁכִּיבֵנוּ יהוה אֱלֹהֵינוּ לְשָׁלוֹם, וְהַעֲמִידֵנוּ מַלְכֵּנוּ לְחַיִּים
וּפְרֹשׂ עָלֵינוּ סֻכַּת שְׁלוֹמֶךָ, וְתַקְּנֵנוּ בְּעֵצָה טוֹבָה מִלְּפָנֶיךָ
וְהוֹשִׁיעֵנוּ לְמַעַן שְׁמֶךָ.

הַשְׁכִּיבֵנוּ *Help us lie down:* This blessing, which has no parallel in the morning service, is a prayer for protection against the hazards of the night.

Shield us and remove from us every enemy,
plague, sword, famine and sorrow.
Remove the adversary from before and behind us.
Shelter us in the shadow of Your wings,
for You, God, are our Guardian and Deliverer;
You, God, are a gracious and compassionate King.
▸ Guard our going out and our coming in,
for life and peace, from now and for ever.
Blessed are You, LORD, who guards His people Israel for ever.

In Israel the service continues with Half Kaddish on page 276.

בָּרוּךְ Blessed be the LORD for ever. Amen and Amen. *Ps. 89*
Blessed from Zion be the LORD *Ps. 135*
who dwells in Jerusalem. Halleluya!
Blessed be the LORD, God of Israel, *Ps. 72*
who alone does wondrous things.
Blessed be His glorious name for ever,
and may the whole earth be filled with His glory. Amen and Amen.
May the glory of the LORD endure for ever; *Ps. 104*
may the LORD rejoice in His works.
May the name of the LORD be blessed now and for all time. *Ps. 113*
For the sake of His great name *I Sam. 12*
the LORD will not abandon His people,
for the LORD vowed to make you a people of His own.
When all the people saw [God's wonders] they fell on their faces *I Kings 18*
and said: "The LORD, He is God; the LORD, He is God."
Then the LORD shall be King over all the earth; *Zech. 14*
on that day the LORD shall be One and His name One.
May Your love, LORD, be upon us, as we have put our hope in You. *Ps. 33*

God, was originally recited as a substitute for the evening Amida – possibly to shorten the evening service in synagogue so that participants could return home before dark. When conditions changed, the prayer was retained. Since it was a substitute for the weekday Amida, it is not said on Shabbat or Yom Tov.

וְהָגֵן בַּעֲדֵנוּ, וְהָסֵר מֵעָלֵינוּ אוֹיֵב, דֶּבֶר וְחֶרֶב וְרָעָב וְיָגוֹן
וְהָסֵר שָׂטָן מִלְּפָנֵינוּ וּמֵאַחֲרֵינוּ, וּבְצֵל כְּנָפֶיךָ תַּסְתִּירֵנוּ
כִּי אֵל שׁוֹמְרֵנוּ וּמַצִּילֵנוּ אָתָּה
כִּי אֵל מֶלֶךְ חַנּוּן וְרַחוּם אָתָּה.
‣ וּשְׁמֹר צֵאתֵנוּ וּבוֹאֵנוּ לְחַיִּים וּלְשָׁלוֹם מֵעַתָּה וְעַד עוֹלָם.
בָּרוּךְ אַתָּה יהוה, שׁוֹמֵר עַמּוֹ יִשְׂרָאֵל לָעַד.

In ארץ ישראל *the service continues with* חצי קדיש *on page 277.*

בָּרוּךְ יהוה לְעוֹלָם, אָמֵן וְאָמֵן: תהלים פט
בָּרוּךְ יהוה מִצִּיּוֹן, שֹׁכֵן יְרוּשָׁלָםִ, הַלְלוּיָהּ: תהלים קלה
בָּרוּךְ יהוה אֱלֹהִים אֱלֹהֵי יִשְׂרָאֵל, עֹשֵׂה נִפְלָאוֹת לְבַדּוֹ: תהלים עב
וּבָרוּךְ שֵׁם כְּבוֹדוֹ לְעוֹלָם
וְיִמָּלֵא כְבוֹדוֹ אֶת־כָּל־הָאָרֶץ, אָמֵן וְאָמֵן:
יְהִי כְבוֹד יהוה לְעוֹלָם, יִשְׂמַח יהוה בְּמַעֲשָׂיו: תהלים קד
יְהִי שֵׁם יהוה מְבֹרָךְ מֵעַתָּה וְעַד־עוֹלָם: תהלים קיג
כִּי לֹא־יִטֹּשׁ יהוה אֶת־עַמּוֹ בַּעֲבוּר שְׁמוֹ הַגָּדוֹל שמואל א, יב
כִּי הוֹאִיל יהוה לַעֲשׂוֹת אֶתְכֶם לוֹ לְעָם:
וַיַּרְא כָּל־הָעָם וַיִּפְּלוּ עַל־פְּנֵיהֶם מלכים א, יח
וַיֹּאמְרוּ, יהוה הוּא הָאֱלֹהִים, יהוה הוּא הָאֱלֹהִים:
וְהָיָה יהוה לְמֶלֶךְ עַל־כָּל־הָאָרֶץ זכריה יד
בַּיּוֹם הַהוּא יִהְיֶה יהוה אֶחָד וּשְׁמוֹ אֶחָד:
יְהִי־חַסְדְּךָ יהוה עָלֵינוּ, כַּאֲשֶׁר יִחַלְנוּ לָךְ: תהלים לג

בָּרוּךְ יהוה לְעוֹלָם *Blessed be the* Lord *for ever:* This pas… Babylonian Jewry at a time when synagogues were … town and were built in the fields outside. This mad… potentially hazardous at night. This prayer, wit…

הוֹשִׁיעֵנוּ Save us, LORD our God, gather us Ps. 106
and deliver us from the nations,
to thank Your holy name, and glory in Your praise.
All the nations You made shall come and bow before You, LORD, Ps. 86
and pay honor to Your name,
for You are great and You perform wonders:
You alone are God.
We, Your people, the flock of Your pasture, will praise You for ever. Ps. 79
For all generations we will relate Your praise.

בָּרוּךְ Blessed is the LORD by day, blessed is the LORD by night.
Blessed is the LORD when we lie down;
blessed is the LORD when we rise.
For in Your hand are the souls of the living and the dead,
[as it is written:] "In His hand is every living soul, Job 12
and the breath of all mankind."
Into Your hand I entrust my spirit: Ps. 31
You redeemed me, LORD, God of truth.
Our God in heaven, bring unity to Your name,
establish Your kingdom constantly
and reign over us for ever and all time.

יִרְאוּ May our eyes see, our hearts rejoice,
and our souls be glad in Your true salvation,
when Zion is told, "Your God reigns."
The LORD is King, the LORD was King,
the LORD will be King for ever and all time.
For sovereignty is Yours,
and to all eternity You will reign in glory,
for we have no king but You.
Blessed are You, [illegible]
the King who in [illegible] constant glory will reign over us
[illegible] His creation [illegible] for ever and all time.

הוֹשִׁיעֵנוּ יהוה אֱלֹהֵינוּ, וְקַבְּצֵנוּ מִן־הַגּוֹיִם תהלים קו
לְהוֹדוֹת לְשֵׁם קָדְשֶׁךָ, לְהִשְׁתַּבֵּחַ בִּתְהִלָּתֶךָ:
כָּל־גּוֹיִם אֲשֶׁר עָשִׂיתָ, יָבוֹאוּ וְיִשְׁתַּחֲווּ לְפָנֶיךָ, אֲדֹנָי תהלים פו
וִיכַבְּדוּ לִשְׁמֶךָ:
כִּי־גָדוֹל אַתָּה וְעֹשֵׂה נִפְלָאוֹת, אַתָּה אֱלֹהִים לְבַדֶּךָ:
וַאֲנַחְנוּ עַמְּךָ וְצֹאן מַרְעִיתֶךָ, נוֹדֶה לְּךָ לְעוֹלָם תהלים עט
לְדוֹר וָדֹר נְסַפֵּר תְּהִלָּתֶךָ:

בָּרוּךְ יהוה בַּיּוֹם, בָּרוּךְ יהוה בַּלָּיְלָה
בָּרוּךְ יהוה בְּשָׁכְבֵנוּ, בָּרוּךְ יהוה בְּקוּמֵנוּ.
כִּי בְיָדְךָ נַפְשׁוֹת הַחַיִּים וְהַמֵּתִים.
אֲשֶׁר בְּיָדוֹ נֶפֶשׁ כָּל־חָי, וְרוּחַ כָּל־בְּשַׂר־אִישׁ: איוב יב
בְּיָדְךָ אַפְקִיד רוּחִי, פָּדִיתָה אוֹתִי יהוה אֵל אֱמֶת: תהלים לא
אֱלֹהֵינוּ שֶׁבַּשָּׁמַיִם, יַחֵד שִׁמְךָ וְקַיֵּם מַלְכוּתְךָ תָּמִיד
וּמְלֹךְ עָלֵינוּ לְעוֹלָם וָעֶד.

יִרְאוּ עֵינֵינוּ וְיִשְׂמַח לִבֵּנוּ
וְתָגֵל נַפְשֵׁנוּ בִּישׁוּעָתְךָ בֶּאֱמֶת
בֶּאֱמֹר לְצִיּוֹן מָלַךְ אֱלֹהָיִךְ.
יהוה מֶלֶךְ, יהוה מָלָךְ, יהוה יִמְלֹךְ לְעֹלָם וָעֶד.
◂ כִּי הַמַּלְכוּת שֶׁלְּךָ הִיא, וּלְעוֹלְמֵי עַד תִּמְלֹךְ בְּכָבוֹד
כִּי אֵין לָנוּ מֶלֶךְ אֶלָּא אָתָּה.
בָּרוּךְ אַתָּה יהוה
הַמֶּלֶךְ בִּכְבוֹדוֹ תָּמִיד, יִמְלֹךְ עָלֵינוּ לְעוֹלָם וָעֶד
וְעַל כָּל מַעֲשָׂיו.

HALF KADDISH

Leader: יִתְגַּדַּל Magnified and sanctified
may His great name be,
in the world He created by His will.
May He establish His kingdom
in your lifetime and in your days,
and in the lifetime of all the house of Israel,
swiftly and soon –
and say: Amen.

All: May His great name be blessed for ever and all time.

Leader: Blessed and praised, glorified and exalted,
raised and honored, uplifted and lauded
be the name of the Holy One,
blessed be He,
beyond any blessing,
song, praise and consolation
uttered in the world –
and say: Amen.

THE AMIDA

The following prayer, until "in former years" on page 296, is said silently, standing with feet together. Take three steps forward and at the points indicated by ᵛ, bend the knees at the first word, bow at the second, and stand straight before saying God's name.

O LORD, open my lips,
so that my mouth may declare Your praise. *Ps. 51*

PATRIARCHS

ᵛבָּרוּךְ Blessed are You, LORD our God and God of our fathers,
God of Abraham, God of Isaac and God of Jacob;
the great, mighty and awesome God, God Most High,
who bestows acts of loving-kindness and creates all,

חצי קדיש

ש״ץ: יִתְגַּדַּל וְיִתְקַדַּשׁ שְׁמֵהּ רַבָּא (קהל: אָמֵן)
בְּעָלְמָא דִּי בְרָא כִרְעוּתֵהּ
וְיַמְלִיךְ מַלְכוּתֵהּ
בְּחַיֵּיכוֹן וּבְיוֹמֵיכוֹן וּבְחַיֵּי דְכָל בֵּית יִשְׂרָאֵל
בַּעֲגָלָא וּבִזְמַן קָרִיב, וְאִמְרוּ אָמֵן. (קהל: אָמֵן)

קהל וש״ץ: יְהֵא שְׁמֵהּ רַבָּא מְבָרַךְ לְעָלַם וּלְעָלְמֵי עָלְמַיָּא.

ש״ץ: יִתְבָּרַךְ וְיִשְׁתַּבַּח וְיִתְפָּאַר וְיִתְרוֹמַם וְיִתְנַשֵּׂא
וְיִתְהַדַּר וְיִתְעַלֶּה וְיִתְהַלָּל
שְׁמֵהּ דְּקֻדְשָׁא בְּרִיךְ הוּא (קהל: בְּרִיךְ הוּא)
לְעֵלָּא מִן כָּל בִּרְכָתָא
/ בעשרת ימי תשובה: לְעֵלָּא לְעֵלָּא מִכָּל בִּרְכָתָא/
וְשִׁירָתָא, תֻּשְׁבְּחָתָא וְנֶחֱמָתָא
דַּאֲמִירָן בְּעָלְמָא, וְאִמְרוּ אָמֵן. (קהל: אָמֵן)

עמידה

The following prayer, until קַדְמֹנִיּוֹת *on page 297, is said silently, standing with feet together. Take three steps forward and at the points indicated by* ˅*, bend the knees at the first word, bow at the second, and stand straight before saying God's name.*

אֲדֹנָי, שְׂפָתַי תִּפְתָּח, וּפִי יַגִּיד תְּהִלָּתֶךָ: תהלים נא

אבות

˅בָּרוּךְ אַתָּה יהוה, אֱלֹהֵינוּ וֵאלֹהֵי אֲבוֹתֵינוּ
אֱלֹהֵי אַבְרָהָם, אֱלֹהֵי יִצְחָק, וֵאלֹהֵי יַעֲקֹב
הָאֵל הַגָּדוֹל הַגִּבּוֹר וְהַנּוֹרָא, אֵל עֶלְיוֹן
גּוֹמֵל חֲסָדִים טוֹבִים, וְקֹנֵה הַכֹּל

who remembers the loving-kindness of the fathers
and will bring a Redeemer to their children's children
for the sake of His name, in love.

Between Rosh HaShana & Yom Kippur: Remember us for life, O King who desires life,
and write us in the book of life –
for Your sake, O God of life.

King, Helper, Savior, Shield:
▾Blessed are You, LORD, Shield of Abraham.

DIVINE MIGHT

אַתָּה גִּבּוֹר You are eternally mighty, LORD.
You give life to the dead
and have great power to save.

The phrase "He makes the wind blow and the rain fall" is added from Simḥat Torah until Pesaḥ. In Israel the phrase "He causes the dew to fall" is added from Pesaḥ until Shemini Atzeret. See laws 49–51.

In fall & winter: He makes the wind blow and the rain fall.
In Israel, in spring & summer: He causes the dew to fall.

He sustains the living with loving-kindness,
and with great compassion revives the dead.
He supports the fallen, heals the sick, sets captives free,
and keeps His faith with those who sleep in the dust.
Who is like You, Master of might,
and to whom can You be compared,
O King who brings death and gives life,
and makes salvation grow?

Between Rosh HaShana & Yom Kippur: Who is like You, compassionate Father,
who remembers His creatures in compassion, for life?

Faithful are You to revive the dead.
Blessed are You, LORD, who revives the dead.

וְזוֹכֵר חַסְדֵי אָבוֹת
וּמֵבִיא גוֹאֵל לִבְנֵי בְנֵיהֶם לְמַעַן שְׁמוֹ בְּאַהֲבָה.

בעשרת ימי תשובה: זָכְרֵנוּ לְחַיִּים, מֶלֶךְ חָפֵץ בַּחַיִּים
וְכָתְבֵנוּ בְּסֵפֶר הַחַיִּים, לְמַעַנְךָ אֱלֹהִים חַיִּים.

מֶלֶךְ עוֹזֵר וּמוֹשִׁיעַ וּמָגֵן.
ׄבָּרוּךְ אַתָּה יהוה, מָגֵן אַבְרָהָם.

גבורות
אַתָּה גִּבּוֹר לְעוֹלָם, אֲדֹנָי
מְחַיֵּה מֵתִים אַתָּה, רַב לְהוֹשִׁיעַ

The phrase מַשִּׁיב הָרְוּחַ *is added from* שמחת תורה *until* פסח. *In* ארץ ישראל *the phrase* מוֹרִיד הַטָּל *is added from* פסח *until* שמיני עצרת. *See laws 49–51.*

בחורף: מַשִּׁיב הָרְוּחַ וּמוֹרִיד הַגֶּשֶׁם / בארץ ישראל בקיץ: מוֹרִיד הַטָּל

מְכַלְכֵּל חַיִּים בְּחֶסֶד
מְחַיֵּה מֵתִים בְּרַחֲמִים רַבִּים
סוֹמֵךְ נוֹפְלִים, וְרוֹפֵא חוֹלִים, וּמַתִּיר אֲסוּרִים
וּמְקַיֵּם אֱמוּנָתוֹ לִישֵׁנֵי עָפָר.
מִי כָמְוֹךָ, בַּעַל גְּבוּרוֹת
וּמִי דּוֹמֶה לָּךְ
מֶלֶךְ, מֵמִית וּמְחַיֶּה וּמַצְמִיחַ יְשׁוּעָה.

בעשרת ימי תשובה: מִי כָמְוֹךָ אַב הָרַחֲמִים
זוֹכֵר יְצוּרָיו לְחַיִּים בְּרַחֲמִים.

וְנֶאֱמָן אַתָּה לְהַחֲיוֹת מֵתִים.
בָּרוּךְ אַתָּה יהוה, מְחַיֵּה הַמֵּתִים.

HOLINESS

אַתָּה קָדוֹשׁ You are holy and Your name is holy,
and holy ones praise You daily, Selah!
Blessed are You, LORD,
the holy God. / *Between Rosh HaShana & Yom Kippur:* the holy King./
(If forgotten, repeat the Amida.)

KNOWLEDGE

אַתָּה חוֹנֵן You grace humanity with knowledge
and teach mortals understanding.

On Motza'ei Shabbat and Motza'ei Yom Tov add:

אַתָּה חוֹנַנְתָּנוּ You have graced us with the knowledge of Your Torah, and taught us to perform the statutes of Your will. You have distinguished, LORD our God, between sacred and profane, light and darkness, Israel and the nations, and between the seventh day and the six days of work. Our Father, our King, may the days approaching us bring peace; may we be free from all sin, cleansed from all iniquity, holding fast to our reverence of You. And

Grace us with the knowledge, understanding
and discernment that come from You.
Blessed are You, LORD,
who graciously grants knowledge.

REPENTANCE

הֲשִׁיבֵנוּ Bring us back, our Father, to Your Torah.
Draw us near, our King, to Your service.
Lead us back to You in perfect repentance.
Blessed are You, LORD,
who desires repentance.

---

distinction?"). In nature there are no sharp boundaries. Day shades gradually into night; winter into spring; life into sentience. According to the Torah, what links man to God is our ability to separate, classify and name, and thus to see order amidst seeming chaos. As we begin the working week, we acknowledge the divine order of creation as the necessary prelude to human acts of creation.

קדושת השם

אַתָּה קָדוֹשׁ וְשִׁמְךָ קָדוֹשׁ
וּקְדוֹשִׁים בְּכָל יוֹם יְהַלְלוּךָ סֶּלָה.
בָּרוּךְ אַתָּה יהוה
הָאֵל הַקָּדוֹשׁ./ בעשרת ימי תשובה: הַמֶּלֶךְ הַקָּדוֹשׁ./

(*If forgotten, repeat the* עמידה.)

דעת

אַתָּה חוֹנֵן לְאָדָם דַּעַת, וּמְלַמֵּד לֶאֱנוֹשׁ בִּינָה.

On מוצאי שבת *and* מוצאי יום טוב *add:*

אַתָּה חוֹנַנְתָּנוּ לְמַדַּע תּוֹרָתֶךָ, וַתְּלַמְּדֵנוּ לַעֲשׂוֹת חֻקֵּי רְצוֹנֶךָ, וַתַּבְדֵּל יהוה אֱלֹהֵינוּ בֵּין קֹדֶשׁ לְחֹל, בֵּין אוֹר לְחֹשֶׁךְ, בֵּין יִשְׂרָאֵל לָעַמִּים, בֵּין יוֹם הַשְּׁבִיעִי לְשֵׁשֶׁת יְמֵי הַמַּעֲשֶׂה. אָבִינוּ מַלְכֵּנוּ, הָחֵל עָלֵינוּ הַיָּמִים הַבָּאִים לִקְרָאתֵנוּ לְשָׁלוֹם, חֲשׂוּכִים מִכָּל חֵטְא וּמְנֻקִּים מִכָּל עָוֹן וּמְדֻבָּקִים בְּיִרְאָתֶךָ. וְ

חָנֵּנוּ מֵאִתְּךָ דֵּעָה בִּינָה וְהַשְׂכֵּל.
בָּרוּךְ אַתָּה יהוה, חוֹנֵן הַדָּעַת.

תשובה

הֲשִׁיבֵנוּ אָבִינוּ לְתוֹרָתֶךָ, וְקָרְבֵנוּ מַלְכֵּנוּ לַעֲבוֹדָתֶךָ
וְהַחֲזִירֵנוּ בִּתְשׁוּבָה שְׁלֵמָה לְפָנֶיךָ.
בָּרוּךְ אַתָּה יהוה, הָרוֹצֶה בִּתְשׁוּבָה.

אַתָּה חוֹנַנְתָּנוּ *You have graced us:* From Talmudic times, this paragraph has been the way of marking Havdala – the transition between holy and secular time – within the Amida prayer. Havdala is repeated as a separate ceremony in the synagogue after prayer, and then again at home. Its positioning here, in the prayer for knowledge, indicates the essential connection between the human mind and the ability to make distinctions ("If there is no knowledge," says the Talmud Yerushalmi [*Berakhot* 5:2], "how can there be

FORGIVENESS

Strike the left side of the chest at °.

סְלַח לָנוּ Forgive us, our Father, for we have °sinned.
Pardon us, our King, for we have °transgressed;
for You pardon and forgive.
Blessed are You, Lord,
the gracious One who repeatedly forgives.

REDEMPTION

רְאֵה Look on our affliction,
plead our cause,
and redeem us soon for Your name's sake,
for You are a powerful Redeemer.
Blessed are You, Lord,
the Redeemer of Israel.

HEALING

רְפָאֵנוּ Heal us, Lord, and we shall be healed.
Save us and we shall be saved,
for You are our praise.
Bring complete recovery for all our ailments,

The following prayer for a sick person may be said here:

May it be Your will, O Lord my God and God of my ancestors, that You speedily send a complete recovery from heaven, a healing of both soul and body, to the patient (*name*), son/daughter of (*mother's name*) among the other afflicted of Israel.

for You, God, King, are a faithful and compassionate Healer.
Blessed are You, Lord,
Healer of the sick of His people Israel.

סליחה

Strike the left side of the chest at °.

סְלַח לָנוּ אָבִינוּ כִּי °חָטָאנוּ
מְחַל לָנוּ מַלְכֵּנוּ כִּי °פָשָׁעְנוּ
כִּי מוֹחֵל וְסוֹלֵחַ אָתָּה.
בָּרוּךְ אַתָּה יהוה, חַנּוּן הַמַּרְבֶּה לִסְלֹחַ.

גאולה

רְאֵה בְעָנְיֵנוּ, וְרִיבָה רִיבֵנוּ
וּגְאָלֵנוּ מְהֵרָה לְמַעַן שְׁמֶךָ
כִּי גּוֹאֵל חָזָק אָתָּה.
בָּרוּךְ אַתָּה יהוה, גּוֹאֵל יִשְׂרָאֵל.

רפואה

רְפָאֵנוּ יהוה וְנֵרָפֵא
הוֹשִׁיעֵנוּ וְנִוָּשֵׁעָה, כִּי תְהִלָּתֵנוּ אָתָּה
וְהַעֲלֵה רְפוּאָה שְׁלֵמָה לְכָל מַכּוֹתֵינוּ

The following prayer for a sick person may be said here:

יְהִי רָצוֹן מִלְּפָנֶיךָ יהוה אֱלֹהַי וֵאלֹהֵי אֲבוֹתַי, שֶׁתִּשְׁלַח מְהֵרָה רְפוּאָה שְׁלֵמָה
מִן הַשָּׁמַיִם רְפוּאַת הַנֶּפֶשׁ וּרְפוּאַת הַגּוּף לַחוֹלֶה/לַחוֹלָה *name of patient*
בֶּן/בַּת *mother's name* בְּתוֹךְ שְׁאָר חוֹלֵי יִשְׂרָאֵל.

כִּי אֵל מֶלֶךְ רוֹפֵא נֶאֱמָן וְרַחֲמָן אָתָּה.
בָּרוּךְ אַתָּה יהוה, רוֹפֵא חוֹלֵי עַמּוֹ יִשְׂרָאֵל.

PROSPERITY

The phrase "Grant dew and rain as a blessing" is said from December 4th (in the year before a civil leap year, December 5th) until Pesaḥ. In Israel, it is said from the 7th of Marḥeshvan. The phrase "Grant blessing" is said from Ḥol HaMo'ed Pesaḥ until December 3rd (in the year before a civil leap year, December 4th). In Israel it is said through the 6th of Marḥeshvan. See laws 52–54.

בָּרֵךְ Bless this year for us, LORD our God,
and all its types of produce for good.
In winter: Grant dew and rain as a blessing
In other seasons: Grant blessing
on the face of the earth, and from its goodness satisfy us,
blessing our year as the best of years.
Blessed are You, LORD,
who blesses the years.

INGATHERING OF EXILES

תְּקַע Sound the great shofar for our freedom,
raise high the banner to gather our exiles,
and gather us together from the four quarters of the earth.
Blessed are You, LORD,
who gathers the dispersed of His people Israel.

JUSTICE

הָשִׁיבָה Restore our judges as at first,
and our counselors as at the beginning,
and remove from us sorrow and sighing.
May You alone, LORD,
reign over us
with loving-kindness and compassion,
and vindicate us in justice.
Blessed are You, LORD,
the King who loves righteousness and justice.
/*Between Rosh HaShana & Yom Kippur, end the blessing:* the King of justice./

ברכת השנים

The phrase וְתֵן טַל וּמָטָר לִבְרָכָה *is said from December 4th (in the year before a civil leap year, December 5th) until* פסח. *In* ארץ ישראל, *it is said from* ז׳ מרחשון. *The phrase* וְתֵן בְּרָכָה *is said from* חול המועד פסח *until December 3rd (in the year before a civil leap year, December 4th). In* ארץ ישראל *it is said through* ז׳ מרחשון. *See laws 52–54.*

בָּרֵךְ עָלֵינוּ יהוה אֱלֹהֵינוּ אֶת הַשָּׁנָה הַזֹּאת
וְאֶת כָּל מִינֵי תְבוּאָתָהּ, לְטוֹבָה
בחורף: וְתֵן טַל וּמָטָר לִבְרָכָה / בקיץ: וְתֵן בְּרָכָה
עַל פְּנֵי הָאֲדָמָה, וְשַׂבְּעֵנוּ מִטּוּבָהּ
וּבָרֵךְ שְׁנָתֵנוּ כַּשָּׁנִים הַטּוֹבוֹת.
בָּרוּךְ אַתָּה יהוה, מְבָרֵךְ הַשָּׁנִים.

קבוץ גלויות

תְּקַע בְּשׁוֹפָר גָּדוֹל לְחֵרוּתֵנוּ
וְשָׂא נֵס לְקַבֵּץ גָּלֻיּוֹתֵינוּ
וְקַבְּצֵנוּ יַחַד מֵאַרְבַּע כַּנְפוֹת הָאָרֶץ.
בָּרוּךְ אַתָּה יהוה, מְקַבֵּץ נִדְחֵי עַמּוֹ יִשְׂרָאֵל.

השבת המשפט

הָשִׁיבָה שׁוֹפְטֵינוּ כְּבָרִאשׁוֹנָה
וְיוֹעֲצֵינוּ כְּבַתְּחִלָּה
וְהָסֵר מִמֶּנּוּ יָגוֹן וַאֲנָחָה
וּמְלֹךְ עָלֵינוּ אַתָּה יהוה לְבַדְּךָ בְּחֶסֶד וּבְרַחֲמִים
וְצַדְּקֵנוּ בַּמִּשְׁפָּט.
בָּרוּךְ אַתָּה יהוה
מֶלֶךְ אוֹהֵב צְדָקָה וּמִשְׁפָּט. / בעשרת ימי תשובה: הַמֶּלֶךְ הַמִּשְׁפָּט./

AGAINST INFORMERS

וְלַמַּלְשִׁינִים For the slanderers let there be no hope,
and may all wickedness perish in an instant.
May all Your people's enemies swiftly be cut down.
May You swiftly uproot, crush, cast down
and humble the arrogant swiftly in our days.
Blessed are You, LORD,
who destroys enemies and humbles the arrogant.

THE RIGHTEOUS

עַל הַצַּדִּיקִים To the righteous, the pious,
the elders of Your people the house of Israel,
the remnant of their scholars,
the righteous converts, and to us,
may Your compassion be aroused,
LORD our God.
Grant a good reward to all
who sincerely trust in Your name.
Set our lot with them,
so that we may never be ashamed,
for in You we trust.
Blessed are You, LORD,
who is the support and trust of the righteous.

REBUILDING JERUSALEM

וְלִירוּשָׁלַיִם To Jerusalem, Your city, may You return in compassion,
and may You dwell in it as You promised.
May You rebuild it rapidly in our days
as an everlasting structure,
and install within it soon the throne of David.
Blessed are You, LORD,
who builds Jerusalem.

ברכת המינים

וְלַמַּלְשִׁינִים אַל תְּהִי תִקְוָה
וְכָל הָרִשְׁעָה כְּרֶגַע תֹּאבֵד
וְכָל אוֹיְבֵי עַמְּךָ מְהֵרָה יִכָּרֵתוּ
וְהַזֵּדִים מְהֵרָה תְעַקֵּר וּתְשַׁבֵּר וּתְמַגֵּר וְתַכְנִיעַ בִּמְהֵרָה בְיָמֵינוּ.
בָּרוּךְ אַתָּה יהוה, שׁוֹבֵר אוֹיְבִים וּמַכְנִיעַ זֵדִים.

על הצדיקים

עַל הַצַּדִּיקִים וְעַל הַחֲסִידִים
וְעַל זִקְנֵי עַמְּךָ בֵּית יִשְׂרָאֵל
וְעַל פְּלֵיטַת סוֹפְרֵיהֶם
וְעַל גֵּרֵי הַצֶּדֶק, וְעָלֵינוּ
יֶהֱמוּ רַחֲמֶיךָ יהוה אֱלֹהֵינוּ
וְתֵן שָׂכָר טוֹב לְכָל הַבּוֹטְחִים בְּשִׁמְךָ בֶּאֱמֶת
וְשִׂים חֶלְקֵנוּ עִמָּהֶם
וּלְעוֹלָם לֹא נֵבוֹשׁ כִּי בְךָ בָטָחְנוּ.
בָּרוּךְ אַתָּה יהוה, מִשְׁעָן וּמִבְטָח לַצַּדִּיקִים.

בניין ירושלים

וְלִירוּשָׁלַיִם עִירְךָ בְּרַחֲמִים תָּשׁוּב
וְתִשְׁכֹּן בְּתוֹכָהּ כַּאֲשֶׁר דִּבַּרְתָּ
וּבְנֵה אוֹתָהּ בְּקָרוֹב בְּיָמֵינוּ בִּנְיַן עוֹלָם
וְכִסֵּא דָוִד מְהֵרָה לְתוֹכָהּ תָּכִין.
בָּרוּךְ אַתָּה יהוה, בּוֹנֵה יְרוּשָׁלָיִם.

KINGDOM OF DAVID

אֶת צֶמַח May the offshoot of Your servant David soon flower,
and may his pride be raised high by Your salvation,
for we wait for Your salvation all day.
Blessed are You, LORD,
who makes the glory of salvation flourish.

RESPONSE TO PRAYER

שְׁמַע קוֹלֵנוּ Listen to our voice, LORD our God.
Spare us and have compassion on us,
and in compassion and favor accept our prayer,
for You, God, listen to prayers and pleas.
Do not turn us away, O our King,
empty-handed from Your presence,*
for You listen with compassion
to the prayer of Your people Israel.
Blessed are You, LORD,
who listens to prayer.

At this point, in times of drought in Israel, say "And answer us" on page 124.

TEMPLE SERVICE

רְצֵה Find favor, LORD our God,
in Your people Israel and their prayer.
Restore the service to Your most holy House,
and accept in love and favor
the fire-offerings of Israel and their prayer.
May the service of Your people Israel always find favor with You.

On Rosh Ḥodesh, say:

אֱלֹהֵינוּ Our God and God of our ancestors, may there rise, come, reach, appear, be favored, heard, regarded and remembered before You, our recollection and remembrance, as well as the remembrance of our ancestors, and of the Messiah son of David Your servant, and of Jerusalem Your holy city, and

משיח בן דוד

אֶת צֶמַח דָּוִד עַבְדְּךָ מְהֵרָה תַצְמִיחַ
וְקַרְנוֹ תָּרוּם בִּישׁוּעָתֶךָ
כִּי לִישׁוּעָתְךָ קִוִּינוּ כָּל הַיּוֹם.
בָּרוּךְ אַתָּה יהוה, מַצְמִיחַ קֶרֶן יְשׁוּעָה.

שומע תפלה

שְׁמַע קוֹלֵנוּ יהוה אֱלֹהֵינוּ
חוּס וְרַחֵם עָלֵינוּ
וְקַבֵּל בְּרַחֲמִים וּבְרָצוֹן אֶת תְּפִלָּתֵנוּ
כִּי אֵל שׁוֹמֵעַ תְּפִלּוֹת וְתַחֲנוּנִים אָתָּה
וּמִלְּפָנֶיךָ מַלְכֵּנוּ רֵיקָם אַל תְּשִׁיבֵנוּ*
כִּי אַתָּה שׁוֹמֵעַ תְּפִלַּת עַמְּךָ יִשְׂרָאֵל בְּרַחֲמִים.
בָּרוּךְ אַתָּה יהוה, שׁוֹמֵעַ תְּפִלָּה.

At this point, in times of drought in ארץ ישראל, say וַעֲנֵנוּ on page 125.

עבודה

רְצֵה יהוה אֱלֹהֵינוּ בְּעַמְּךָ יִשְׂרָאֵל, וּבִתְפִלָּתָם
וְהָשֵׁב אֶת הָעֲבוֹדָה לִדְבִיר בֵּיתֶךָ
וְאִשֵּׁי יִשְׂרָאֵל וּתְפִלָּתָם בְּאַהֲבָה תְקַבֵּל בְּרָצוֹן
וּתְהִי לְרָצוֹן תָּמִיד עֲבוֹדַת יִשְׂרָאֵל עַמֶּךָ.

On ראש חודש*, say:*

אֱלֹהֵינוּ וֵאלֹהֵי אֲבוֹתֵינוּ, יַעֲלֶה וְיָבוֹא וְיַגִּיעַ, וְיֵרָאֶה וְיֵרָצֶה וְיִשָּׁמַע, וְיִפָּקֵד וְיִזָּכֵר זִכְרוֹנֵנוּ וּפִקְדוֹנֵנוּ וְזִכְרוֹן אֲבוֹתֵינוּ, וְזִכְרוֹן מָשִׁיחַ בֶּן דָּוִד עַבְדֶּךָ, וְזִכְרוֹן יְרוּשָׁלַיִם עִיר קָדְשֶׁךָ, וְזִכְרוֹן כָּל עַמְּךָ

of all Your people the house of Israel – for deliverance and well-being, grace, loving-kindness and compassion, life and peace, on this day of Rosh Ḥodesh. On it remember us, LORD our God, for good; recollect us for blessing, and deliver us for life. In accord with Your promise of salvation and compassion, spare us and be gracious to us; have compassion on us and deliver us, for our eyes are turned to You because You, God, are a gracious and compassionate King.

וְתֶחֱזֶינָה And may our eyes witness
Your return to Zion in compassion.
Blessed are You, LORD,
who restores His Presence to Zion.

THANKSGIVING

Bow at the first nine words.

מוֹדִים We give thanks to You,
for You are the LORD our God and God of our ancestors
for ever and all time.
You are the Rock of our lives,
Shield of our salvation from generation to generation.
We will thank You and declare Your praise for our lives,
which are entrusted into Your hand;
for our souls, which are placed in Your charge;
for Your miracles which are with us every day;
and for Your wonders and favors at all times,
evening, morning and midday.
You are good –
for Your compassion never fails.
You are compassionate –
for Your loving-kindnesses never cease.
We have always placed our hope in You.

בֵּית יִשְׂרָאֵל, לְפָנֶיךָ, לִפְלֵיטָה לְטוֹבָה, לְחֵן וּלְחֶסֶד וּלְרַחֲמִים, לְחַיִּים וּלְשָׁלוֹם בְּיוֹם רֹאשׁ הַחֹדֶשׁ הַזֶּה. זָכְרֵנוּ יהוה אֱלֹהֵינוּ בּוֹ לְטוֹבָה, וּפָקְדֵנוּ בוֹ לִבְרָכָה, וְהוֹשִׁיעֵנוּ בוֹ לְחַיִּים. וּבִדְבַר יְשׁוּעָה וְרַחֲמִים, חוּס וְחָנֵּנוּ וְרַחֵם עָלֵינוּ וְהוֹשִׁיעֵנוּ, כִּי אֵלֶיךָ עֵינֵינוּ, כִּי אֵל מֶלֶךְ חַנּוּן וְרַחוּם אָתָּה.

וְתֶחֱזֶינָה עֵינֵינוּ בְּשׁוּבְךָ לְצִיּוֹן בְּרַחֲמִים.
בָּרוּךְ אַתָּה יהוה, הַמַּחֲזִיר שְׁכִינָתוֹ לְצִיּוֹן.

הודאה

Bow at the first five words.

מוֹדִים אֲנַחְנוּ לָךְ
שָׁאַתָּה הוּא יהוה אֱלֹהֵינוּ וֵאלֹהֵי אֲבוֹתֵינוּ לְעוֹלָם וָעֶד.
צוּר חַיֵּינוּ, מָגֵן יִשְׁעֵנוּ
אַתָּה הוּא לְדוֹר וָדוֹר.
נוֹדֶה לְּךָ וּנְסַפֵּר תְּהִלָּתֶךָ
עַל חַיֵּינוּ הַמְּסוּרִים בְּיָדֶךָ
וְעַל נִשְׁמוֹתֵינוּ הַפְּקוּדוֹת לָךְ
וְעַל נִסֶּיךָ שֶׁבְּכָל יוֹם עִמָּנוּ
וְעַל נִפְלְאוֹתֶיךָ וְטוֹבוֹתֶיךָ שֶׁבְּכָל עֵת
עֶרֶב וָבֹקֶר וְצָהֳרָיִם.
הַטּוֹב, כִּי לֹא כָלוּ רַחֲמֶיךָ
וְהַמְרַחֵם, כִּי לֹא תַמּוּ חֲסָדֶיךָ
מֵעוֹלָם קִוִּינוּ לָךְ.

On Ḥanukka:

עַל הַנִּסִּים [We thank You also] for the miracles, the redemption, the mighty deeds, the salvations, and the victories in battle which You performed for our ancestors in those days, at this time.

בִּימֵי מַתִּתְיָהוּ In the days of Mattityahu, son of Yoḥanan, the High Priest, the Hasmonean, and his sons, the wicked Greek kingdom rose up against Your people Israel to make them forget Your Torah and to force them to transgress the statutes of Your will. It was then that You in Your great compassion stood by them in the time of their distress. You championed their cause, judged their claim, and avenged their wrong. You delivered the strong into the hands of the weak, the many into the hands of the few, the impure into the hands of the pure, the wicked into the hands of the righteous, and the arrogant into the hands of those who were engaged in the study of Your Torah. You made for Yourself great and holy renown in Your world, and for Your people Israel You performed a great salvation and redemption as of this very day. Your children then entered the holiest part of Your House, cleansed Your Temple, purified Your Sanctuary, kindled lights in Your holy courts, and designated these eight days of Ḥanukka for giving thanks and praise to Your great name.

Continue with "For all these things."

On Purim:

עַל הַנִּסִּים [We thank You also] for the miracles, the redemption, the mighty deeds, the salvations, and the victories in battle which You performed for our ancestors in those days at this time.

בִּימֵי מָרְדְּכַי In the days of Mordekhai and Esther, in Shushan the capital, the wicked Haman rose up against them and sought to destroy, slay and exterminate *Esther 3* all the Jews, young and old, children and women, on one day, the thirteenth day of the twelfth month, which is the month of Adar, and to plunder their possessions. Then You in Your great compassion thwarted his counsel, frustrated his plans, and caused his scheme to recoil on his own head, so that they hanged him and his sons on the gallows.

Continue with "For all these things."

וְעַל כֻּלָּם For all these things may Your name be blessed and exalted, our King, continually, for ever and all time.

Between Rosh HaShana & Yom Kippur: And write, for a good life,
all the children of Your covenant.

Let all that lives thank You, Selah! and praise Your name in truth,
God, our Savior and Help, Selah!
▾Blessed are You, Lord, whose name is "the Good"
and to whom thanks are due.

בחנוכה:

עַל הַנִּסִּים וְעַל הַפֻּרְקָן וְעַל הַגְּבוּרוֹת וְעַל הַתְּשׁוּעוֹת וְעַל הַמִּלְחָמוֹת שֶׁעָשִׂיתָ לַאֲבוֹתֵינוּ בַּיָּמִים הָהֵם בַּזְּמַן הַזֶּה.

בִּימֵי מַתִּתְיָהוּ בֶּן יוֹחָנָן כֹּהֵן גָּדוֹל חַשְׁמוֹנַאי וּבָנָיו, כְּשֶׁעָמְדָה מַלְכוּת יָוָן הָרְשָׁעָה עַל עַמְּךָ יִשְׂרָאֵל לְהַשְׁכִּיחָם תּוֹרָתֶךָ וּלְהַעֲבִירָם מֵחֻקֵּי רְצוֹנֶךָ, וְאַתָּה בְּרַחֲמֶיךָ הָרַבִּים עָמַדְתָּ לָהֶם בְּעֵת צָרָתָם, רַבְתָּ אֶת רִיבָם, דַּנְתָּ אֶת דִּינָם, נָקַמְתָּ אֶת נִקְמָתָם, מָסַרְתָּ גִבּוֹרִים בְּיַד חַלָּשִׁים, וְרַבִּים בְּיַד מְעַטִּים, וּטְמֵאִים בְּיַד טְהוֹרִים, וּרְשָׁעִים בְּיַד צַדִּיקִים, וְזֵדִים בְּיַד עוֹסְקֵי תוֹרָתֶךָ, וּלְךָ עָשִׂיתָ שֵׁם גָּדוֹל וְקָדוֹשׁ בְּעוֹלָמֶךָ, וּלְעַמְּךָ יִשְׂרָאֵל עָשִׂיתָ תְּשׁוּעָה גְדוֹלָה וּפֻרְקָן כְּהַיּוֹם הַזֶּה. וְאַחַר כֵּן בָּאוּ בָנֶיךָ לִדְבִיר בֵּיתֶךָ, וּפִנּוּ אֶת הֵיכָלֶךָ, וְטִהֲרוּ אֶת מִקְדָּשֶׁךָ, וְהִדְלִיקוּ נֵרוֹת בְּחַצְרוֹת קָדְשֶׁךָ, וְקָבְעוּ שְׁמוֹנַת יְמֵי חֲנֻכָּה אֵלּוּ, לְהוֹדוֹת וּלְהַלֵּל לְשִׁמְךָ הַגָּדוֹל.

Continue with וְעַל כֻּלָּם.

בפורים:

עַל הַנִּסִּים וְעַל הַפֻּרְקָן וְעַל הַגְּבוּרוֹת וְעַל הַתְּשׁוּעוֹת וְעַל הַמִּלְחָמוֹת שֶׁעָשִׂיתָ לַאֲבוֹתֵינוּ בַּיָּמִים הָהֵם בַּזְּמַן הַזֶּה.

בִּימֵי מָרְדְּכַי וְאֶסְתֵּר בְּשׁוּשַׁן הַבִּירָה, כְּשֶׁעָמַד עֲלֵיהֶם הָמָן הָרָשָׁע, בִּקֵּשׁ
לְהַשְׁמִיד לַהֲרֹג וּלְאַבֵּד אֶת־כָּל־הַיְּהוּדִים מִנַּעַר וְעַד־זָקֵן טַף וְנָשִׁים בְּיוֹם אסתר ג
אֶחָד, בִּשְׁלוֹשָׁה עָשָׂר לְחֹדֶשׁ שְׁנֵים־עָשָׂר, הוּא־חֹדֶשׁ אֲדָר, וּשְׁלָלָם
לָבוֹז: וְאַתָּה בְּרַחֲמֶיךָ הָרַבִּים הֵפַרְתָּ אֶת עֲצָתוֹ, וְקִלְקַלְתָּ אֶת מַחֲשַׁבְתּוֹ,
וַהֲשֵׁבוֹתָ לּוֹ גְּמוּלוֹ בְּרֹאשׁוֹ, וְתָלוּ אוֹתוֹ וְאֶת בָּנָיו עַל הָעֵץ.

Continue with וְעַל כֻּלָּם.

וְעַל כֻּלָּם יִתְבָּרַךְ וְיִתְרוֹמַם שִׁמְךָ מַלְכֵּנוּ תָּמִיד לְעוֹלָם וָעֶד.

בעשרת ימי תשובה: וּכְתֹב לְחַיִּים טוֹבִים כָּל בְּנֵי בְרִיתֶךָ.

וְכֹל הַחַיִּים יוֹדוּךָ סֶּלָה, וִיהַלְלוּ אֶת שִׁמְךָ בֶּאֱמֶת הָאֵל יְשׁוּעָתֵנוּ וְעֶזְרָתֵנוּ סֶלָה.

בָּרוּךְ אַתָּה יהוה, הַטּוֹב שִׁמְךָ וּלְךָ נָאֶה לְהוֹדוֹת.

PEACE

שָׁלוֹם רָב Grant great peace to Your people Israel for ever,
for You are the sovereign LORD of all peace;
and may it be good in Your eyes
to bless Your people Israel
at every time, at every hour, with Your peace.

Between Rosh HaShana & Yom Kippur: In the book of life, blessing, peace and prosperity,
may we and all Your people the house of Israel be remembered
and written before You for a good life, and for peace.*

Blessed are You, LORD, who blesses His people Israel with peace.

**Between Rosh HaShana and Yom Kippur outside Israel, many end the blessing:*
Blessed are You, LORD, who makes peace.

Some say the following verse (see law 60):
May the words of my mouth and the meditation of my heart *Ps. 19*
find favor before You, LORD, my Rock and Redeemer.

אֱלֹהַי My God, *Berakhot 17a*
guard my tongue from evil and my lips from deceitful speech.
To those who curse me, let my soul be silent;
may my soul be to all like the dust.
Open my heart to Your Torah
and let my soul pursue Your commandments.
As for all who plan evil against me,
swiftly thwart their counsel and frustrate their plans.
Act for the sake of Your name; act for the sake of Your right hand;
act for the sake of Your holiness; act for the sake of Your Torah.
That Your beloved ones may be delivered, *Ps. 60*
save with Your right hand and answer me.
May the words of my mouth *Ps. 19*
and the meditation of my heart find favor before You,
LORD, my Rock and Redeemer.

Bow, take three steps back, then bow, first left, then right, then center, while saying:
May He who makes peace in His high places,
make peace for us and all Israel – and say: Amen.

ברכת שלום

שָׁלוֹם רָב עַל יִשְׂרָאֵל עַמְּךָ תָּשִׂים לְעוֹלָם
כִּי אַתָּה הוּא מֶלֶךְ אָדוֹן לְכָל הַשָּׁלוֹם.
וְטוֹב בְּעֵינֶיךָ לְבָרֵךְ אֶת עַמְּךָ יִשְׂרָאֵל
בְּכָל עֵת וּבְכָל שָׁעָה בִּשְׁלוֹמֶךָ.

בעשרת ימי תשובה: בְּסֵפֶר חַיִּים, בְּרָכָה וְשָׁלוֹם, וּפַרְנָסָה טוֹבָה
נִזָּכֵר וְנִכָּתֵב לְפָנֶיךָ, אֲנַחְנוּ וְכָל עַמְּךָ בֵּית יִשְׂרָאֵל
לְחַיִּים טוֹבִים וּלְשָׁלוֹם.*

בָּרוּךְ אַתָּה יהוה, הַמְבָרֵךְ אֶת עַמּוֹ יִשְׂרָאֵל בַּשָּׁלוֹם.

During the עשרת ימי תשובה in חוץ לארץ, many end the blessing:

בָּרוּךְ אַתָּה יהוה, עוֹשֵׂה הַשָּׁלוֹם.

Some say the following verse (see law 60):

תהלים יט יִהְיוּ לְרָצוֹן אִמְרֵי־פִי וְהֶגְיוֹן לִבִּי לְפָנֶיךָ, יהוה צוּרִי וְגֹאֲלִי:

ברכות יז. אֱלֹהַי
נְצֹר לְשׁוֹנִי מֵרָע וּשְׂפָתַי מִדַּבֵּר מִרְמָה
וְלִמְקַלְלַי נַפְשִׁי תִדֹּם, וְנַפְשִׁי כֶּעָפָר לַכֹּל תִּהְיֶה.
פְּתַח לִבִּי בְּתוֹרָתֶךָ, וּבְמִצְוֹתֶיךָ תִּרְדֹּף נַפְשִׁי.
וְכָל הַחוֹשְׁבִים עָלַי רָעָה
מְהֵרָה הָפֵר עֲצָתָם וְקַלְקֵל מַחֲשַׁבְתָּם.
עֲשֵׂה לְמַעַן שְׁמֶךָ, עֲשֵׂה לְמַעַן יְמִינֶךָ
עֲשֵׂה לְמַעַן קְדֻשָּׁתֶךָ, עֲשֵׂה לְמַעַן תּוֹרָתֶךָ.
תהלים ס לְמַעַן יֵחָלְצוּן יְדִידֶיךָ, הוֹשִׁיעָה יְמִינְךָ וַעֲנֵנִי:
תהלים יט יִהְיוּ לְרָצוֹן אִמְרֵי־פִי וְהֶגְיוֹן לִבִּי לְפָנֶיךָ, יהוה צוּרִי וְגֹאֲלִי:

Bow, take three steps back, then bow, first left, then right, then center, while saying:

עֹשֶׂה שָׁלוֹם/ בעשרת ימי תשובה: הַשָּׁלוֹם/ בִּמְרוֹמָיו
הוּא יַעֲשֶׂה שָׁלוֹם עָלֵינוּ וְעַל כָּל יִשְׂרָאֵל, וְאִמְרוּ אָמֵן.

יְהִי רָצוֹן May it be Your will, LORD our God and God of our ancestors,
that the Temple be rebuilt speedily in our days, and grant us a share in Your Torah.
And there we will serve You with reverence,
as in the days of old and as in former years.
Then the offering of Judah and Jerusalem *Mal. 3*
will be pleasing to the LORD as in the days of old and as in former years.

On Motza'ei Shabbat (except when Yom Tov or Erev Pesaḥ falls in the following week), the Leader continues with Half Kaddish (below, until ◂), then "May the pleasantness" on page 316.
On Motza'ei Shabbat when Yom Tov falls in the following week, the service continues on page 322.
On other evenings the Leader says Full Kaddish:

FULL KADDISH

Leader: יִתְגַּדַּל Magnified and sanctified may His great name be,
in the world He created by His will.
May He establish His kingdom
in your lifetime and in your days,
and in the lifetime of all the house of Israel,
swiftly and soon –
and say: Amen.

All: May His great name be blessed for ever and all time.

Leader: Blessed and praised,
glorified and exalted,
raised and honored,
uplifted and lauded be
the name of the Holy One,
blessed be He, beyond any blessing,
song, praise and consolation
uttered in the world –
and say: Amen. ◂

May the prayers and pleas of all Israel
be accepted by their Father in heaven –
and say: Amen.